Shadow Banking

Shadow banking – a system of credit creation outside traditional banks – lies at the very heart of the global economy. It accounts for over half of global banking assets, and represents a third of the global financial system. Although the term 'shadow banking' only entered public discourse in 2007, the importance and scope of this system is now widely recognised by the international policy-makers. There is, however, much less consensus on the origins of the shadow banking system, what role it plays in global political economy and the optimal approach to regulating this complex segment of finance. This volume addresses these questions.

Shadow Banking is the first study to bring together the insights from financial regulators, practitioners and academics from across the social sciences. The first part traces the evolution and ongoing confusion about the meaning of 'shadow banking'. The second section draws major lessons about shadow banking as posed by the financial crisis of 2007–09, providing comparative analyses in the US and Europe, and attempts to establish why shadow banking has emerged and matured to the level of a de facto parallel financial system. Finally, the third part goes beyond current regulatory concerns about shadow banking and explains why it is 'here to stay'.

This volume is of great importance to political economy, banking and international political economy.

Anastasia Nesvetailova is Director of City Political Economy Research Centre, City University of London, UK. Her main research and teaching interests lie in the area of international political economy, finance and financial crises, regulation and governance.

Routledge Critical Studies in Finance and Stability
Edited by Jan Toporowski, School of Oriental and
African Studies, University of London, UK

The 2007–8 Banking Crash has induced a major and wide-ranging discussion on the subject of financial (in)stability and a need to revaluate theory and policy. The response of policy-makers to the crisis has been to refocus fiscal and monetary policy on financial stabilisation and reconstruction. However, this has been done with only vague ideas of bank recapitalisation and 'Keynesian' reflation aroused by the exigencies of the crisis, rather than the application of any systematic theory or theories of financial instability.

Routledge Critical Studies in Finance and Stability covers a range of issues in the area of finance including instability, systemic failure, financial macroeconomics in the vein of Hyman P. Minsky, Ben Bernanke and Mark Gertler, central bank operations, financial regulation, developing countries and financial crises, new portfolio theory and New International Monetary and Financial Architecture.

For a full list of titles in this series, please visit www.routledge.com/series/RCSFS

Shadow Banking

Scope, Origins and Theories

Edited by Anastasia Nesvetailova

Routledge
Taylor & Francis Group

LONDON AND NEW YORK

First published 2018 by Routledge

2 Park Square, Milton Park, Abingdon, Oxfordshire OX14 4RN
52 Vanderbilt Avenue, New York, NY 10017

Routledge is an imprint of the Taylor & Francis Group, an informa business

First issued in paperback 2018

British Library Cataloguing in Publication Data
A catalogue record for this book is available from the British Library

Library of Congress Cataloging in Publication Data
A catalog record for this book has been requested

ISBN: 978-1-138-20153-8 (hbk)
ISBN: 978-0-367-14037-3 (pbk)

Typeset in Times New Roman
by Swales & Willis, Exeter, Devon, UK

Contents

Figures

Tables

Contributors

Viktoria Baklanova is senior adviser at US Treasury.

Elias Bengtsson is a Senior Lecturer at Halmstad University, Sweden. He previously held positions at the European Central Bank and the Swedish central bank.

Antoine Bouveret is an economist at the International Monetary Fund.

Ewald Engelen is Professor of Financial Geography at the University of Amsterdam, Netherlands.

Daniela Gabor is Professor of Economics at Bristol Business School, UK.

Thorvald Grung Moe is senior adviser at Norges Bank and a research associate at Levy Economics Institute of Bard College, USA.

Robert Guttmann is Professor of Economics at Hofstra University and University of Paris-Nord, France.

Sara Hsu is Associate Professor of Economics at the University of New Paltz, USA.

Natalia Kaurova is Associate Professor at the Financial University under the Government of the Russian Federation, Moscow, Russia.

Oliver Kessler is Professor of Political Science at the University of Erfurt, Germany.

Jianjun Li is Professor of Finance at Central University of Finance and Economics in Beijing, China.

Photis Lysandrou is Professor Emeritus at London Metropolitan University and a Research Fellow at City Political Economy Research Centre (CITYPERC), City, University of London, UK.

Anastasia Nesvetailova is Professor of IPE at City, University of London, UK.

Ronen Palan is Professor of International Political Economy, City, University of London, UK.

Zoltan Pozsar is senior macro strategist at Credit Suisse.

Joseph Tanega is Professor of Law at the University of Westminster, UK.

Jan Toporowski is Professor of Economics and Finance at SOAS, University of London, UK.

Duncan Wigan is Assistant Professor of Political Economy at Copenhagen Business School, Denmark.

Benjamin Wilhelm is a doctoral candidate at the University of Erfurt, Germany.

Abbreviations

ABCP	Asset-backed commercial paper
ABS	Asset-backed securities
BCBS	The Basel Committee of Banking Supervision
BIS	The Bank for International Settlements
CBRC	The China Banking Regulatory Commission
CCP	Central Clearing Counterparty
CDO	Collateralised debt obligations
CDS	Credit default swaps
CMU	The Capital Markets Union
CRM	Credit risk mitigation
CRMA	Credit risk mitigation agreement
CRMW	Credit risk mitigation warranty
EC	The European Commission
FDIC	The Federal Deposit Insurance Corporation
FRBNY	The Federal Reserve Bank of New York
FSB	The Financial Stability Board
FVC	Financial vehicle corporations
GSE	Government sponsored enterprise
HMRC	Her Majesty's Revenue and Customs
HNWI	High-net worth individuals
HQLA	High-quality liquid assets
IOSCO	The International Organization of Securities Commissions
LIBOR	The London Interbank Offered Rate
LLR	Lender of last resort
LTI	Loan to income
LTV	Loan to value
MFI	Micro-finance institution
MMLR	Market makers of last resort
MMF	Money market fund
NAV	Net asset value
OTC	Over-the-counter (derivatives)
OTD	Originate to distribute model
QE	Quantitative easing
REIT	Real Estate Investment Trust
SIV	Special investment vehicle
SPE	Special purpose entities
SPV	Special purpose vehicle
TARP	Troubled Asset Relief Programme
UCITS	Undertakings for Collective Investments in Transferable Securities

Abbreviations

Introduction

Shadow banking
The political economy of financial innovation

Anastasia Nesvetailova

In August 2007, the world's leading monetary and financial policymakers gathered for their annual symposium – a major international event organised by the Federal Reserve (Fed) – in Jackson Hole, Wyoming. The agenda for the meeting was set by the challenge of dealing with the consequences of the imploding housing bubbles that had built up in most of the 34 countries represented at the conference. The first shockwaves of the unfolding financial meltdown only made this complex aspect of financial regulation more pressing. Being a central banker or a minister of finance is hardly ever an easy job. Yet in principle, the regulators and policymakers did have some common ground, awareness and even tools that in 2007 could help them mitigate the consequences of the imminent burst of the asset bubble. Or at least, many of them thought so. Things however, were about to become much more complicated.

A leading financier, Paul McCulley, gave a speech on financial instability. The housing bubbles and their consequences, he argued, may not be the tallest challenge confronting the central bankers in August 2007. According to McCulley, the real problem requiring attention and action was the growth of 'a set of financial intermediaries that lie outside the realm of traditional banks', or as he called it, the shadow banking system, which 'drove one of the biggest lending booms in history, and collapsed into one of the most crushing financial crises we've ever seen' (McCulley 2009: 1). He explained that the shadow banking system was a highly complex and unaccounted for web of financial entities, levered investment conduits, products and structures that paralleled the growth of the asset and housing markets and over time, mutated into a de facto parallel financial universe that operated legally yet entirely outside the regulatory realm. Few had any idea about the size, contents and scope of this shadow banking system. Fewer still understood its significance and implications for economic stability and public policy.

In the months and years that followed the 2007 Fed gathering in Jackson Hole, regulators, finance experts and academics rose to the challenge of addressing the problem of shadow banking and, as it would turn out, its industrial proportions. Between 2007 and now, as their institutions were preoccupied with the practical side of managing the crisis (injecting liquidity into the markets, arranging bank bailouts, managing cooperation on the transatlantic level to deal with the European stage of the crisis), leading minds in the regulatory class and academics from various fields (law, finance, political economy, sociology) have been working towards an understanding of the phenomenon of shadow banking, its size, scope, functions and varieties. Many further studies have delved into the deeper questions about the origins of this parallel financial system and its structural place in the global economy.

This volume presents a synthesis of these efforts, tracing the evolution of shadow banking research from the initial efforts to map, scope and quantify this complex phenomenon, to providing further theoretical and historical analyses of the functions and the role of the shadow banking system in what is commonly known as the financialised capitalism of the late twentieth to early twenty-first centuries.

The agenda of this book

Almost immediately after Paul McCulley first coined the term shadow banking, it became clear that the phrase was concomitantly a stroke of genius and an unfortunate choice of words. 'Shadow' banking resonates with shady banking, ascribing rather pejorative connotations to an important segment that had become essential for the functioning of the global banking system. As a grand metaphor, the term has captured hearts and minds, yet shadow banking is neither shady nor shadowy. Most of the emergent literature implies that 'shadow banking' is a misnomer. In fact, the more we know about the shadow banking industry, the more we realise that a better suited metaphor would have been that of 'mirror banking': shadow banks and shadow banking operations reflect the functions of traditional banks, yet in reverse. While for instance, traditional banks are assumed to be taking in short-term deposits and converting them into long-term loans, shadow banks do the opposite: they take in long-term savings (e.g. pension fund liabilities) and transform them into short-term savings. If traditional banks take in liquid deposits (e.g. cash and similar instruments) and transform them into less liquid securities, shadow banks do the opposite: through a combination of financial and legal operations they transform illiquid assets (such as mortgages or car loans) into apparently liquid financial securities.

At the same time, McCulley's concept of shadow banking would prove to be ingenious. Despite, or maybe because of, the ambiguities of meaning, in the space of just a few years, the study of shadow banking has evolved from the initial efforts to visualise this largely undetected and unregulated web of financial intermediation and delineate its functions, to comparative and theoretical analyses of shadow banking practices across national borders, and their structural place in the global economy. Importantly, it has also awakened the regulators to the challenges posed by the complex and still evolving network of financial intermediation that had been largely undetected up until the crisis of 2007–09.

It also would transpire that although it was McCulley who gave the complex phenomenon of financial innovation its name in 2007, shadow banking had been on the radar of some analysts of the financial system for a while (e.g. Rajan 2005). What then, is 'shadow banking' and what role does a financial system dependent on shadow banking play in the economy? This volume addresses these questions, collating a range of analytical and theoretical perspectives on the phenomenon of shadow banking and finance more generally. The arguments developed in this book, while representing a multi-disciplinary field of expertise, tend to converge on the idea that shadow banking, in its varieties, has become a vital part of financial capitalism. This recognition, in turn, invites further considerations about key concepts in finance and political economy. Overall, the studies collected here not only present the emergent schools of thought on shadow banking but together, represent a systematic effort to address and theorise the phenomenon of financial innovation – up to now, a loosely defined process commonly associated with competition, progress and economic growth driven by finance.

With this major premise, this volume distinguishes three major phases in the evolving literature on shadow banking, focused respectively, on three distinct sets of questions:

1   What is shadow banking and how does it work?
2   What led to the emergence of the shadow banking system, and what are the mechanisms of its rapid expansion since the late 1980s?
3   What, if any, are the structural roots of the shadow banking system, and what lessons does its evolution present to existing paradigms of finance and financial capitalism?

To anticipate, two major conclusions derive from the survey of the debates presented in this book. On the one hand, the long-term consequences of the rise and spread of shadow banking and its institutions are only beginning to be understood fully, both in the framework of economic theory and in the context of regulatory topography of post-crisis economies. On the other, understanding shadow banking is important not only because of the subject matter itself or the risks associated with the shadow banking system. At a broader level, research in shadow banking addresses the so far under-examined and poorly understood phenomenon of financial innovation. It is a great puzzle for those who study finance and banking that despite being the very lifeblood of financial capitalism, up until very recently financial innovation has remained under-researched and, therefore, poorly understood. In fact, it was the lack of critical understanding or even a tradition of academic thought on financial innovation that explained why the crisis of 2007–09 was largely unanticipated by the economic mainstream (Lawson 2009; Mirowski 2013; Nesvetailova 2010).

Reflecting this research agenda, this volume is structured into three parts. Part I summarises the key insights from the first wave of studies on the scope of the shadow banking system. It presents key debates on shadow banking, placing them in the geographical context, and focusing mainly on quantitative and functional dimensions of the shadow banking system and its entities. The degree of effort and access to data needed in the efforts to map the phenomenon of shadow banking have meant that on the whole, the first stage of shadow banking research has been led by financial regulators, market and policy practitioners (see chapters by Pozsar, Baklanova and Tanega, and Moe in this volume). An instructive fact in the context of global efforts to re-regulate the financial system, it also has led many to argue that the post-crisis regulatory efforts are marked by a tangible shift in the balance of power between private market and public authorities (chapters by Bouveret and Bengtsson in this volume), and the new identity and mission of central banks governing the elastic system of privately generated liquidity and credit (Moe in this volume).

Examining the scope, the elements and varieties of the shadow banking system in detail, Chapters 1 to 6 suggest that both globally (2015 estimates by the Financial Stability Board (FSB) put the size of the global shadow banking system at \$137 trillion, or over 40 per cent of the world financial system)[1] and in its regional varieties, shadow banking is a crucial segment of the economic system. As such, it cannot be dismissed as an outcome of undisciplined behaviour of individual bankers or even as an outgrowth of financial speculation more generally (see chapters by Gabor, and Baklanova and Tanega, and Engelen). Indeed, although most well-known maps of shadow banking stress its Anglo-European origins, recent studies have pointed out that shadow banking accounts for up to 40 per cent of financing in the emerging economies in Eastern Europe; anecdotal evidence suggests that the share of non-bank loans in China may have risen to 79 per cent in 2010 and has grown further since (see contributions by Li and Hsu, by Gabor and by Kaurova). In the emerging markets in turn, the term 'shadow banking' covers a range of alternative financial practices such as leasing and factoring companies, credit unions, cooperative banks, microfinance companies and pawn shops and is thus distinct from the concept as used in the context of advanced financialised capitalism (Ghosh *et al.* 2012).[2] China has experienced the fastest growth of shadow banking activities, and even in the economies affected by the crisis – Europe, UK, the Netherlands – shadow banking has either stayed around its 2008 levels, or grown further. It is clear therefore, that shadow banking has been playing an important function in the global chain of financial intermediation, both before and after the crisis of 2007–09. While in the USA the sphere of shadow banks has shrunk in the wake of the 2007–09 crisis, in some jurisdictions, notably the EU, shadow banking activities have grown from 2009 onwards. In other words, available data suggest that shadow banking is a complex and still evolving economic and financial phenomenon that is not confined to the dynamics of the 2007–09 crisis, and thus requires a more serious historical and theoretical discussion.

Part II of the volume takes up this challenge, analysing the factors behind the rise of the shadow banking system. Chapters 7 to 10 summarise the major approaches to the study of shadow banking developed over the past few years in different academic fields, including political science, law and socio-legal studies of finance, economics and business. As this part of the book suggests, the regulators, finance experts, political scientists and legal economists share the view that, fundamentally, the shadow banking system is the outcome of the problem of regulatory arbitrage in global finance. In finance, arbitrage opportunities are pursued by a variety of tactics, including restructuring transactions, financial engineering, geographical and, crucially, juridical relocation and arbitrage.

One of the major consequences of the financial system's ability to escape or augment existing regulations is the problem of systemic risk. Major bank failures during 2007–09 occurred at a nexus of traditional and shadow banking systems. This highlighted new dimensions and sources of systemic risk in finance, as well as myriad other problems posed by the universe of unregulated credit mechanisms and entities. The FSB for instance, specified several major risks associated with a system of credit intermediation that involves entities and activities outside the regular banking system, which in turn raises (i) systemic risk concerns associated with maturity/liquidity transformation, leverage and flawed credit risk transfer, and/or (ii) regulatory arbitrage concerns (FSB 2011). Both sets of issues are related to the practice of leverage and securitisation in shadow banking, an activity that, while yielding economic benefits for its users, creates the problem of unsustainable and perhaps more crucially, undetected debt structures.

At the same time, more critical approaches to shadow banking and the processes it entails have found regulatory arbitrage reasoning rather delimited. Shadow banks and networks perform funding functions that are vital for the activity of official banks, and regulatory arbitrage theories, while insightful of finance's ability to thrive in 'in between' regulatory niches, cannot fully account for the scale, diversity and centrality of shadow banking in today's economy. Indeed, the shadow banking system had expanded not only in the run-up to the 2007–09 crisis but also in its wake. Reflecting these concerns and critique, Part III of this book presents a third body of scholarship on shadow banking. Chapters 11 to 14 bridge research in heterodox economics, political economy, sociology and related fields, addressing the political-economic agenda raised by the phenomena of shadow banking. While the scope of concrete questions addressed by these contributions is wide-ranging, altogether, Part III of the volume suggests that the phenomenon of shadow banking has to be understood as an important institutional outcome of a longer and larger historical process of financial innovation. Reflecting this vision, the third stage of shadow banking research has centred on the question of the significance of shadow banking for the study of finance and financial processes in the economy of the twenty-first century.

The political economy of financial innovation: shadow banking and the financial crisis

The first generation of literature on shadow banking (published mostly between 2007 and 2010) rests on two major arguments. First, shadow banking is only ostensibly a recent problem. As Robert Guttmann and Jan Toporowski, among others, explain in their contributions to this volume, shadow banking is a manifestation of a much longer chain of institutional transformations in the banking industry. The most significant of these shifts is the transition from the 'originate to hold' to 'originate and distribute' model of banking and the rise of universal mega-banks.[3] Often captured by the academic term 'financialisation', these transformations meant that starting in the early 1980s, the business of banking stopped being . . . boring.

A typical bank in the 1950s–1960s was in the tedious business of 'maturity transformation'. It was taking in deposits (liabilities) and extending loans to borrowers (assets). This 'originate to hold' model of banking (often called the 3–6–3 model of banking[4]) meant that the banks extending loans to a variety of borrowers were motivated to understand the risk profiles of its borrowers. The loans lent out were registered on the asset side of the bank's balance sheet, and the variety of risks that may affect the money lent to the borrower and the borrower themselves, was thus directly affecting the bank's balance sheet and its financial position. In academic terms this position is understood as the constraints associated with deposit-making capacities and the so-called 'acceptance function' (Kregel 2010).[5]

Things changed dramatically with the introduction of new financial regulations in the 1980s and the spread of new technologies and cadre in finance. The new business principle in finance and banking has become known as the 'originate to distribute' (OTD) model of banking. Under the new model, the bank originated a variety of loans with a variety of clients, and then shifted (sells) the risks associated with these loans to other participants in the financial system whose business it was to manage those risks. The opportunities offered by the OTD model meant that banking was no longer boring, and instead, became an exciting and highly prestigious area of finance. Along with deregulatory shifts in the financial industry, a major factor in this transformation has been new financial techniques and, in particular, the practice of securitisation (bundling up several tranches of illiquid loans together and converting them into liquid financial securities).

Under the OTD model of banking, securitisation enabled large complex financial institutions to extend huge volumes of home mortgages and credit card loans to non-prime borrowers. Universal banks were effectively (i) originating consumer and corporate loans, (ii) packaging loans into asset backed securities and collateralised debt obligations (CDOs), (iii) creating over-the-counter (OTC) derivatives whose values were derived from loans, and (iv) distributing the resulting securities and other financial instruments to investors. Large complex financial institutions used the OTD strategy to maximise their fee income, reduce their capital charges and transfer the risks associated with securitised loans to investors. Since they also followed reckless lending policies in the commercial real estate and corporate sectors, they retained some residual risks, and with the collapse of securitisation markets in mid-2007, universal mega-banks were exposed to significant losses (Wilmarth 2009: 963–964). Altogether, a set of legal and financial techniques of risk management and securitisation enabled banks to pool together a variety of assets, many of which were of very low credit quality, and, by redistributing these assets off the books, to reduce the levels of risk in their portfolios. Or at least, this was the idea until the crisis broke out in August 2007. The ensuing crisis has revealed, as McCulley observed, the interconnectedness between the official banking system and its less understood shadow segment. It also exposed the many fragile nodes of the global financial network that combined official and shadow banking in long and opaque chains of credit intermediation.

It was not the mere fact that regulated banks may be dependent on their shadow financial creations, but the sheer complexity underpinning the financial network that emerged as one of the most sobering lessons of the financial crisis of 2007–09. Up until the events of 2007–09, complexity, both in organisational and in technical sense, has been widely assumed to be a necessary and healthy component of a thriving financial system in advanced capitalism. Financial technologies and products were seen as a unique sphere of economic activity, where innovation, engineering and specialised expertise produced a highly sophisticated system befitting the great variety of risks. The expertise and talent required to deal with this complexity were, in turn, handsomely rewarded. In the USA, since the late 1980s through to 2007, bankers' pay relative to non-banking professional salaries swelled from almost parity to 1.7 times (Philippon and Reshef 2009). Even after the crisis, despite public outcry, continuing scandals and some restrictions on pay and bonuses, investment banks globally still paid their staff an average of £212,000 in 2012 – higher than a decade ago and 4.6 times the remuneration in the insurance sector. In the UK in 2011, the highest earners in banking received on average bonuses of 3.5 times their base salary in 2011, down from 6.1 times in the year before, according to the data collected by the European Banking Authority (Schafer 2013).

The global credit crisis showed that complexity had become a crucial social and even cultural tool of opacity, employed by financial elites in efforts to isolate themselves in 'silos of silence' (Tett 2016). Professional jargon, heavy mathematics and scientific tools served as barriers to the transparency of the often controversial yet profitable business of financial innovation (Palan and Nesvetailova 2014). Ironically, though perhaps not surprisingly, in the largely self-governed financial system, this complexity would prove implosive: the increasing sophistication and precision of financial practices were paralleled by growing ignorance about the actual developments in finance. In the midst of the 2007–09 meltdown, possibly for the first time in modern economic history, regulators, senior managers and academics resorted to the concept of complexity to excuse and even justify their ignorance about the developments in the financial system in general and in their own institutions in particular (Datz 2012).

The recognition that an undetected and opaque network of financial cells and channels played a leading role in the global financial meltdown has served to empower national and international financial regulatory bodies. It is indeed remarkable that the first generation of scholarship on shadow banking has been led by the regulators themselves (chapters by Pozsar, Bouveret, Bengtsson and Moe in this volume). The efforts to scope the prudential and functional issues arising from the shadow banking system have helped produce refined regulatory maps which in the post-2007 world inform thinking at the monetary and financial regulatory institutions. In parallel, the apparent lack of due attention to this phenomenon of shadow banking in the run-up to 2007–09, has also demonstrated how scarce conceptual knowledge on financial innovation actually is.

One reason for this, according to Awrey (2012), is that up until the crisis, financial innovation was too often assumed to be driven by the demand of economic agents for new financial techniques and products. It was therefore deemed a natural, organic and ultimately progressive element of capitalist development.

Under this general paradigm, there was little dedicated conceptual knowledge developed about financial innovation per se. At best, it was viewed as a universal and homogenising engine of economic growth (e.g. Shiller 2006, 2012). At worst, financial innovation was deemed not to merit specialised academic research.[6]

How can the impact of the first stage of shadow banking research be summarised? The ongoing monitoring and analyses of the evolving network of shadow banks have helped visualise and quantify the shadow banking system, revealing in the process its complexity and global dimensions. Gradually, these efforts, while still continuing, have matured into a debate about the origins and regulatory challenges of the shadow banking system. In the framework of this volume, this debate is presented as a second wave of literature on shadow banking.

Where does it come from? An emergent mainstream view of the shadow banking system

While it evolved broadly in parallel with the initial efforts to frame and map the phenomenon of shadow banking, the second generation of scholarship on shadow banking (circa 2009–2012) has focused on a specific question: how can we explain the emergence, growth and apparent global significance of this phenomenon? In addressing this question, a certain consensus on the origins of shadow banking has emerged, led primarily by legal scholars (Dorn, Awrey, Gorton, Merrick, etc.), sociologists (e.g. Engelen this volume; Engelen *et al.* 2011; Polillo 2013) and political scientists (e.g. Helleiner and Pagliari 2011). Most of the observers converge that the shadow banking system is a cumulative result of regulatory arbitrage. Arbitrage and regulatory avoidance are widely recognised as two major driving factors behind the emergence and growth of the shadow banking network. Yet the specific role of regulatory arbitrage in the shadow banking universe has been interpreted in two different ways.

To some, shadow banking suggests that existing financial regulations are too cumbersome and simply not fit for purpose in the financial system of the twenty-first century. In this interpretation, obsolete, arcane or inadequate regulatory norms and policies had unwittingly given rise to the phenomenon of shadow banking. As Victoria Chick writes, regulations which were intended to strengthen the balance sheets of banks by weighting assets by risk, thus rewarding the holding of safe assets, actually drove risky assets off the balance sheet. As a reaction to Basel rules, securitisation was undertaken not just in a small part of bank operations when banks needed liquidity, but on such a scale as to change the whole way banks operate (Chick 2008: 6–7). From a technique employed by individual desks at individual banks in very specific transactions (like for instance, in dealing with the problem of default risk of corporate clients), securitisation evolved into an industry that allowed banks to identify, pursue and sell off a whole new variety of risks (like subprime mortgages), without taking responsibility for the risks (e.g. Tett 2009).[7]

To others, the vast and complex network of shadow banking units and operations indicates that it is the behaviour of key financial agents (the innovators, or 'bricoleurs' (Ertürk and Solari 2007)) that drives this process by corrupting existing rules and boundaries. The major premise of these accounts is that the financial industry has attained its position of power and influence in today's capitalism, not only because of its direct capacity (capital) to effect or bargain for political outcomes and compromises, but also because it has been able to capture and subsequently change the policy agenda of major political bodies, nationally and internationally (Pagliari 2013). According to Awrey (2012), this supply-driven pattern of financial innovation, particularly dominant in the past few decades, has been marked by two tendencies: the accelerating pace of financial innovation and capture of monopoly-like rents through 'shrouding', or embracing complexity. Seen from this angle, financial innovation through shadow banking has only accelerated longer historical trends, by lengthening the credit creation process itself and adding layers of opacity onto it.

The analyses presented in this volume, while engaging with these two major arguments on the origins of shadow banking, suggest that the deeper roots of the complex phenomenon can be best understood in a different framework. Under closer examination, it appears that the shadow banking system is not a response to financial regulation or arbitrage, but is the outcome of the ongoing quest of finance for being 'elsewhere' and even better, 'nowhere', both for tax and regulatory purposes (Palan and Nesvetailova 2014). At its global core, the shadow banking system is closely embedded in the world of offshore financial havens, which, in turn, have long anchored the globalisation of finance (Palan *et al.* 2010). Richard Murphy explains that the assumption that the secrecy world – the universe of offshore financial havens – is geographically located is simply not correct. It is instead:

> [a] space that has *no specific location*. This space is created by tax haven legislation that assumes that the entities registered in such places are 'elsewhere' for operational purposes, i.e. they do not trade within the domain of the tax haven, and no information is sought about where trade actually occurs.
>
> (Murphy 2009: 2)

In this perspective, special conduits such as special purpose vehicles, special investment vehicles and CDOs, which form a key part of the shadow banking system, are in fact a much more structural phenomenon of global finance and existing systems of financial reporting and accounting.

Over time, the debate about the origins of the shadow banking system has crystallised in the emergent academic discussion about financial innovation. It is quite clear that mainstream academic research in finance and economics was ill-equipped or simply inadequate, to address the problems of financial innovation generally, and innovation through shadow banking in particular. In 2009, Queen Elizabeth II famously asked an audience of esteemed economists at the London School of Economics why no one had seen the crisis coming. The question fell onto an awkward silence.

Before 2007, few economists were interested in asking any questions about any crisis: in most textbooks and policy briefs, crises were the sort of topics that interested Marxists and other academic 'outcasts'. When crises did occur, they were attributed to 'exogenous factors', such as natural disasters, economic changes in neighbouring economies or some other 'outside' shocks, typically associated with less developed countries and their corrupt political regimes. Indeed, despite the fact that financial crises have occurred with some regularity since the early 1980s, it would take the near breakdown of the financial systems advanced in the North Atlantic to home in the controversies and costs of private financial innovation. Both at the micro-level (e.g. the alphabet soup complex and toxic securities invented by financial institutions) and in the macroeconomic context (e.g. reliance on OTC strategies and off-balance sheet operations), financial innovation has been central to the evolution of the shadow banking system.

Along with the continuing economic recession, the role of shadow banking in questioning policy dogmas is indisputable (Turner 2012, 2013). The second generation of scholarship on shadow banking, by shifting the focus from shadow banking entities to the shadow banking as a global systemic phenomenon, has opened up analytical and policy space for interdisciplinary research in finance and further strengthened so-called heterodox approaches in economics and finance, including, most prominently, Keynesian and post-Keynesian theories of money and credit (Chick and Dow 2001; Lawson 2009). One of the big conceptual dilemmas concerning financial innovation in particular is the question of whether financial intermediation through shadow banking *creates* new money and wealth or simply redistributes credit between existing parties.

In this book, the work addressing these important questions is summarised under the broad heading of a third-generation scholarship on shadow banking. While built upon data and information generated by the first phase of efforts to map the shadow banking system, and unavoidably overlapping with the analyses of regulation, competition and arbitrage in finance, the new stage of scholarship is quite distinct. As Part III of this volume suggests, it not only presents an original conceptual reading of shadow banking, but also contributes to a new understanding of financial innovation more broadly.

Banking on the future: the structural demand for financial innovation

The third stream of scholarship on shadow banking is built around an idea that challenges most prevailing beliefs and assumptions about finance, credit and money. It is the notion that far from being uniquely fluid, boundless, harmonious and footless, finance has an in-built structural problem. This thinking suggests that the financial system had reached the limits of its natural growth *as a system* and has been seeking a way to expand.

A key hypothesis that informs this literature is that in today's financialised or 'money manager' capitalism (Minsky 1996; Wray 2009), and especially in the environment of low yield since the late 1990s, the aggregate demand for financial assets consistently outstrips the supply of available capital. Just like the proverbial cats left in charge of the milk, with the end of capital controls in 1971–73, financiers were left in charge of controlling and limiting the available capital, in the face of the growing demand for their assets. A prudent approach to resolving this dilemma would require that only sound financial assets are created and traded, and that existing regulations and market practices safeguard this key principle. Importantly, in doing so, financiers would have to limit their own earnings and profits. Many of them opted for a different route: financial innovation.

Benign approaches to financial innovation understand it as a complex set of techniques, institutions and processes that include, but are not confined to, the invention of new financial products and securities; the creation or augmentation of a market by new financial instruments; the emergence of new types of financial institutions; and structural shifts within financial institutions themselves. More critical views though argue simply that at its heart, 'financial innovation is . . . the subversion of existing routines, rules, and boundaries' (Polillo 2013).

The reasoning on which this vision rests appears counterintuitive. We have grown accustomed to thinking about global finance as virtually boundless. Most of the academic literature on globalisation, financialisation and the international capital markets developed over the past 20 or 30 years, suggests that finance and money are the most globalised, boundless and fluid spheres of the global economy, where a click of a computer mouse can transfer billions of dollars across borders, and where a few hours of work by a team of brilliant mathematicians and financial geeks can create a multi-million dollar security. Academic research has also often suggested that finance has been leading the globalisation trend, and that the sphere of global money and finance has thrived because of a lack or due to the removal of regulations and national barriers (Cerny 1991), often causing financial and economic crises around the world (Gowan 1999; Greider 1997; Harvey 1982; Soederberg 2004). Indeed, the argument about the so-called 'global savings glut' remains one of the most cited explanations for the subprime mortgage crisis and the global credit crunch (Bernanke 2005).

However, under closer examination, finance is in fact one of the most over-regulated spheres of the global economy. The growth and expansion of seemingly boundless capital markets and, especially, of the official banking system, are actually constrained by national tax rules, monetary policies, the fundamentals of the 'real economy', investor sentiment, social and political factors, demographics, etc. One recent manifestation of the consequences of such constraints is the problem of collateral scarcity – the lack of high-quality, readily available capital in the form of liquid securities that can be used for lending and securitisation in particular (Singh 2011). Although having many roots, the scarcity of eligible collateral is commonly seen to be becoming more acute as a consequence of tighter financial regulation introduced in the wake of the 2007–09 crisis. New regulations on liquidity and capital requirements imply that the supply of 'sound' collateral is, in principle, limited (Houben and Slingenberg 2013). One of the key insights of this emergent literature is the idea that for the agents of financial innovation themselves, profit-making may not be the only goal. Innovations today may also be driven by non-pecuniary motivations and objectives (such as competition for reputation, prestige and even sabotage) that, in turn, generate tensions and conflicts within the class of innovators themselves (Polillo 2013: 364). In this process, non-monetary factors, such as jurisdictional fragmentation and facilities created in the process of accommodating the fiscal needs of the economy, now serve as part of the institutional framework of the shadow banking system, contributing to its growth and evolution (Palan and Wigan this volume).

Part III of this book presents the intellectual perspectives that follow from this argument. Its academic origins lie in theories of endogenous finance and hetero-dox political economy. As the essays here imply, the major function of the shadow banking system is to ensure the acceptability of debt instruments in various forms. This angle helps us see that in a broader historical context, activities conducted through and by shadow banking entities are not confined to the financial practices of the 2002–07 lending boom, but can be understood as a continual process of:

> [o]ff-bank balance sheet credit intermediation and maturity and liquidity
> transformation activities conducted by bank owned or sponsored entities in
> the capital and money market domains for the primary purpose of expand-
> ing the rate of production of yield bearing debt securities required by the
> global investor community.
>
> (Lysandrou and Nesvetailova 2014: 4)

In parallel, and contrary to more established traditions of thought on global finance (those stressing the homogenising impact of financial inclusion, the prin-ciple of 'time-space compression', the growing concentration of financial power as well as the seemingly ubiquitous drive of financialisation), the third strand of shadow banking research echoes those views that argue that the global financial system, while elastic, is now defined by fragmentation, over-specialisation and hierarchies, rather than on any single cohesive force.

Together, the three strands of research presented here help explain the diversity and evolving scope of the shadow banking system, the role of regulatory arbitrage in its rise and expansion, and the political economy of shadow banking as the very infrastructure of the debt-anchored financial system today.

Notes

1 The FSB uses an aggregate 'MUNFI' (monitoring universe of non-bank financial inter-mediation) measure of the assets of other financial intermediaries (OFIs), pension funds and insurance companies in 20 jurisdictions and the euro area. In aggregate, the FSB notes, the insurance company, pension fund and OFI sectors all grew in 2014, while banking system assets fell slightly in US dollar terms (FSB 2015: 2).
2 In China for instance, the concept 'total social financing' is used to capture a range of alternative mechanisms of credit provision.
3 In the new era of 'originate and distribute' banking, banks had no incentives to con-trol and account for the variety and quality of risks they themselves originated, simply because they were able to shift them off to other financial intermediaries.
4 The so-called 3–6–3 rule describes how bankers would give 3 per cent interest on depos-itors' accounts, lend the depositors' money at 6 per cent interest and be on the golf course by 3 p.m.

5 Receipt of public deposits and the creation of liquidity by commercial banks.
6 The crisis would also reveal that the basis of empirical studies of financial innovation is rather thin. For instance, in their survey article (2004) reviewing the state of the studies of innovation, Frame and White fund only two dozen empirical articles addressing financial innovation, 14 of which had been written since 2000. As the authors observed then, to the best of their knowledge, 'there are no articles attempting to rank financial institutions by their innovative tendency or to measure the effect of innovative tendency on long run market yields to the institutions' common shares' (cited in Dew 2007: 2–3).
7 This perspective corresponds to longer-held views about the incapacity and futility of bank regulations that, while aimed at making the system safer, have always produced some unintended consequences.

References

Awrey, D. (2012) *Toward a Supply-Side Theory of Financial Innovation.* Oxford Legal Studies Research Paper, no. 44/2012. Available at: https://papers.ssrn.com/sol3/papers.cfm?abstract_id=2094254. Last accessed: 13.01.2017.

Bernanke, B. (2005) *The Global Saving Glut and the U.S. Current Account Deficit.* Speech at the Sandridge Lecture, Virginia Association of Economics, Richmond, Virginia, March 10, and the Homer Jones Lecture, St. Louis, Missouri, 14 April. Available at: www.federalreserve.gov/boarddocs/speeches/2005/200503102/. Last accessed: 13.01.2017.

Cerny, P. (1991) 'The Limits of Deregulation: Transnational Interpenetration and Policy Change'. *European Journal of Political Research*, 19(2/3), pp. 173–196.

Chick, V. (2008) 'Could the Crisis at Northern Rock Have Been Predicted? An Evolutionary Approach'. *Contributions to Political Economy*, 28(1), pp. 115–124.

Chick, V. and S. Dow (2001) 'Formalism, Logic and Reality: A Keynesian Analysis'. *Cambridge Journal of Economics*, 25(6), pp. 705–721.

Datz, G. (2012) 'The Narrative of Complexity in the Crisis of Finance: Epistemological Challenge and Macroprudential Policy Response'. *New Political Economy*, 18(4), pp. 1–21.

Dew, J. K. (2007) *Why are Profits from Financial Innovation So Difficult to Identify? Innovation Clusters and Productive Opacity.* NFI Working Paper, no. 2006-WP-13. Available at: https://papers.ssrn.com/sol3/papers.cfm?abstract_id=946452. Last accessed 21.04.2017.

Engelen, E., I. Ertürk, J. Froud, S. Johal, A. Leaver, M. Moran, A. Nilsson and K. Williams (2011) *After the Great Complacence: Financial Crisis and the Politics of Reform.* Oxford, UK: Oxford University Press.

Ertürk, I. and S. Solari (2007) 'Banks as Continuous Reinvention'. *New Political Economy*, 12(3), pp. 369–388.

FSB (2011) *Shadow Banking: Strengthening Oversight and Regulation.* Recommendations of the Financial Stability Board, 27 October. Available at: www.fsb.org/wp-content/uploads/r_110412a.pdf. Last accessed: 13.01.2017.

FSB (2015) *Global Shadow Banking Monitoring Report.* Basle, Switzerland: Financial Stability Board, November. Available at: www.fsb.org/2015/11/global-shadow-banking-monitoring-report-2015/. Last accessed: 13.01.2017.

Ghosh, S., I. Gonzalez del Mazo and İ. Ötker-Robe (2012) *Chasing the Shadows: How Significant Is Shadow Banking in Emerging Markets?* World Bank, Economic Premise Report, no. 88. Available at: http://siteresources.worldbank.org/EXTPREMNET/Resources/EP88.pdf. Last accessed: 13.01.2017.

Gowan, P. (1999) *The Global Gamble: Washington's Faustian Bid for World Dominance*. London: Verso.

Greider, W. (1997) *One World, Ready or Not: The Manic Logic of Global Capitalism*. London: Penguin Books.

Harvey, D. (1982) *Limits to Capital*. London: SAGE.

Helleiner, E. and S. Pagliari (2011) 'The End of an Era in International Financial Regulation? A Post Crisis Research Agenda'. *International Organization*, 65(1), pp. 169–200.

Houben, A. C. F. J. and J. W. Slingenberg (2013) *Collateral Scarcity and Asset Encumbrance: Implications for the European Financial System*. Financial Stability Review, Banque de France. Available at: www.bis.org/publ/cgfs49.pdf. Last accessed: 13.01.2017.

Kregel, J. (2010) *No Going Back: Why We Cannot Restore Glass-Steagall's Segregation of Banking and Finance*. Levy Institute of Bard College, Public Policy Brief, no. 107. Available at: www.levyinstitute.org/publications/no-going-back-why-we-cannot-restore-glass-steagalls-segregation-of-banking-and-finance. Last accessed: 13.01.2017.

Lawson, T. (2009) 'The Current Economic Crisis: Its Nature and the Course of Academic Economics'. *Cambridge Journal of Economics*, 33, pp. 759–777.

Lysandrou, P. and A. Nesvetailova (2014) 'The Role of Securities in the Shadow Banking System: A Disaggregated View'. *Review of International Political Economy*, 22(2), pp. 257–279.

McCulley, P. (2007) *Teton Reflections*. Pimco, August/September. Available at: www.pimco.com/insights/economic-and-market-commentary/global-central-bank-focus/teton-reflections. Last accessed: 20.12.2016.

McCulley, P. (2009) *The Shadow Banking System and Hyman Minsky's Economic Journey*. Pimco, May. Available at: www.pimco.com/insights/economic-and-market-commentary/global-central-bank-focus/the-shadow-banking-system-and-hyman-minskys-economic-journey. Last accessed: 13.01.2017.

Minsky, H. (1996) *Uncertainty and the Institutional Structure of Capitalist Economies*. Levy Economics Institute of Bard College, Working Paper, no. 155. Available at: www.levyinstitute.org/pubs/wp155.pdf. Last accessed: 13.01.2017.

Mirowski, P. (2013) *Never Let a Serious Crisis go to Waste: How Neoliberalism Survived the Financial Meltdown*. London: Verso.

Murphy, R. (2009) *Defining the Secrecy World. Rethinking the Language of 'Offshore'*. Tax Justice Network. Working Paper. Available at: www.financialsecrecyindex.com/PDF/SecrecyWorld.PDF. Last accessed: 13.01.2017.

Nesvetailova, A. (2010) *Financial Alchemy in Crisis*. London: Pluto.

Pagliari, S. (2013) 'A Wall Around Europe? The European Regulatory Response to the Global Financial Crisis and the Turn in Transatlantic Relations'. *Journal of European Integration*, 35(4), pp. 391–408.

Palan, R. and A. Nesvetailova (2014) *Elsewhere, Ideally Nowhere: Shadow Banking and Offshore Finance*. CITYPERC Working Paper Series, No. 2014–01. Available at: http://openaccess.city.ac.uk/3085/. Last accessed: 13.01.2017.

Palan, R., R. Murphy and C. Chavagneux (2010) *Tax Havens: How Globalization Really Works*. Ithaca, NY: Cornell University Press.

Philippon, T. and A. Reshef (2009) *Wages and Human Capital in the U.S. Financial Industry: 1909–2006*. NBER Working Paper, no. 14644. Available at: www.nber.org/papers/w14644. Last accessed: 13.01.2017.

Polillo, S. (2013) *Conservatives vs. Wildcats: A Sociology of Financial Conflict*. Stanford, CA: Stanford University Press.

Rajan, R. (2005) *Has Financial Development Made the World Riskier?* IMF Working Paper, September. Available at: https://core.ac.uk/download/pdf/6970619.pdf. Last accessed: 13.01.2017.

Schafer, D. (2013) 'Bonuses Fall Significantly for Bankers Earning More than €1m'. *Financial Times*, 15 July.

Shiller, R. (2006) *Irrational Exuberance*. New York: Crown Business.

Shiller, R. (2012) *Finance and the Good Society*. Princeton, NJ: Princeton University Press.

Singh (2011) *Velocity of Pledged Collateral: Analysis and Implications*. IMF Working Paper, no. WP/11/256. Available at: http://nowandfutures.com/large/VelocityOf PledgedCollateral-wp11256(repo_hypothecation)(imf).pdf. Last accessed: 13.01.2017.

Soederberg, S. (2004) *The Politics of the New International Financial Architecture: Reimposing Neoliberal Domination in the Global South*. London: Zed Books.

Tett, G. (2009) *Fool's Gold: How Unrestrained Greed Corrupted a Dream, Shattered Global Markets and Unleashed a Catastrophe*. New York, London: Little, Brown.

Tett, G. (2016) *The Silo Effect: The Peril of Expertise and the Promise of Breaking Down Barriers*. New York: Simon and Schuster.

Turner, A. (2012) *Shadow Banking and Financial Instability*. Cass Business School Lecture. Available at: www.cass.city.ac.uk/__data/assets/pdf_file/0014/120308/004-Cass-Lecture-201203105-2.pdf. Last accessed: 13.01.2017.

Turner, A. (2013) *Debt, Money, and Mephistopheles: How Do We Get Out of this Mess?* Speech at the Cass Business School, 6 February. Available at: www.fca.org.uk/ publication/archive/debt-money-mephistopheles-speech.pdf. Last accessed: 12.01.2017.

Wilmarth, A. (2009) 'The Dark Side of Universal Banking: Financial Conglomerates and the Origins of the Subprime Financial Crisis'. *Connecticut Law Review*, 41(4), pp. 963–1050.

Wray, R. (2009) 'The Rise and Fall of Money Manager Capitalism: A Minskian Approach'. *Cambridge Journal of Economics*, 33(4), pp. 807–828.

Part I

Scoping the shadow banking system

1 Shadow banking

A view from the USA

Zoltan Pozsar

Shadow banking is a widely discussed topic but is not well understood. It is the subject of intense regulatory scrutiny but is not yet clearly defined. Shadow banking means one thing for academics and another for regulators. And it refers to different sets of institutions depending on whom we ask: for banks, shadow banks are hedge funds; for hedge funds, shadow banks are money funds; and for money funds, shadow banks are too-big-to-fail banks. Shadow banking it thus seems is a relative concept: whichever institution is more levered than another is a shadow bank, but in an absolute sense shadow banks do not seem to exist.

The source of this confusion is perhaps the fact that the term "shadow banking" has never been defined. The term was coined by Paul McCulley who described it as:

> [t]he whole alphabet soup of levered up non-bank investment conduits, vehicles and structures. Unlike regulated real banks, who fund them-selves with insured deposits, backstopped by access to the Fed's discount window, unregulated shadow banks fund themselves with uninsured com-mercial paper, which may or may not be backstopped by liquidity lines from real banks.
>
> (see McCulley 2007)

But to emphasize again, this was a description and not a definition of shadow banking. Implicit in McCulley's description were three observations that would later guide the emerging literature on shadow banking. These were that shadow banking involves (1) tradable bonds versus hold-to-maturity loans on the asset side; (2) uninsured, wholesale money market instruments versus insured, retail deposits on the liability side; and (3) levered, non-bank intermediaries that do not have access to liquidity and credit backstops from the Fed and the FDIC versus traditional banks (henceforth banks) that do.

Works that followed took McCulley's description and implicit observations on the assets, liabilities and lack of backstops of levered, wholesale-funded non-bank intermediaries as a starting point, but still did not define shadow banking but rather mapped and described the asset and funding flows in it (see Pozsar 2008).

This map was later expanded (see Pozsar *et al*. 2010) to include the repo market (McCulley's description included only the commercial paper market); to add more institutional detail; and to show how the private liquidity and credit puts (provided by banks and CDS protection sellers, respectively) that were meant to backstop the shadow banking system that failed during the crisis and ended up being replaced with a 360-degree set of public backstops through the Fed's 13(3) facilities and U.S. Treasury's guarantees.

Pozsar (2008) and Pozsar *et al*. (2010) saw the essence of shadow banking in a "securitization-based credit intermediation process" where the functions of credit, maturity and liquidity transformation are performed through daisy-chains of various intermediaries' balance sheets as opposed to a single balance sheet in the case of banks.

Credit transformation – the transformation of credit-risky assets into credit-safe (Treasury note-like) assets – was performed through the prioritization and tranching of loan portfolios' cash flows on the balance sheet of securitization trusts (or special purpose vehicles).[1]

Maturity transformation – the transformation of long-term assets into short-term (Treasury bill-like) assets – was performed through the funding of portfolios of bonds with short-term money market instruments on the balance sheet of non-bank intermediaries.

Liquidity transformation – the transformation of portfolios of short-term money market instruments into at par on demand instruments – was performed on the balance sheet of wholesale cash intermediaries, or money market funds (henceforth money funds).

Importantly, the interpretation of the term "liquidity" in the context of shadow banking should be different from its typical interpretation. In the context of banking and shadow banking, the appropriate interpretation is "at par on demand" liquidity and not market or funding liquidity where liquidity is measured by the tightness of bid-offer spreads; the immediacy with which buy and sell orders can be executed; depth, that is the size of a transaction that can be executed without affecting prices; and resilience, that is, the tendency of prices to return to normal. In other words, in the context of shadow banking, the meaning of the term liquidity is best interpreted from the perspective of the demands of the institutional cash investors funding the system and not from the perspective of the intermediaries being funded.

In describing these three functions the focus of Pozsar (2008) and Pozsar *et al*. (2010) was to emphasize the credit intermediation aspects of shadow banking, and how its essence was to involve money market investors averse to holding long-term, credit-risky private loans in the funding of exactly such loans. But in retrospect, this was too narrow a perspective. Meanwhile, research progressed along the lines of exploring each of the functional areas of shadow banking, but separately, in silos. Thus, corresponding to shadow credit transformation is the literature on "safe asset" shortages (see, for example, Caballero 2010 and Bernanke *et al*. 2011). Corresponding to shadow maturity transformation is the literature on repo (see, for example, Gorton and Metrick 2009).

And corresponding to shadow liquidity transformation is the literature on money funds (see, for example, McCabe 2010).

But from the perspective of understanding what shadow banking – not its components, not its functions, but the system as a whole – was about and why it arose in the first place, one can identify four shortcomings of this body of academic literature and their offspring. Consider the following observations. First observation: these works were written from a micro perspective. A macro perspective describing how the sum of the system's three functions was greater than its parts was lacking.

Namely, shadow banking – similar to traditional banking – involves the creation of money-like (henceforth shadow money) claims.[2] And shadow money is the joint product of credit, maturity and liquidity transformation through what could be called a process of risk "stripping" (see Claessens *et al.* 2012). The concept of risk stripping is the flip side of how the shadow banking system engaged credit and duration risk averse money market investors in funding the extension of long-term credit to the private sector. But instead of focusing on the workings of the credit intermediation process, risk stripping explains how credit-risky, term bonds were turned into "riskless" shadow money claims.

Thus, a portfolio of loans is securitized – this is credit transformation, or credit-risk stripping. The credit-safe (Treasury note-like) tranche of this loan pool is then funded in the wholesale money market through the issuance of money market instruments – this is maturity transformation, or duration risk stripping. These credit-safe, short-term (Treasury bill-like) money market instruments are eligible investments for money funds which, in turn, issue stable value (or $1 net asset value ($1 NAV)) liabilities against a portfolio of such credit-safe, short-term instruments – this is liquidity transformation, or market-risk stripping.

These $1 NAV liabilities (or shadow money claims) were considered to be credit-safe, short-term and liquid (which in the context of this chapter simply means "at par on demand") instruments with zero credit, zero duration and zero market risk that functioned in the financial eco-system as if they were money – a perception also reflected in the Fed's H.6 money supply measure[3] (note that in light of our discussion above, "at par on demand" instruments are simply a subset of credit-safe, short-term instruments, namely those with zero credit, zero duration and zero market risk. Credit-safe, short-term instruments still have some of these risks, but much less than credit-risky, long-term bonds).

Second observation: these works focused solely on private credit (securitized and re-securitized private credit) and failed to broaden the thinking about shadow banking to public credit. Specifically, no attention was paid to the fact that the shadow banking system tried to replicate public money creation through purely private means. And no parallels were drawn between the facts that from a balance sheet perspective, public (or fiat) money is backed by credit-safe Treasuries, and not any type of Treasuries but short-term Treasury bills (the Fed's predominant type of asset until the crisis). Also, that public money essentially amounts to holding portfolios of Treasury bills through a "veil" of zero credit, zero duration and zero market-risk liabilities (which may be currency or reserves) issued by the central bank, and that in a similar fashion shadow money claims were backed by credit-safe Treasury-like instruments, and not any type of Treasury-like instruments but short-term, Treasury bill-like instruments (issued by non-bank intermediaries to fund long-term bonds and money funds' main type of asset). And finally, that shadow money claims essentially amount to holding portfolios of Treasury bill-like instruments through a "veil" of zero credit, zero duration and zero market risk (or $1 NAV) liabilities issued by money funds.[4]

Of course, the money-ness of public and shadow money claims is not the same: the former is backed by Treasury bills and the latter only by Treasury bill-like instruments, and the former is created by the central bank at will and the latter represents borrowed funds; but these parallels are instructive nonetheless. In fact, this chapter uses them as an entry point for a deeper understanding of shadow banking and the larger eco-system within which it exists.

Third observation: these works all focused on shadow banking from the supply side, asking what was wrong with the system (safe asset provision via securitization; repo and short-term funding; and money funds) but not what underlying problem the system arose to solve and how this problem could have been solved differently.

A demand side perspective to shadow banking – asking who (that is, what types of investors) were funding the system and why – was missing, and the raison d'être of the "shadows" was assumed to be simply "regulatory arbitrage and search for yield" (on the demand side, see Pozsar 2011, 2012; and Claessens *et al.* 2012).

Fourth observation: these works ignored the fact that safe assets are not the same as credit-safe, short-term assets and at par on demand assets. As a result, the shortage of safe assets came to mean a shortage of credit-risk free assets, and the literature (see Krishnamurthy and Vissing-Jorgensen 2010 and IMF 2012) missed the systemically far more important shortage of credit-safe, short-term assets and their at par on demand subset demanded by institutional cash investors averse to holding not only credit, but also duration and market risk (see Pozsar 2011).

It is the shortage of credit-safe, short-term and at par on demand assets where credit, duration and market-risk stripping intersect and the essence of shadow banking is clearly visible.

In light of the observations above, to help clear the confusion around shadow banking, the system can be defined as one of "money market funding of capital market lending" (see Mehrling *et al.* 2013). The term "money market funding of capital market lending" is a synthesis of both the credit intermediation and "money" creation aspects of shadow banking, and it also meshes remarkably well with McCulley's implicit observations on bonds versus loans, and uninsured wholesale money market instruments versus insured deposits.

As such, Mehrling *et al.*'s description is an excellent candidate for an official definition of shadow banking and superior to the terms "market-based financing" or "market-based credit intermediation" which leave out the crucial detail of the type of market (money or capital) where financing is being conducted. However, "money market funding of capital market lending" involves both bank and non-bank intermediaries and as such cannot be a definition of shadow banking without amendments. Banks, unlike shadow banks, have access to the Fed, and shadow banking – according to McCulley 2007 – involves intermediaries with no access to the Fed. Shadow banking could thus be defined as a subset of "money market funding of capital market lending". Namely, it is "money market funding of capital market lending by non-banks" or more precisely "non-banks with managed balance sheets but without reserve accounts at the Fed" (see Fisher 2012).

Notes

1 The term "safe asset" (popularized by the works of Caballero 2010, Krishnamurthy and Vissing-Jorgensen 2010 and more recently the IMF 2012) is misleading as it only refers to the likelihood of an asset's default. However, assets carry other risks too, such as duration risks. The term "credit-safe" aims to address the fact that credit-safe assets may not be safe from a duration risk perspective (Fisher 2012). Truly safe assets have zero credit, zero duration and zero market (or liquidity) risk. In the context of this chapter, safe assets are reserves and insured deposits.
2 Only the central bank and insured banks create money. Everyone else in the financial eco-system borrows money. The claims representing these borrowings are money-like (hence shadow), but not money in a strict sense.
3 In observing that money funds' liabilities were considered to be "at par on demand" (that is, stable value), this chapter is simply making an observation of a fact. As this chapter argues, stable value money fund shares are not money and should not be considered money in a strict sense.
4 Shadow money claims other than $1 NAV liabilities are overnight repos and, importantly, uninsured checking accounts. These instruments will be discussed in later parts of this chapter.

References

Bernanke, B., C. Bertaut, L. P. DeMarco and S. Kamin (2011) *International Capital Flows and the Return to Safe Assets in the US, 2003–2007*. International Finance Discussion Paper, no. 1014. Available at: www.federalreserve.gov/pubs/ifdp/2011/1014/ifdp1014. pdf. Last accessed: 16.12.2016.

Caballero, R. J. (2010) *The "Other" Imbalance and the Financial Crisis*. NBER Working Paper, no. 15636. Available at: www.nber.org/papers/w15636.pdf. Last accessed: 16.12.2016.

Claessens, S., Z Pozsar, L. Ratnovski and M. Singh (2012) *Shadow Banking: Economics and Policy*. IMF Staff Discussion Note. Available at: www.imf.org/external/pubs/ft/ sdn/2012/sdn1212.pdf. Last accessed: 16.12.2016.

Fisher, P. R. (2012) "Thoughts on Debt Sustainability: Supply and Demand Keynote Remarks". In F. Allen, A. Gelpern, C. Mooney and D. Skeel (eds) *Is US Government Debt Different?* Philadelphia, PA: FIC Press.

Gorton, G. B. and A. Metrick (2009) *Securitised Banking and the Run on Repo*. Working Paper, no. 15223. Available at: www.nber.org/papers/w15223.pdf. Last accessed: 16.12.2016.

IMF (2012) *Global Financial Stability Report*. Chapter 3. Available at: www.imf.org/ external/pubs/ft/gfsr/2012/01/pdf/c3.pdf. Last accessed: 16.12.2016.

Krishnamurthy, A. and A. Vissing-Jorgensen (2010) *The Aggregate Demand for Treasury Debt*. Working Paper. Available at: www.cemfi.es/ftp/pdf/papers/Seminar/demand treas_may122010_jperevision.pdf. Last accessed: 16.12.2016.

McCabe, P. E. (2010) *The Cross Section of Money Market Fund Risks and Financial Crises*. Finance and Economics Discussion Series, Federal Reserve Board, Washington, DC. Available at: www.federalreserve.gov/pubs/feds/2010/201051/201051pap.pdf. Last accessed: 16.12.2016.

McCulley, P. (2007) *Teton Reflections*. Newport Beach, CA: PIMCO.

Mehrling, P., Z. Pozsar, J. Sweeney and D. H. Neilson (2013) *Bagehot was a Shadow Banker: Shadow Banking, Central Banking, and the Future of Global Finance*. Working Paper. Available at: https://ssrn.com/abstract=2232016. Last accessed: 16.12.2016.

Pozsar, Z. (2008) *The Rise and Fall of the Shadow Banking System*. Regional Financial Review, Moody's. Available at: www.economy.com/sbs. Last accessed: 16.12.2016.

Pozsar, Z. (2011) *Institutional Cash Pools and the Triffin Dilemma of the U.S. Banking System*. IMF Working Paper. Available at: www.imf.org/external/pubs/ft/wp/2011/wp11190.pdf. Last accessed: 16.12.2016.

Pozsar, Z. (2012) "A Macro View of Shadow Banking: Do T-Bill Shortages Pose a New Triffin Dilemma?", in F. Allen, A. Gelpern, C. Mooney and D. Skeel (eds) *Is US Government Debt Different?* Philadelphia, PA: FIC Press.

Pozsar, Z., T. Adrian, A. Ashcraft and H. Boesky (2010) *Shadow Banking*. Federal Reserve Bank of NY Staff Reports, no. 458. Available at: www.newyorkfed.org/medialibrary/media/research/staff_reports/sr458_July_2010_version.pdf. Last accessed: 16.12.2016.

2 The transformation of banking

Robert Guttmann

The financial crisis of 2007–09, brutal and deep as it was, hit everyone by surprise. We can accept that most economists could not have foreseen this tragic event, wedded as they are to a minimalist view of finance as passive residual and comprising efficient markets. More troubling is that bankers themselves had, for the most part, no clue what was brewing. While there were clear signs of an unsustainable US housing bubble emerging already in 2005–06, it was not at all obvious that its demise would trigger such an avalanche of instability on a truly global scale. This begs the question of how and why trouble in a relatively minor slice of the bond market, namely the downgrading of some mortgage-backed securities following a spike in subprime-mortgage defaults during the first quarter of 2007, set off a bullet ricocheting across various financial markets and credit channels to bring the entire world economy to the brink of collapse.[1]

The answer was given to us by the crisis itself. As is generally true with systemic crises (see, for instance, the Great Depression of the 1930s or stagflation in the 1970s), their precise unfolding reveals hitherto hidden realities of fragility, rupture, and contagion. In this case, we were confronted with the existence of a subterranean credit system of vast proportions whose unstable and intertwined nature not even its creators had grasped until it was too late. This system, now generally referred to as the "shadow banking system" (SBS), is a dangerous beast inasmuch as it thrives in hiding and beyond constraint, but is ready to spill over into the real economy at any time (both on the up- and down-swing sides of the latter's cyclical growth process). Unless we come to terms with this new dimension of global finance, we will not master our own fate.

Network finance

As Nesvetailova explains in the introduction to this volume, the term "shadow banking" has been attributed to Paul McCulley of fixed-income trader Pimco, who coined it in 2007 while referring to "the whole alphabet soup of levered up non-bank investment conduits, vehicles, and structures". Given its prominent role in the crisis of 2007/08, "shadow banking" has since become a major object of attention by national bank regulators (Federal Reserve, Bank of England, European Central Bank, etc.) as well as global rule-setting organizations, notably the Bank for International Settlements (BIS), the International Organization of Securities Commissions, and the Financial Stability Board (FSB). These authorities have recently agreed on an official definition of "shadow banking" as involving "entities and activities structured outside the regular banking system that perform bank-like functions" or, to put it in more compressed form, as "non-bank credit intermediation".[2]

Even though that definition of "shadow banking" does pinpoint accurately its key nature of mobilizing credit beyond the purview of regulators, it does imply something sinister going on. That negative connotation of something improper or illegal (as in "shadowy") is, however, not the only bias. I see two more possible inaccuracies embodied in the above definition. One is its emphasis on non-bank institutions, such as money-market funds, hedge funds, and structured-investment vehicles, as if "shadow banking" was separated from traditional banks which, as we shall see further below, it is decidedly not. And the other is a descriptive bias. By presenting "shadow banking" as a collection of "investment conduits, vehicles, and structures" or as an amalgam of "entities" and "activities", we presume their separate existence parallel to each other as if they were not intertwined so as to render the whole more than the sum of its parts.

What we need hence is a more systemic view of "shadow banking" as a transformational phase in the evolution of our financial system and one profoundly linked to traditional banking (instead of an alternative to it). In opting for such a systemic view, we could do worse than starting with a series of remarkable studies of "shadow banking" conducted in recent years by the research staff of the Federal Reserve Bank of New York.[3] These are especially noteworthy for having constructed a topography of the SBS in all its complexities. When looking at these Federal Reserve Bank of New York "maps" of the SBS, we can see that the principal vehicles of this subterranean credit system – its actors (money-market mutual funds, investment conduits, structured-investment vehicles, hedge funds, broker-dealers, finance companies, etc.) as well as its instruments (wholesale money-market instruments, repos, asset-backed securities, and so forth) – form intricate webs of funding affiliations and intermediation chains. It may therefore be opportune to characterize the SBS as *network finance*.

While it is fair to argue that all finance is ultimately composed of networks, those define neither *indirect finance* (involving commercial banks taking deposits and making loans) nor *market finance* (comprising securities markets, market-making investment banks, and the institutional investors buying securities) as such. In contrast, in shadow banking, it is the network that counts as its defining feature by the transferring and sharing of risks through chains of maturity or credit intermediation.

The term "network finance" is also useful inasmuch as it allows us to apply network theory to matters of finance. The rapid propagation of network analysis since the late 1990s has already brought forth interesting contributions to key questions pertaining to finance, such as how social ties between corporate managers and institutional investors shape investment decisions, how investment banks organize the underwriting of securities, how financial institutions share risks, or how incidences of financial instability trigger contagion.[4] While these studies shed new light on important issues such as systemic risk, the role of informal ties in investment decisions or corporate governance, or the modus operandi of certain financial institutions, they do not deal specifically with shadow banking. Yet network analysis can usefully highlight key features of SBS and so help us better understand this still relatively obscure dimension of modern finance. I am particularly interested in what this approach can bring to the questions of financial innovation, universal banking, and systemic crisis.

Financial innovation

While economists have in recent decades focused increasingly on innovation as a key driving force of growth, they have paid comparatively scant attention to the issue of financial innovation. As a matter of fact, it is fair to argue that there exist strong biases in our profession that prevent us from taking this issue as seriously as we should. Standard economic models developed for finance, such as the Modigliani-Miller theorem of capital structure or the capital asset pricing model, focus solely on securities. They explain why investors may prefer some type of security compared to another, but have little to say as to why a new type of security may emerge. Financial innovation is in this context often reduced to a question of improved mathematical application, as happened with the explosion of option trading following the introduction of the Black-Sholes model, or new technology, as occurred with the introduction of ATM machines or electronic money. In any case, economists have repeatedly expressed a negative bias towards financial innovation as enhancing rent-seeking but adding little to productivity growth.[5]

In contrast, I favour a Minskian view of financial innovation exerting significant (pro-cyclical) macro-economic influence by facilitating higher levels of debt-financed spending, only to lead to a build-up of risks and eventual crisis.[6] Profit-seeking financial institutions use innovation to make it easier for themselves and their clients to operate with greater amounts of debt, and the success of their efforts supports a higher level of aggregate demand in the economy. But this spending- and income-creation enhancement makes those actors also less conscientious of the greater risks incurred in conjunction with more leverage. In the process, and this is at the core of the "financial instability hypothesis" developed by Hyman Minsky (1992), economic actors end up with higher debt servicing charges that make them more vulnerable (or, as Minsky put it, more "financially fragile") to revenue-reducing shocks. Significant financial crises occur when a relatively large number of economic actors have reached this fragile stage of Minsky's so-called "Ponzi finance" position where revenues no longer suffice to meet even debt servicing charges and so necessitate new debt to service old debt.

But I also believe that it is useful to look at the micro-level specificities of financial innovation. That activity is far different from industrial innovation. Whereas the latter involves tangible products on which innovators have often spent considerable effort before obtaining promising results, the former typically involves just contractual arrangements and thus far lower sunk costs. Because of their intangible nature, financial innovations do not typically get assigned intellectual property rights. Both their intrinsic copiability and lack of legal protections limit any first-comer advantages. Financial innovators thus have an interest in making their innovation less easily and/or less rapidly copied. They can slow the catching-up capacities of imitators by making their innovations as opaque, as complex, and/or as customized as possible. Shadow banking accommodates these characteristics. It encourages opacity by operating off-balance-sheet. It facilitates complexity, both in the design of the financial claims and how these circulate, by typically bringing many players together who are given considerable freedom to experiment in the absence of regulatory constraints and accounting rules. And it fosters customization by avoiding the standardization needs of claims traded in public exchanges (e.g. government bonds, corporate stocks) in favour of broker-dealer networks which can accommodate in personalized fashion a much greater variety of funding arrangements for their clients.

This last point deserves closer attention. We need to understand clearly the differences between public exchanges and broker-dealer networks, often referred to as "over-the-counter markets (OTC)". Exchanges are run by a central rule-making authority, have third-party clearing facilities, trade standardized products, and maintain transparently accessible prices under all circumstances. In contrast, the OTC "markets" involve bilateral deals between two parties who agree with each other on all the terms of their trades and settle those among themselves without third-party assistance. These parties have the freedom to customize their transactions and even keep their prices hidden from others. Their dealings "over-the-counter" are in effect off-exchange trades between parties bound together in inter-dealer networks. These differences in the trading of financial instruments are one reason why it makes sense to juxtapose *market finance* (public exchanges) and *network finance* (dealer networks). Since the ultimate success of many financial innovations depends on their rapid diffusion, it is often easier to achieve such scale by setting up less costly and more flexible dealer networks than the more complex, regulated, and transparent public exchanges.

Regulatory dialectic

Another crucial aspect of financial innovation is its regulation-evading intent. We have many examples where financial innovations were launched to move their users beyond regulatory constraints. As a matter of fact, we can clearly discern a sort of "regulatory dialectic" here. Financial institutions innovate in order to escape regulations. Having succeeded in that effort, they then tend to use their newly found freedoms excessively to the point of triggering a crisis. The damage caused by such irresponsible behaviour prompts the authorities to re-regulate what has now become a clearly untenable situation.[7] As we shall explore further in this section, all the main pillars of the SBS have arisen in the course of such regulatory dialectic.

The first time we see this process come to the fore was during the 1960s, when hitherto tightly regulated commercial banks created two avenues of massive regulatory circumvention – first a global private banking network known as the "Eurocurrency markets", followed by the introduction of new money-market instruments through which banks could borrow additional funds on short notice. Those two new sources of funds transformed the post-war regime of nationally administered credit-money that had been put into place by Roosevelt's monetary reforms (Emergency Banking Act of 1933, Glass Steagall Act of 1933, Bank Act of 1935).[8] That regime had been centred around commercial banks attracting deposits, thereby gaining reserves, setting aside a certain fraction of those reserves to meet withdrawal needs (i.e. so-called "fractional-reserve banking"), and then using their excess reserves to make loans. This intermediation process, characterized earlier as "indirect finance", assured endogenous money creation by commercial banks in response to the public's demand for credit, which the central banks tended to accommodate as much as possible. Having tied the banks' money-creation activity to their profit motive (when turning zero-interest (excess) reserves into interest-yielding loan assets), central bankers kept a tight rein on that process to minimize the propensities of profit-seeking bankers for instability and inequality. At that point, US commercial banks had been essentially shut out of financial markets, which were in turn organized by investment banks. Other industrial nations, such as Germany, Japan, or the United Kingdom, had not explicitly separated *indirect finance* (i.e. commercial banking) and *market finance* (i.e. investment banking) as the US had done with Glass Steagall. But in those countries, banks established close ties to industrial firms while suppressing the scope of financial markets so as to keep alternative funding channels for corporations in check, as exemplified by Germany's "Hausbank" or Japan's "keiretsu".

The Eurocurrency markets

In the 1960s, US banks found a very convenient way to circumvent all of their regulatory constraints in one swoop – geographic branching restrictions, interest-rate ceilings on bank deposits and loans, separation of commercial and investment banking – when London sought to extend its global financial centre role by accepting bank deposits and loans denominated in US dollars. This so-called "Eurodollar market" redirected US dollars in international circulation, a by-product of the dollar-based international monetary system known as Bretton Woods, from the official payments system of central banks to a new private banking network operating (ultimately globally) beyond the reach of the national monetary authorities. In the absence of any regulatory costs, transnational banks operating in the Eurocurrency market were able to offer their global clientele higher deposit rates and lower loan rates while at the same time still earning better spreads than in the highly regulated domestic banking system. No surprise then that this more attractive intermediation channel soon began to draw funds away from the less lucrative domestic banking circuits. In a way, it is fair to say that the creation of the Eurodollar market in 1960 marked the beginning of shadow banking, organized by a network of transnational banks linked to each other through the two computerized payments systems of SWIFT and CHIPS encompassing the Eurocurrency market.[9]

Since then the Euromarket has been a primary catalyst for financial globalization, spearheading the internationalization of capital. On top of its original layer of indirect finance (time deposits, loans) the transnational banks have added layers of market finance, in particular, globally traded floating-rate notes and sovereign debt. Not constrained by any regulatory barriers, it did not take long for Eurobanks to drive excessive behaviour to the point of crisis. Rapidly evolving in the late 1960s into a highly effective vehicle of global speculation thanks to the ease of moving funds across countries and currencies, the Euromarket brought down the fixed-rate regime of Bretton Woods in a series of devastating attacks on the dollar (March 1968, August 1971, March 1973). The messy transition to a new system of floating exchange rates in the mid-1970s transformed currency speculation from attacks on unsustainable pegs to a daily search for capital gains from correctly anticipated exchange-rate movements and thereby into a major profit centre of transnational banks and multinational corporations. At times, speculators failed, and their losses threatened to bring down banks as happened in 1974 with Germany's Herstatt Bank. In the wake of that bank's collapse, the Eurocurrency markets froze up. This crisis prompted leading central banks to meet under the aegis of the BIS and agree to improved coordination during crises, the so-called Basel Concordat of 1975. The BIS was thus transformed into the role of global coordinator for the world's leading central banks, a role that got dramatically enhanced with the 1988 Basel Accord establishing a new regime of globally coordinated banking regulations in the aftermath of a painfully long sovereign-debt crisis triggered by the Euromarket's excessive recycling of petro-dollars – the LDC debt crisis of 1982–1989.

Borrowed liabilities

One of the primary uses of the Euromarket early on consisted of US banks moving the local funds of their largest (corporate and wealthy individual) clients off-shore, where the domestic Regulation Q interest-rate ceilings did not apply and so yielded better returns, and then re-borrowing those funds from their Euromarket subsidiaries abroad. Such substitution of deposit liabilities by borrowed liabilities soon took on a much larger scale, as banks introduced during the 1960s a variety of new funding instruments – large-denomination time deposits that could be re-sold to third parties before maturity ("negotiable CDs"), excess reserves that could be re-loaned to banks with reserve deficiencies ("federal funds"), short-term bonds ("commercial paper"), to name a few. These new money-market instruments made it possible for banks to pursue more aggressive expansion goals. Rather than having to keep highly liquid, but low-earning assets (i.e. cash reserves, Treasury bills) on hand to meet withdrawal needs arising from their deposit liabilities, they could now free themselves from this liquidity constraint on their asset side by borrowing in the money markets whenever they needed to.

They could access those borrowed liabilities on short notice to match any short-falls from their deposit liabilities relative to their asset base. Such access to the money markets allowed banks to set higher asset-growth targets and invest in higher-yielding, but less liquid assets.

The burgeoning money markets received a shock in 1975 with the introduction of money-market funds (MMFs) in the United States. Sponsored initially by mutual funds, those MMFs attracted savers by treating them as sharehold-ers who earn money-market rates on their fund shares. As long as the banks had interest-rate ceilings (Regulation Q) imposed on them, the MMFs could offer more attractive returns and thereby divert large amounts of funds from banks. In order to fight this massive disintermediation, US banks pushed suc-cessfully for a phase-out of Regulation Q ceilings in the early 1980s and then offered competitive money-market deposit accounts and/or introduced their own MMFs. Since those funds did not enjoy deposit-insurance protection by the FDIC and emergency support from the Fed, they tried to make up for that competitive disadvantage by offering limited cheque-writing privileges on their fund-share accounts and guaranteeing a net asset value of one dollar per share. Their success has greatly boosted demand for money-market instruments and so supported much larger money-market trading volumes.

These money markets, including Eurocurrencies, have at their centre the inter-bank market where the world's leading banks can fund each other on a daily basis. This "market" operates in a highly decentralized fashion as a loose network where banks negotiate bilateral funding deals without central supervision. Apart from the major international banks, the interbank "market" network also includes, albeit to a much more limited extent, smaller regional banks, other financial institutions, and multinational corporations. Much of the global interbank "market" comprises foreign exchange transactions and is thus the principal locus for the funding of currency speculation, a large-volume and highly leveraged activity that remains a significant profit centre for financial institutions and companies alike. It should be noted that the interbank market and the web of additional money-market seg-ments it supports enabled during the 1990s and 2000s many second-tier banks and non-bank institutions to fund aggressive expansion of their balance sheets in an effort to catch up with the market leaders. This all came to a sudden halt in September 2008 when, following losses suffered from the bankruptcy of Lehman Brothers, America's oldest money-market fund known as Reserve Primary could not maintain its promised one dollar net asset value and so triggered a panic run on other MMFs which froze the world's money markets. Suddenly cut off from wholesale funding, the most aggressive borrowers found themselves in a brutal liquidity squeeze which some of them did not survive (e.g. Northern Rock, Fortis, Dexia, Hypo Real Estate). More recently, the world's money markets have been shaken by revelations that the world's twenty leading banks setting the interbank rate known as LIBOR (London Interbank Offer Rate) had rigged rate submissions for their own benefit, especially during the credit crunch of 2008. That scandal shed dramatic light on an insider network in blatant collusion to manipulate the world's most important money-market rate serving as the benchmark for a good many other short-term interest rates – "network finance" as its most criminal, and a horrible indictment of the world's leading bankers' proclivity to run their industry as a cartel.[10]

The repo market

In another misnomer where a supposed "market" is in reality a network, banks have structured a secured loan as a repurchase agreement where one party sells a packet of securities to another party with the promise to buy those back at a slightly higher price shortly thereafter. This practice of swapping securities for cash began with the central banks' collateralization of emergency loans which turned into a more standard monetary-policy tool in the context of open-market operations and then spread from the central bank's network of primary dealers to other banks and eventually to the universe of financial institutions at large. Today the repo market in the US alone has grown to the astronomical volume of $5 trillion, with a crisis-induced contraction during 2008–09 already fully put behind. The enormous popularity of repo transactions stems from allowing sell-ers to turn their securities into loan collateral and hence into cash while giving buyers access to securities for a prescribed period of time and a pre-determined rate of return at low risk.

Such bilateral repurchasing agreements do carry counterparty risk, which can be mitigated by a third party, typically a clearinghouse, stepping in to assume that risk. The spread of such tri-party repos in recent years has expanded the range of securities acceptable as collateral and boosted access to the repo market for a much larger number of players. Such expansion has also brought riskier practices. For one, it has become more common to see investors buy securities and then scramble for a repo transaction to pay for that acquisition with borrowed funds. This works as long as the returns earned on the securities serving as collateral exceed repo rates paid on the loans, a situation likely to persist as long as quan-titative easing by the world's leading central banks keeps money-market rates artificially low and securities prices rising. Any future tightening of monetary policy may cause sharp reversals in those spreads and so trigger a shock in the repo market. Another dangerous practice is rehypothecation where the same bun-dle of securities serves more than once as collateral, thus supporting a chain of repo transactions. We have good evidence that the super-fast growth of the SBS just before the crisis was largely driven by rehypothecation. The extent to which this practice multiplies counterparty risk became clear with the collapse of MF Global in October 2011 where the firm had used collateral belonging to its clients to fund its risky expansion.

We also have learned from the ongoing crisis in the Eurozone that the repo market has some resilience, with less creditworthy borrowers able to continue funding as long as they are willing to accept "haircuts" (i.e. lower valuations for their securities and hence above-par collateral). As we have seen in the case of Greek and Cypriot banks, this practice presumes continued funding support of those high-risk institutions by the central bank which can thereby pressure troubled banks more easily into restructuring. Still, to the extent that MMFs remain dominant buyers/lenders in the repo market, its resilience depends on their willingness and ability to provide funds. European banks suffered a great deal of pressure from the growing reluctance of US MMFs to fund them during 2011 and 2012, and the MMFs themselves are vulnerable to sudden runs as long as they are rigidly committed to a fixed net asset value.

Derivatives

In 1973, the world moved from fixed (government-set) exchange rates to flexible (market-determined) exchange rates, followed in 1979 by the deregulation of interest rates. Since then, both prices of money have shown great volatility, prompting the introduction of financial derivatives which enabled its users to hedge their exposures to adverse exchange- or interest-rate movements by locking in these rates today. On the other side of the ledger, highly leveraged derivative contracts have attracted speculators betting on the future direction of these price movements. Here we must distinguish between two types of derivatives that emerged after 1980. One category comprises futures and options, which are traded as standardized contracts in public exchanges. These are part of the aforementioned "market finance". The other consists of a growing variety of OTC derivatives that are designed to meet the specific needs of the two parties engaged in that transaction, giving them the customized and opaque features typifying "network finance".

Early on, OTC derivatives consisted largely of swaps allowing interested parties to transform claims (e.g. debt-for-equity swaps) or exchange cash flows associated with claims (e.g. interest-rate swaps) for desired portfolio adjustments. Later on, in response to massive regulatory arbitrage by banks trying to bypass the risk-adjusted capital requirement at the centre of the aforementioned Basel Accord of 1988, we see an explosion of a new type of OTC derivative, so-called credit derivatives. Banks responded to this new regulatory principle of the BIS by selling off their safer loans, for which they would have put aside less capital on their own than required by the Basel rules, and keeping on their books riskier loans which the capital requirement of Basel undercapitalized. This circumvention strategy, a classic example of regulatory dialectic, spawned two crucial financial innovations. The banks could get rid of their better loans by bundling them together into marketable securities, thus boosting the burgeoning practice of securitization. And they could seek credit-risk protection for their riskier loans remaining on the books by acquiring credit-default swaps (CDSs), thereby dramatically increasing the demand for this new type of loan-default insurance.

The latter experienced meteoric rise in the run-up to the crisis of 2008, perhaps an indication that the Minskian pattern of growing financial fragility fuelled the need to mitigate greater credit risks with protection against default losses. But that crisis also illustrated the extent to which the pre-crisis growth of CDSs was fuelled by a number of practices that went far beyond the original intent of these swaps. In such a credit-default swap, the protection buyer makes a series of payments ("fees" or "spread") to the seller who promises to compensate the buyer in the event of a default or other credit event (e.g. restructuring, or even just a drop in the borrower's credit rating). This is a straight hedge against default risk. But parties can also acquire CDS contracts if they have no insurable interest whatsoever relating to the debt in question, thereby turning the swap into a tool of speculation. Such "naked" CDSs allow investors to speculate on the creditworthiness of debtors or short-sell bonds, and they soon came to absorb 80 per cent of the multi-trillion CDS volume. Hedge funds in particular have found naked CDSs to be an irresistible means for speculative gains during and in the aftermath of a major crisis when many debtors face questions about their creditworthiness. More broadly speaking, naked CDSs have given rise to *synthetic finance* whereby investors can run several speculative strategies on bonds without owning the underlying debt instruments.[11] Apart from having raised speculation to a whole new level, CDSs are also controversial through their signalling effect whereby rising CDS spreads indicate market expectations of declining creditworthiness to put more pressure on already troubled debtors. And, unlike traditional insurers, sellers of CDSs do not have to have the cash ready for eventual payouts, which proved disastrous for AIG, triggering the biggest bail-out of the crisis.

Securitization

Much has already been said about securitization, the bundling of loans against which asset-backed bonds can be issued. This practice has enabled banks to replace volatile interest-spread income with more stable fee income, transfer risk to third parties, and speed up the turnover of their loans. The explosive growth of mortgage-backed securities (MBSs) during the last stages of America's great housing bubble in 2005 and 2006 owed much to various extensions of that innovation. In a powerful example of *structured finance*, which in its most general usage involves complex financial instruments (e.g. derivatives, securitized instruments) to respond in customized fashion to the unique financing needs of debtors that traditional funding instruments could not satisfy, banks would pool together MBSs and issue collateralized debt obligations (CDOs) against them.[12] They would then split up CDOs into tranches of different riskiness, with the senior tranches shielded from losses until the junior tranches were wiped out. This practice enabled senior tranches to carry triple-A ratings even though they contained many riskier debts in the underlying bundle backing them. The different CDO tranches each had their own network of issuers and buyers, with hedge funds in particular gobbling up the riskier junior tranches. New issues of CDOs were further accelerated by tying those to CDSs, a combination of synthetic and structured finance which greatly facilitated investor access to CDOs and streamlined how those structured instruments were created. Moreover, bank-sponsored special-investment vehicles issued shorter-term asset-backed commercial paper (ABCP) and used thereby mobilized funds in support of longer-term MBSs and CDOs. This web of linkages explains how a default wave among riskier subprime mortgages triggered a tsunami-like shock wave all the way to the money markets of the world, first eroding the credibility of MBSs, rendering many CDOs impossible to value, spilling losses into the CDS network, and endangering proper servicing of ABCPs which in turn triggered back-up credit lines in the commercial-paper market provided by the banks.

Universal banking

When looking at those financial innovations discussed above in their entirety, it is clear that they transformed banking. Securities have replaced loans as the principal form of credit, with their issue increasingly tied to the process of money creation. Their markets, whether for money-market instruments, equity shares, bonds, currencies, or derivatives, have moved beyond self-regulated public exchanges trading standardized claims to broker-dealer networks offering customized arrangements that meet the specific needs of individual portfolios. Financial engineering has combined with major advances in information and communication technologies to design an explosively growing variety of financial instruments and circulate them in network-based "markets". As participation in (pension, mutual, hedge, and private-equity) funds became the primary vehicle for savings in lieu of bank deposits, we ended up with large institutions of speculative intent ready to hook up with the dealer networks for their share of the gains. These funds provide the liquidity for even the most esoteric and insider-biased network "markets". All this is driven by relentlessly rent-seeking financial innovation with its propensities for complexity, opacity, and customization.

In this new world of finance, it is perhaps no longer enough to think of "shadow banking" as this somewhat sinister underground funding machine separated from old-style banking. No, it is part and parcel of how the world's leading banks operate today. These transnational institutions are after all nowadays *universal banks*, having used a combination of regulation-evading financial innovation and political muscle to gain regulatory permission (e.g. the European Commission's Second Banking Directive of 1989, the US Financial Services Modernization Act of 1999) for spanning the entire range of financial services and funding arrangements. As such, they integrate commercial banking, investment banking, insurance, fund management, and payment services. In other words, when you look at the internal structure of the world's top banks, you can see that they combine tightly regulated indirect finance (commercial banking), self-regulated market finance (investment banking), and unregulated network finance (shadow banking) under one roof so as to exploit various scale, scope, and network economies. These economies have led to a dramatic increase in concentration, with the world's top thirty (truly universal) banks grabbing much larger market shares across all three segments of finance. Able to direct money creation towards securities markets and dealer networks, the banks can finance their own self-expansion. In the process, they interact with a variety of more specialized institutions (e.g. hedge funds, MMFs) with whom they share their gains in a complex relation of interdependence and conflict. The universal banks compete and cooperate at the same time, forming a de facto cartel that is capable of exacting a steadily growing share of the total income pie through a variety of rent-seeking activities generating spreads, fees, commissions, trading profits, and so forth. We only have to look at how the top bankers pay themselves and their strategic employees to witness such cartel-based formation of monopoly rents at work.

The structural transformation of banking over the last thirty years has inexorably altered the modus operandi of advanced capitalist economies, yielding what I have elsewhere termed *finance-led capitalism*.[13] This system is prone to asset bubbles, with potentially heavy fall-out when those burst. Its sectoral composition, with self-expanding finance at its strategic centre, invites continuous redistribution in favour of financial capital income, which leaves industrial profit shares intact only at the expense of steadily declining wage shares. Such functional income redistribution yields also much greater gaps between the super-rich and the rest of the personal-income distribution pie. On a global scale, the dominance of speculative finance has caused vast short-term cross-border flows of "hot money" crowding out productive investment and trade – the proverbial "tail wagging the dog". Chronic imbalances between debtor nations and creditor nations are thereby locked in, with America's status as the leading debtor nation supported by the rest of the world using the US dollar as principal reserve asset and international medium of exchange. Chronic US balance-of-payments deficits underwrite the export-led growth strategies of emerging-market economies (notably China) and neo-mercantilist industrial economies (Germany, Japan) as those nations recycle their surpluses to finance America's deficits. In this matrix of global asymmetries, other debtor nations such as those on the southern periphery of the Eurozone, in the Arab world, or Central Asia, are getting brutally squeezed as global finance abandons them.

Universal banks are now the masters of our (finance-led) capitalist system. Ironically, the crisis has only reinforced their power as they were bailed out by their governments at huge taxpayer expense, a second tier of potential competitors got knocked out, and post-crisis restructuring encouraged further integration across the different segments of finance (see the disappearance of America's once-independent investment banks). They remain too big to fail, too inter-connected to supervise or regulate, and too complex to manage. Finance just absorbs too many resources and too much income, at the expense of much-needed investment and resource allocation towards the world's pressing problems of climate change, jobs, education, health, and infrastructure. Its dominance, thriving on the debt dependence of governments, industries, and households all facing comparatively stagnant revenues, makes our economic system more prone to pronounced boom-bust cycles and income inequalities – a politically explosive mix and difficult policy challenge.

Re-regulation

With the regulatory dialectic at work once again, the systemic crisis we faced in 2007–09 has now been followed by new initiatives to re-regulate finance – America's Dodd-Frank Act of 2010, Britain's Bank Reform Bill of 2012, the EU's new Capital Requirement Directive (CRD IV) of 2013, and globally the new Basel III regime of 2010–19. These efforts at re-regulation have obviously tried to draw relevant lessons from the crisis, demanding better safety buffers, greater disclosure of information, and more reasonable incentive structures (e.g. executive compensation, rating agencies). They have introduced three new regulatory principles pertaining to universal banks: a strengthening of bank capital coupled with leverage limitations and liquidity cushions whose resilience will be subject to regular stress tests; an enhanced regulatory and supervisory focus on systemically important financial institutions; and resolution authority to deal with failing institutions short of taxpayer bail-outs. All these principles will be put to the test in due course, I am sure. The regulatory authorities have also committed themselves to macro-prudential regulation of systemic risk which finance trends may pose to the health of the economy as a whole. The success of this novel approach will depend on interpretation capacity of worrisome trends amidst a flood of data (do bank regulators have a good theory of systemic crisis à la Minsky?) and effective tools to alter these trends. Perhaps most important, but least discussed, among the new regulatory efforts is the realization that shadow banking needs to be made more transparent and its network "markets" rendered more resilient. The most shocking fact in the unfolding of the crisis was the sudden disintegration of network-based "markets" for asset-backed securities, credit derivatives, and repos in the face of sudden trouble. The links between the nodes in those financial networks hold only if the actors trust their counterparties and are confident that promises made are kept. The links break when trust is shaken and confidence erodes. There will be a lot of experimentation to figure out how best to reorganize these "markets", either by turning networks into public exchanges or, at least, injecting third-party clearing and settlement facilities absorbing counterparty risk into these networks. As happened with the high-yield ("junk") bond market after the destruction of the Drexel-led insider network in 1990, securitization and credit derivatives may ultimately end up in better-managed set-ups.

Still, the re-regulation effort has a long way to go before we shall know its effectiveness. Its new principles have yet to withstand the test of time, and there are serious doubts with regards to each one of those being adequate or feasible. The complexity of financial institutions has been matched by equally complex regulation, which may seriously hamper its enforceability. It would have been better to rely on simpler rules applied to the structure of universal banks. First steps were made in that direction with Dodd-Frank's Volcker rule banning proprietary trading by banks and obliging them to have a more hands-off link with hedge funds; the EU's Liikanen rules for mandatory isolation of high-risk trading, better management incentives, and bail-in mechanisms to bolster resolution; and the UK's Vickers proposal to ring-fence commercial banking from the other two pillars of universal banks. We thus have three bank-structure proposals to compare, with Liikanen in the middle between the weaker Volcker rule and the much stronger Vickers model. The world will eventually want to converge towards a single structure standard, in which case we might argue in favour of another Glass-Steagall-type isolation of commercial banking from investment banking à la Vickers. At that point, we shall have to revisit the question of shadow banking with renewed urgency, as it straddles both.

Notes

1 For a tentative sequencing of that ricochet path, see Randall Dodd (2007) or Robert Guttmann (2011).
2 See FSB (2012: 2).
3 We are talking here specifically about Zoltan Pozsar *et al.* (2010), Adrian and Ashcraft (2012a), as well as Adrian and Ashcraft (2012b).
4 See in this context the useful contribution of Allen and Babus (2009) which provides us with an up-to-date survey of the literature on network analysis as applied to financial institutions and markets.
5 See Paul Krugman (2007, 2009) or *The Economist* (2012a).
6 This more nuanced, eminently pro-cyclical view of financial innovation can already be found in the early work of Hyman Minsky (1957, 1980).
7 This dialectic of regulatory evasion, excess behaviour, crisis, and re-regulation has been well captured by Kane (1981, 2012).
8 Elsewhere (Guttmann 1994), I have analysed Roosevelt's reforms of money and banking as in effect creating a new monetary regime replacing the collapsed gold standard. This regime can be characterized as "nationally administered" inasmuch as it relied on government regulators exerting tight control over their local commercial banks while keeping interest rates low and exchange rates fixed.
9 SWIFT, for Society of Worldwide International Financial Telecommunication, deals with the data-transmission protocol for cross-border fund transfers, while CHIPS, for Clearing House International Payments System, settles foreign-exchange transactions among Eurobanks. The inner workings of the Eurodollar system were well analysed early on by Frydl (1982).
10 As pointed out in the *New York Times* (2012) and *The Economist* (2012b), the LIBOR scandal was the work of a market-manipulating insider network comprising the world's leading banks in collusion with each other and their favoured clients.
11 For new post-crisis applications of synthetic finance, indicating that this new type of speculative activity is here to stay, see Delos (2012).
12 For a very good explanation of structured finance, in particular CDOs, see Coval *et al.* (2012).
13 See Guttmann (2008, 2009, 2016).

References

Adrian, T. and A. B. Ashcraft (2012a) *Shadow Banking: A Review of the Literature*. Federal Reserve Bank of New York, Staff Report, no. 580. Available at: www.newyorkfed.org/medialibrary/media/research/staff_reports/sr580.pdf. Last accessed: 20.12.2016.

Adrian, T. and A. B. Ashcraft (2012b) *Shadow Banking Regulation*. Federal Reserve Bank of New York, Staff Report, no. 559. Available at: www.newyorkfed.org/medialibrary/media/research/staff_reports/sr559.pdf. Last accessed: 20.12.2016.

Allen, F. and A. Babus (2009) "Networks in Finance". In P. R. Kleindorfer and Y. Wind (eds) *The Network Challenge: Strategy, Profit, and Risk in an Interlinked World*. New York: Pearson Prentice Hall.

Coval, J., J. Jurek and E. Stafford (2012) *The Economics of Structured Finance*. Harvard Business School. Working Paper, no. 09–060. Available at: http://hbs.edu/faculty/Publication%20Files/09–060.pdf. Last accessed: 06.01.2017.

Delos, T. (2012) "Synthetic Route has Real Appeal". *Financial Times*, March 23. Available at: www.ft.com/content/1ba104a4-6dc7-11e1-b98d-00144feab49a. Last accessed 21.04.2017.

Dodd, R. (2007) "Subprime: Tentacles of a Crisis". *Finance & Development*, 44(4), pp. 15–19.

Frydl (1982) "The Eurodollar Conundrum". *Federal Reserve Bank of New York Quarterly Review*, Spring, pp. 11–19.

FSB (2012) *Global Shadow Banking Monitoring Report*. Financial Stability Board. Report. Available at: www.financialstabilityboard.org/publications/r_121118c.pdf. Last accessed: 20.12.2016.

Guttmann, R. (1994) *How Credit-Money Shapes the Economy: The United States in a Global System*. Armonk, NY: M. E. Sharpe.

Guttmann, R. (2008) "A Primer on Finance-Led Capitalism and Its Crisis". *Revue de la Régulation*, 3/4. Available at: http://regulation.revues.org/5843. Last accessed: 06.01.2017.

Guttmann, R. (2009) "Asset Bubbles, Debt Deflation, and Global Imbalances", *International Journal of Political Economy*, 38(2), pp. 46–69.

Guttmann, R. (2011) "The Collapse of Securitisation: From Subprimes to Global Credit Crunch". In C. Gnos and L. P. Rochon (eds) *Credit, Money and Macroeconomic Policy: A Post-Keynesian Approach*. Cheltenham, UK: Edward Elgar, pp. 45–55.

Guttmann, R. (2016). *Finance-Led Capitalism: Shadow Banking, Re-Regulation, and the Future of Global Markets*. Palgrave Macmillan: New York.

Kane, E. J. (1981) "Accelerating Inflation, Technological Innovation, and the Decreasing Effectives of Banking Regulation". *Journal of Finance*, 36(2), pp. 355–367.

Kane, E. J. (2012) *The Inevitability of Shadowy Banking*. Paper presented at the Federal Reserve Bank of Atlanta. Financial Markets Conference, April 10. Available at: https://papers.ssrn.com/sol3/papers.cfm?abstract_id=2026229. Last accessed 21.04.2017.

Krugman, P. (2007) "Innovating Our Way to Financial Crisis". *New York Times*, December 3. Available at: www.nytimes.com/2007/12/03/opinion/03krugman.html. Last accessed 21.04.2017.

Krugman, P. (2009) "Money for Nothing". *New York Times*, April 26. Available at: www.nytimes.com/2009/04/27/opinion/27krugman.html. Last accessed 21.04.2017.

Minsky, H. (1957) "Central Banking and Money Market Changes", *Quarterly Journal of Economics*, 71(2), pp. 171–187.

Minsky, H. (1980) "Capitalist Financial Processes and the Instability of Capitalism", *Journal of Economic Issues*, 14(2), pp. 505–523.

Minsky, H. (1992) *The Financial Instability Hypothesis*. Jerome Levy Institute. Working Paper, no. 74. Available at: http://levyinstitute.org/pubs/wp74.pdf. Last accessed: 06.01.2017.

New York Times (2012) "Behind the Libor Scandal". July 10. Available at: www.nytimes.com/interactive/2012/07/10/business/dealbook/behind-the-libor-scandal.html. Last accessed 21.04.2017.

Pozsar, Z., T. Adrian, A. Ashcraft and H. Boesky (2010) *Shadow Banking*. Staff Report, no. 458. Federal Reserve Bank of New York. Available at: www.newyorkfed.org/medialibrary/media/research/staff_reports/sr458.pdf. Last accessed: 20.12.2016.

The Economist (2012a) "Financial Innovation: Playing with Fire". February 25. Available at: www.economist.com/node/21547999. Last accessed 21.04.2017.

The Economist (2012b) "The Rotten Heart of Finance". July 7. Available at: www.economist.com/node/21558281. Last accessed 21.04.2017.

3 How shadow banking became non-bank finance

The conjectural power of economic ideas

Ewald Engelen

A mass of Latin words falls upon the facts like soft snow,
blurring the outline and covering up all the details.

(George Orwell, 1946)

Events, my dear boy, events . . .

(Harold Macmillan, 1956)

Introduction

On 18 February 2015, the European Commission (EC) presented a Green Paper that was to provide more detail of its new, post-crisis flagship project, the Capital Markets Union (CMU). The Green Paper was all about 'investment', 'funding', 'access', 'growth', 'development', 'infrastructure', 'equity': the many good things that the EU in general and the Eurozone in particular was so disastrously lacking and so desperately needed (EC 2015). The main recipients of all these good things would be Europe's small- and medium-sized enterprises, which were mentioned no fewer than 46 times. Notable for its absence was any mention of 'shadow banking', for that was precisely what the CMU tried to do: more credit intermediation by non-bank lenders, in other words: more shadow banking.

The Commission's CMU, which is currently under construction by the European Council and the European Parliament, and in close collaboration with the financial industry (see Engelen and Glasmacher 2016), is merely the latest instance of a sweeping reframing of what was perceived as extremely dangerous, risky, opaque and desperately in need of regulatory oversight in the immediate aftermath of the crisis. In those early days, shadow banking was held responsible for a global run on the banks through the backdoor and was hence seen as one of the main causes of the financial crisis (Gorton and Metrick 2010), while one of the first papers to attempt to map the intricate credit intermediation schemes set up in the shadow banking system clearly demonstrated their origins in regulatory arbitrage purposes, suggesting an intentional attempt to circumvent regulatory oversight (Pozsar *et al.* 2010). As the example of the CMU suggests, a decade later shadow banking is instead seen as the key to unlocking growth and kickstarting job creation. From one of the main problems of the global financial system it has become the solution to make finance again serve the real economy. How did this sweeping reconceptualization come about? Who was responsible for it? What discursive means did they use? And why did they do it? Those are the questions this chapter tries to answer.

To do so, it tracks the reframing of shadow banking in a fairly straightforward, chronological order through a discussion of the linguistic shifts its definition has experienced over time in the academic literature as well as in the formal reporting of the Financial Stability Board (FSB), the Basel-based regulator that was mandated by the G20 in the autumn of 2010 to map shadow banking, identify its risky parts and propose new regulation. The second section then discusses the conjuncture which made this reframing possible and adds to the growing literature on the conditionality of the power of (economic) ideas. The final section concludes.

The story of shadow banking

The precrisis history

The term 'shadow banking' was coined in the late summer of 2007 by Paul McCulley of bond investor Pimco, during the annual Federal Reserve summit in Jackson Hole, Wyoming, which was dedicated to Housing, Housing Finance and Monetary Policy. McCulley used the term to refer to the special investment vehicles (SIVs), conduits and special purpose vehicles (SPVs) that banks used to securitize and offload their assets, attract funding and arbitrage around regulation:

> And in the current circumstance, it's called a run on what I've dubbed the 'shadow banking system' – the whole alphabet soup of levered up non-bank investment conduits, vehicles, and structures. Unlike regulated real banks . . . *unregulated shadow banks* fund themselves with *uninsured* commercial paper, which may or may not be *backstopped by liquidity lines from real banks*. Thus, the shadow banking system is particularly vulnerable to runs.
>
> (McCulley 2007, my emphasis)

What is crucial in McCulley's first take on shadow banking is that it emphasizes the 'unregulated' and 'uninsured' nature of shadow banking, while the reference to the 'alphabet soup' of conduits, vehicles and structures contains the recognition that shadow banking is predominantly about regulatory arbitrage undertaken by large banks. This is corroborated by McCulley's reference to 'runs' as well as by his statement that some of these structures (but not all of them) are 'backstopped by liquidity lines from real banks'. In this initial definition, shadow banking is closely tied to 'real banking', serves predominantly arbitrage purposes, lacks regulatory oversight and is highly vulnerable to panics, manias and crises.

The first to take up McCulley's definition and use it to attempt a more encompassing mapping of the shadow banking system was Zoltan Pozsar, a US trained economist of Hungarian descent, in a paper called the *Rise and Fall of the Shadow*

Banking System that was published in the July 2008 edition of Moody's Regional Financial Review (Pozsar 2008). In that paper Pozsar relates the rise of shadow banking to structural transformations in credit intermediation by banks: from on-balance intermediation to 'originate-and-distribute', which requires the use of off-balance sheet intermediaries such as conduits and structured investment vehicles (SIVs) and in that sense further develops McCulley's definition:

> By borrowing short and lending long, conduits and SIVs were involved in the classic bank business of maturity transformation. In this sense, conduits and SIVs were *an alternative form of traditional banking*, the crucial difference being that these alternative banks were not funded by depositors, but by investors in the wholesale funding market and that maturity transformation did not occur on bank balance sheets but through capital markets in off-balance-sheet vehicles *outside the purview of regulators* . . . Another crucial difference was that the safety net that is available to regulated banks . . . were [sic!] unavailable for the shadow banking system of SIVs and conduits, and no alternatives existed.
>
> (Pozsar 2008: 17, my emphasis)

Again the emphasis is on shadow banking as being unregulated and uninsured. What is new is the description of shadow banking as 'an alternative form of traditional banking', suggesting the possibility of not only risks but also functionalities. Moreover, the paper introduced the balance sheet approach to the different off-balance sheet vehicles and the way they are linked to regular banks, which was made famous through an op-ed by Gillian Tett in the *Financial Times* about a longer paper in the same vein that Pozsar did with Thomas Adrian, Adam Ashcraft and Hayley Boesky for the Federal Reserve Bank of New York in 2010 and which later on strongly influenced the approach of the FSB.

The academic take on shadow banking

In the immediate aftermath of the bankruptcy of Lehman Brothers, the attention shifted to the ecosystem of the interbank markets, which, in hindsight, was blamed for the buildup of excessive leverage before the crisis and for serving as channels of contagion between banks and jurisdictions after the crisis. The first paper that looked at shadow banking through a crisis lens dates from July 2009, was written by Tobias Adrian from the Federal Reserve Bank of New York and Hyun Song Shin from the BIS and Princeton University. As the title, *The Shadow Banking System: Implications for Financial Regulation*, already indicates, the optic was very much about analyses of what went wrong to prevent similar meltdowns in the future.

   While refusing to provide a definition (in fact: shadow banking only figures four times in the paper), this is the first paper where shadow banking is explicitly linked to capital markets. As its first sentences indicates:

The distinguishing mark of a modern financial system is the increasingly *intimate ties between banking and the capital markets*. The success of macro-prudential regulation will depend on being able to internalise the externalities that are generated in the shadow banking system.

(Adrian and Shin 2009: 1, my emphasis)

While the crucial role of commercial banks as originators of the shadow banking system is recognized throughout the paper – in fact, the authors warn that prudential regulation after the crisis that only looks at banks is prone to fail (Adrian and Shin 2009: 15) – their offhand association of shadow banking with capital markets more general, suggesting an easy overlap between the two, can be seen to already prefigure its later transformation into non-bank finance.

The next instalment of our story has already been mentioned, namely the famous 2010 switchboard paper Pozsar *et al.* produced for the Federal Reserve Bank of New York. In that paper the authors not only presented a more elaborate version of the shadow banking switchboard that Pozsar had provided in his 2008 paper, but they also tried to go beyond McCulley's descriptive definition and provide a more systematic, theory-based definition of shadow banking. Using insights from Merton (1977) and Merton and Bodie (1993), the authors define shadow banking as the opposite of credit intermediation with 'official enhancements', in the form of public deposit guarantees, which require on-balance sheet intermediation (Pozsar *et al.* 2010: 5).

We define shadow credit intermediation to include all credit intermediation activities that are *implicitly enhanced, indirectly enhanced or unenhanced by official guarantees*.

(Pozsar *et al.* 2010: 6, my emphasis)

The sort of entities these kinds of implicit, indirect or no enhancements refer to are, for instance, mortgage-backed securities emitted by Freddy Mac and Fannie Mae (implicit enhancements), the bonds emitted by off-balance sheet vehicles used by banks in securitization (indirect enhancements) and the credit intermediation activities of non-banks such as asset managers and money-market funds through the emission of asset-backed commercial paper on repo markets as well as securities lending by custodians to allow for shorting and other trading strategies. The authors then go on to identify three distinct 'sub-systems' within shadow banking: 'internal shadow banking', 'external shadow banking' and 'parallel shadow banking'. Again, these are defined by their relationship to banking entities with a direct, explicit public backstop.

This paper proved seminal not only because of its detailed overview of the mechanics of the cash flows moving through the shadow bank-based credit intermediation chain, but also for its attempt at a definition that zoomed in on the activities undertaken in the shadow banking system. Moreover, like the Adrian paper discussed above, Pozsar *et al.* clearly situate shadow banking thus defined within a larger historical transformation process of the financial system, from being bank-based to becoming market-based. As the first two sentences of the abstract read:

> The rapid growth of the market-based financial system since the mid-1980s changed the nature of financial intermediation. Within the market-based financial system, 'shadow banks' have served a critical role.
>
> (Pozsar *et al.* 2010)

The year 2010 also saw the publication of a second key text in the discursive history of shadow banking. The American economists Gary Gorton and Andrew Metrick, both from Yale School of Management, demonstrated how the shadow banking universe during the crisis had become prone to similar kinds of cascading panics on the side of wholesale counterparties as happened in the 1930s among retail customers. In this paper, Gorton and Metrick (2009) extended their earlier concept of 'securitized banking' to encompass a larger universe of non-bank banks:

> [Shadow banking] performs the same functions as traditional banking, but the names of the players are different, and the regulatory structure is light or non-existent. In its broadest definition, shadow banking includes such familiar institutions as investment banks, money-market mutual funds, and mortgage brokers; some rather old contractual forms, such as sale-and-repurchase agreements (repos); and more esoteric instruments such as asset-backed securities (ABSs), collateralized debt obligations (CDOs), and asset-backed commercial paper (ABCP).
>
> (Gorton and Metrick 2010: 261–262)

While more descriptive than theoretical, the importance of the paper lies in its implied regulatory politics. Shadow banking was no longer framed as the outcome of regulatory arbitrage but as the result of the secular transformation of the US financial system: from based-based finance to 'securitized banking', partly as a result of the secular changes in the preferences of financial agents, especially for 'efficient, bankruptcy-free collateral in large financial transactions' (Gorton and Metrick 2010: 267). The authors stress that it does not make sense to aim to rewind history and 'reverse earlier changes' to the wiring of the financial system. Not only is that impossible, it is undesirable, as the authors explicity state (ibid.). Instead, Gorton and Metrick 'take the broad outlines of the system as given and ask how the current regulatory structure could be adapted to make the system safer without driving its activity into a new unregulated darkness' (ibid.).

Here, we have the first explicit academic attempt to reframe shadow banking as a new form of credit intermediation, which, despite regulatory failures, is perceived as being more efficient than bank-based credit intermediation, in the sense that it allows for a better accommodation of the financial preferences of agents. Together with the Pozsar *et al.* (2010) and Adrian and Shin (2009) papers, the Gorton and Metrick (2010) paper belongs to the top three of the most quoted papers on 'shadow banking' according to Google Scholar.

The regulatory response

While academic reflection on shadow banking continued uninterrupted (Google Scholar gives no fewer than 10,400 results as at 24 March 2015), from 2010 the action moved increasingly to the regulatory backrooms. Paul Tucker, Deputy Governor for Financial Stability at the Bank of England at the time, was the first high level regulator to publicly speak about shadow banking. At a January 2010 seminar in London, Tucker called for a better map of shadow banking to be able to contain future contagion risks: 'I do not have all the answers to these questions, so my goal this evening is to push them up the agenda' (Tucker 2010).

This call was heeded by the supranational community of banking regulators and was rapidly taken over by politicians. At the Seoul Summit of November 2010, the G20 decided that there was a pressing need to have an overview of the scale, scope and shape of shadow banking:

> With the completion of the new standards for banks, there is a potential that regulatory gaps may emerge in the shadow banking system. Therefore, we called on the FSB to work in collaboration with other international standard setting bodies to develop recommendations to strengthen the regulation and oversight of the shadow banking system by mid-2011.
>
> (G20 2010)

Since then, the FSB, under the directorship of Mark Carney, former governor of the Bank of Canada and current Governor of the Bank of England, has produced a series of reports on shadow banking (FSB 2011, 2012a, 2012b, 2012c, 2013a, 2013b, 2014a, 2014b), both to inform and to propose. Below I briefly quote the definitions of shadow banking provided in these subsequent reports in order to highlight the wider reassessment of which they speak.

In the first report of November 2011, shadow banking is defined as:

> [t]he system of credit intermediation that involves entities and activities outside the regular banking system.

Six months later, in April 2012, the definition is more or less the same:

> The 'shadow banking system' can broadly be described as 'credit intermediation involving entities and activities outside the regular banking system'.

However, the FSB have added a telling footnote, stating:

> It is important to note the use of the term 'shadow banking' is not intended to cast a pejorative tone on this system of credit intermediation. The FSB has chosen to use the term 'shadow banking' as this is most commonly employed and, in particular, has been used in the earlier G20 communications. Alternative terms used by some authorities or market participants include 'market-based financing' or 'market-based credit intermediation'.

This is the first indication that the FSB is uncomfortable with the negative connotations of 'shadow banking' and is aware of the existence of more neutral synonyms – 'neutral' of course as seen from the perspective of the banking community.

In November 2012, the definition is extended with two crucial riders:

> The 'shadow banking system' can broadly be described as 'credit intermediation involving entities and activities (fully or partially) outside the regular banking system' or non-bank credit intermediation in short. Such intermediation, appropriately conducted, provides *a valuable alternative to bank funding that supports real economic activity* (my emphasis).

Here, shadow banking is officially equated with non-bank credit intermediation and hence rendered harmless in a rhetorical sense. Moreover, it is presented as an alternative means of financing 'real economic activity' and hence as the functional equivalent to credit intermediation by banks.

One year later, this definition is extended:

> The shadow banking system can broadly be described as credit intermediation involving entities and activities outside the regular banking system. Intermediating credit through non-bank channels can have important advantages and contributes to the financing of the real economy, but such channels can also become a source of systemic risk, especially when they are structured to perform bank-like functions (e.g. maturity transformation and leverage) and when their interconnectedness with the regular banking system is strong. Therefore, *appropriate monitoring* of shadow banking helps to mitigate the build-up of such systemic risks (my emphasis).

In other words, there is nothing intrinsically wrong with shadow banking (or better: non-bank credit intermediating) if 'appropriately conducted'. And to ensure that it is 'appropriately conducted' the FSB will ensure 'appropriate monitoring'.

In the summer of 2014, the rhetorical transformation of shadow banking into 'market-based finance' was more or less complete. In an op-ed piece in the *Financial Times* of 15 July 2014, titled: 'The need to focus a light on shadow banking is nigh', Mark Carney argued that it was about time to develop a more balanced regulatory approach to shadow banking:

> Our approach to reform recognises that an effective financial system needs intermediation outside the traditional banking sector. When conducted appropriately, it can be a valuable alternative to, and provide competition for, banks in funding the real economy. Diversifying sources of finance makes the provision of the credit that is essential for growth more plentiful and more resilient . . . The goal is to replace a shadow banking system prone to excess

and collapse with one that contributes to strong, sustainable balanced growth of the world economy . . . Now is the time to take shadow banking out of the shadows and to create sustainable market-based finance.

(Carney 2014)

Carney had signed off the piece both as Governor of the Bank of England and as chairman of the FSB, suggesting broad consensus among the central banking elite about the undesirability of eradicating shadow banking disguised as the need for alternative channels of funding.

This position received its official blessing in November 2014 with the publication of a new FSB report, revealingly titled: *Progress Report on Transforming Shadow Banking into Resilient Market-Based Financing*. In that report the FSB states:

> Transforming shadow banking into resilient market-based financing has been one of the core elements of the FSB's regulatory reform agenda to address the fault lines that contributed to the global financial crisis and to build safer, more sustainable sources of financing for the real economy.

No matter that this aim has never been explicitly stated as such before, nor that the crisis-related concerns which gave 'shadow banking' its name in the first place have never been put to rest, nor that the case for 'market-based finance' as a 'more sustainable source of financing for the real economy' has never been convincingly made.

The EC's Green Paper, mentioned in the introduction and meant to develop a European copy of the American non-bank ecosystem formerly known as shadow banking, clearly signals the political success of this new frame. In a mere five years shadow banking has mutated from something that stood at the root of the Great Financial Crisis of 2008 ('a bank run through the back door') into something that is a solution for a broken bank-based credit intermediation system which could 'contribute to strong, sustainable balanced growth for the world economy'. How did this happen? And even more important: why did it happen *when* it happened?

Explaining the new frame

As Keynes famously noted, policy makers unwittingly run the danger of being 'the slave of some defunct economist', in the sense that their worldviews, problem definitions and policy solutions indirectly derive from 'primitive economisms' which are rooted in old, long forgotten pieces of economic theorizing. What Keynes implies here is that the power of ideas works in a straightforward, hierarchically based manner: from academia to policy makers, from the brain to the hands. An increasing number of studies has contested this simplified view. Beginning with Peter Hall, who showed that the political power of Keynesian ideas depended crucially on the accessability of policy-making arenas by academic economists

(Hall 1989), a veritable cottage industry has developed in international political economy (see Blyth 2002, 2012; Seabrooke and Tsingou 2009; Chwieroth 2010; Gabor 2013; Dellepiane-Avellaneda 2014; Ban 2015 to name a few), sociology (see Fligstein 2001; Fourcade 2006, 2009; MacKenzie 2006, 2009; Fourcade and Khurana 2013; Fourcade *et al.* 2014; Heilbron *et al.* 2014; Hirschman and Popp Berman 2014 to name a few) and even economics itself (see Mirowski and Phlewe 2009; Mirowski 2013; Zingales 2013), which looks more precisely into the conditions that determine the power of (economic) ideas.

In their recent review of this literature, the economic sociologists Hirschman and Berman suggest that one of the main areas of overlap between the three different research strands in this literature (politics and ideas, sociology of professions and expertise, science and technology studies) is that the conjuncture actually matters:

> Economists' policy recommendations are more likely to have effects under some conditions than others. In particular, economists will have a greater influence in situations that are ill-defined, including both situations of crisis and moments early in the policy process, during the problem definition and agenda-setting phases.
>
> (Hirschman and Berman 2014: 788)

In other words, policy makers are more susceptible to economic advice if existing paradigms have been discredited by events and if a policy response has not yet been articulated. Moreover, as Hirschman and Berman note, its success is enhanced if it succeeds in framing a particular problematic as technical rather than political, i.e. as an issue of coordination rather than distribution (Scharpf 1997).

These conditions are certainly pertinent to our case. The conjuncture under which the three most-cited academic papers on shadow banking were written and published (Adrian and Shin in July 2009, Poszar *et al.* in July 2010, Gorton and Metrick in October 2010), clearly fits the bill. Former economic policy paradigms, especially the ones undergirding the Great Moderation from before the crisis, were in disarray as they had failed their promises of dispersed risk and robust financial markets. While what had caused the disarray, as became increasingly evident in the immediate aftermath of the crisis, namely a run on the interbank market through repo and asset-backed commercial paper, had remained invisible to national and supranational regulators.

Similarly, the initial policy response focused almost exclusively on dealing with the solvency and liquidity constraints large banks faced. The Basel Committee of Banking Supervision quickly developed a number of consultation papers to address these issues and was relatively effective in pushing these through (Young 2012; Blom 2014; Engelen 2015a, 2015b). Shadow banking, however, was a different matter, and since the discovery of the existence of a shadow banking system and its role in the crisis was rather late in the day, this was a nascent policy field where the articulation of a coherent policy response was up for grabs in late 2008, throughout 2009 and even in early 2010.

As Helleiner has noted, it was at the November 2008 G20 meeting that the slumbering Financial Stability Forum was upgraded to the FSB with an expanded membership, a more extensive secretariat and a wider mandate (Helleiner 2010). However it took until the G20 summit in Seoul, South-Korea, in November 2010 before the FSB was explicitly mandated to track developments in shadow banking. Finally, as clearly came to the fore in Poszar *et al.* 2010 with its elaborate balance sheet-based approach to credit intermediation in shadow banking, the problematic of shadow banking was presented as an engineering problem (insufficient backstops, too much complexity, not enough transparency) looking for a technical fix, not a political one with wider distributive causes and consequences.

Finally, part of the explanation is also the huge divergence post-crisis between the aggregate economic performance of the Eurozone and the US. While the crisis had ignited over rehypothecated American mortgage-backed securities losing their market value, it was the Eurozone that experienced the sharpest economic contraction (2.8 versus 4.5 per cent in 2009). Moreover, while the US economy quickly rebounded and succeeded in avoiding a second contraction, the Eurozone in 2011 again lost momentum and in 2012 entered into a second contraction, resulting in a cumulative growth differential between 2008 and 2015 with the US economy of no less than 8.6 per cent. Mistimed ('frontloaded') and misdesigned (too many tax increases) austerity is clearly to blame for this (Blyth 2012).

In a desperate attempt to deflect electoral anger, European policy makers frantically looked for alternative stories that could help 'explain' the dismal economic performance of the Eurozone. Excessive dependence on banks which had to rebuild their balance sheets after the crisis due to the absence of a US-style alternative credit intermediation channel fitted that bill perfectly. It shifted the blame from depressed demand due to austerity to restricted credit supply due to the US financial crisis and too much reliance on bank lending which had historically developed and for which, hence, noone could be blamed.

Conclusion

Eight years into a crisis that is far from over, it has become obvious that the tide of new regulation has more or less run its course. In an interview with the *Financial Times*, the secretary-general of the BIS said in late March 2015, that:

> The avalanche of post-crisis banking regulation is coming to an end and most of the uncertainties weighing on the financial industry will be dealth with in the next year.
>
> (*Financial Times* 2015)

Compared to the dramatic regulatory changes that were enacted in the immediate aftermath of the Great Depression (Glass-Steagall, Government Sponsored Enterprises, Deposit Guarantees, huge public infrastructure projects as well as the establishment of crucial parts of the US welfare state), the political response to the Great Recession has been notably feeble. Basel III has not succeeded in radically transforming a banking business model built on high profitability through excessive leverage, huge balance sheets, implicit state guarantees, long and fragile chains of credit intermediation and obfuscating complexity. Neither have additional collateral requirements and demands for more standardization on repo and asset-backed securities markets. Moreover, as this chapter has shown, shadow banking is on the verge of largely escaping the regulatory pushback and has during the arc of the crisis been successfully reframed from villain to saviour. Europe's CMU, which is currently moving through the legislative process, is a case in point.

By avoiding the mistakes of the 1930s and shoring up the international banking system, central bankers may well have saved the world from disaster, but at the same time have politically anesthetized citizens and politicians. Hence, the absence by and large of any concerted political effort to shrug off the socio-economic as well as political burden of too much finance. Moreover, in a financialized world where households depend crucially on financial markets for their assets (pension funds) as well as liabilities (mortgages), there may well be a different political dynamic which works against a large scale uprooting of finance. The 'democratization of debt' creates strong political incentives to keep credit lines open, and credit and funding cheap (Mian and Sufi 2014; see also Fuller 2015). Financialization creates its own constituencies.

This may well be a more powerful, albeit indirect explanation for why the reframing happened. If a large and growing segment of the electorate depends crucially on rising asset prices to take out and pay off debt, and hence to maintain living standards, the political will to enforce deleveraging policies (increased loan-to-value and loan-to-income ratios, end to tax deductibility of debt, increase capital buffers) may quickly erode, despite the demonstrated dangers of financialization. That is to say that in a financialized world, the interests of citizens and banks are essentially aligned, forcing politicians to tread carefully when preventing future financial crises. Since cheap credit for households requires cheap funding for banks, politicians face strong incentives to leave the ecosystem of SPVs, SIVs and conduits in peace.

References

Adrian, T. and H. Shin (2009) *The Shadow Banking System: Implications for Financial Regulation*. Financial Stability Review. Available at: www.newyorkfed.org/research/staff_reports/sr382.html. Last accessed 05.04.17.

Ban, C. (2015) 'From Designers to Doctrinaires. Staff Research and Fiscal Policy Change at the IMF'. In G. Morgan, P. Hirsch and S. Quack (eds.) *Elites on Trial*. Research in the Sociology of Organizations, Volume 43. Bingley, UK: Emerald Group Publishing Limited, pp. 337–369.

Blom, J. (2014) 'Banking'. In Mugge, D. K. (ed.) *Europe and the Governance of Global Finance*. Oxford, UK: Oxford University Press, pp. 35–52.

Blyth, M. (2002) *Great Transformations: Economic Ideas and Institutional Change in the Twentieth Century*. Cambridge, UK: Cambridge University Press.

Blyth, M. (2012) *Austerity: The History Of a Dangerous Idea*. Oxford, UK: Oxford University Press.

Carney, M. (2014) 'The Need to Focus a Light on Shadow Banking is Nigh'. *Financial Times*, June 15. Available at: www.ft.com/content/3a1c5cbc-f088-11e3-8f3d-00144feabdc0. Last accessed 21.04.2017.

Chwieroth, J. (2010) *Capital Ideas: The IMF and the Rise of Financial Liberalisation*. Princeton, NJ: Princeton University Press.

Dellepiane-Avellaneda, S. (2014) 'The Political Power of Economic Ideas: The Case of "Expansionary Fiscal Contractions"'. *The British Journal of Politics and International Relations*, 17(3), pp. 391–418.

EC (2015) *Building a Capital Markets Union*. Green Paper. Available at: http://eur-lex.europa.eu/legal-content/EN/TXT/PDF/?uri=COM:2015:63:FIN&from=EN. Last accessed: 06.01.2017.

Engelen, E. (2015a) 'Don't Mind the Funding Gap: What Dutch Post Crisis Storytelling tells Us about Elite Politics in Financialized Capitalism'. *Environment and Planning A*, 47(8), pp. 1606–1623.

Engelen, E. (2015b) 'Three-Dimensional Power in a Post-Democratic Age: Elite Battle over Dutch Shadow Banking'. *Theory, Culture and Society*. Forthcoming. Available at: www.researchgate.net/publication/276027049_Three-Dimensional_Power_in_a_Post-Democratic_Age_Elite_Battle_over_Dutch_Shadow_Banking. Last accessed 21.04.2017.

Engelen, E and A. Glasmacher (2016) 'Simple, Transparent and Standardized: Narratives, Law and Interest Coalitions in Regulatory Capitalism'. Paper presented at MPiFG workshop on 'Financial Innovation, Diffusion and Institutionalisation: the Case of Securitisation', Cologne, 10–12 June 2016.

Financial Times (2015) 'End in Sight for Post-Crisis Banking Reform, Says Basel Head'. March 29. Available at: www.ft.com/content/dcedd782-d4a7-11e4-8be8-00144feab7de. Last accessed 21.04.2017.

Fligstein, N. (2001) *The Architecture of Markets: An Economic Sociology of Twenty-First Century Capitalist Societies*. Princeton, NJ: Princeton University Press.

Fourcade, M. (2006) 'The Construction of a Global Profession: The Transnationalization of Economics'. *American Journal of Sociology*, 112(1), pp. 145–194.

Fourcade, M. (2009) *Economists and Societies: Discipline and Profession in the United States, Great Britain and France, 1890s to 1990s*. Princeton, NJ: Princeton University Press.

Fourcade, M. and R. Khurana (2013) 'From Social Control to Financial Economics: The Linked Ecologies of Economics and Business in Twentieth Century America'. *Theory and Society*, 42, pp. 121–159.

Fourcade, M., E. Ollion and Y. Algan (2014) *The Superiority of Economists*. MaxPo Discussion Paper, no. 14/3. Available at: www.maxpo.eu/pub/maxpo_dp/maxpodp 14–3.pdf. Last accessed: 06.01.2017.

FSB (2011) *Shadow Banking: Scoping the Issues. A Background Note of the Financial Stability Board*. Financial Stability Board. Available at: www.fsb.org/2011/04/shadow-banking-scoping-the-issues/. Last accessed: 20.12.2016.

FSB (2012a) *Strengthening the Oversight and Regulation of Shadow Banking*. Progress Report to G20 Ministers and Governors. Financial Stability Board. Available at: www.fsb.org/wp-content/uploads/r_111027a.pdf?page_moved=1. Last accessed: 20.12.2016.

FSB (2012b) *Securities Lending and Repos: Market Overview and Financial Stability Issues*. Interim Report of the FSB Workstream on Securities Lending and Repos. Financial Stability Board. Available at: www.fsb.org/wp-content/uploads/r_120427. pdf. Last accessed: 20.12.2016.

FSB (2012c) *Global Shadow Banking Monitoring Report 2012*. Financial Stability Board. Available at: www.fsb.org/2012/11/r_121118c/. Last accessed: 20.12.2016.

FSB (2013a) *An Overview of Policy Recommendations for Shadow Banking*. Available at: www.financialstabilityboard.org/2013/08/r_130829a. Last accessed: 20.12.2016.

FSB (2013b) *Global Shadow Banking Monitoring Report*. Available at: http://www.financialstabilityboard.org/2013/11/r_131114. Last accessed: 20.12.2016.

FSB (2014a) *Global Shadow Banking Monitoring Report*. Available at: www.financialstabilityboard.org/2014/11/global-shadow-banking-monitoring-report-2014. Last accessed: 20.12.2016.

FSB (2014b) *Progress Report on Transforming Shadow Banking into Resilient Market-Based Financing*. Available at: http://www.financialstabilityboard.org/2014/11/progress-report-on-transforming-shadow-banking-into-resilient-market-based-financing. Last accessed: 20.12.2016.

Fuller, G. W. (2015) 'Who's Borrowing? Credit Encouragement vs. Credit Mitigation in National Financial Systems'. *Politics and Society*, 43(2), pp. 241–268.

G20 (2010) *The G20 Summit Leader's Declaration*. Available at: www.g20.utoronto.ca/summits/2010seoul.html. Last accessed: 20.12.2016.

Gabor, D. (2013) *Shadow Interconnectedness: The Political Economy of (European) Shadow Banking*. SSRN Working Paper. Available at: https://papers.ssrn.com/sol3/papers.cfm?abstract_id=2326645. Last accessed: 20.12.2016.

Gorton, G. and A. Metrick (2009) *Securitized Banking and the Run on Repo*. NBER Working Paper, no. 15233. Available at: www.nber.org/papers/w15223.pdf. Last accessed: 20.12.2016.

Gorton, G. and A. Metrick (2010) *Securitized Repo and the Run on Banks*. Yale ICF Working Paper, no. 09–14. Available at: www.moodys.com/microsites/crc2010/papers/gorton_run_on_repo_nov.pdf. Last accessed: 20.12.2016.

Hall, P. (1989) *The Political Power of Economic Ideas: Keynesianism across Nations*. Princeton, NJ: Princeton University Press.

Heilbron, J., J. Verheul and S. Quack (2014) 'The Origins and Early Diffusion of "Shareholder Value" in the United States'. *Theory and Society*, 43(1), pp. 1–22.

Helleiner, E. (2010) 'What Role for the New Financial Stability Board? The Politics of International Standards after the Crisis'. *Global Policy*, 1(3), pp. 282–290.

Hirschman, D. and E. Popp Berman (2014) 'Do Economists Make Policies? On the Political Effects of Economics'. *Socio-Economic Review*. Vol. 12(4), pp. 779–811.

MacKenzie, D. (2006) *An Engine, Not a Camera: How Financial Models Shape Markets*. Harvard, MA: MIT Press.

MacKenzie, D. (2009) *Material Markets*. Oxford, UK: Oxford University Press.

McCulley, P. (2007) *Teton Reflections*. Pimco, August/September. Available at: www.pimco.com/insights/economic-and-market-commentary/global-central-bank-focus/teton-reflections. Last accessed: 20.12.2016.

Merton, R. (1977) 'An Analytic Derivation of ohe Cost of Deposit Insurance and Loan Guarantees: An Application of Modern Option Pricing Theory'. *Journal of Banking and Finance*. Vol. 1, pp. 3–11.

Merton, R. and Z. Bodie (1993) *Deposit Insurance Reform: A Functional Approach*. Carnegie-Rochester Conference Series on Public Policy, no. 38. Available at: https://pdfs.semanticscholar.org/cdb1/362fa977e8cfc165fb043098288c423f68eb.pdf. Last accessed: 06.01.2017.

Mian, A. and A. Sufi (2014) *House of Debt*. Princeton, NJ: Princeton University Press.

Mirowski, P. (2013) *Never Let a Serious Crisis Go to Waste: How Neoliberalism Survived the Financial Meltdown*. London: Verso.

Mirowski, P. and D. Phlewe (2009) (eds) *The Road to Mont Pelerin. The Making of the Neoliberal Thought Collective*. Harvard, MA: Harvard University Press.

Pozsar, Z. (2008) *The Rise and Fall of the Shadow Banking System*. Available at: www. economy.com/sbs. Last accessed: 20.12.2016.

Pozsar, Z., T. Adrian, A. Ashcraft and H. Boesky (2010) *Shadow Banking*. Federal Reserve Bank of New York Staff Report, no. 458, July. Available at: www.newyorkfed.org/medialibrary/media/research/staff_reports/sr458.pdf. Last accessed: 20.12.2016.

Scharpf, F. (1997) *Games Real Actors Play: Actor-Centered Institutionalism*. Oxford, UK: Westview Press.

Seabrooke, L. and E. Tsingou (2009) 'Power Elites and Everyday Politics in International Financial Reform'. *International Political Sociology*, 3(4), pp. 457–461.

Tucker, P. (2010) *Shadow Banking, Financing Markets and Financial Stability*. Speech. Available at: www.bankofengland.co.uk/publications/Documents/speeches/2010/speech420.pdf. Last accessed: 20.12.2016.

Young, K. L. (2012) 'Transnational Regulatory Capture? An Empirical Examination of the Transnational Lobbying of the Basel Committee on Banking Supervision'. *Review of International Political Economy*, 19(4), pp. 663–688.

Zingales, L. (2013) 'Preventing Economists' Capture'. In Carpenter and Moss (eds) *Preventing Regulatory Capture: Special Interest Influence and How to Limit It*. Cambridge, UK: Cambridge University Press, pp. 124–151.

4 Shadow banking, German banking and the question of political order

Oliver Kessler and Benjamin Wilhelm

Introduction

The 2007–09 crisis made visible how banks, rating agencies and non-bank actors, such as hedge funds or money market mutual funds, have created a new network around practices of securitisation and repurchase agreements. Even though these transformations were widely known about by the early 2000s, it is only after 2007 that they were associated with the 'shadow banking system' (see Munteanu 2010; Pakravan 2011; Pozsar 2008).[1] Shadow banking is a conceptual innovation of this crisis. It is predominantly defined as a 'functional' equivalent to the traditional banking system as it offers practically the same 'functions' as the traditional banking system but lacks access to the latter's public funding and stabilisation mechanisms.[2] Whether we deal with volatile investment streams, the innovations in financial practices, or the dynamic reconfiguration of the global financial system, shadow banking is a crucial aspect of understanding the current debacle that now stands behind many calls for tighter regulation and monitory procedures in financial markets (Claessens *et al.* 2012; EC 2012; ECB 2013; FSB 2013a, 2013b; IMF 2013; Liikanen 2012).

Since 2009, shadow banking has moved on to the front pages of newspapers and has become a highly debated topic in the global regulation discourse, the subject of publications from the International Monetary Fund, the Bank for International Settlements, the Financial Stability Board and the European Commission. Of course, nobody disputes the political relevance of both shadow banking practices as well as on-going auditing practices that move claims off balance sheets. Yet, it is quite interesting to note that the 'official' literature around shadow banking puts forward the claim that the shadow banking system has de-stabilised markets by creating new information asymmetries as, for instance, the BIS indicates:

> Regarding the market implications, information asymmetries are the fuel that feeds financial panics. In the 2007–09 crisis, we saw contagion ignited by uncertainty over counterparty exposures – not knowing who will bear losses should they occur. Transparency and information are the keys to any solution, including for markets.
>
> (BIS 2010: 17)

Even though we certainly do not want to negate the existence of these asymmetries, it is quite surprising that the classic 'topos' of 'information asymmetry' explains the new phenomenon of shadow banking equally as well as the infamous Lemon market.[3] It seems that if instabilities manifest themselves, the same vocabulary around moral hazard, adverse selection and misaligned incentives is applied, regardless of whether we deal with the Asian Crisis, bubbles in the real estate market or shadow banking practices. And everywhere, the solutions already seem to be known: more transparency, tighter regulation, more data. The normative appeal of transparency makes it hard to argue against it, let alone take a somewhat more critical stance: who would argue for fewer data and less transparency?

Yet, at the same time, this normative dimension at the same time suggests that more is at stake than simply finding the right cure to a new problem. When we look at what the concept of information asymmetry *does* (and not whether it is an adequate description), we suggest that this economic concept does far more than just provide a neutral description of contemporary practices: to focus on information instability is to refer to modern microeconomic models (including the now classic market and government failure literature). This reference in itself is neither a good nor a bad thing, but it has three repercussions: first, these models are performative (for several aspects see MacKenzie *et al.* 2007). The concept of information asymmetry then, in a way, determines what the problem is and what the range of possible solutions looks like. Thus, what the current reform debate includes and excludes, what the discussion makes (in)visible and how the challenges are positioned are related to the episteme of the disciplinary knowledge of (mainstream) economics. It creates a demand for economic expertise, because it is economics and not anthropology or sociology that can deal effectively with problems identified as, for instance, 'moral hazard'. Second, these models are based on the assumption that markets could – in principle – be stable. Even if practitioners may believe otherwise and become fully aware that instabilities are related to financial practices, the efficient market hypothesis is perpetuated on the semantic level insofar as 'stability' is equated with 'efficiency' (Fama 1970; Shleifer 2000). Financial instability is thus not inherent to financial practices but is due to other factors, such as the lack of states' will to regulate markets effectively.[4] Third, through its formalism, economic theory takes the identity of actors as a given. It abstracts from diagnostic processes where actors have to figure out what is actually the case. The structure of the game, the actors' interests and their formation, is common knowledge (e.g. Lépinay 2007). Thereby, these models abstract from the social dimension of financial practices, i.e. the net of continuously reorganised connections between actors on the basis of models, financial instruments and 'regulations' that create a specific spatio-temporality of financial markets (Kessler and Wilhelm 2013).

Although we certainly welcome recent initiatives to tighten regulations and do not argue, we should pursue a hands-off approach; we argue that regulation needs to take into account the aforementioned practical consequences of economic rationality. Moreover, we suggest that such an alternative stance highlights different dynamics that counteract the success aspired to current reform proposals. Hence, to question the efficient market hypothesis, to consider the social dimension of finance and to understand instability as endogenous to financial practices makes the regulation of shadow banking an even more challenging issue than 'asymmetric information' suggests.

In relation to the shadow banking system, the current strategy to abstract from the social dimension of financial practices leads to a reification of the shadow banking system itself: it is understood as a field or problem that can be clearly distinguished, managed and quantified. To recognise and take seriously the social dimension allows us to see that the term 'shadow banking' highlights different aspects in relation to space, time and agency. These three contexts also define distinct regulatory tasks that otherwise are thrown together: the determination of spatial government structures, the political consequences of different temporalities and the advent of new, as well as the evolution of current, actors.

In order to foster this argument, this contribution is divided into three sections. The first section discusses the three meanings of shadow banking in relation to space, time and agency and shows that regulation becomes an eternal task rather than a one-time solution to a set of given problems. Taking Germany as an example, the second section shows that the current attempt to 'regulate' shadow banking 'creates' ambiguities in precisely these areas: the demarcation of space, the management of different temporalities, and the identification and regulation of actors. The final section summarises the argument and tries to outline an alternative approach incorporating the social dimension of financial practices and how it relates to political order.

Three meanings of shadow banking

As many contributions to this volume reiterate, shadow banking is a relatively new invention, which emerged in the context of the crisis (see, in particular, Adrian and Shin 2009, 2010; McCulley 2007; Pozsar 2008, 2011).[5] The current literature defines and frames it as a new system of financial intermediation where the traditional banking system and shadow banking perform the same economic function (Pozsar *et al.* 2012: 11): both provide credit, maturity and liquidity transformation. This literature mentions two major differences between the traditional and the shadow banking systems that sets them apart. In the traditional banking system, financial intermediation is visible on the bank's balance sheet: they receive deposits (passive side of the balance sheet) and issue loans (active side of the balance sheet). In the shadow banking system, financial intermediation is organised by an entire chain of agencies and actors where securitisation allows individual banks to move loans off their balance sheets (for a more detailed overview, see Pozsar *et al.* 2012: 10).[6] Second, while the traditional banking system is stabilised by and linked to public funding (especially by the Federal Reserve System in the US), it is the private sector that has to provide for sufficient liquidity and stability in the shadow banking system (Pozsar *et al.* 2012: 3).[7] Hence, information and monitoring are derived from market-based pricing within a market-based credit system.

The crisis has led to a fundamental reassessment of the shadow banking system. While private liquidity provisions were seen as stabilising financial markets so that risks could be hedged more efficiently, it is now argued retrospectively that to disperse risks means relocating risks affecting the whole banking sector (see Adrian and Shin 2009: 11). Through the concept of shadow banking, it is possible to articulate pleas for tighter regulation of financial markets.

In this section, we show that the very term 'shadow banking' can be seen from three different perspectives: shadow banking can be conceptualised as a specific space constituting the problem of transnational financial relations. The primary regulatory task is then to delineate and fix the regulatory space. Shadow banking can be conceptualised in temporal terms. Financial practices impact on temporal understandings of financial infrastructures and governance. The regulatory task here is to make different temporalities congruent. Last but not least, shadow banking can be conceptualised in terms of the advent of new actors, such as special investment vehicles, hedge funds and other so-called non-bank financial institutions. Here, regulators have to 'capture' these new actors as well as their evolution by making them subject to regulation. In the following paragraphs, we want to outline these three contexts and identify the distinct regulatory tasks, before the final section takes the example of Germany to show in detail the limits and implications of the current approach to banking regulation.

Shadow banking as a particular space

The spatiality of shadow banking comes to the fore when it is framed as a specific space that is separate from traditional banking, for example by using tax havens and 'offshore' as opportunities for 'regulatory arbitrage'. Consequently, supervision and monitoring of shadow banks is significantly more difficult than the traditional, predominantly nation-based system. This difficulty is exacerbated through practices of securitisation that trespass on national confines (Gorton *et al.* 2012). Structured and securitised tranches (as collateralised debt obligations) are sold on a global scale, and associated practices do not stop at national borders. In this sense, to talk about a US, German, French or British shadow banking system is problematic in much the same way as we might identify different nationally defined varieties of capitalism. Although often discussed in these terms, national borders do not 'cut off' chains and relations of shadow banking practices. On the contrary, shadow banking is rather constituted by a globally overreaching network.

For the IMF, on the other hand, nation states are the primary focus and are assumed to be in charge of their own banking systems (IMF 2010: 39). If countries stabilise their domestic banking system, this should also reduce systemic risks (IMF 2011: 14). At the same time, the existence of different political frameworks does not provide the means to "address systemic risks" or to secure "too-important-to-fail institutions" (IMF 2010: 9). Or as Cerutti *et al.* (2011: 3) put it: "Much of the data needed for identifying and tracking international linkages, even at a rudimentary level, is not (yet) available, and the institutional infrastructure for global systemic risk management is inadequate or simply non-existent". The complexities of cross-country relations and monetary flows cannot be described adequately due to a lack of information which, in turn, has brought about a new set of surveillance measures initiated by the IMF (IMF 2008: chapter 3). The collecting of more information as well as expanding practices to provide information will be a task for years to come. This also requires the introduction of new monitoring structures in order to exchange information about the global shadow banking system and its evolution (FSB 2011: 5).

The continuing task for regulatory bodies is to break down global flows and delineate clear-cut jurisdictions. Yet, all attempts to include certain institutions and practices must immediately come to terms with how to deal with the excluded and external relations and actors. The moment when authorities try to 'close' a space, new connections and new loopholes are created that link entities across jurisdictions in new ways.

Shadow banking as a specific temporal order

Financial intermediation regulates time by providing liquidity today in exchange for future revenues. The transformation of long maturity assets into short-term financial products has been made increasingly possible by non-bank financial intermediaries through securitisation (FSB 2012a: 8). The regulatory measures of the Basel Accords supported and unintentionally accompanied such a reformatting of the international credit system (Du Plessis 2011: 11). Shadow banking allowed for maturity transformation beyond national supervision and created money, for instance short-term liabilities in the form of (synthetically) constructed commercial papers. As the BIS (2011: 15) confirms:

> Shadow banks have the potential to generate substantial systemic risk because they can be highly leveraged and engage in significant amounts of maturity transformation while being closely linked to commercial banks. And, as the name suggests, the shadow banks can do all of this in ways that are less than completely transparent.

This led to a highly liquid financial market based on the exchange of commercial papers. The exchange value of such papers could be sustained, as the risks associated with these financial products could be contained through hedging strategies (for instance, through credit default swaps).

This combination of commercial papers and insurances 'constituted' a distinctive temporality of shadow banking. On the one hand, as a market-based valuation system, it allowed commercial papers (in combination with tailored default insurances) to be treated as 'money-like' assets, because it was assumed that all information would be readily taken into consideration. When all available information is (believed to be) included in the current price, then speed is only limited by the technical restrictions of glass fibre and calculation capacities – hence the importance of automated algorithm trading today.[8]

This temporal concept defines the regulatory task as being to structure the way in which future developments, changes and uncertainties are 'accounted' for and regulate the temporal structure of different capital flows. At the moment, proposals try to regulate the capital structure of financial actors directly (most prominently by the implementation of Basel III standards), or 'artificially' reduce the temporality of financial transactions. The proposal for a financial transaction tax (the so-called Tobin tax) in the European context (see the proposed directive of the EC 2013) presents one example around which the temporality of financial transactions is being debated. However, regulating the temporalities of financial streams as well might go along with financial actors' attempts to 'optimise' their business models by creating new financial categories and instruments. Just as shadow banking is very much the result of financial actors' attempts to circumvent capital requirements by getting funds off their balance sheets, the attempt to regulate their temporal structure will stimulate new innovations, followed by the production of new temporalities.

Shadow banking as a set of actors

The demand for regulation of the shadow banking system focuses not only on control over cross-border interactions and maturity transformations, but also on the transparency and visibility of actors' positions within the shadow banking system (Adrian and Ashcraft 2012: 4). The identification of actors is important in two ways: first, there is the quest to identify 'systemically important banks', i.e. to identify those institutions that are so deeply connected within the global financial system that their financial positions needs to be made known to regulators (BCBS 2011). Second, and for our discussion more importantly, financial markets are characterised by the continuous advent and decay of specific types of actors within financial markets. From this perspective, shadow banking is associated with a new complexity of new types of (and chains between) actors that have hitherto not been on the regulators' radar.

Proposals to fix and make visible the set of actors face two difficulties. First, even though regulatory measures want "to extend the regulatory perimeter beyond traditional financial institutions to cover shadow banks" (BIS 2011: 15), it is also acknowledged that processes of shadow banking can, potentially, stabilise the traditional banking system (FSB 2012b). From this perspective, the existence of the shadow banking system might not be a bad thing, in general and the 'transformation' of shadow banking into 'traditional' banking would be counterproductive. Second, in order to stabilise the shadow banking system, supervision requires information about and risk assessments for all included actors (Caruana 2012: 10; Fontaine and Garcia 2012: 12). One expression of this is the call for global legislation regarding finance (FSB *et al.* 2011: 6). This requires a common definition of categories by which these agencies can be distinguished and regulated accordingly. However, these categories are not passive descriptions but actually alter the field they want to describe. For example, the attempt to define the capital ratios of specific agents via the Basel Accords did not succeed in stabilising the financial system. On the contrary, these regulatory measures provided the basis for the creation of new entities and expanded the shadow banking system.

Taking these three contexts together, shadow banking can be seen as a *space* that has to be understood and clarified (Borio *et al*. 2011: 52); it can be seen as a specific temporality *and* it can be associated with the advent of new actors. In the next section, we show how these three dimensions play out by looking at the German jurisdictional context more closely.

Performing German shadow banking

The last section identified three contexts with distinct regulatory tasks. All point in one direction: the idea that regulation will specify comprehensive boundaries to tame and control financial practices is problematic. Hence, equally problematic is the idea that there exists a 'right' set of adjustments that make financial markets work perfectly well. Instead, we suggest that regulation and practices have to be seen in a more 'dialectic' relationship. By dialectic we mean that regulation changes the complexity of shadow banking and that this altered complexity then creates new realities and crisis dynamics asking for new regulatory measures. Thus shadow banking cannot simply be 'tamed', but attempts for incremental changes will induce changes, new practices and new contingencies. Hence, the shadow banking system is the very product of the dialectic relation and not a designed outcome of regulation. The current approach (as outlined earlier) – to regulate shadow banking by focusing on given entities or 'things' and thereby presupposing given actors – underestimates the way in which connections between those entities change rapidly. In other words, this task underestimates the extent to which new regulations will simply induce a reorganisation of financial markets that might lead to a change in their complexity but not change the overall logic.[9] In order to become more specific, we turn now to one example of how regulation is translated into the specific jurisdictional context of Germany through the frequently and recently revised German Banking Act.

Even though we do not want to reiterate the history of the German Banking Act, there is one important matter to note beforehand: regulation is neither the result of a grand 'institutional' design, nor is it driven by a functional logic of the market. The same holds true for this example. The story of the German Banking Act displays the contingent reiteration of crises and political responses. For example, from its very beginning, formal banking regulation has been a reaction to the German banking crisis of 1931. In 1934, Germany started to centralise the supervision related to (thrift-)banking activities. This legislation became effective in 1935, and for the first time it covered all banking activities under the supervision of the Ministry of Economics. After the Second World War, the UK and the US in particular reversed the centralisation of supervision in Germany and delegated it to the regional level. Only in 1957 was a step towards centralisation taken when the Bundesbank was created following a merger of its regional counterparts. Apart from the Bundesbank, the "Kreditwesengesetz", implemented in 1961, constituted a new supervisory agency on the federal level, the "Bundesaufsichtsamt", attached to the Ministry of Economics (for a detailed study, see Von Georg 2013). Later, in 1972, this agency was transferred to the Ministry of Finance. Until 2002, the agency's sole concern was the supervision of credit institutions. However, immediately after the dotcom bubble burst, three German supervisory bodies responsible for supervising the lending and credit system (BAKred) and the insurance industry (BAV), as well as securities trading (BAWe) were merged into one institution to be responsible for the supervision of the German financial market, the Federal Financial Supervisory Authority (BaFin). The BaFin and the Bundesbank remain the key regulatory and supervisory bodies for financial actors to this day at the national level (BaFin 2010). In short, we can see that supervision is also a history of competing authorities, for instance, the Länder vis-à-vis the federal state, between different federal ministries and between the Central Bank and BaFin.[10] In the context of the Eurocrisis, the Banking Act has been the main site where new capital requirements (CRD IV), new supervisory agencies (ESAs) and new definitions of financial practices (Solvency II, MiFid II and AIMD), as well as the new supervisory coordination under the umbrella of the so-called banking union, are translated into German law. To see how it works and the counter-dynamics this translation produces, let us turn now to the reform of the German Banking Act.

Spaces of German shadow banking

The spatial problem of shadow banking was described earlier as a conflict between the global reach of financial practices and the demarcation of national spaces. This section shows how the German Banking Act defines and delimits its regulatory space, while at the same time incorporating links and relations that paradoxically reach beyond its jurisdiction. It is not only the German case that indicates supervision is an amalgam of national and European, as well as global standards all referring to relationships between different supervisory bodies and legal constraints. In this sense, the German Banking Act is also a product of its own restrictions. For example, we can read that:

> If an enterprise domiciled outside Germany maintains a branch in Germany which conducts banking business or provides financial services, that branch shall be deemed to be a credit institution or a financial services institution. If the enterprise maintains several branches in Germany, they shall be deemed to be one institution.
>
> (Bundestag 2013: Section 53)

Here we see how the German Banking Act tried to delimit the concept of credit institutions to its own jurisdiction, while at the same time having to take into account the existence of foreign institutions. The Banking Act thereby not only defines and regulates financial institutions within its own jurisdiction but also conditions how the transnational constellation of (financial) firms is to be captured. Thereby, on the one hand, the legal document decides about the limits of legal, illegal as well as legally undefined practices across borders. The jurisdiction of the Banking Act is thus not – by itself – similar to Germany as a specific territory. Rather, the link between legal and political spaces is much more contingent. At the same time, this implies that other 'national' regulation (or Banking Acts) 'trespasses' over national borders. How these different Acts then relate to each other gives rise to a new complexity and eventually legal problems as they don't 'fit'. Hence, the way, for example, that UK regulation deals with the existence of Deutsche Bank and its branches in the UK, and the way in which Germany deals with the existence of British banks and their branches in Germany, opens up specific ways for these banks to structure (or restructure) their business models in order to benefit from loopholes and inconsistencies that are produced at the intersection of these different Banking Acts. For example, new instruments, products and practices question the relationship between foreign and national institutions or reconfigure them in new ways (alas, the meaning of national contexts for financial practices is continuously changing through new instruments and financial practices). Consider in this context, for example, the role of credit default swaps that allow for profits from cash flows from institutions in other countries without actually having to buy shares in those institutions. This example is only indicative of a larger problem of how legal boundaries allow and constrain financial exchange across and beyond jurisdictional borders, not because individual Banking Acts 'deal' with these practices conclusively 'within' the Act, but rather at the margins where several Acts 'meet'. Hence different legal conditions exist in parallel, but the practice of finance – especially through market-based credit systems – connects these legal spheres and creates new demand for transnational coordination.

At this point, the particular problem within the European Union does not relate to the formulation or production of directives or regulations, but rather European law needs to be translated into national laws where these directives and regulations can be made to operate differently according to the specific national contexts in which they now need to work. The same holds true for global standards. Global financial standards were adopted by the EU and were then forwarded to national authorities. In the end, the very requirement for various translations (of global, regional, national or transnational norms and regulations) shows that the idea of an existing and homogenous space, that at best is also identical to the national space, is only an ideal or – to be more precise – an imaginary that motivates further and further regulation and the management of borders. For instance, in the German context, one operational mode to translate financial regulation is provided by the regulation of trading and banking books, which leads us to a temporal logic of the governance and practice of banking.

Time of German shadow banking

The difference between the trading and banking books of a financial institution relates to the capital structure of financial institutions.[11] The trading book requires a different capital provision to that of the banking book. Therefore, management of the balance sheet is strongly related to what kinds of financial practices are pursued and what kind of financial products are being bought at a distinct point in time. In that way, financial products and their regulation manage these temporal differences. The differences between the trading and banking books are also taken to demarcate the distinction between short-term and long-term investments by the bank.[12] The differences between the trading and banking books provide an incentive to engage with shadow banking through financial innovations as they expand the action space for (external) management of the balance sheet. Through this structure, financial products are governed differently depending on whether they are considered to be short- or long-term investments.

Since 2006, it is the German Ministry of Finance that decides (under certain conditions) what instruments belong to which category. Whereas before it needed an actual change of legal texts to alter the categories, it is now within the prerogative of the government to change this by "statutory order".[13] Throughout the several changes of the German Banking Act since 2006,[14] this procedure has been continuously extended to other issues and areas. This, of course, is not only a shift from legislative to the executive power, but it means that the Ministry is now able to influence the temporality of financial streams through accounting procedures related to the balance sheets of financial institutions. Apart from the separation of traditional and shadow banking procedures, this also influences the politics of financial regulation by changing the decision and power structures of national institutional contexts. This is also true for lower-level decision processes – for instance, for liquidity requirements. In this case (since 2007 and instead of the Ministry of Finance) it is the BaFin in consultation with the Bundesbank that is able to specify the conditions for liquidity requirements. Since 2009, they have been allowed to ask for further liquidity provisions if the institution concerned seems to lack liquidity under the prevailing conditions specified in the German Banking Act. Since 2014, also in line with the implementation of CRD IV requirements, the BaFin is able to shorten the reporting period and extend the reporting obligations regarding liquidity.

The change in the temporal logic of banking also affects the practices of shadow banking, as it impacts on what can be traded profitably under regulatory practices. To be more explicit, the regulation of the internal practice of banking forces banks, on the one hand, to comply with new regulatory expectations while, on the other, they now use these different temporalities to manage their accounts. Hence, the temporal differences enable or even force banks to create new strategies for managing the positions on and off their balance sheets (cf. Bundestag 2013: Section 2, 11). This temporal dimension shows how banking, shadow banking and regulatory bodies are related and how changes in the temporal structure impact on how shadow banking 'works' for the traditional banking sector.

During and after the crisis, the German Banking Act underwent several changes in order to adapt to the new global standard-setting through European re-regulation of the banking sector. More recent changes to the German Banking Act include the sharing of more information at the European level by national supervisors (Section 7a, 3), as well as a division of the banking sector through the new category of so-called "CRR-institutions", which means that these institutions fall within the scope of the Capital Requirements Regulation (EC 2013). This, in turn, sets further requirements for how the differences between the trading and the non-trading book are to be handled by financial institutions. However, how the new institutional and regulatory framework impacts on financial practices and thereby also the reconfiguration of transnational shadow banking practices beyond recent mapping exercises (Jackson and Matilainen 2012) is still to be researched. The new temporal order of this new regulation might trigger new strategies to organise the temporality of trading practices in relation to capital requirements and therefore further financial innovations on and off the balance sheet.

For the regulation of shadow banking practices, this means that it is not only a passive description of how accounting must be more transparent and how capital ratios must be applied to specific exposures. It is also the governance of temporality beyond the regulatory designs of the German Banking Act.

Agencies of shadow banking

Associated with the production of spatial and temporal aspects of banking is the need to identify new actors. For example, national authorities need to define the location as well as the associated properties of, e.g. "credit institutions" or "financial services institutions". The German Banking Act from 2006 onwards refers to the BaFin as the main institution able to define the category in which companies are to be placed and hence according to which regulation they are subject. Needless to say, the category to which they are ascribed has important repercussions for the business model of the various firms, as how actors are defined impacts on their capacity to buy and sell specific financial products. How financial products are made, changed, traded, produced etc. will make these categories work for the institutions. Hence, the very act of categorisation impacts on the way in which these categorised actors behave in the market, the products that are exchanged in it and the way in which actors relate to one another (or how institutions 'break up' or redefine themselves in order to escape these straitjackets). Yet, categorisation is not a one-way street. To the extent to which classification depends on actors' practices (for example, exposure, audit, trading practices), actors can react and change their practices in order to be 'repositioned'. Then, for instance, the difference between insurance from banking and investment actors is located in the capital structure, not in the actual services provided by the products they offer. Insurance, for instance, is then provided by the hedging strategies of banks, whereas credit can be generated by insurance companies through repurchasing government bonds. Hence the difference between "deposit-taking institutions" or "risk-pooling institutions" (Carmichael and Pomerleano 2002) is oriented towards their financial products off and on their balance sheets as much as in the actual services provided.

The Banking Act categorises different actors and puts them into 'sectors' on the basis of their capital structure. Actors now have the incentive to comply with specific ratios applicable to one category – so that the regulatory demands and their internal business model 'fit'. In this way, the German Banking Act structures and positions the financial actors. A financial conglomerate, for example, as a combination of diverse financial activities operating in different financial sectors, can issue a range of possible capital adequacy statements depending on which kind of 'firm' and activities are 'assembled'. Even though one assumes that capital adequacy statements are 'under supervision' by the federal agencies, their supervisory power is limited to the extent to which actors can redefine themselves.[15] Germany tries to respond to this 'inconsistency' by providing a separate governance structure for financial conglomerates:

> The Federal Ministry of Finance shall be authorised to issue in consultation with the Deutsche Bundesbank more detailed provisions by way of a statutory order that does not require the consent of the upper house of parliament (Bundesrat) on determining the adequate own funds . . . in particular concerning [for instance] the permissible composition of own funds.
>
> (Bundestag 2013: Section 10b, 1)

Indeed, since July 2013, the German Banking Act includes the category of "mixed financial holding companies" (Bundestag 2013: Section 10), which encompasses different functions and financial institutions. It is the composition of the balance sheets that provides the rationale to determine under which regulatory regime such a company is placed. The actual placement connects several decision-making layers, such as the European and national levels or different national and European agencies.

Hence, depending on the way supervision is executed and on the categories defined within the German Banking Act, it is producing a static model of possible actors subject to its law. This in turn also relates to the possible relationship between these different actors. Agency within financial markets depends on differences between the regulatory framework (and the knowledge it produces and presupposes), the practices 'on the ground' (and the knowledge they produce) and the way in which these practices 'know' about the regulations put in place. Here, shadow banking is one strategy to put that knowledge into practice. Nevertheless, shadow banking within Germany was not as widespread as in other jurisdictions (in contrast to, especially, the US):

> [b]ecause of the broad regulatory approach taken in the German Banking Act (Kreditwesengesetz) and other financial market regulations. Moreover, tax regimes and differences in administrative practices are further key reasons why shadow banking entities are more likely to be located in foreign financial centres than in Germany . . . Risks are created not only by the existence of indirect contagion channels, especially via the financial markets, but also by direct interlinkages, such as through loans and subsidiaries.
>
> (Bundesbank 2012: 67)

The supervision of shadow banking mainly focuses on balance sheets and the counterparties of entities involved in the shadow banking system. A German perspective on these balance sheets is, however, hardly able to clarify how German institutions are related to the global or international shadow banking system. This is not only because of the different definitions of shadow banking within different jurisdictions connected through financial practices to German banks, but "moreover, it is impossible to fully rule out the possibility that a certain percentage of foreign banks acting as counterparties are actually MMFs. The available data, however, are not granular enough to reach any substantive conclusions" (Bundesbank 2012: 72). Again, the regulation of shadow banking is driven by 'completing' the knowledge about its entities. It is the lack of data about the exact configuration of its agents that hinders comprehensive regulation. The German Banking Act provides some of the categories through which financial institutions can be classified, practices attached and capital ratios prescribed. But the dynamic process of regulation as well as the ongoing differences in practically and regulatory produced knowledge is rather seen as a problem, in contrast to designating this difference as a constitutive function of the financial as well as the shadow banking system.

Conclusion: political order and shadow banking

As indicated in the discussions on the threefold production of shadow banking in general as well as in the more concrete reconstruction concerning the legal reconfiguration of the German context, both variations point to the political order around new forms of banking: How has political order enabled shadow banking practices? How is it produced by the interdependence of new governance and banking structures? And, finally, how can the political order be conceptualised in order to integrate the spatial, temporal and subjectivity conceptions?

The debate on shadow banking is not simply a technical debate on how to regulate these institutions and financial instruments, it also opens up a debate about authority, the boundary of state authority and the rationality of markets. It is here that the autonomy and power of financial markets are renegotiated. However, it is not a debate that includes the wider public or public authorities and where they meet to decide 'rationally' on financial policies. It is a debate about where economic models and concepts define the terms and outlook of financial reforms: the concepts of incentive misalignments, transparency, market failure and asymmetric information (predominantly in the form of moral hazard) have exclusionary powers by defining the horizon of possible reform and constituting a technical debate and functional logic. The primary question, then, is only how to solve the various problems – preferably without political interference. The politics of shadow banking is not simply related to what states do, it also points to specific groups of experts related to central banks or international financial institutions (in particular the IMF, BIS and FSB) that, based on disciplinary defined knowledge, can 'fix' shadow banking to such an extent that the definition of key problems, the meaning of shadow banking and the road ahead are already framed by their own analysis.

In this contribution we have connected the notion of shadow banking with the reproduction of the German jurisdiction in order to understand how authority and legitimacy are produced within the financial system. Therefore, we first traced how shadow banking and the non-shadowy part evolved and are differentiated. Second, we provided an overview of how shadow banking is embedded into current German banking regulation. Third, this opened up a discussion of legitimacy and authority and how these political concepts are connected to the knowledge production within the realm of financial regulation. Therefore, this contribution enables a political discussion of financial regulation as an integral part of the performance of the political order itself.

It is a specific political order, associated with the shadow banking system, that creates a technical vocabulary where economic models are central to providing financial and regulatory solutions. That means it is a political order that transforms a financial crisis into a functional one, where further questions about authority, the public or even the legitimacy of (economic) knowledge are sidelined, hidden and 'legitimately' excluded. We argued that this strategy is based on a specific episteme that leads us down a wrong alley: economic models and resulting regulation are notoriously blind to both the social conditions that make them (and the communication through them) possible and the practical consequences of applying them to specific problems. Hence, the assumption is that regulation is possible, finite and a technical problem to be solved as soon as economists can do their magic tricks. Yet, by pointing towards the social conditions of economic knowledge in its various forms and guises (as economic expertise, economic models or economic concepts), we suggest that regulation is not an easy task: it is essentially a utopian project, a Sisyphus task that will not extinguish uncertainty or crisis in financial markets.

Notes

1 The term shadow banking is said to have been coined by Paul McCulley. For fuller description of his views on what shadow banking means, see this interview: McCulley (2013).
2 In particular, the literature points to the function of credit, maturity and liquidity transformation (e.g. FSB 2012c: 2).
3 For an argument proposing uncertain information as the constitutive function of financial production, see Esposito (2012).
4 Even though officials may openly challenge the view today that financial markets are self-stabilising around existing equilibria, this implies that the efficient market hypothesis is perpetuated on a conceptual level insofar as the literature is based on a semantic link between stability and efficiency: stable markets are efficient, instabilities thus create inefficiencies. Alas, crises can only be 'failures' of otherwise stable and efficient markets.
5 This section is based on Kessler and Wilhelm (2013).
6 Due to space limitations, we cannot present these steps in detail. See Pozsar *et al.* (2012) for a discussion.
7 Of course, this is only a rather crude distinction: banks in the traditional sector are often linked indirectly to shadow banking. Thus, if a bank suffers from negative consequences in the shadow banking system, it may turn to public authorities nevertheless. This of course raises the question of how the shadow banking system and the traditional banking system are linked and connected. But this cannot be dealt with in this contribution.

8 For an overview and more detailed discussion of the role of algorithms in financial markets, see Lenglet (2011).
9 The conclusion is not 'no regulation', but rather regulation that clearly de-connects (i.e. forbids) certain connections and does not focus only on specific actors such as hedge funds.
10 Things get even more complicated when we look at the impact of the EU. From 1992 onwards, increasing harmonisation and coordination took place. On the one hand, it was the introduction of the principle that institutions are regulated by their home countries; on the other hand, capital requirements were aligned between member states' jurisdictions.
11 The differences between trading and banking books (basically long-term assets vs the more short-term trading positions) have been a central concern for re-regulation after the financial crisis: "The [Basel Committee for Banking Supervision] believes that the definition of the regulatory boundary has been a source of weakness in the current regime. A key determinant of the existing boundary has been banks' effectively self-determined intent to trade, an inherently subjective criterion that has proved difficult to police and insufficiently restrictive from a prudential perspective in some jurisdictions. Coupled with large differences in capital requirements against similar types of risk on either side of the boundary, the overall capital framework proved susceptible to arbitrage in the run-up to the crisis" (BCBS 2013: 6).
12 The distribution of short- and long-term financial instruments on balance sheets relates to capital requirement ratios and therefore to the profitability of a bank. Hence, through balance sheet management and outsourcing practices, profitability and capital requirements can be adjusted (BCBS 2013: 8).
13 The German translation of 'Rechtsverordnung' – a legal function specified in German Basic Law (GG Article 80) that permits the federal government, federal minister or regional governments to establish a statutory order under certain conditions.
14 The Banking Act has been revised 47 times since 2006, the most recent changes taking place on 2 January 2014.
15 For instance, it qualifies to choose between different calculation methods, in this case between: "(a) method 1: Accounting consolidation method; (b) method 2: Deduction and aggregation method; (c) method 3: Book value/Requirement deduction method; or (d) combination of methods 1 to 3" (Bundestag 2013, section 10b, 3).

References

Adrian, T. and A. B. Ashcraft (2012) *Shadow Banking Regulation.* Federal Reserve Bank of New York Staff Reports, no. 559. Available at: www.newyorkfed.org/medialibrary/media/research/staff_reports/sr580.pdf. Last accessed: 16.01.2017.

Adrian, T. and H. S. Shin (2009) *The Shadow Banking System: Implications for Financial Regulation.* Federal Reserve Bank of New York Staff Report, no. 382. Available at: www.newyorkfed.org/medialibrary/media/research/staff_reports/sr382.pdf. Last accessed: 06.01.2017.

Adrian, T. and H. S. Shin (2010) *The Changing Nature of Financial Intermediation and the Financial Crisis of 2007–09.* Federal Reserve Bank of New York Staff Report, no. 439. Available at: www.newyorkfed.org/medialibrary/media/research/staff_reports/sr439.pdf. Last accessed: 06.01.2017.

BaFin (2012) *BaFin is Ten Years Old: From Lightning Birth to Maturity.* Federal Financial Supervisory Authority Report. Available at: www.bafin.de/SharedDocs/Veroeffentlichungen/EN/Fachartikel/2012/fa_bj_2012-05_bafin_jubilaeum_en.html. Last accessed: 19.12.2013.

BCBS (2011) *Global Systemically Important Banks: Assessment Methodology and the Additional Loss Absorbency Requirement – Rules Text*. Basel Committee on Banking Supervision. Available at: www.bis.org/publ/bcbs207.htm. Last accessed 21.04.2017.

BCBS (2013) *Consultative Document – Fundamental Review of the Trading Book: A Revised Market Risk Framework*. Basel Committee on Banking Supervision. Available at: www.bis.org/publ/bcbs207.pdf. Last accessed: 06.01.2017.

BIS (2010) *BIS 80th Annual Report*. Bank for International Settlements. Available at: www.bis.org/publ/arpdf/ar2010e.pdf. Last accessed: 16.01.2017.

BIS (2011) *BIS 81st Annual Report*, June 2011. Bank for International Settlements. Available at: www.bis.org/publ/arpdf/ar2011e.pdf. Last accessed: 16.01.2017.

Borio, C., R. McCauley and P. McGuire (2011) *Global Credit and Domestic Credit Booms*. BIS Quarterly Review, September. Available at: www.bis.org/publ/qtrpdf/r_qt1109f.pdf. Last accessed: 16.01.2017.

Bundesbank (2012) *Financial Stability Review 2012*. Frankfurt am Main, Germany: Deutsche Bundesbank.

Bundestag (2013) *Banking Act (Gesetz über das Kreditwesen, Kreditwesengesetz – KWG)*. Available at: www.gesetze-im-internet.de/kredwg/BJNR008810961.html. Last accessed: 19.12.2013.

Carmichael, J. and M. Pomerleano (2002) *The Development and Regulation of Non-Bank Financial Institutions*. Washington, DC, World Bank Publications. Working Paper. Available at: https://ideas.repec.org/b/wbk/wbpubs/15236.html. Last accessed: 16.01.2017.

Caruana, J. (2012) *Building a Resilient Financial System*. Keynote Speech at the 2012 ADB Financial Sector Forum on 'Enhancing Financial Stability – Issues and Challenges', Manila, 7 February. Available at: www.bis.org/speeches/sp120208.pdf. Last accessed: 16.01.2017.

Cerutti, E., S. Claessens and P. McGuire (2011) *Systemic Risks in Global Banking: What Available Data Can Tell Us and What More Data are Needed?* IMF Working Paper, no. 11/222. Available at: www.imf.org/external/pubs/ft/wp/2011/wp11222.pdf. Last accessed: 16.01.2017.

Claessens, S., Z. Pozsar, L. Ratnovski and M. Singh (2012) *Shadow Banking: Economics and Policy*. IMF Staff Discussion Note. Available at: www.imf.org/external/pubs/ft/sdn/2012/sdn1212.pdf. Last accessed: 16.12.2016.

Du Plessis, S. (2011) *Collapse. The Story of the International Financial Crisis, its Causes and Policy Consequences*. Stellenbosch Economic Working Papers, no. 02.11. Available at: www.ekon.sun.ac.za/wpapers/2011/wp022011/wp-02–2011.pdf. Last accessed: 16.01.2017.

EC (2012) *Green Paper: Shadow Banking*. European Commission, COM(2012) 102 Final. Available at: http://ec.europa.eu/internal_market/bank/docs/shadow/green-paper_en.pdf. Last accessed: 16.01.2017.

EC (2013) *Regulation (EU) No 575/2013 of the European Parliament and of the Council of 26 June 2013 on Prudential Requirements for Credit Institutions and Investment Firms and Amending Regulation (EU) No 648/2012*. European Council. Available at: http://eur-lex.europa.eu/eli/reg/2013/575/oj. Last accessed 21.04.2017.

ECB (2013) *Enhancing the Monitoring of Shadow Banking*. European Central Bank, Monthly Bulletin, February. Available at: www.ecb.europa.eu/pub/pdf/other/art2_mb201302en_pp89-99en.pdf. Last accessed: 16.01.2017.

Esposito, E. (2012) "The Structures of Uncertainty: Performativity and Unpredictability in Economic Operations". *Economy and Society*, 42(1), pp. 102–129.

Fama, E. F. (1970) "Efficient Capital Markets: A Review of Theory and Empirical Work". *Journal of Finance*, 25(2), pp. 383–417.

Fontaine, J. S. and R. Garcia (2012) "Bond Liquidity Premia". *Review of Financial Studies*, 25(4), pp. 1207–1254.

FSB (2011) *Shadow Banking: Scoping the Issues. A Background Note of the Financial Stability Board*. Financial Stability Board. Available at: www.fsb.org/2011/04/shadow-banking-scoping-the-issues/. Last accessed: 20.12.2016.

FSB (2012a) *Strengthening the Oversight and Regulation of Shadow Banking*. Progress Report to G20 Ministers and Governors. Financial Stability Board. Available at: www.fsb.org/wp-content/uploads/r_111027a.pdf?page_moved=1. Last accessed: 20.12.2016.

FSB (2012b) *Securities Lending and Repos: Market Overview and Financial Stability Issues*. Interim Report of the FSB Workstream on Securities Lending and Repos. Financial Stability Board. Available at: www.fsb.org/wp-content/uploads/r_120427. pdf. Last accessed: 20.12.2016.

FSB (2012c) *Global Shadow Banking Monitoring Report 2012*. Financial Stability Board. Available at: www.fsb.org/2012/11/r_121118c/. Last accessed: 20.12.2016.

FSB (2013a) *Strengthening Oversight and Regulation of Shadow Banking: An Overview of Policy Recommendations*. FSB Report. Available at: www.ny.frb.org/research/epr/12v18n2/1207peri.pdf. Last accessed: 12.01.2017.

FSB (2013b) *Global Shadow Banking Monitoring Report*. FSB Report. Available at: www.financialstabilityboard.org/publications/r_131114.htm. Last accessed: 12.01.2017.

FSB, IMF and BIS (2011) *Macroprudential Policy Tools and Frameworks – Progress Report to G20*. Financial Stability Board, International Monetary Fund and Bank for International Settlements Report, October. Available at: www.imf.org/external/np/g20/pdf/102711.pdf. Last accessed: 12.01.2017.

Gorton, G. B., S. Lewellen and A. Metrick (2012) *The Safe-Asset Share*. NBER Working Paper Series, no. 17777. Available at: www.nber.org/papers/w17777. Last accessed: 16.01.2017.

IMF (2008) *IMF Annual Report 2008: Make the Global Economy Work for All*. Washington, DC: IMF.

IMF (2010) *IMF Annual Report 2010: Supporting a Balanced Global Recovery*. International Monetary Fund Report. Available at: www.imf.org/external/pubs/ft/ar/2010/eng/pdf/ar10_eng.pdf. Last accessed: 16.01.2017.

IMF (2011) *IMF Annual Report 2011: Pursuing Equitable and Balanced Growth*. International Monetary Fund Report. Available at: www.imf.org/external/pubs/ft/ar/2011/eng/. Last accessed: 16.01.2017.

IMF (2013) *Global Financial Stability Report 2013*. International Monetary Fund Report. Available at: www.imf.org/External/Pubs/FT/GFSR/2013/02/pdf/text.pdf. Last accessed: 16.01.2017.

Jackson, C. and J. Matilainen (2012) *Macro-Mapping the Euro Area Shadow Banking System with Financial Sector Balance Sheet Statistics*. IFC Conference on Statistical Issues and Activities in a Changing Environment, Basel (28–29 August). Available at: www.bis.org/ifc/events/6ifcconf/jacksonmatilainen.pdf. *Last accessed 21.04.2017.*

Kessler, O. and B. Wilhelm (2013) "Financialisation and the Three Utopias of Shadow Banking". *Competition & Change*, 17(3), pp. 248–264.

Lenglet, M. (2011) "Conflicting Codes and Codings: How Algorithmic Trading Is Reshaping Financial Regulation". *Theory, Culture & Society*, 28(6), pp. 44–66.

Lépinay, V. (2007) "Decoding Finance: Articulation and Liquidity around a Trading Room". In D. A. F. MacKenzie, F. Muniesa and L. Siu (eds) *Do Economists Make*

Markets? On the Performativity of Economics. Princeton, NJ: Princeton University Press, pp. 87–127.

Liikanen, E. (2012) *Reforming the Structure of the EU Banking Sector*. High-level Expert Group Report. Available at: http://ec.europa.eu/finance/bank/docs/high-level_expert_group/report_en.pdf. Last accessed 12.01.2017.

MacKenzie, D. A., F. Muniesa and L. Siu (2007) *Do Economists Make Markets? On the Performativity of Economics*. Princeton, NJ: Princeton University Press.

McCulley, P. (2007) *Teton Reflections*. Pimco, August/September. Available at: www.pimco.com/insights/economic-and-market-commentary/global-central-bank-focus/teton-reflections. Last accessed: 20.12.2016.

McCulley, P. (2013) *Shadow Banking: An Interview with Paul McCulley*. Available at: www.youtube.com/watch?v=sCfhaPT_71k. Last accessed: 16.01.2017.

Munteanu, I. (2010) *Systemic Risk in Banking: New Approaches Under the Current Financial Crisis. MPRA Paper*. Available at: https://mpra.ub.uni-muenchen.de/27392/. Last accessed: 16.01.2017.

Pakravan, K. (2011) "Global Financial Architecture, Global Imbalances and the Future of the Dollar in A Post-Crisis World". *Journal of Financial Regulation and Compliance*, 19(1), pp. 18–32.

Pozsar, Z. (2008) *The Rise and Fall of the Shadow Banking System*. Available at: www.economy.com/sbs. Last accessed: 20.12.2016.

Pozsar, Z. (2011) *Institutional Cash Pools and the Triffin Dilemma of the U.S. Banking System*. IMF Working Paper. Available at: www.imf.org/external/pubs/ft/wp/2011/wp11190.pdf. Last accessed: 16.12.2016.

Pozsar, Z., T. Adrian, H. Boesky and A. Ashcraft (2012) *The Traditional Banking System has Three Actors: Savers, Borrowers, and Banks*. Federal Reserve Bank of New York, Staff Reports, no. 458. Available at: www.newyorkfed.org/medialibrary/media/research/staff_reports/sr458.pdf. Last accessed: 16.12.2016.

Shleifer, A. (2000) *Inefficient Markets: An Introduction to Behavioral Finance*. Oxford, UK: Oxford University Press.

Von Georg, J. R. (2013) *Die Entstehung des Kreditwesengesetzes Von 1961*. Berlin: Peter Lang.

5 Shadow banking in China
Instruments, issues, trends

Jianjun Li and Sara Hsu

Introduction

The shadow banking system can be defined as financial intermediaries that conduct maturity, credit and liquidity transformation outside of the traditional bank lending system. It often includes newly innovated products and instruments. The Chinese shadow banking system has a special function in credit creation; most shadow banking institutions supply loans backed by money collection instruments rather than certificates of deposit. The Chinese shadow banking system includes informal finance[1] as well as trust companies, small loan companies, bonding companies, financial companies, and financial leasing companies. In this chapter, we describe China's shadow banking instruments, and then discuss data and measurement issues in quantifying the system and its components. The Chinese shadow banking system has evolved since 2007, and grew rapidly in the wake of the global crisis.

In 2014, the wider aggregate comprising "other financial intermediaries" in 20 jurisdictions and the euro area grew to reach $80 trillion, from $78 trillion in 2013 (FSB 2015). The Chinese shadow banking system grew rapidly until 2014, when China entered an economic downturn. According to PBOC data for 2011, shadow financial activity in China, which has increased over the past ten to twenty years, accounted for 12.83 trillion RMB (excluding informal finance), or $2.14 trillion US dollars. Since 2007, China has experienced supply side innovations with the creation of new financial products. China has also undergone demand side changes due to continuing limitations on credit provided by the banking sector. The latter is important to recognize—demand for more credit has given way, since reform and opening up, to a growing informal finance sector, which is a characteristic of developing countries but unique in its manifestation. The shadow banking sector has arisen with increased exposure to innovations in other countries and with the search for profits on the part of banks, as well as a search for returns on the part of individuals and institutional investors.

Kane (2012: 6) has defined "shadow-y" banking as including firms with products or charters that are not ruled by law, that are in fact designed to fall outside regulation, and that can be redesigned to exploit future gaps if necessary. Kane also writes that:

[a]lmost anything that carries an explicit or implicit government guarantee can be swapped in great volume and . . . high volume establishes the equivalent of a squatter's right because authorities are reluctant to roll back innovations once they have achieved widespread use.

Hence unregulated financial sectors have been known to persist because enforcing laws against them would leave a gaping hole. In China, shadow banking institutions are increasingly integral aspects of day to day finance. Transparency would attenuate some of the negative effects that may be caused by the growth of shadow banking.

In this chapter, we first discuss the importance of financial data in monitoring finance. Then we describe and examine the types of shadow banking instruments in China, existing availability of data, and gaps in data that render quantifying the shadow banking sector overall and in terms of risk a challenge. We do not discuss the informal financial sector per se, which contains myriad types of organizations and is even more challenging to quantify.

Importance of data in financial monitoring

As the most recent global crisis has revealed, obtaining and utilizing data on financial transactions is essential in monitoring the system for risk. No model of systemic or institutional risk is an accurate reflection of reality without sufficient data. As Cecchetti *et al.* (2010: 1) note:

Data are the eyes and ears we use to see and hear what is happening in the financial and economic world. Anecdotes, introspection, personal experience and modeling can help us figure out where to look and organize our thoughts. In the end, though, it is the data that tell us what is going on. Without [data], we are deaf and blind, which makes us dumb (in both senses of the word).

They go on to argue that data requirements should be able to fulfil the following requirements:

- that central banks can monitor use of their currency;
- that policy makers can monitor for systemic financial risk; and
- that financial market participants can improve market discipline.

For this, balance sheet data, equity prices and credit spreads, counterparty exposures, financial market price and quantities, and macroeconomic data are essential points of reference. Cerutti *et al.* (2012) also discuss essential components of data gathering, but from a global perspective. For firms that operate globally, they recommend that detailed foreign credit exposures (including off balance sheet exposures) be collected.

Lack of market-priced data in particular can "break" a market once a crisis occurs. Consider the issue created during the 2008 crisis as a result of trading over the counter. Structured securities, derivatives, commercial paper, municipal bonds, and securitized students loans, all traded over the counter, were enormously difficult to price once the crisis adversely affected all markets. Without a unified market and corresponding transparency, price discovery became impossible. In a financial system with insufficient markets for instruments, coupled with a lack of data on individual historical asset transactions and other price and stability indicators, the potential for amplification of a negative shock is large.

There is another point to make with specific reference to China. Even where data are available to party officials in China, a corresponding lack of availability to the public, particularly to scholars and analysts, as well as to financial market participants, can create large issues of uncertainty. Currently, the government keeps private individual firm data and makes available only aggregated, industry-level data. The presence of off balance sheet and risky transactions within some of these firms is of great concern. Leaving analysis of financial risk and monitoring solely to officials who are privy to the data greatly limits the evaluation and understanding of both firm-level and systemic risk.

There is a great lack of data that are made public in China, and absence of information pervades many types of shadow banking instruments, from money market funds to trust products. The shadow banking system in China, however, is quite different from that in the United States or Europe. Rather than being comprised of extensive numbers of asset-backed securities and a widely used repo market, the Chinese shadow banking system contains a wide variety of instruments that are less sophisticated and less liquid. In the section below, we review the types of shadow banking instruments used in China. One should pay particular attention to the type of market in which the instrument is traded and to the size of assets under management in each category, for both of these features impact the degree to which a presence or lack of data can build risk.

Shadow banking instruments

There are many types of shadow banking instruments in China, including asset-backed securities, money market funds, repurchase agreements, commercial paper, wealth management products, trust products (including Real Estate Investment Trusts (REITs)), leveraged leases, negotiable securities, and financial guarantee instruments. While some of these have been used for some time, several products, including the wealth management and trust products, have grown up only recently due to regulatory changes and dwindling sources of growth following the global financial crisis. Below, we describe each of these instruments.

Asset-backed securities. The asset-backed securities market is small in scale in comparison to that in the US. Asset-backed securities in China consist of mortgage securities approved by the PBOC and the Chinese Banking Regulatory Commission, and enterprise asset securities developed by securities companies and traded mainly through the interbank bonds market. The trading scale of nonperforming asset securities is even smaller, but with the credit asset securitization pilot restarting in 2012 it had increased to 20 billion RMB by the end of 2012. In 2013, the scale of loans for securitizing was 50 billion RMB. By 2015, the stock of asset-backed securities reached 639.6 billion RMB; among them, enterprise asset securities reached 226.4 billion RMB.

Money market funds. China's money market funds developed rapidly after 1998. The money market consists of the repurchase market, the commercial paper market, and the bond and bill market, among other instruments (including government issued debt). Aggregated data for negotiable securities, repurchase agreements, commercial paper, corporate bonds, and medium-term notes is available through the database built by the China Central Depository & Clearing Co. Ltd under the guidance of the Ministry of Finance of China.

Repurchase agreements. China has two repurchase agreement (repo) markets, the exchange-traded repo market and the interbank repo market. These markets mainly exist for individuals or institutions to borrow or lend money, rather than securities. Repo rates on identical types of transactions varied between these two markets between 2000 and 2005, demonstrating market segmentation in this area (Fan and Zhang 2007). Two reasons for this segmentation in the repo market are given: high exchange repo rates are linked to new stock market issues, while interbank repo rates follow the trends of the macro economy. In addition, larger amounts of volatility in the exchange-traded repo market result in the payment of additional risk premiums due to this uncertainty.

Repurchase agreements are used in China by institutions for short-term financing and by the central bank as a tool in open market operations (Fan and Zhang 2007). China's repo market began in 1993, using Treasuries as collateral. Interbank trading began in 1997 with Treasuries, policy financing bonds, and central bank notes as collateral. Commercial banks were at that time forbidden from trading in repurchase agreements on the stock exchange (Xie 2002).

The most common repo maturity type has been one week, although repos with maturities of less than one week have been traded on the exchange market, and three-week and two-month repos have been traded on the interbank market (Fan and Zhang 2007). With an increase in the speed of financial market processing, the scale of repos traded grew quickly; They measure in at 2.67 trillion RMB (91.4 percent traded on the interbank market, and 8.6 percent on the stock exchange market) in 2002 and it reached 566.18 trillion RMB (78 percent traded on the interbank market, and 22 percent on the stock exchange market) in 2015, with an average annual increase rate above 40 percent. Since 2010, the trading scale of the exchange market has grown rapidly because individual investors were allowed to take part in repo trading.

Commercial paper market. The commercial paper market consists of bills issued by large corporations including enterprises, listed companies, and securities companies in order to raise funds. Large enterprises, such as state-owned enterprises, issue commercial paper in the interbank bond market and the maturity is one year. By 2012, the stock scale of commercial paper was 832.7 billion RMB, which had increased 65.7 percent over what it was in 2011. In 2012, securities companies began to issue commercial paper for liquidity management with maturities of 90 days to 270 days. This broker-dealer commercial paper scale was 29.5 billion RMB in 2012. Some large state-owned enterprises have issued super- and short-term commercial paper in the interbank market since 2010. The scale reached 15 billion RMB in that year and 45 billion in 2011, but there was a big bang increase in 2012, reaching 353 billion RMB. Super commercial paper is welcomed by large enterprises because its maturity lasts from 7 to 270 days, which supplies a flexible instrument for managing financial liquidity. The total stock of commercial paper, super commercial paper, and securities company commercial paper exceeded 1.5 trillion RMB in 2013 and increased to 2.47 trillion RMB in 2015.

Corporate bonds. Highly rated corporate bonds are very liquid instruments. The corporate bond market measured in at 1.7 trillion RMB in total bonds outstanding at the end of 2015. Corporate bond issuance is approved by the China Securities Regulatory Commission. Bonds can be issued for any purpose and can amount to 40 percent of the corporation's net assets at the end of the previous accounting year (Pessarossi and Laurent 2011).

Bankers' acceptance bills. Enterprises also issue bankers' acceptances for short-term financing. This kind of bill became a debt instrument under the tight credit policy in China. At the end of 2005, the balance of undiscounted bankers' acceptances was 2.4 billion RMB, but had reached 5.85 trillion RMB at the same time in 2015. Bankers' acceptance bills have been used increasingly outside of trade transactions in recent years. In 2015, with stock prices increasing rapidly, some money from bill discounting went into the stock market. The bill case of Agricultural Bank of China showed that 3.918 billion RMB went into stock trading and could not be taken back after the stock crash.

Medium-term notes. Medium-term notes (MTNs) are debt securities offered to the public and issued by corporations after they are registered and approved by the regulatory authorities. In April 2008, the PBOC allowed state enterprises to issue RMB 39.2 billion in MTNs, and the scale of issuance reached 167.2 billion. In the next four years, the issuance scale grew rapidly and the outstanding volume was 2.63 trillion RMB in 2013. MTNs are the most important types of collateral assets in repo transactions, and its market quota is 77 percent. By 2015, the balance of MTNs had reached 4.16 trillion RMB.

Private placement notes, small- and medium-sized enterprises (SME) collective notes and asset-backed notes. Non-financial corporations have issued private placement notes (PPNs) in the interbank market since 2011. The private placement note maturity is from six months to three years. By 2012, the balance of PPNs was 450.2 billion RMB, but only 89.9 billion RMB at the end of 2011. By 2015, this had reached 2.1 trillion RMB.

Starting from 2009, SMEs were permitted to issue SME collective notes in the interbank market and stock exchanges. This note requires two to ten enterprises to form a unified issuer under the same note name. In past three years (2010–2012), the scale was 2.1 billion, 3.5 billion, and 4.3 billion RMB, respectively. Since 2012, enterprises can issue asset-backed notes (ABNs) in the interbank market. Fourteen enterprises issued ABNs of 5.7 billion RMB in that year. By the end of 2015, the number had grown to 15.9 billion RMB. Aggregated data for PPNs and credit derivatives is available through the Shanghai Clearing House database.

Credit derivatives. In China, derivatives have developed slowly because regulatory authorities are afraid of risks that may be brought about by the derivatives market. Commodity futures appeared at the beginning of the 1990s. The top three categories of derivatives include interest rate, currency, and stock market derivatives (Gao and Sun 2012). The derivatives market was approved for operation by the State Council on October 12, 1990 (Gao and Sun 2012). Unfortunately, a number of trading markets appeared and were not well organized, experiencing breaches such as illegal trading and market manipulation. Therefore, in 1993, the State Council reduced the number of actively trading markets to three, including the Shanghai Futures Exchange, Dalian Commodity Exchange, and the Zhengzhou Commodity Exchange, and reduced the number of instrument types that could be traded on these exchanges.

On December 29, 2000, the China Futures Association was established, creating a self-regulatory agency for the futures market (Gao and Sun 2012). The China Financial Futures Exchange was built on September 8, 2006, and the Stock Index Futures began on April 16, 2010. Now China has four exchanges and agricultural, precious metals, energy, chemical, and financial futures are traded on the four exchange markets. The futures market reached a trading volume of 171 trillion RMB in 2012. China currently lacks an options market.

Credit derivative instruments include two types: credit risk mitigation warrants (CRMW) and credit risk mitigation agreements (CRMA). The (CRM) product was established in 2010 as one type of credit derivative. The CRMA is a nontraditional financial risk management instrument that provides credit protection to the seller in a financial agreement. The first CRMA was set up with a nominal capital of 1,840 million RMB. Debt types included short-term and medium-term bills and bank loans. The CRMA was set with a one-year term period. On November 23, 2010, the China Bond Insurance Co., Ltd, the Bank of Communications, and Minsheng Bank established the first CRMW, with a nominal capital of 480 million RMB. Hence both types of CRM products were established.

CRM business volume remains relatively low. Although CRM products have not grown rapidly, they have played a vital role in China's money market. This is because China's money market financial structure has created an extreme dependence by firms on bank credit. CRM tools are playing an increasing role as other types of asset credit risks expand. In addition, CRM tools also make it possible for SMEs to dilute credit risk.

Commercial banks comprise 75 percent of CRMW traders. Other trading companies include negotiable securities companies and asset management companies. CRMA nominal capital was 1,990 million RMB as of February 2010, and there were no CRMA transactions in 2011. CRMW nominal capital equalled 730 million RMB in 2010 and dropped to 130 million RMB in 2012.

Data on derivatives such as futures is available from the individual exchanges on a daily, weekly, or monthly basis, and from the China Securities Regulatory Commission on a monthly basis, but in aggregate form.

Wealth management products (WMPs) including those sold through banks, securities companies, and insurance companies. Commercial bank WMPs are linked to stocks and bonds, interest rate instruments, bills, credit assets, commodities, exchange rate instruments, and other asset bases. These can be denominated in RMB or foreign currencies.

In 1999, investments in WMPs were relatively scarce, and the fund scale was small at 132 billion RMB. However, in 2004, the Bank of China promoted the first foreign currency financial product, and, later that year, the Everbright Bank issued the first RMB financial product. Following that, many other banks promoted their own WMPs and the market grew rapidly. By 2013, the banking WMPs' stock was more than 10 trillion RMB, and there were 47,000 WMPs, valued at 25 trillion RMB, and the number of issuers had increased from 12 in 2004 to 97 in 2011. Most products are currently issued in RMB (nearly 95 percent). By the end of 2015, the banking WMPs' stock was over 23.5 trillion RMB.

In 2004, most WMPs sold were medium- and long-term products, whereas after that period through 2012, short-term products, particularly 1–3 month products, increased in the market share. This implies that customers began to prefer short-term income over this period, as long-term financial risk increased. The largest increase over the period took place in bond WMPs, while the smallest increase was in commodity WMPs.

China's rising middle class has given way to new financial market investors, individuals that may not have large amounts of wealth to invest, and who may not have much knowledge of the market. Specialized wealth management funds have been created to meet their needs, some of which are on the esoteric side. For example, the China Construction Bank created an investment product based on the art industry, while Minsheng Bank sold a product based on white liquor. Shenzhen Development Bank also created a financial product based on white wine with an investment period of one year. Personalized financial management products satisfy a wide range of demands.

China's WMPs are recorded off bank balance sheets, and individual bank sales of WMPs are not disclosed to the public, although the products are quantified on aggregate. Better disclosure of these products, in terms of specific bank holdings and characteristics, would help the public to predict the viability of these instruments.

Trust products. Trust company products range from securities, equity investments, and trust loans, while funds are used to finance real estate and business investment. Trust funds may be divided into the single trust fund, which caters to an individual, possibly an institutional investor, and the collective trust fund, which caters to a group of investors. The collective trust fund is based on common financial goals, and may be channeled into an equity investment trust, a securities investment trust, a loan trust, or other types of trusts. For the trust industry, 2010 was the best year, experiencing a growth of 196 percent. Policies in 2010 that limited growth of bank trust cooperation WMPs contributed to the growth of the trust industry. Collective trust products released in 2010 amounted to 2,213 products with a total of 399.76 billion RMB, while those released in 2012 amounted to 6,167 products totaling 1016.07 billion RMB.

REITs are a type of trust which carries out investment in real estate management and operations. China does not have REITs that rank at the international standard, but rather has similar REIT products that are denoted as Quasi-Real Estate Investment Trusts, or Q-REITs. Q-REITs are trust companies that carry out investment in real estate and real estate management, with most transactions being associated with government-owned real estate.

China's real estate trust products are in their initial stages of development. The need for funding in property development is large, and REITs satisfy only a part of the demand. Increasing diversity may help satisfy some of the demand.

In the second half of 2003, the Chinese government implemented a series of macroeconomic regulation and control policies to improve quality of the real estate industry. This resulted in an increase in real estate funds. Credit quotas were also set on commercial bank real estate transactions to control property development loans. Commercial banks thus were caught between controlling risk and attempting to satisfy demand.

The commercial property development loan amount increased from 2,380 billion RMB in 2004 to 10,730 billion RMB in 2011, in step with an increase in property development. In 2003, China distributed 84 real estate trust products with a total of 7.8 billion RMB. In 2011, 1,062 products existed altogether with a total scale of 274 billion RMB. In 2012, the total scale reached 316 billion RMB. As of 2011, the real estate trust average yearly returns ratio was as high as 10.09 percent.

Like WMPs sold by banks, trust products are not disclosed on an individual firm basis; rather, information on trust products is only viewable by the public in aggregate form. This is of concern to investors who hold products from particular firms. The recent spate of trust product failures has increased concern over the lack of transparency in the trust sector.

Leveraged leases. Financial leases are created when firms use bank loans, their own funds, or stock funds to purchase equipment and lease them out at a high interest rate. The financial lease, also known as a leveraged lease, is used in aviation, shipping, medical services, printing, the equipment industry, and construction. The leveraged lease is a tripartite contract that allows the lessor to purchase goods from a third party that are repaid by the lessee. The leveraged lease is paid with principal and interest. The lease can end when the lessee purchases the good, the good is re-leased, or when the lease is broken. The purchase of the good is the most common way in which a lease ends.

From the tenant's perspective, the leveraged lease is regarded as a temporary purchase of property rights. For the lessor, the leveraged lease service is a type of highly leveraged investment tool, with an average leverage of about 11 percent. The lessor may also enjoy preferential tax policies. The leveraged lease industry is a global industry, and a large one, amounting in 2007 to 582 billion US dollars. China's leveraged lease industry has experienced large growth, even during the global financial crisis.

Financial leasing companies' members consist mainly of bank or financial enterprises. China had 560 leveraged lease companies in 2012, which were concentrated in the eastern coastal provinces and cities, and in a few interior key cities. By 2011, the leveraged leases' service scale amounted to 930 billion RMB and increased to 1.55 trillion RMB in 2012. The leasing industry is concentrated in aviation ships and large machinery, and the industry has broad prospects for expansion into areas such as property development, medical equipment, and railway transportation. Aggregated annual data for leveraged leases is available through the annual report of the China Leasing Alliance.

Negotiable securities. Negotiable securities companies manage financial products based on stocks and bonds with distributed risk and income. The negotiable securities company sets up an asset management plan to invest in government bonds, bond market funds, the stock market fund, and corporate bonds. Customers investing in asset management plans are required to invest in funds of at least 50,000 RMB. Securities traders group products into large-scale products, which manage a larger pool of funds, and small scale products, which do not surpass 1 billion RMB.

Negotiable securities funds accounted for 265.7 billion RMB in 2012. Large commercial banks are also involved, including the China Construction Bank, ICBC, Bank of Communications, Bank of China, and China Merchant Bank. State-owned banks dominate.

The negotiable securities market is presently somewhat limited in scale, since it faces strong supervision. CSRC has gradually begun to relax supervision, which is expected to increase the size of the market over time.

Financial guarantee instruments. Financing guarantee companies provide a credit guarantee service, managing credit risk and taking responsibility for the risk. Competitiveness of the financing guarantee company is determined by the amount of capital in case and risk control. Financing guarantee companies may be divided into financial bonding companies and non-financial bonding companies. The former provides a guarantee for the fund holder and the latter is not directly engaged with the loan itself, but guarantees advanced payments and commercial contracts for example.

In China, financing guarantee company risk became an issue in 2011, with increased policies to prevent property price bubbles and inflation. Tight monetary policies and tightened real estate market supervision occurred. Informal finance increased as bank lending declined. Some financing guarantee companies lent money to informal financial markets. This increased the riskiness of financing guarantee companies. For example, the Henan province credit guarantee industry based in Zhengzhou saw a rise in financing guarantee companies from 100 in 2007 to over 1,640 in 2010, with registered capital of 57 billion RMB. Unlike financing guarantee companies in other regions, in Henan the companies are densely interwoven with informal finance. A crisis among four large-scale financing guarantee companies erupted in 2011, involving an amount of 2,450 million RMB. These companies went out of business, and there were 23 companies that had absorbed public deposits surpassing 10 billion RMB, accounting for 1 in 6 of registered capital of bonding companies in Henan. Failures of guaranteed loans due to the economic slowdown surged in 2014, and guaranteed loans became a large proportion of nonperforming loans.

The industry thereafter has prospered, supporting SMEs. In recent years, some financing guarantee companies have also engaged in informal lending, making it difficult to supervise and track financial activity in these institutions. Financing guarantee companies have engaged in riskier activity, and have aroused supervisory organizations to examine them more carefully. Additional policies and measures were implemented in 2011 to strengthen financing guarantee company supervision. The Banking Regulatory Commission has increased attention to bonding companies' risk. Most provinces and cities have also acted to adopt supervisory measures since 2010.

Financing guarantee companies are increasing in scale and strength, with higher levels of registered capital in cash daily. The number of small- and medium-sized financing guarantee companies increased from 3,336 in 2006 to 4,817 in 2010. Between these dates, capital in cash rose by 3.15 times, amounting to 391.5 billion RMB in 2010. The number of households participating in the industry has increased from 210,000 in 2006 to 350,000 in 2010. The financing guarantee business outstanding reached 1.55 trillion RMB by the end of 2012 and exceeded 1.9 trillion RMB by the end of June 2013. Aggregated annual data for financial guarantee instruments is through the research report of the China Guarantee Association.

A source of financing guarantee companies' capital is institutional investor funds. Enterprises are partial to financing guarantee companies because the rate of return is high. The populace itself invested in financing guarantee companies, with individuals getting family and friends to put their funds into the companies. Financing guarantee companies have been able to obtain funds at a low interest rate from banks and extend loans to individuals at a higher interest rate, earning a big profit. Acting as an intermediary, the financing guarantee company takes a big risk because they cannot gain refinancing from the central bank. Financing guarantee companies engaging in the real estate market also seek high returns at a very high risk. Financing guarantee companies have also provided bridging loans to companies that could not repay their bank debts. Some financing guarantee companies have also absorbed funds for investment in the stock market or for venture capital institutions. This activity has also moved financing guarantee companies away from traditional guarantee services. In Henan, some real estate businesses even register through financing guarantee companies to obtain financing. The Henan financing guarantee industry faced mounting risks. Employees lacked the necessary industry knowledge. Due to high returns, private capital flowed into the industry. The Henan province Financing Guarantee Association, created in September 2002, has not played a proper role in preventing this activity. Financing guarantee companies have lost competitiveness due to increased perceived risky behavior.

China's shadow banking instrument data issues

The modern financial sector is a whole system that includes securitization and repo markets in the shadow banking sub-system. The core of the shadow banking system includes special purpose vehicles (SPVs) used for conducting securitization and repo transactions. Both traditional banks and most non-bank financial intermediaries are conducting shadow banking transactions off balance sheet and out of the scope of monitoring and regulation. In China, the central bank and China Banking Regulatory Commission are able to obtain all banks' and most non-bank financial institutions' balance sheets and financial statements. But most of these financial statements, except those of listed banks, trusts and leasing corporations, are not open to the public. Listed financial corporations are relatively few in number. Hence scholars, analysts and market participants cannot use these data for analysis. Only aggregate industry data can be obtained through public channels.

Since the subprime mortgage crisis began, the shadow banking system became a very hot subject in China. Data on shadow banking instruments are very important to financial regulatory authorities. Most countries and international financial organizations such as the BIS and European Securitization Forum started to gather statistics on shadow banking data. In China, shadow banking instrument data are scattered across different departments and are not easy to obtain. For example, data on securities, repurchase agreements, commercial paper, and ABNs are issued by China Central Depository and Clearing Co., Ltd, Shanghai Clearing House, and China Securities Depository and Clearing Corporation Limited. These institutions issue monthly or quarterly reports, and the summary data are open to the public. But more detailed data cannot be obtained—data such as asset holding structure information is viewable only by the government.

Chinese shadow banking instruments include WMPs issued by banks, negotiable securities companies, and trust companies, but there is incomplete statistical data on these kinds of products. The China Banking Regulatory Commission (CBRC) requests that all banks submit the data through internal channels, but does not make all of the data open to the public. Some individual pieces of data can be gathered from databases and research reports, but there is no way to obtain certain types of data, such as negotiable securities' wealth management product data, at this time. It is necessary to build a unified database on the shadow banking system in China. This should gather data on shadow banking instruments' issuance and amounts outstanding, shadow banks' balance sheets and financial statements, credit sizing, and other information. The data should also be made available to the public.

What is more, many WMPs are created through SPVs, off the balance sheets of banks and securities companies. The bank trust WMPs in particular are formed as SPVs. But since 2012, this product was prohibited.

Below, we illustrate aggregated data on shadow banking instruments. Shadow banking instruments can be classified into two kinds—the first kind includes instruments issued by different institutions on the interbank market and on exchanges, including stock exchanges and futures exchanges. These include ABS, MMF, CP, SCP, ABN, PPN, CRMW, and MSECN.[2] These data can be found through the National Association of Financial Market Institutional Investors, the Shanghai Clearing House (SCH), China Central Depository & Clearing Co. Ltd (CCDC), China Securities Depository and Clearing Co. Ltd (CSDC) and the China Trustee Association (CTA). The second kind of instrument is

Table 5.1 China's shadow banking instruments data (Stock of products, Unit: 100 million RMB)

Year	2005	2006	2007	2008	2009	2010	2011	2012	2013	2014	2015
REPOs on the interbank market	3810.34	3872.47	8170.64	7988.55	9490.13	13529.62	22277.75	21924.7	28447.82	34427.96	44473.11
REPOs on the exchange market	64.72	42.43	50.26	66.49	98.44	191.83	560.61	948.93	3059	6000	9600
ABS	①	187.74	324.05	551.06	398.58	182.32	95.27	192.62	349.47	2952.96	6396.92
MMF (net value)	1867.9	794.88	1110.46	3891.74	2595.27	1532.77	2948.95	7570.41	8802.2899	21873.84	45761.68
CP	1380.5	2667.1	3203.1	4203.1	4561.05	6530.35	5023.5	8326.97	8433.2	10565.93	9637
SCP	—	—	—	—	—	150	450	3531	4729	6999.5	14666.4
Securities companies CP	—	—	—	—	—	—	—	295	824.9	1076.9	451
PPN	—	—	—	—	—	—	899	4502.3	9495.88	17811.84	21567.29
ABN	—	—	—	—	—	—	—	57	96.3	167.9	158.9
MTN	—	—	—	1672	8622	13536	18742.7	24922	29846.5	33753.3	41655.2
SMECN	—	—	—	—	12.65	55.12	93.68	145.02	94.17	55.07	10.26
CRMW	—	—	—	—	—	6.9	7.3	1.3	n.a	n.a	n.a
Undiscounted Bankers' acceptances	24	1500	6701	1064	4606	23346	10271	10499	7755	–1198	–9100
Banking financial management products	5000	5000	5000	8200	17000	27700	45900	71000	95000	150000	235000
Trust products	2113	3617	9622	12442.5	20557	30404.55	48114.38	74705.55	109071.11	139799.1	163036.2
Securities company financial management products	—	—	—	—	—	n.a②	2818.68	18900	51900	79700	118800
Financial leases	n.a	80	240	1550	3700	7000	9300	15500	21000	32000	43000
Loans from small loan businesses	—	n.a	n.a	n.a	766.41	1975.05	3914.74	5921.38	8191.27	9420.38	9411.51
Financial guarantee instruments	n.a	n.a	n.a	n.a	n.a	13746	19120	n.a	n.a	n.a	n.a
Total③	10430.5	13917.6	31341.0	38005.9	65911.8	111916.6	154209.7	242630.6	387095.9	545406.7	754525.5

Source: CCDC, SCH, CSDC, and CTA.

Note: ① "—" means nonexistent. ② n.a means the data should exist but is not available. ③ The total number excluding financial guarantee business.

issued by banks, trust companies, securities companies, leasing companies, and micro-lending companies. These include instruments such as bank WMPs, non-discounted bills, trusts, leases, and small loans. These data are controlled by the PBOC, the CBRC and the CSRC. We can view these data below, in Table 5.1.

From Table 5.1, we can see that the shadow banking instruments have developed rapidly in past ten years. There was a turning point in 2010 after the impacts of the global financial crisis subsided in China—the scale of the shadow banking sector in 2010 was 11.19 trillion RMB, nearly double that of 2009. After two years, the scale doubled again; the size of shadow banking instruments to bank assets was 25 percent at the end of 2012. Compared to the sizes of the American and European shadow banking sectors, the Chinese shadow banking sector is not large, but has grown very quickly after the crisis (see Figure 5.1 below). Currently, the size of the shadow banking sector in 2015 was 75.45 trillion RMB.

Figure 5.1 shows the ratio of the value of shadow banking instruments to the total banking assets from 2005 to 2015. Over this period, the formal Chinese banking system developed quickly, with total assets growing from 37.47 trillion RMB to 194.2 trillion RMB, with an average rate of increase of 18 percent; however, shadow banking instruments grew more quickly, from 1.04 trillion RMB to 75.45 trillion RMB at an average rate of increase of 53 percent. During the financial reform and interest rate marketization process, financial innovation has pushed the shadow banking system to develop faster.

Without a robust regulatory system, the risks of shadow banking may accumulate as fast as shadow banking develops. For example, there are currently more than 20 trust projects in solvency crisis, because funds for these projects were channeled into the coal mining and real estate sectors, which have faced financial trouble. Since the second half of 2011, the Chinese economy began to decline

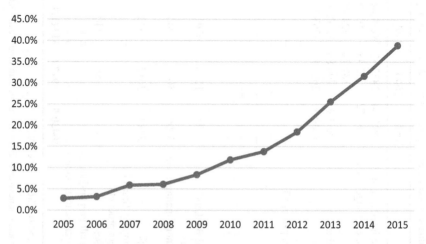

Figure 5.1 Ratio of shadow banking instruments to banking assets in China.

and many enterprises met with financial and business difficulties. They could not repay bonds or loans linked to WMPs and trust products. Therefore, the credit risk was transferred to the financial market. How to manage these instrument related risks and avoid systemic risk is a key issue confronting the Chinese government.

Conclusion

In China, the shadow banking system is different from that in the US and Europe in terms of the size of securitization and length of existence. Shadow banking instruments have swelled in variety and number from 2005 on. Types of shadow banking instruments include WMPs, trusts, which developed very quickly after 2008, and repurchase agreements, among others. The scale of repo trading is currently very large; it is an important liquidity management instrument for banks, financial companies, and large enterprises. Data on shadow banking instruments are scattered throughout different institutions and departments, and the most detailed data cannot be obtained through public channels. Micro-level data, such as data on balance sheets and financial statements, can be seen only by regulatory authorities for non-listed corporations. Therefore, it is important to build a unified database on the shadow banking system in China, that is made available not only to the government but to the public as well. A lack of data presents a threat to shadow banking system stability and makes it difficult for investors to maintain confidence in purchasing such instruments.

Since 2014, China has been gathering data on its shadow banking. This will enhance the public's access to financial information, although the details of the new data platform have not been disclosed, and it is unclear whether the platform will encompass all aspects of shadow banking, particularly at a disaggregated level. If it does not, the data issue will remain an ongoing problem.

Notes

1 Financing of small and medium enterprises by unregistered or non-bank-registered institutions.
2 In the Chinese bond market, there are many instruments similar to those in the American bond market—for example, CP, MTN, MSECN, and ABN, but only CP and MTN are used as collateral in repo transactions.

References

Cecchetti, S. G., I. Fender and P. McGuire (2010) *Toward A Global Risk Map*. BIS Working Paper, no. 309. Available at: www.bis.org/publ/work309.htm. Last accessed: 19.12.2016.

Cerutti, E., S. Claessens and P. McGuire (2012) *Systemic Risks in Global Banking: What Can Available Data Tell Us and What More Data Are Needed?* BIS Working Paper, no. 376. Available at: www.bis.org/publ/work376.htm. Last accessed: 19.12.2016.

Fan, L. and C. Zhang (2007) "Beyond Segmentation: The Case of China's Repo Markets". *Journal of Banking and Finance*, 31, pp. 939–954.

FSB (2015) *Transforming Shadow Banking into Resilient Market-Based Finance*. Financial Stability Board Report. Available at: www.fsb.org/2015/11/fsb-publishes-reports-on-transforming-shadow-banking-into-resilient-market-based-finance/. Last accessed: 19.12.2016.

Gao, H. and Y.-J. Sun (2012) "Research of Derivatives Markets Development in China". *Advances in Applied Economics and Finance*, 2(3), 407–413.

Kane, E. J. (2012) *The Inevitability of Shadowy Banking*. Paper presented at the Federal Reserve Bank of Atlanta, Financial Markets Conference, April 10. Available at: https://papers.ssrn.com/sol3/papers.cfm?abstract_id=2026229. Last accessed 21.04.2017.

Pessarossi, P. and W. Laurent (2011) *Choice of Corporate Debt in China: The Role of State Ownership*. BOFIT Discussion Papers, no. 29. Available at: https://papers.ssrn.com/sol3/papers.cfm?abstract_id=2079457. Last accessed: 19.12.2016.

Xie, D. (2002) "Analysis of the Development of China's Money Market". *China & World Economy*, 1, pp. 29–37.

6 The two shadow banking systems in Russia

Natalia Kaurova

Introduction

More than 20 years after the breakdown of the command economy, Russia remains a cash-based society. At the same time, since the mid 2000s in particular, it has been in transition to a financialised capitalism. Just like in more mature financialised economies, the problem of the shadow banking sector in Russia has come to the fore in the wake of the 2007–08 crisis. In the context of the maturing financial capitalism in Russia, the crisis has demonstrated the limited capacity of the central bank to address financial instability which stems from the increased interdependence of banks and companies in the real economy. Nearly ten years after the start of the global credit crunch, it is evident that the lessons of the 2007 crisis have not been fully recognised. In particular, the phenomenon of shadow banking remains a major challenge for monetary and financial authorities world-wide, including in countries of advanced financial capitalism, like the USA, UK and countries in Europe, but also in the emerging economies (India, Turkey, Indonesia, Argentina and Saudi Arabia) where non-bank financial intermediation is relatively low (typically below 20 per cent of GDP) yet has been expanding rapidly over the past few years.

This chapter focuses on the de facto two shadow banking systems in Russia today. On the one hand, there is an intricate world of grey credit and payment networks that has evolved in parallel with the economic transition of the 1990s, and works as a core pillar of the underground economic turnover. On the other, as a consequence of the financial liberalisation of the 1990s, and in particular with the deepening of financial relations since the mid 2000s, the financialisation of the Russian economy has brought expansion of bank and non-bank financial intermediation. Thus, while one dimension of shadow financial intermediation in Russia is quite specific to the economic and governance problems of an emerging market, the second facet of the shadow financial system is a result of the country's integration into the global financial system. Just like in more mature markets, it involves multiple linkages and innovations between financial institutions, the activities of which are non-transparent, unregulated and poorly recorded in the official data.

Shadow banking and the Russian macroeconomy

While the definitions of shadow banking in Russia remain as vague as they are in other contexts, in the post-command economic reality of Russia, where the official financial system remains centred on the state and a handful of state-owned banks, the shadow banking industry has assumed a rather distinct function. Unlike in more advanced economies, the activities of the Russian shadow banking system are associated with the organisation and maintenance of the partially illegal market of cash circulation. In Russia, like in some other emerging markets, a large part of the shadow financial system is centred on the turnover of illegal cash: money laundering, legalisation of 'dirty' cash flows, money in support of different types of the shadow economy, the financing of terrorism, corruption, channelling profits to offshore havens, etc. According to official data of Russia's statistical agency Rosstat, the grey economy amounts to up to 16–17 per cent of GDP. If one includes the corruption component, some experts estimate that the shadow financial turnover in Russia can account for between 40 and 46 per cent of GDP,[1] or 27–30 trillion roubles. This does suggest that the tension between the formal and the grey in Russia is widespread across all major sectors of economic activity.

A number of studies confirm the correlation between the share of cash payments and the size of the shadow economy in the country (Schneider *et al.* 2010). According to the BIS, Russia is one of three countries in the world with the highest proportion of cash money in circulation (M0) in relation to GDP. According to the European Central Bank, the rate of non-cash payments per capita in Russia is one of the lowest in Europe. More than half of payments for retail goods and services in Russia are made in cash. According to the Ministry of Finance of Russia, the amount of cash in the country's monetary turnover is about 23 per cent,[2] while in developed countries this figure is only 10.7 per cent and does not exceed 15 per cent even in emerging markets.

Most monitoring agencies confirm that Russia remains a cash-based economy, with 89.6 per cent of respondents using cash in daily payments and transfers. About 50.1 per cent of respondents never use non-cash forms of money, and only 15.9 per cent prefer non-cash-based transactions.[3] The use of electronic payment terminals in Russia lags far behind their use in economies at a comparable level of development; the population coverage of electronic terminals is one of the lowest in the world.

The large presence of the shadow economy entails the loss of tax revenue and an additional burden on public authorities. Estimates suggest that in 2015, the loss of tax revenue due to the shadow economy in Russia amounted to more than 5 trillion rubles, while the total direct costs of the Russian economy associated with cash turnover amounted to about 1.1 per cent of GDP (or more than 880 billion rubles in 2013). Currently, about 900 billion rubles ($15 billion) of illegal cash turnover fall on the shadow payment system, or grey payment platforms, the activities of which are opaque and not regulated. The national legislation[4] allows entities with low equity capital[5] to undertake very opaque activities to receive

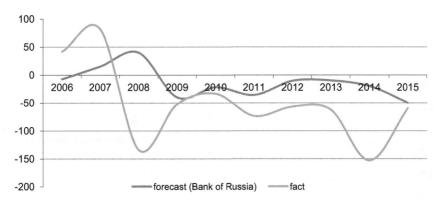

Figure 6.1 Capital flight from Russia, billion $.

cash (nobody knows who owns these terminals, how they are cleared and whether the sums are deposited with a credit institution). Moreover, these activities are typically conducted without licences or any other authorisation documents.

Persistent capital flight is another perennial problem associated with the Russian shadow economy. The year 2014 saw the peak of capital flight out of Russia ($153bn, equivalent to 13 per cent of GDP). In 2015, the outflow of capital decreased by 2.7 times to $59.6bn, which is mostly accounted for by a substantial reduction in Russia's foreign debt as a result of the ruble's devaluation and international sanctions.

According to the Central Bank of Russia, in 2013, net capital outflow from Russia amounted to $62.7 billion, an increase of 14.8 per cent compared to 2012 (in 2012 – $56.8 billion). In 2011, this figure reached $84.2 billion, up from $33.6 billion in 2010. In 2009 it amounted to $56.9 billion, and in the crisis year of 2008 it set the first record of $126 billion. Thus, in 2011 there was an increase in the net outflow of capital to just over 4 per cent of GDP, compared to 2.3 per cent in 2010. The record high figure of almost 9 per cent of GDP in 2008 exceeds the level of capital flight of 2011. As a result, over the period of 2008–2015, capital outflow was more than $693.8 billion, which exceeds almost twice the size of the annual budget of Russia in 2015 in current prices and 59 per cent of GDP. It is also highly likely that the real amount of money withdrawn from the country vastly exceeds the sums officially recorded by the Bank of Russia.

According to official statistics, almost half of capital outflows are associated with the private sector's interest payments on external debts that have been growing steadily recently, as well as the purchase of foreign assets by Russian enterprises. The foreign debt of Russian banks and other corporations amounts to over 92 per cent of the country's total foreign debt.

Russia's external debt includes government and private sector debts. Governmental foreign debt totalled $50.9bn, with the debt of Russian banks at $148.92 billion (a 29 per cent decrease over one year). However, the largest share

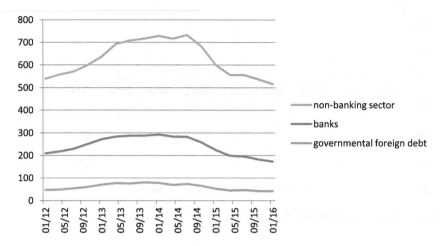

Figure 6.2 Russia's foreign debt, billion $.

of external debt falls on the non-banking sector, where it amounts to $326.19 billion (a decrease of 23 per cent per year and a decrease of 26 per cent since 2014).[6] At a rate of 5–7 per cent per annum, such debt service can cost up to $30–51 billion every year, the equivalent to half of the total capital flight from the country. Russia's external debt (which increased to $529.70 bn in the first quarter of 2017 from $518.70 bn in the fourth quarter of 2016) is high, and in the context of lower commodity prices, threatens the stability of the economy.

A deepening of the internal capital market is a factor that may help sustain the trend of lower foreign indebtedness. However, spare liquidity which can be directed to build such a market is scarce. In the meantime, the shrinking taxation base in the country (due to demographic changes and lower oil revenues) has precipitated a structural shift away from the extractive industries. In the context of fiscal rigidities (most fiscal transfers include social and military expenditure which are impossible to change without inviting political tensions), such structural shifts will inevitably lead to higher internal and external borrowings in the countries that have not aligned with the 2014 sanctions regime.

According to the former chairman of the Central Bank of Russia, Sergei Ignatiev, questionable transactions account for about 60 per cent of the outflow of capital from Russia. These are associated with drug trafficking, grey imports, bribes and kickbacks to officials, as well as tax evasion. The phenomenon of capital flight is so opaque and uncontrollable for Russia that some government officials have recently suggested renaming the problem of "capital flight" as the phenomenon of "transfer of funds". Against the backdrop of chronic underfunding of the economy and the infrastructure, the massive outflow of capital leads to an increase in the share of foreign loans in the structure of foreign investment, which has jumped from 45 per cent in the early 2000s to almost 90 per cent in 2011, effectively putting Russia in the situation of a debt trap (Bashkatova 2014).

Up to now, foreign borrowings remain the dominant form of foreign investment in the Russian economy. Between 2000–2016, on average about 80 per cent of foreign investments were directed towards the extractive industries, trade, finance and insurance sectors. The private and the public sectors are equally exposed to the risks of the debt trap. A solution to the problem is imperilled by the fundamental problems of the domestic economy: the impoverishment of the population, failures of small- and medium-sized enterprises against unfavourable conditions for Russia's core exports – oil, gas and other raw materials.

Against this background, the Russian shadow banking industry includes four major levels of activity:

1 The legal shadow financial market (the so-called 'white' market), which in addition to certain segments of the financial market operating outside the control and supervision of the official bank regulators, also includes transactions in the captive bank clusters, micro-financing operations, as well as government guarantees for loans extended to state-affiliated financial institutions and other economic operations carried out by oligarchic financial groups.
2 The illegal shadow banking market (the 'grey' market) – operations and transactions undertaken by financial institutions and other market actors that are legitimate in principle, yet lead to, or facilitate, a semi-legal and unidentified export of capital, opaque ownership structures, tax evasion, etc.
3 Criminal shadow banking market (the 'black' market), including illegal activities of financial institutions aimed at money laundering, movement of dirty money, etc.
4 Fictitious shadow banking segment: various corruption schemes, involving corrupt ties for obtaining preferences, privileges and subsidies from the state, etc.

Among the agents of the grey credit system in Russia, the most significant are the following:

1 Pawn shops, or *lombards* (according to expert estimates, the annual credit turnover of pawnshops is about $1 billion). With the expansion of consumer credit in the country, which stems from the increasing demand for borrowing and loosened borrowing conditions, the cases of illegal activities associated with money laundering through cash flight are becoming more frequent (according to Rosfinmonitoring).
2 "Functional" fronts or technical companies usually represented by offshore entities that are designed to transfer credit to simulate a low concentration of loan portfolio, and to conceal the risks or the purpose of loan, etc. These companies typically perform a number of specific functions, such as withholding information from a wide range of individuals, regulatory arbitrage (to evade prudential requirements as well as to understate the level of risk by cooking the books, or to withdraw "bad assets" from the balance sheet), and tax avoidance and evasion.

3   Construction companies, which accumulate money borrowed from indi-
    viduals for the purposes of primary construction and development. Since
    2005, the financial activities of these companies are regulated by a spe-
    cial law.[7] This legislation aims to prevent financial and building pyramid
    schemes. It sets requirements to register the contract to ensure ways
    of enforcing contractual obligations and accounting for the use of the
    funds, and to register the term property transfer, house warranty, pen-
    alties for violation of the contract and other insurance and customer
    protection measures. Nevertheless, it is estimated that the share of the so-
    called "grey" schemes used to attract funds in circumvention of the law
    accounted for 90 per cent of all sales of new buildings in Moscow and the
    Moscow region.[8]

Among the regulated entities of the shadow banking sector in Russia, which are
subject to weaker regulatory requirements than traditional banks, the following
institutions play a key role:

1   Micro-finance institutions (MFIs) which are increasingly expanding their
    activity. In 2010, a new law institutionalised micro-finance organisations and
    gave a new impetus for the development of financial infrastructure in small
    cities and towns of Russia. This law is aimed at facilitating control over the
    debt market, promoting competition in the micro-credit sector, while pro-
    tecting the rights and interests of borrowers from abuses by moneylenders.
    Official data suggest that the number of MFIs has grown significantly since
    2010. In the first half of 2013, there were 3,260 MFIs registered officially,
    or 29 per cent more than the previous year. The year 2012 saw a twofold
    increase in the number of registered MFIs.

In absolute terms, MFIs dominate the Russian financial system: they comprise
39 per cent of the country's financial institutions. As of July 2016, there were
3,560 MFIs, which is almost 4 times the number of banks in the country. The
micro-finance industry also grows much more dynamically than the banking sector. This can be attributed to the high demand for loans by small- and
medium-sized businesses, together with the public appetite for consumer and
payday loans, as well as to significantly higher interest rates on the loans.[9]
    The volume of loans issued by MFIs is estimated at 60 billion rubles (an
increase of 51 per cent compared to 2015). In January-October 2012 the rapid
growth of the micro-finance market enabled several MFIs to successfully issue
debt securities to raise funds, which created a precedent. The potential for this
credit segment is vast: some estimates suggest it can expand by 40 per cent a year
to about RUR 350 billion ($6bn). The prognosis is based on the fact that about 70
per cent of the population living in small urban centres are not served by banks,
while the crossover between the banking system and micro-finance is no more
than 25 per cent. The tightening of bank lending standards prompted an expansion
of micro-finance lending to the individual entrepreneurs. As of 2015, the share of

loans to individuals was 84 per cent of the total portfolio of MFIs (7.8 per cent was loans to individual entrepreneurs, 8.2 per cent to corporate clients).

A large volume of arrears and overdue loans is a key issue of the micro-finance market. The relative youth of the micro-finance market in Russia is mirrored in the lack of professional practice of portfolio management in these companies, as well as to often ad hoc efforts to collect debts. Currently, the Central Bank of Russia (CBR) is putting efforts into improving the transparency and organisation of this segment of the shadow credit market. In particular, in 2015, the CBR introduced reserve requirements for micro-finance companies that could count towards tax obligations and the system of reporting was changed. This effectively makes MFIs de facto equivalent to credit organisations, making the industry more transparent and regulated.

The dynamics of micro-finance companies show that this remains one of the most dynamically growing areas of the financial system in Russia. And while there were some signs of saturation of this market in 2015, lower numbers of new companies in this segment can be accounted for by a much stricter regulatory approach by the authorities. At present, the micro-finance market in Russia appears to be on the verge of being integrated into the official, regulated financial systems of the country.

There are some elements in Russia that remain opposed to micro-finance. The Duma has a draft law tabled to the parliamentarians which would ban the activity of micro-finance companies in Russia. The reasons for the ban originate in predatory lending – namely, large numbers of loans given to low income households in the context of a worsening socio-economic climate in the country. The growth of micro-financing leads to the growth of net indebtedness and debt servicing payments in the lower income groups of the population and, therefore, lower living standards. According to CBR, in 2015 the average value of payday

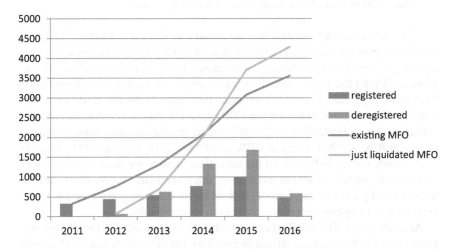

Figure 6.3 Registered and liquidated MFIs in Russia. Pcs.

loans (up to 1 month to the value of 30,000 roubles) went down by 46.1 per cent to 605.2 per cent. There is a potential for a reduction in aggregate demand and, as a result, lower economic stimuli for growth and development.

2   Despite the fact that the total number of corporate credit organisations is second largest in Russia, they represent only 17 per cent of the total number of financial institutions. The segment of alternative micro-finance companies is not regulated effectively and is not transparent. As of July 2016, the CBR reported that between 2002–2016, out of 6,192 registered consumer credit organisations, only 2,483 were active. There have been 1,620 agricultural credit cooperatives established since 2002, and out of 75 housing cooperatives set up since 2007, only 60 are active today.
3   From July 2014, the CBR is the regulatory of pawn companies (lombards). Up to now, however, there are no official statistics on this area of shadow banking. According to the register of credit organisations, there are around 7,000 pawn shops in Russia. In 2015, the CBR addressed regulatory and reporting problems in 85 per cent of them. Therefore, in the near term, we are likely to see serious changes in the pawn market, mostly connected to reducing the overall number of these institutions (in 2015 the CBR initiated closure of 784 pawn shops) and tightening of their regulation and transparency.[10]
4   Issuers of electronic money. The sphere of e-money has been growing rapidly in Russia over the past few years. According to J'son & Partners Consulting, the e-money market in Russia demonstrates steady growth. The average annual growth of turnover of e-money in Russia between 2012 and 2014 was 53 per cent. It is anticipated that by 2019 the growth of this market will bring the total volume of e-money turnover to more than 1.1 trillion rubles.[11] Between 2014 and 2015, the number of operations with electronic money was 1,100 million, to the total value of 1 billion rubles.[12]

The number of transactions and the total amount of electronic money transferred have been growing steadily. For this reason, in 2011, the CBR began to regulate e-money issuers and the circulation of electronic funds on the basis of special legislation.[13] Under this legislation, all issuers of electronic money (e-cash operators) have to be registered as credit institutions (including non-bank credit organisations) and are required to inform the CBR about the launch of electronic transfer activities. As of September 2011, only credit institutions can issue electronic money in Russia.[14] According to CBR, as of May 2016, there are 101 operators of electronic money in Russia. At the same time, despite the increased regulatory focus on the sphere of electronic money, there are many transactions that are not covered by existing regulations, such as electronic money payments between legal entities or hybrid operations carried out by non-banks.

According to CBR and Rosfinmonitoring, the illegal liquidation of e-money purses recently has assumed serious proportions. On the basis of one investigation by Webmoney, the users access the system of transferring money from e-purses to bank cards and accounts. It is expected that Russian lawmakers will pass a law that would require the non-identified e-money purses to be linked to the bank accounts of clients. This would increase transparency and solve the anonymity problems of this segment, potentially making it more attractive to regulated banks.

Key elements of the legal shadow market in Russia

Twenty years after the collapse of command economy, Russia is still primarily a cash-based economy, in transition to a financialised capitalism. This explains why credit intermediation outside the regulated banking system, or the shadow banking system as defined by the FSB, remains underdeveloped in Russia as compared with the countries of advanced capitalism. A handful of state-owned banks dominate the Russian financial system, and alternative investment funds are not sufficiently developed. In 2016, total assets of the Russian banking sector accounted for 103.6 per cent of the country's GDP. In five years, the volume of assets increased by 30 per cent (from 73 to 103.6 per cent of GDP), in ten years it practically doubled (45.1 per cent in 2006). The financial sphere has demonstrated fast rates of growth (35.2 per cent in 2015; 16 per cent in 2014; 12 per cent in 2013; 19.6 per cent in 2012), surpassing the growth in trade (−10.1 per cent in 2015, 1.1 per cent in 2013 and 3.8 per cent in 2012), mining (1.1 per cent in 2015, 0.9 per cent in 2013) and manufacturing (−2.7 per cent). In parallel, the share of gross savings in the country's GDP has remained far lower and demonstrates a tendency towards further shrinkage (from 25.5 per cent in 2008 to 20.4 per cent in 2015) than the share of final consumption, which is increasing (from 66.8 per cent in 2008 to 71.6 per cent in 2015).

Russia's economic growth is severely undermined by the sparse access Russian corporations have to the internal capital market, alternative funding sources and risk insurance mechanisms. These problems stem from the shallow penetration of financial relations into the 'real' economy and the restrictions to accessing foreign credit due to the 2014 sanctions, as well as lower commodity export revenues.

Development of the internal capital market becomes a strategic priority for the country in the face of the external economic context and internal brakes on faster growth. This in turn, has to be seen in the context of the traditional dominance of the banking sector in Russia: the assets of the banking systems in Russia account for more than 65 per cent of assets in the country. If one includes the assets of the CBR, this figure rises to 90 per cent of the total financial system. This share is growing incrementally. The other segments of the financial market are marginal. The range of financial services is also rather narrow and accessible mostly to only large companies.

Yet despite its infancy, the Russian shadow banking industry accommodates different types of hedge funds, private equity funds and investment divisions of traditional banks, money market funds, broker-dealers, issuers of asset-backed commercial paper (ABCP), special purpose entities and other non-bank financial intermediaries, including insurance companies and pension funds. These agents conduct transactions with credit default swaps, collateralised debt obligations, OTC derivatives, repos and other complex structured financial products. Against the background of finance-led growth, the large size of the underground economy and the grey banking sector, the presence of such specialised financial structures poses a serious challenge not only to financial regulation, but to economic stability as a whole. Specifically, four segments of the legal shadow banking system in Russia are notable.

1   Hedge funds. The Russian hedge fund industry remains in its infancy. It was only in 2007 that it became legally possible to set up a hedge fund in Russia. In 2010, the regulations were introduced that govern the structure and composition of hedge funds and institutional investors.

If globally, 10–13,000 hedge funds control over $2.8 trillion world-wide, in Russia only 100 are registered, with a mere 60 of them functioning, according to the data of ratings agencies. This puts the scale of the Russian hedge fund sector of 2013 at the level of the American hedge fund industry as it was in 1984. Russian hedge funds tend to be small, and around 90 per cent of their assets are accounted for by HNWIs seeking to diversify the yield on their investments. In the West, in contrast, around 90 per cent of the hedge fund assets come from institutional investors. Every year in Russia, about five to seven new hedge funds are launched, which is insignificant by international standards. Under Russian law, a hedge fund is classified as a type of mutual fund. Many fund managers register hedge funds in offshore havens (primarily the Cayman Islands), partly with the aim of widening the scope of investment instruments the fund can work with, as well as seeking taxation and regulatory arbitrage benefits. In addition, there is a tendency in Russian companies to use hedge funds to help manage the company, in order to provide risk management in the import-export business and to address the issues of financial engineering.

Interestingly, in light of the recent downturn in the global hedge fund sector, many investors prefer to work with individual fund managers or invest in projects in the real economy.

Recent years have seen an increase in activity of foreign hedge funds operating in Russia. Those invested in the Russian market reported profits of 29 per cent. The total volume of investments in the Russian capital markets was 8 times higher than in China and 16 times higher than in India. The profitability of the Russian financial market is increasingly contrasted by the fact that the Russian stock has proved to be amongst the most volatile in the world.

2   Direct investment funds. A key role in the development of direct investment funds is played by the Russian Direct Investment Fund founded in June 2011 with equity capital of $10 billion. Its main purpose is to attract foreign investments into leading companies in the fast-growing sectors of the Russian economy. Typically, such inflows come from institutional investors, private equity firms and sovereign wealth funds.

3   Investment divisions of banks. In Russia, the major banks are universal. The capitalisation of the Russian stock market, which over the period from 1999 to 2013 grew 20 times from $40 to $772 billion, centred on state-owned banks. From 2013 onwards, the Russian stock market has been on a negative trend. As of 2015, the capitalisation of the Russian stock market fell to $400 billion, which is minuscule by international standards. According to the *Transforming World Markets* report published by Bank of America Merrill Lynch, the Russian stock market is of comparable size to that of Finland, Italy and Spain. In addition to its small size, the Russian stock market is increasingly concentrated, with 6 per cent of its value accounted for by the top ten companies.

The main instrument in the Russian capital market is repo (around 177 trillion rubles, or 84.7 per cent of total market turnover), with the corporate bond market significantly lower (around 8 trillion rubles). From 2015, there has been a trend for the massive closure of brokerages: there has been on average one broker company liquidated per day.

At the same time, since autumn 2013, the number of banks in Russia has been in steady decline. In 2013, 26 commercial banks lost their licences; in 2014, 89; in 2015, 101 commercial banks lost their licences. Over a 15-year period, the number of banks shrank twofold (from 1,311 in 2001 to 707 in 2016). The main reasons cited by the CBR when withdrawing the banks' licences are difficulties in processing customers' payment orders, unreliability of reporting data and documents, reductions in the core capital of the banks, and aggressive credit strategies. In addition, some of the banks were associated with 'suspicious' activities, often involving money laundering, transfer pricing and capital flight, as well as other opaque schemes. While analysts tend to agree that tighter monitoring and control over the commercial banks and their activities promote transparency in Russian banking, some speculate that the administrative approach to 'bank cleansing' may eventually lead to a return to a Soviet-style one-level banking system.

4   Mutual funds (PIFs) and funds of funds. A mutual fund brings together investors' funds that are managed by a special management company. In Russia, as of 1Q 2016, there were 714 registered mutual funds, of which 324 were closed, 358 were open and 32 were term funds. The total value of mutual fund assets was 605.6 billion rubles.

Other specialised non-bank financial intermediaries, including insurance companies and pension funds, play an important role in the shadow financial system in Russia. Russia's insurance market has historically lagged behind the banking system in Russia, and is mostly represented by insurance organisations, mutual insurance societies (10 in total as of early 2016, down from 12 in 2015) and insurance brokers (134 in early 2016; down from 151 in 2015).

In the Russian market, the number of insurance companies has been declining. In the first half of 2013 their number amounted to 454; 404 in 2014; and 334 in 2015.

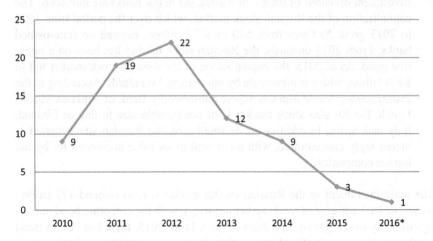

Figure 6.4 Yearly growth of insurance contributions, %.

Source: RAEX.

In 2015, the CBR revoked the licences of 70 insurance companies, or 16.5 per cent of the sector players.

At the same time, recently the activity of insurance companies has been marked by the growing ratio of insurance payments to premiums, high commission fees paid to insurance intermediaries, as well as by increased business costs. The slowdown of the economy, lower incomes and aggregate demand have affected the insurance market. In 2014 the ratio of total insurance premiums to GDP was 1.39 per cent; in 2015 this figure had declined to 1.27 per cent. The total value of insurers' assets is about 2 per cent of GDP.

This trend leads to small- and medium-sized insurers disappearing from the market, contributing to a greater concentration. Recently, there has been a marked trend for top companies to merge into conglomerates (typically uniting banks, pension funds, funds of funds and insurance companies under one roof). As in other types of economies, this tendency leads to a greater concentration of risk sources and, therefore, potential nodes of systemic risk in the Russian financial system, and points to the shadow financial sector as one of its main sources. This may increase capital flight from the industry and undermine financial stability of the overall financial system in Russia.

In addition to the low financial literacy of the population and demand for investables, there is a low capitalisation of the domestic capital market, a limited range of derivative financial instruments and illiquidity of securities. These problems, in turn, imperil the progress of securitisation as a risk mitigation technique. The official registration procedure for new securities issuance is also rather complex, while management companies are not sufficiently transparent, which limits their attractiveness to market participants.

Regulatory challenges of shadow banking in Russia

From a regulatory point of view, there are two paradoxes of shadow banking in Russia. First, although it accommodates most of the participants of the financial system, Russia's shadow banking system is anchored in the country's banking system which, in turn, is rather concentrated. At the same time, because the shadow financial sector operates outside the scope of bank regulation, it complicates the overall assessment of risks in the financial system and undermines the existing set of regulatory measures employed by the regulator. The evolution of the shadow banking sector in Russia in recent years has been largely uncontrolled. This has given rise to significant risks, the scope and level of which cannot be adequately assessed by the business community and financial regulators. In the event of a sharp deterioration in the liquidity of the Russian financial system, even the relatively small volume of shadow banking activity can become a source of systemic risk at any given time because it is closely related to all entities holding financial institutions. Continuous adequate monitoring and systemic oversight might help to partially mitigate the risks posed by the shadow banking system and enable the regulators to promptly identify them. It may also help further reduce the negative impact on the monetary policy, while also aiding the collection of tax revenues into the federal budget.

Second, while there has been no or little systemic oversight of shadow banking in Russia, at times localised regulation was excessive and disproportionate. It is important, therefore, to draw lessons from the recent developments in Russia and other emerging markets, with the aim of designing an effective system of regulation both globally and nationally. In Russia, it is only in late 2013 that the idea of a mega-regulator, a financial supervisory authority on the basis of the central bank, became feasible. The new Russian mega-regulator combines the Russian Central Bank and what used to be the Federal Service for Financial Markets. The major functions of the new regulatory body include supervision of the commercial banks and control over non-bank financial institutions, including insurance companies, asset management companies, pension funds, brokerage firms and MFIs.

The role of the mega-regulator in Russia has only just started to develop fully. It is envisaged that it will serve as the foundation for an integrated financial governance system. Yet fundamentally, the governance of risk in such a complex arrangement depends on the readiness of the authorities to act on emergent risks in this complex network, and prevent these risks from transforming into a systemic risk. In this sense, the mission of the new mega-regulator is rather secondary to the more pertinent issue of the vision of financial governance. In the absence of full information, a thorough analytical base and a paradigm of financial governance, despite its relative financial immaturity, the Russian economy remains exposed to the risks stemming from the complexity of financial networks. This is a particular concern, because in the emerging economy of Russia, financial stability is inevitably linked to economic security, as the currently unfolding episode of US-imposed financial sanctions illustrates.

The new regulatory body has not yet fully shaped its approach to the specifics of the shadow banking sector in Russia (not even at the level of a coherent definition and the classification of groups). There is no consistent analysis and monitoring of the activities of key players of shadow banking, whereas the approach to regulation and control of the individual segments of the shadow financial system are still being formulated. Far too often in Russia, the understanding of the financial sector and the principles of its regulation are based on the rather uncritical, direct translation of foreign reports and academic publications into Russian. In fact, the CBR is currently analysing foreign experience in monitoring and control of the shadow banking system, its legal foundations and the operations of its key participants. Such transliterations are rarely adapted to the specific context of the Russian market and often contain no analyses which could be relevant to Russia. By way of an example, the reports of the CBR on the activities of the shadow banking sector tend not to analyse this market as a whole, but rather treat it as consisting of discrete agents interacting with one another (e.g. MFIs, pawnshops, closed credit mutual funds, construction companies and SPVs, technical intermediaries, hedge funds, private equity firms, money market funds and ABCP funds, private pension funds, etc.). The lack of system-wide monitoring and the focus on the relationships, both within and beyond a given segment, do not allow the establishment of a reliable evaluation of its development. As a result, the impact of external shocks on the Russian economy is offset not by the relatively successful policy mix and governance approaches, but by Russia's incomplete integration into the global financial system and the small size of national financial markets. Therefore, in the present conditions when the economic growth fuelled by consumer credit bubbles has given way to debt deflation, it is essential to find a model that can explain the relationship and feedback mechanisms between the financial sector and the wider economic system.

For instance, only a small part of the financial flows is spent on goods and services. The bulk goes to purchase financial securities and other assets, or is used to further increase interest-bearing debt by simplifying lending conditions, as other possibilities for direct investment, as a rule, have been exhausted. Therefore, an urgent task today for the Russian financial regulators, is to identify the channels through which the increase of asset liquidity affects asset prices more than the prices of consumer goods. The growth of the debt / equity ratio also negatively affects the quality of loan portfolios, prompting banks to seek new creditors and, in the process, become further alienated from the real economy. This, in turn, adds to the potential for systemic risk. In this situation, and against the backdrop of the theoretical fallacies of open economy macroeconomics and the lack of alternative models, policy-makers are unable to make informed governance decisions, prevent debt bubbles or deal effectively with the subsequent depression. High interest rates and other financial expenditure put the real economy on a downward economic spiral, keeping the prices of raw materials high, while putting pressure on the markets, wages and employment. The two divergent price trends (in asset prices and commodity prices), created the need to find an answer to the question: how does credit expansion push asset prices up, while causing debt deflation.

A more adequate financial paradigm would require a modification to existing approaches to the analysis of monetary policy. An alternative vision should incorporate a clearer distinction between money and loans spent on goods and services, and those spent on financial assets and debt servicing. Creating a more realistic model should also reflect the evolution of financialisation in a given economic system, and to treat the economy and the financial sector (including the shadow banking component) as a network of distinct yet interacting sectors.

Conclusion

If in advanced economies the regulation of the shadow banking industry is a tall challenge for the regulators because of the vested interests and complexity and opacity of the sector, in the context of Russia these problems are further compounded by the centrality of a shadow financial sphere that serves the underground or illegal economy. At the same time, it is clear that it is important for Russia to develop a strategic vision of macro-prudential analysis and financial regulation. Here, the main structural challenge for financial regulation in Russia is twofold. On the one hand, there is a significant presence of an illegal (grey) shadow economy; on the other, the shadow banking sector is a developing network of credit channels driven by financial innovation and financialisation. Here, analysts identify several objectives: increasing the transparency of the shadow banking system; the creation of a regulatory, informational and methodological platform for expanding the scope of prudential supervision (of banks and non-bank entities); and reducing opportunities for regulatory arbitrage. Several specific steps towards such a reform in Russia are worth noting:

1 Improving the quality of the statistical base and, in particular, compiling statistics on flows of funds between sectors. Consolidated statistics on flows of funds would help in the efforts to identify the structure and size of the shadow banking system. In this area, it would be useful for Russia to use the experience of countries such as the USA, UK, Germany, etc. For this purpose, it is necessary to maintain the balances of financial instruments and financial market sectors, including the components of the shadow financial system – a feature currently missing from the range of monitoring instruments in Russia. Changes need to be introduced to the balance sheet and accounting reports by firms; it is essential to revive the system of inter-sectoral balances, containing a comprehensive description of inter-sectoral relations and structural developments in the Russian economy by sectors and products (Rosstat was due to begin publishing the data of inter-sectoral balances in Russia in 2016).
2 Reclassification and expansion of the register and classifier of economic activities and financial companies.
3 Introduction of soft (random) observations of financial companies, which would allow their financial risks to be assessed (primarily, liquidity risk and credit risk) from the perspective of the real economy.

Better regulation and oversight of the shadow banking sector entities, in turn, would require:

1   Improving the quality of consolidated, systematic supervision of financial group holdings, within the mandate of the various regulators. It is necessary, for instance, to establish joint integrated oversight and information sharing between the Bank of Russia and the Ministry of Finance, the Federal Financial Monitoring Service.
2   Improvement of legislation in the field of individual elements of the shadow banking sector, primarily with respect to construction companies, issuers of electronic money, credit and mutual funds, etc.

The size of the grey economy in Russia is an important indication of the quality of the official regulatory regime in the country. The tightening of the regulatory stances observed over the past few years tends to invite negative reactions from the market, while the grey economy appears to be sufficiently adaptable to new regulatory standards. The cleansing of the financial system launched by the CBR has not brought about the decrease in grey economic activity as such, but rather led to an integration of the grey economy into the official system as business simply flows over to the largest commercial banks and financial companies.

Therefore, while the specific contours and challenges of shadow banking in Russia are shaped by the legacy of transition and the post-Soviet political economy, a path towards a more adequate financial regulation and governance involves steps that are being developed and implemented in more mature economies. Increasing transparency, fuller information, a reform of financial reporting standards and fuller, systemic oversight of the dynamic networks that connect the economy and the financial system, constitute critical steps towards a more efficient financial and economic governance in the post-2009 Russia.

Notes

1   According to analysts Global Financial Integrity. Available at: www.gfintegrity.org/wp-content/uploads/2013/02/Russia_Illicit_Financial_Flows_and_the_Role_of_the_Underground_Economy-HighRes.pdf. Last accessed: 12.01.2017.
2   http://info.minfin.ru/monetary.php. The cash in the country's monetary turnover is about 25–23 per cent, rather stable over the last five years.
3   Report based on the joint study by the Bank of Russia and National Agency for Financial Research: "Payment and Clearing Systems: Analysis and Statistics. Retail Payment Services consumer behaviour", No. 42, 2014.
4   Federal Law of 03.06.2009 No. 103-FZ "On the Activities of Individuals Receiving Payments by Payment Agents".
5   10,000 rubles for legal entities and no capital restrictions for individual entrepreneurs.
6   Calculated according to Russia's balance of payments.
7   Federal Law No. 214-FZ "On Participation in the Shared Construction of Apartment Buildings and Other Real Estate and on Amendments to Certain Legislative Acts of the Russian Federation".
8   Such a widespread use of various schemes designed to bypass existing laws is primarily to do with regulatory loopholes and the system of relations prevailing in the

construction industry. Another major reason for the use of such "grey" schemes is the desire to reduce the tax base and to allow the payment of penalties to co-investors in the event of a delay in completion of the project.

9 In 2012, there were cases when micro-loans were taken out by financially literate citizens from micro-finance companies in the branches of "Russian Post" at unprecedentedly high interest rates – from 10,000 to 473 billion per cent per annum. See www.cbr.ru/Press/?PrtId=event&id=197&PrintVersion=Y.

10 The actual interest payments on debt built into hundreds and even thousands of percent per annum.

11 "Brief Overview of the Russian e-Currency Market. First Half of 2014", J'son & Partners Consulting, Market Watch. October 2014.

12 http://cbr.ru/statistics/p_sys/print.aspx?file=sheet001.htm&pid=psrf&sid=ITM_30245.

13 Federal Law of 27 June 2011 No. 161-FZ "On the National Payment System"; Federal Law of 03.06.2009 No. 103-FZ "On the Activities of Individuals Receiving Payments by Payment Agents"; Bank of Russia Instruction of 15.09.2011 No. 137-I "On Mandatory Ratios of Non-Bank Credit Organizations Entitled to Money Transfers without Opening Bank Accounts and Other Related Banking Operations and the Peculiarities of the Russian Bank Oversight of Their Implementation"; Directive of the Central Bank of Russia from 14.09.2011 No. 2693 "On the Procedure for Monitoring Operators Remittance in a Credit Institution: The Activities of the Bank Payment Agents"; Directive of the Central Bank of Russia from 14.09.2011 No. 2694 "On the Procedure for Notifying the Bank Russian Operator of Electronic Funds to Start the Implementation of Electronic Transfer of Funds".

14 There is a requirement for minimum equity capital: no less than 2 per cent, calculated as the ratio of equity to total liabilities together with the statutory liquidity ratio, no less than 100 per cent, calculated as the ratio of liquid assets to be received in the next 30 days to total liabilities.

References

Bashkatova, A. (2014) "External Debt and Offshore Exsanguainated Economy". *Nezvisimaya Gazeta*, 20 January. Available at: www.ng.ru/economics/2014-01-20/4_dolgi.html. Last accessed 21.04.2017.

Schneider, F., A. Buehn and C. E. Montenegro (2010) *Shadow Economy All over the World: New Estimates for 162 Countries from 1999 to 2007*. Working Paper, no. 322. Department of Economics, University of Chile. Available at: *elibrary.worldbank.org/doi/pdf/10.1596/1813-9450-5356. Last accessed 21.04.2017.*

Part II
Crisis and beyond
Shadow banking and its origins

Part II

7 The shadow banking system during the financial crisis of 2007–08

A comparison of the US and the EU

Antoine Bouveret[1]

Introduction

The financial crisis started in August 2007 with a run on US asset-backed commercial paper (ABCP) that quickly spread to the interbank market (Acharya *et al.* 2009; Covitz *et al.* 2013). ABCP issuers were unable to refinance their assets (including asset-backed securities (ABS) and mortgage loans) with short-term paper as investors were concerned about the quality of the underlying assets due to the collapse of the US housing market. The financial turbulence expanded to other financial markets such as the ones for repurchase agreements (repo), ABS and mortgage-backed securities, and then to the interbank market as ABCP and ABS issuers had contingent credit lines with sponsor banks. Those events lead eventually to the collapse of Lehman Brothers in September 2008, and required the placing into government conservatorship of government sponsored enterprises (GSEs) Freddie Mac and Fannie Mae as well as emergency lending facilities to AIG. It is only after the Federal Reserve Board and governmental bodies implemented a whole set of liquidity facilities available to entities outside of the banking sector, and established the Troubled Asset Relief Program (TARP), that the run started to wane.[2] As emphasized by Pozsar *et al.* (2010):

> The liquidity facilities of the Federal Reserve and other government agencies' guarantee schemes were a direct response to the liquidity and capital shortfalls of shadow banks and, effectively, provided either a backstop to credit intermediation by the shadow banking system or to traditional banks for the exposure to shadow banks.

The financial crisis has been the result of a combination of factors[3] that includes search for yields and global imbalances (Bernanke 2011), market misconduct and inadequate regulation (Levine 2010). On top of that, the 'shadow banking sector' has also played a significant role. In particular, by performing bank-like activities such as credit intermediation, liquidity and maturity transformation, it had significantly contributed to the US housing bubble. For example, financial companies granted loans extensively as they were able to move them out of their balance sheets by transferring the assets to special purpose vehicles that got funding by securitizing the assets by issuing ABS. Given that those loans were no longer held on the balance sheet of financial companies, the latter were not incentivized to monitor the borrowers, contributing to the expansion of the subprime market. Those risks were amplified by the development of complex products (such as collateralized debt obligations) that repackaged these ABS and the general underestimation of risks, in important ways interrelated with the strong reliance on external ratings provided by credit rating agencies which proved to be inadequate. When the US housing market collapsed and mortgage borrowers were no longer able to repay their loans, holders of securitized products backed by mortgage loans started to experience sharp losses, and the whole shadow banking system experienced a run that eventually led to the financial crisis.[4]

This significant role played by the shadow banking sector in the US has been emphasized by Adrian and Shin (2009). They estimate that market-based holdings of home mortgages amounted to around USD 7 trillion in 2008Q1, while bank-based holdings added up to a total of around USD 3.2 trillion.

While performing bank-like activities, shadow banks did not have access to liquidity backstops such as central bank lending facilities and deposit guarantees, and they were therefore greatly exposed to runs. The high reliance of shadow banks on short-term funding markets, as well as the high interconnectedness with the banking system, increased the vulnerability of the financial system as a whole. Moreover, before the crisis, there had been no general understanding of the role played by shadow banks: "These risks [linked to shadow banks] grew rapidly in the period before the crisis, in part because the regulators – like most financial firms and investors – did not fully understand or appreciate them" (Bernanke 2010).[5] As a result, during the financial crisis, policy responses by central banks, and later on by Treasuries, were partly ineffective, at least until Lehman Brothers' collapse in September 2008, due, in particular, to the lack of an overall view of the shadow banking sector. For example, in August 2007, the Federal Reserve's first response was to reduce the primary credit rate offered to banks using the discount window to cope with the freeze in the interbank market. However, as this facility was only available to banks and not to shadow banks, it did not even manage to significantly reduce the symptoms, let alone cure the disease.

During the financial crisis, the US shadow banking system declined dramatically. Total liabilities were reduced by USD 5 trillion between 2008Q1 and 2010Q4, according to Pozsar *et al.* (2010). One particular feature of the financial crisis was that the collapse of the US shadow banking system spread quickly in the US to European financial markets, due to the high degree of interconnectedness between US and European financial markets linked to the role played by US and European investment banks. The collapse of the US shadow banking system spread quickly from the US to the European financial system, due to the high degree of interconnectedness between US and European financial institutions linked to the role played by US and European investment banks. However, the European shadow banking system did not collapse to the same extent during the financial crisis.

This feature is puzzling given that the overall evolution of financial markets in the US and in the EU during the financial crisis was somewhat similar. This chapter provides an explanation by looking at the evolution of the components of the shadow banking system and, in particular, the surge in securitization that occurred in the EU in 2008. By proving indirect liquidity backstops to shadow banking activities at an early stage, especially since ABS were eligible for refinancing operations, the European Central Bank (ECB) supported the shadow banking system. A similar route was followed by the Fed and the Bank of England but only after September 2008, by the implementation of specific liquidity facilities.

The first section discusses the definition of the shadow banking sector and ways to measure it, the second section provides estimates for the US and Europe and the third section focuses on the role played by central banks during the financial crisis. The final section concludes.

Scoping the shadow banking system

The first attested use of the expression 'shadow banking system' seems to have been made at the Federal Reserve of Kansas's annual symposium in Jackson Hole, Wyoming in August 2007:

> [u]nlike regulated banks, who fund themselves with insured deposits, back-stopped by the access to the Fed's discount window, unregulated shadow banks fund themselves with un-insured commercial paper, which may or may not be backstopped by liquidity lines from real banks. Thus, the shadow banking system is particularly vulnerable to runs.
>
> (McCulley 2007)

Following the same focus on run risk, for Pozsar *et al.* (2010), the shadow banking sector can be defined as "financial intermediaries that conduct maturity, credit, and liquidity transformation without access to central bank liquidity or public sector credit guarantees". In other words, the shadow banking sector encompasses all non-bank financial institutions that perform bank-like activities, are not subjected to the same regulatory and prudential requirements as banks, and also do not have access to public safety nets and therefore are particularly exposed to runs.[6]

Following the mandate put forward by the G20 at the November 2010 Summit, the FSB released a note aiming at defining the shadow banking system (FSB 2011), which is relatively close to the previous approaches: "the system of credit intermediation that involves entities and activities outside the regular banking system".[7] The FSB has also provided a narrower definition whereby the shadow banking system is:

> [a] system of credit intermediation that involves entities and activities outside the regular banking system, and raises i) systemic risk concerns, in particular by maturity/liquidity transformation, leverage and flawed credit risk transfer, and/or ii) regulatory arbitrage concerns.

In practice, the FSB narrow definition is tricky to operationalize. On the one hand, by focusing on activities and entities that raise systemic risk concern, it relies on

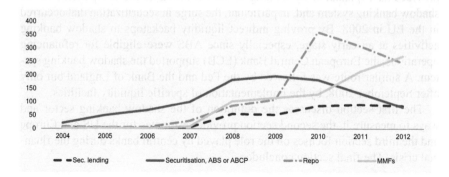

Figure 7.1 Low systemic risk concerns linked to shadow banking before 2007–2008.

Sources: Factiva, ESMA.

Note: Number of articles referring to 'shadow banking' or 'financial stability' or 'systemic risk' and the specific components identified above in Business and Consumer Services or Banking and Credit or Accounting and Consulting or Insurance newspapers.

the ability of observers to assess this risk. In other words, using this definition, one may have arrived at a very low estimate of the size of the shadow banking system in 2007, given that at the time there was generally no systemic risk concerns associated with securitization or the repo market. Anecdotal evidence is provided in Figure 7.1, which shows that before 2008 there was hardly any business article linking repo, securities lending or money market funds to systemic risk or financial stability.

The definitions of the shadow banking system presented above are based on a functional approach[8] whereby it is the very functions performed by the shadow banking system that are central rather than their institutional type (e.g. hedge funds or structured investment vehicles). Nevertheless, the FSB note provides an institution-based description that includes hedge funds, insurance companies and credit rating agencies.

Lately, Mehrling *et al.* (2013) define shadow banking as "money market funding of capital market lending" and summarize the three main features of shadow banking: i) no direct public backstop, ii) money market funding of capital market borrowing, and iii) market pricing. One issue with this definition is that it is difficult to operationalize as it requires access to data at the balance sheet level in order to link money market funding (liabilities) to capital market lending (assets).

The definition of shadow banking used in this chapter relies on institutions and financial instruments that are used to perform bank-like activities (maturity and liquidity transformation), as well as credit transformation, without any *direct* public backstop. In particular, this definition includes securitization due to the credit, maturity and liquidity transformations it allows, as well as securities lending and repo transactions given that they allow maturity and liquidity transformation, and finally money market funds as they perform liquidity and (somewhat) limited maturity transformation. All those instruments and entities are potentially exposed to run risk. Moreover, unlike the FSB definition, there is no 'subjective' assessment linked to this definition (such as 'flawed credit risk transfer' or 'systemic risk concerns').

To assess the size of the shadow banking system, the definition has to be operationalized. Two main approaches have been followed in the existing literature. The 'subtractive approach' defines the shadow banking system as a residual (see, for example, Bakk-Simon 2012; ECB 2013; FSB 2011). The whole financial system is split between banks, insurance corporations and pension funds, public sector financial entities and other financial intermediaries. The latter category is taken as a proxy for shadow banking, even though it mixes very different entities such as brokers and derivatives dealers as well as leasing corporations. Furthermore, this approach focuses exclusively on entities rather than activities. The use of the 'subtractive approach' is linked to the fact that existing statistics, especially at the European level, tend to focus on credit institutions (banks) and insurance companies, while the remaining financial entities (with the exception of investment and money market funds) are merged into an "other financial intermediaries" category.[9]

The 'additive approach' used in this chapter pursues the mapping of the shadow banking system by looking at its individual components such as securitized products and securities lending transactions. This approach has been used by Pozsar *et al.* (2010) and Adrian and Ashcraft (2012) for the US, and by Bouveret (2011) for the European Union. It allows the identification of each of the components. One drawback, as in the case of the 'subtractive approach', is that shadow banking is not assessed as a system.

The shadow banking system can be decomposed into several subcomponents. The securitization-based shadow credit intermediation involves several instruments[10] and institutions that perform bank-like activities, as pictured in Figure 7.2. Loan pools transferred to (or originated by) the shadow banking sector are securitized in the form of ABS where the ABS structure is not exposed to maturity mismatch. Those ABS can be purchased by other entities and funded through ABCP, implying a "resecuritisation process" (Pozsar *et al.* 2010), or through other alternatives such as repo (Gorton 2009). Finally, those instruments are purchased by money market investors (such as money funds and securities lenders).

Therefore, the instruments used during the securitization process are crucial components of the shadow banking sector, along with short-term instruments such as repo and securities lending transactions that expose the shadow banking system to run risk.[11] One of the main issues is linked to data gaps, for the US but even more for the EU. The ECB provides data for the euro area, but they are not entirely fit for assessing the shadow banking system. Data on securitization can be sourced from ECB financial vehicle corporations, but the collection started only in 2009Q4, therefore we rely on the data provided by Association for Financial Markets in Europe (AFME). For the repo market, the main dataset for Europe is the half-yearly survey from ICMA, although ICAP through its Brokertec platform provides some transaction-level data but only for short maturities, and the ECB money market survey also provides some qualitative information. For securities lending, the Risk Management Association provides quarterly data, while Markit allows subscribers to retrieve aggregate and individual information on securities lending.[12]

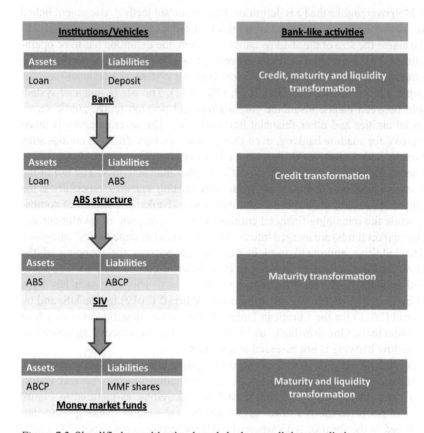

Figure 7.2 Simplified securitization-based shadow credit intermediation.

A comparison of the US and EU shadow banking system during the financial crisis

As of end-2012, the US shadow banking system amounted to USD 14.6tn,[13] down 30 per cent from a peak of USD 20.6tn in 2008Q1 (Figure 7.3). The European shadow banking system totalled EUR 8.2tn as of 2012Q4 (Figure 7.4), and experienced an 8 per cent decline over the same period.

One important feature is that the European shadow banking system accounts for less than 20 per cent of EU banks' liabilities against 100 per cent for the US. This partly reflects different financial systems where, in the US, funding is more market-based whereas in Europe it remains mostly bank-based. The US shadow banking system peaked in 2008Q2 and has experienced a sharp decline (−30 per cent) since then. The European shadow banking system remained more stable during the crisis, with the exception of 2008Q4, and reached a level end-2012 that was similar to 2006Q4.

As shown in Table 7.1, the decline of the US shadow banking system was mostly linked to the fall in ABS that accounted for 45 per cent of the decrease,

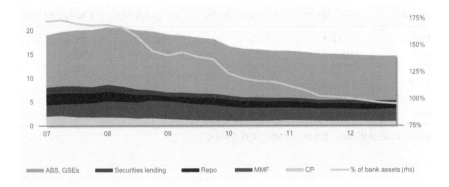

Figure 7.3 US shadow banking system.

Sources: FED Flow of Funds, ESMA.

Note: Size of shadow banking system proxied by liabilities of ABS issuers, GSEs and pool securities (ABS, GSEs), open commercial paper (CP), size of the US repo market, securities borrowed by broker dealers and liabilities of Money Market Funds (MMF), USD tn.

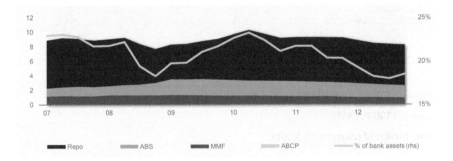

Figure 7.4 European shadow banking system.

Sources: ECB, AFME, ICMA, ESMA

Note: Size of shadow banking system proxied by amounts of Asset-Backed Securities (ABS) and Asset-Backed Commercial Paper (ABCP) outstanding, size of the EU repo market and liabilities of Money Market Funds (MMF).

and the run on short-term securities markets (repo, ABCP and securities lending) that explained 43 per cent of the decline. Regarding the European shadow banking system, the decline was largely linked to the repo market and money market funds, but ABS increased during the period.

In terms of composition, the share of short-term instruments (repo, securities lending and ABCP) declined significantly in the US due to the run that they experienced during the crisis. In Europe, the share of each component remained roughly stable, with the notable exception of securitization whose share increased during the financial crisis from 12 per cent in 2006 to 26 per cent in 2008.

Table 7.1 Evolution of the US and EU shadow banking systems (2012Q4 – 2008Q1)

Amounts	US (USD bn)	Change US (%)	EU (EUR bn)	Change EU (%)
MMF	−732.9	12%	−360.5	46%
Repo	−1003.5	16%	−832.0	106%
ABS	−2738.6	45%	422.9	−54%
ABCP	−832.3	14%	−12.7	2%
Sec lending	−789.5	13%	N/A	N/A
Total	−6096.8	100%	−782.3	100%

Sources: Federal Reserve, ICMA, AFME, ECB, ESMA.

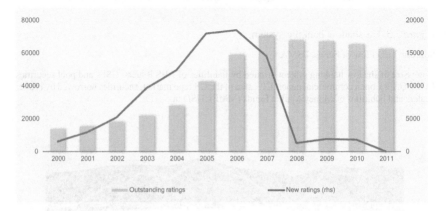

Figure 7.5 Ratings of RMBS in the US.

Sources: CEREP, ESMA.

Note: Number of ratings for US RMBS.

The decline of US housing prices in 2007 and the increase in the delinquency rates of subprime borrowers led to the collapse of residential mortgage-backed securitization (RMBS) in the US. This can be seen in Figure 7.5, while just for the year 2006 there were 18,000 new RMBS ratings, new ratings in 2008 were fewer than 1,500. The same trend can be observed in Europe, although absolute figures were lower.

One of the driving factors was the sharp deterioration of the credit quality by RMBS tranches. For the year 2006, while more than 90 per cent of US RMBS were rated investment grade (and 50 per cent AAA), five years later only 4 per cent remained investment grade (and 1 per cent AAA) and 50 per cent defaulted (Figure 7.6). The same deterioration occurred in Europe, although no default was recorded (Figure 7.7).

Therefore, given that the credit quality of US and European RMBS decreased at the same time, it is striking that securitization issuance totally collapsed in the US in 2008, with a 56 per cent decline between 2007 and 2008, while in Europe it reached historical highs during the same period, with a 35 per cent increase.

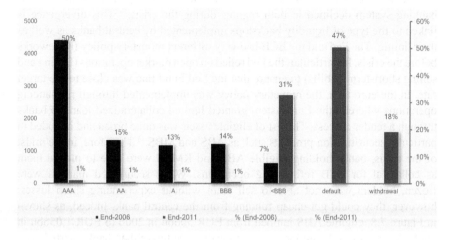

Figure 7.6 US RMBS ratings.

Sources: CEREP, ESMA.

Note: S&P Credit ratings of US RMBS for the 2006 vintage.

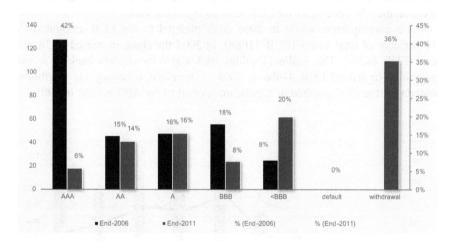

Figure 7.7 European RMBS ratings.

Sources: CEREP, ESMA.

Note: S&P Credit ratings of European RMBS for the 2006 vintage.

The role of central banks' liquidity backstops to the shadow banking system

The divergence in the evolution of shadow banking systems in the US and in the EU during the financial crisis is mainly linked to securitization. In the US, this component declined by USD 2.8tn between 2008Q1 and 2012Q4, accounting for 45 per cent of the decline of the shadow banking system (Table 7.2). However, in

Europe, it increased by around EUR 420bn. The other components of the shadow banking system declined in both regions during the crisis.[14] This divergence is linked to the type of liquidity backstops implemented by central banks as well as their timing. The Fed and the ECB had very different monetary policy frameworks before the crisis. In particular, the Fed relied on open market operations (buying and selling short-term T-bills) to ensure that the Fed Fund rate was close to the target rate. In the euro area, the monetary policy was implemented through refinancing operations whereby the Eurosystem granted limited collateralized loans to banks through a tender process. The list of eligible assets was quite broad and included in particular securitization products such as ABS and MBS.[15] Therefore, in the midst of the crisis, banks holding eligible ABS and RMBS were able to pledge them as collateral for ECB refinancing operations. While securitized markets were frozen, holders were not able to sell them without experiencing sharp losses; however, they could get cheap funding from the central bank. Indeed, as shown in Figure 7.8, eligible ABS jumped from EUR 506bn in 2006 to EUR 1,056bn in 2008, despite a significant increase in spreads.[16] On top of that, banks started issuing ABS and RMBS only for pledging them as collateral with the ECB. This is evidenced by the sharp increase in retained ABS issuance which peaked at 99 per cent in 2008 against 47 per cent in 2007 as shown in Figure 7.9. Given that no private investors were willing to buy newly issued ABS in 2008, banks retained them on their balance sheet for ECB refinancing operations.

As a consequence, while in 2006 ABS pledged to the ECB amounted to 11 per cent of total assets (EUR 110bn), in 2008 the share increased to 28 per cent (EUR 440bn). This indirect liquidity backstop to the shadow banking sector amounted to around EUR 410bn in 2008.[17] Therefore, relatively lax eligibility criteria for the ECB resulted in significant support to the ABS market in 2008.

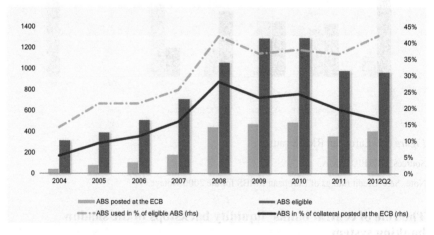

Figure 7.8 Eligibility of ABS in the euro area.

Sources: ECB, ESMA.

Note: EUR bn.

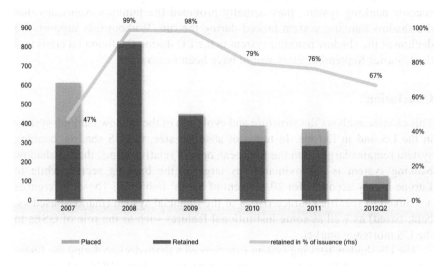

Figure 7.9 ABS issuance in Europe.

Sources: AFME, JPMorgan, ESMA.

Note: Issuance of ABS, in EUR bn.

In the US, the Federal Reserve followed the same route by designing liquid-ity backstops that were implemented only after September-October 2008. The Federal Reserve facilities were targeted at specific entities and activities such as ABCP and money market funds with the Asset-Backed Commercial Paper Money Market Mutual Fund Liquidity Facility (AMLF), the Commercial Paper with the Commercial Paper Funding Facility (CPFF) and the ABS with the Term Asset-Backed Securities Loan Facility (TALF). Overall, those facilities amounted to USD 395bn in December 2008 (Table 7.2).

Interestingly, the ECB provided liquidity support only for banks holding eli-gible collateral, while the Federal Reserve also implemented facilities aimed at non-bank institutions. This could reflect the features of the two financial systems, with a larger role played by markets in the US but also a broader scope of inter-vention in the US compared to Europe.

Table 7.2 Fed facilities (USD bn)

Amounts	*31/12/2008*
CPFF	334
TALF	0
PDCF	37
AMLF	24
Total	395

Sources: Federal Reserve, ESMA.

While those liquidity programmes were not explicitly targeted at the shadow banking system, they actually provided the liquidity backstops that the shadow banking system lacked during the run. Without this support, the decline of the shadow banking system in the EU during the financial crisis and the US after September 2008 would have been far sharper.

Conclusion

This chapter analyses the structure and evolution of the shadow banking system in the US and in Europe. In terms of absolute size, the US shadow banking system remains larger than the European one. In relative terms, the US shadow banking system is approximately as large as the banking sector, while in Europe it only accounts for 20 per cent of banks' liabilities. These differences are linked to specific characteristics of the financial system (market-based vs. bank-based) as well as some institutional features such as the role of GSEs in the US mortgage market.

The US shadow banking system experienced a sharp decline during the financial crisis, especially for its short-term components such as ABCP and repo. The European shadow banking system did not collapse, in contrast, despite a sharp deterioration in credit ratings for securitized instruments. One of the driving factors was the eligibility of ABS for ECB refinancing operations that provided incentives to banks to issue ABS that were retained and later pledged to the ECB. While the Federal Reserve and other central banks followed similar policies, those tools were not available at an early stage. The flexible monetary policy framework of the ECB allowed it to support the shadow banking system, even without having a global understanding of the system. This was due to the high interconnectedness between banks and shadow banks which since then has been under the scope of the Financial Stability Board, which has put forward recommendations to limit it.

One of the lessons of the financial crisis was that it was extraordinary liquidity support by central banks as well as Treasuries that helped to reduce the run on the shadow banking system. On-going regulatory discussions aim at reducing run risk on shadow banking entities and activities, but two issues remain open: i) how can the shadow banking system contribute to the funding of the real economy? and ii) how would public authorities react to a run on shadow banking in the future, given the difficult accountability issues to taxpayers and citizens that were raised by the extraordinary support provided during the financial crisis?

Appendix

Table 7.3 Data used to map the shadow banking system

	US	European Union
Money Market Mutual Funds Liabilities	Flow of Funds Table L.119 (FED)	Aggregated balance sheet of euro area Money Market Funds (ECB)
Issuers of ABS	Flow of Funds Table L.124 (FED)	AFME Securitisation data report

Liabilities of GSEs	Flow of Funds Table L.122 and L.123 (FED)	N/A
Repo market	Flow of Funds Table L.207 (FED)	ICMA Half-yearly survey
Commercial Paper outstanding	Flow of Funds Table L.208 (FED)	STEP program (ECB)
Securities lending	Flow of Funds Table L.230 (FED)	N/A
Commercial banks' liabilities	Flow of Funds Table L.209 (FED)	Liabilities of euro area MFI excluding the Eurosystem and liabilities of non-participating Member States' monetary financial institutions excluding National Central Banks (NCBs)

Notes

1 International Monetary Fund, email: abouveret@hotmail.com. The views expressed are those of the author and do not necessarily represent the views of the IMF, its Executive Board, or IMF management. The author thanks Steffen Kern for his comments on an earlier version of the chapter as well as seminar participants at the Cass Business School Conference on Shadow Banking: A European Perspective.

2 See Cecchetti (2009) for an overview of the Federal Reserve's response to the crisis and more details on the timeline on the Federal Reserve of Saint Louis website at http://timeline.stlouisfed.org/index.cfm?p=timeline.

3 See Acharya *et al.* (2009) for a discussion of the causes of the crisis.

4 See Adrian and Shin (2008, 2010), Brunnermeier (2009), Gorton (2009), Gorton and Metrick (2010a, 2010b) and Acharya *et al.* (2010).

5 The BIS (2008: 138) makes a similar claim: "Moreover, as evidence has accumulated that the financial system as a whole is no longer functioning effectively, those charged with prudential oversight must also ask themselves what went wrong. How, for example, could a huge shadow banking system emerge without provoking clear statements of official concern? Perhaps, as with processes for internal governance, it is simply that no one saw any pressing need to ask hard questions about the sources of profits when things were going so well".

6 In particular, while banks produce informationally insensitive debt by creating deposits, shadow banks are supposed to produce informationally insensitive debt by securitization and repos. However, during the financial crisis, debt issued by shadow banks became informationally sensitive as investors started to sell securitized assets that were previously perceived as risk-free (see Gorton (2009) for further details).

7 FSB (2011: 2).

8 See Merton and Bodie (1995).

9 As explained by Bouveret (2011) "a proxy for shadow banking can be calculated . . . by adding the sector comprising 'non-monetary financial intermediaries other than insurance corporations and pension funds' (OFIs) to the figure for 'MMFs' and then subtracting 'investment funds other than MMFs'".

10 This section presents a very simplified version of shadow credit intermediation; see Pozsar *et al.* (2010) for a detailed description.

11 Tucker (2010) uses the same framework by including MMF, ABCP, SIV, finance companies and the securities lending and repo markets.

12 See Bouveret *et al.* (2013) for further details on data gaps linked to securities financing transactions.

13 Further details on the data used to assess the size of the shadow banking system are provided in the Appendix.

14 For the non-securitization components of the shadow banking system, the divergence was also linked to lower reliance on ABCP in Europe (outstanding amounts peaked at EUR 58bn in 2008Q1 against USD 1.1tn in the US).

15 During the financial crisis, the ECB did not change its framework, but rather started providing unlimited liquidity at a fixed rate.

16 This point is also made by Albertazzi *et al*. (2011): "Much ABS issuance in Italy (and in the euro area) since the end of 2007 has been related to their use as collateral in Eurosystem refinancing operations. According to informal estimates from market participants, approximately 90% of euro-denominated ABS issued in 2008 seems to have been used as collateral for ECB liquidity standing facilities rather than sold to the markets".

17 This amount is computed based on outstanding ABS posted at the ECB. A haircut of 7 per cent (average of the 2–12 per cent haircut on ABS in 2008) is then applied to this amount.

References

Acharya, V., T. Cooley, M. Richardson and I. Walter (2009) "Manufacturing Tail Risk: A Perspective on the Financial Crisis of 2007–2009". *Foundations and Trends in Finance*, 4(4), pp. 247–325.

Acharya, V., P. Schnabl and G. Suarez (2010) *Securitization without Risk Transfer*. NBER Working Paper, no. 15730. Available at: http://pages.stern.nyu.edu/~pschnabl/public_html/AcharyaSchnablSuarez2013.pdf. Last accessed: 06.01.2017.

Adrian, T. and A. B. Ashcraft (2012) *Shadow Banking: A Review of the Literature*. Federal Reserve Bank of New York Staff Report, No. 580. Available at: www.newyorkfed.org/medialibrary/media/research/staff_reports/sr580.pdf. Last accessed: 06.01.2017.

Adrian, T. and H. S. Shin (2008) *Financial Intermediary Leverage and Value-at-Risk*. Federal Reserve Bank of New York Staff Report, No. 338. Available at: www.aeaweb.org/conference/2010/retrieve.php?pdfid=481. Last accessed: 06.01.2017.

Adrian, T. and H. S. Shin (2009) *The Shadow Banking System: Implications for Financial Regulation*. Federal Reserve Bank of New York Staff Report, no. 382. Available at: www.newyorkfed.org/medialibrary/media/research/staff_reports/sr382.pdf. Last accessed: 06.01.2017.

Adrian, T. and H. S. Shin (2010) *The Changing Nature of Financial Intermediation and the Financial Crisis of 2007–09*. Federal Reserve Bank of New York Staff Report, no. 439. Available at: www.newyorkfed.org/medialibrary/media/research/staff_reports/sr439.pdf. Last accessed: 06.01.2017.

Albertazzi, U., G. Eramo, L. Gambacorta, and C. Salleo (2011) *Securitization Is Not That Evil After All*. Bank of Italy Working Paper, no. 796. Available at: https://ideas.repec.org/p/bdi/wptemi/td_796_11.html. Last accessed: 06.01.2017.

Bakk-Simon, K., S. Borgioli, C. Girón, H. Hempell, A. Maddaloni, F. Recine and S. Rosati (2012) *Shadow Banking in the Euro Area: An Overview*. European Central Bank Occasional Paper, no. 133. Available at: www.ecb.europa.eu/pub/pdf/scpops/ecbocp133.pdf. Last accessed: 06.01.2017.

Bernanke, B. (2010) *Economic Challenges: Past, Present, and Future*. Speech at the Dallas Regional Chamber, 7 April. Available at: www.federalreserve.gov/newsevents/speech/20100407a.htm. Last accessed: 06.01.2017.

Bernanke, B. (2011) *Global Imbalances: Links to Economic and Financial Stability*. Speech at the Banque de France, 18 February. Available at: www.federalreserve.gov/newsevents/speech/bernanke20110218a.htm. Last accessed: 06.01.2017.

BIS (2008) *78th Annual Report*. Available at: www.bis.org/publ/arpdf/ar2008e.htm. Last accessed: 06.01.2017.

Bouveret, A. (2011) *An Assessment of the Shadow Banking Sector in Europe*. SSRN Paper. Available at: https://papers.ssrn.com/sol3/papers.cfm?abstract_id=2027007. Last accessed: 06.01.2017.

Bouveret, A., J. Jardelot, J. Keller, P. Molitor, J. Theal and M. Vital (2013) *Towards a Monitoring Framework for Securities Financing Transactions*. ESRB Occasional Paper, no. 2. Available at: www.esrb.europa.eu/pub/pdf/occasional/20130318_occasional_paper_2.pdf?99e4d453977078d79270e659cce29cd3. Last accessed: 06.01.2017.

Brunnermeier, M. (2009) "Deciphering the Liquidity and Credit Crunch 2007–2008". *Journal of Economic Perspectives*, 23(1), pp. 77–100.

Cecchetti, S. (2009) "Crisis and Responses: The Federal Reserve in the Early Stages of the Financial Crisis". *Journal of Economic Perspectives*, 23(1), pp. 51–75.

Coval, J., J. Jurek and E. Stafford (2009) "The Economics of Structured Finance". *Journal of Economic Perspectives*, 23(1), pp. 3–25.

Covitz, D., N. Lang and G. Suarez (2013) "The Evolution of a Financial Crisis: Collapse of the Asset-Backed Commercial Paper Market". *Journal of Finance*, 68(3), pp. 815–848.

ECB (2013) *Enhancing the Monitoring of Shadow Banking*. Monthly Bulletin. February, pp 89–99. Available at: www.ecb.europa.eu/pub/pdf/other/art2_mb201302en_pp89–99en.pdf. Last accessed: 06.01.2017.

FSB (2011) *Shadow Banking: Scoping the Issues*. 12 April. Available at: www.fsb.org/2011/04/shadow-banking-scoping-the-issues/. Last accessed: 06.01.2017.

Gorton, G. (2009) *Slapped in the Face by the Invisible Hand: Banking and the Panic of 2007*. Paper Presented at the Federal Reserve Bank of Atlanta's 2009 Financial Markets Conference: Financial Innovation and Crisis, May 11–13. Available at: www.frbatlanta.org/-/media/documents/news/conferences/2009/financial-markets-conference/gorton.pdf. Last accessed: 06.01.2017.

Gorton, G. and A. Metrick (2010a) *Securitized Banking and the Run on Repo*. Yale ICF Working Paper, No. 09–14. Available at: www.moodys.com/microsites/crc2010/papers/gorton_run_on_repo_nov.pdf. Last accessed: 06.01.2017.

Gorton, G. and A. Metrick (2010b) *Regulating the Shadow Banking System*. Brookings Papers on Economic Activity. Fall, pp 261–312. Available at: www.brookings.edu/wp-content/uploads/2010/09/2010b_bpea_gorton.pdf. Last accessed: 06.01.2017.

Levine, R. (2010) *An Autopsy of the U.S. Financial System*. NBER Working Paper, no. 15956. Available at: https://core.ac.uk/download/pdf/6611623.pdf?repositoryId=153. Last accessed: 06.01.2017.

McCulley, P. (2007) *Teton Reflections*. PIMCO Global Central Bank Focus. Available at: www.pimco.com/insights/economic-and-market-commentary/global-central-bank-focus/teton-reflections. Last accessed: 06.01.2017.

Mehrling, P., Z. Pozsar, J. Sweeney and D. H. Neilson (2013) *Bagehot was a Shadow Banker: Shadow Banking, Central Banking, and the Future of Global Finance*. Working Paper. Available at: http://econ.as.nyu.edu/docs/IO/26329/Mehrling_10012012.pdf. Last accessed: 06.01.2017.

Merton, R. and Z. Bodie (1995) *A Conceptual Framework for Analyzing the Financial Environment*. In D. B. Crane (ed.) *The Global Financial System*. Harvard, MA: Harvard Business Press.

Pozsar, Z., T. Adrian, A. Ashcraft and H. Boesky (2010) *Shadow Banking*. Federal Reserve Bank of New York Staff Report, no. 458. Available at: www.newyorkfed.org/medialibrary/media/research/staff_reports/sr458.pdf. Last accessed: 06.01.2017.

Tucker, P. (2010) *Shadow Banking, Financing Markets and Financial Stability*. Speech at the Bank of England, 21 January. Available at: www.bis.org/review/r100126d.pdf. Last accessed: 06.01.2017.

8 European money market funds

A study of the market micro-processes[1]

Viktoria Baklanova and Joseph Tanega[2]

Introduction

The importance of money market funds in the US and Europe emerged during the financial crisis,[3] with new regulations aimed at changing the industry structure world-wide proposed in 2012 and, after a number of revisions, re-proposed in 2016.[4] The ability of these funds to transmit funding risk drew the attention of regulators and academic researchers.[5] Despite all the attention these funds have received in recent years, a common de jure definition of a money market fund remains elusive. Indeed, our study across European jurisdictions reveals that there exist numerous versions of money market funds in as many countries. Nevertheless, we believe that if our aim is to improve market structure, then a proper analysis from a regulatory perspective should begin with the de facto structure of the functioning markets. Thus, we offer an initial abstraction of the de facto market with a few broad strokes of money market funds practice.

Money market funds essentially are low-risk collective investment schemes that serve as a conservative investment option for risk-averse investors and a temporary safe storage for cash. Figure 8.1 presents the main features of a money market fund structure.

Figure 8.1 depicts the flow of investments into a money market fund in exchange for shares and dividends. A money market fund, in turn, invests the proceeds from the sale of its shares in securities issued by various entities such as banks, corporations, and municipal and state governments that could be located in any country. When investors need their cash back, the process is reversed. To raise cash, a money market fund may rely on due proceeds from securities or sell its portfolio assets in the secondary market.[6] Because money market funds only invest in high quality securities[7] with short maturities, generally within one year, it is expected that a money market fund would be able to sell its assets without incurring material losses.[8] Therefore, investors in a money market fund expect to sell their shares back to the fund with no loss on the purchase price. This expectation explains the essential beneficial characteristics of money market funds to investors: they are collective investment schemes that provide safety of principal, and liquidity and yield consistent with short-term market rates.[9] In the US, which accounts for the largest share of money market funds' assets under management,[10]

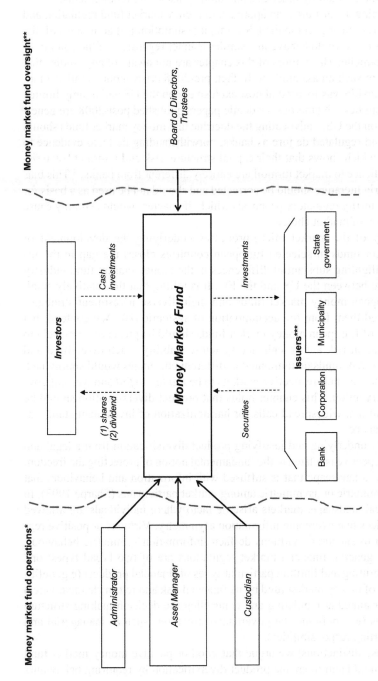

Figure 8.1 Money market fund structure.

Note:

* Operational support could structured differently depending on jurisdictional requirements

** Oversight could be provided in a different form depending on jurisdictional requirements

*** Issuers of securities purchased by money market funds are not necessarily entities located in the US or the EU, but could be organised/registered in different countriesMoney

money market funds are defined under federal securities laws by referring to their principal characteristics, which include limitations on investment risks, specific operational and accounting practices, and unique disclosure requirements.[11]

In developing a pan-European approach to money market fund regulation and taking cues from their peers in the US, a major assumption is that in times of distress, shareholders would behave in a similar manner regardless of the country of the fund's domicile. The authors of this chapter are not aware of any studies that would confirm such an assumption. In fact, pre-2008 crisis money market fund-related scholarship was focused almost exclusively on the US and mainly limited to financial studies.[12] Numerous academic papers published post-2008 are generally focused on the US,[13] advocating the doctrine that money market funds should be lumped and regulated de jure as banks, notwithstanding de facto evidence to the contrary which shows that their capital structure, risk and return characteristics, and resilience to market turmoil are entirely different from banks.[14] This bias in the scholarly literature should be corrected and should not be used as a basis for regulators to justify regulatory proposals which, if enacted, would certainly cause the destruction of market choice.

Our study of the market micro-processes underlying the development of money market funds in selected European countries closes the gap in the literature, highlighting substantial differences in the money market fund industry infrastructure between the US and the EU. It is telling that the relatively small size of European money market funds and their diverse investment strategies have protected them from the accumulation of systemic risk. We contend that the diversity of European money market funds should be preserved precisely to reduce contagion risk and to enhance systemic stability. Such diversified and relatively low-risk funds denominated in different currencies would simply lack the significance in their respective markets to be *too big to fail* and warrant government intervention. This chapter holds that product diversification should be promoted and that widespread calls for harmonization of investment standards should be resisted.

The theory underlying and justifying product diversification from a legal and financial perspective is related to the fundamental notion of protecting the freedom of contract in a landscape that is suffused with information and behaviours that are either symmetric or asymmetric among market participants (Sharpe 1993). In this theoretical landscape, markets arise de facto where individuals are allowed to make choices that overcome information asymmetry. Virtuous or positive regulations tend to encourage virtuous de facto information symmetric behaviour. However, in general, financial market regulations are of two broad types: one aimed at permitting and limiting particular types of financial products (e.g. defining the types of money market fund by its financial risk and return characteristics) and the other aimed at regulating and controlling the decision-making structure of institutions (e.g. defining the governance structures, such as managerial and internal reporting responsibilities).

Given these distinctions, we argue that good or positive money market fund regulations should aim to enable product diversification by requiring behaviours which enhance product transparency for the benefit of investors. That is, regulations in the financial world should encourage risk symmetry and arbitrage, and positive money market fund regulations should encourage the social comity of de facto market participation. Conversely, money market fund regulations that discourage market participation should be strongly limited. For example, calls for the harmonization of investment standards tend to lessen market product choice, and may, if implemented, lead to immediate market failure.

The rest of this chapter is organized as follows: the first section is the introduction and presents the generic definition of money market funds and discusses our theoretical premises. The second section outlines the historical background for the development of money market funds in selected European countries. The third section examines the harmonization initiatives with respect to European money market funds. It also offers a critical view of these initiatives on the grounds of their limited benefits to the local investment communities and general concerns related to aggregation of systemic risk.

Origin of European money market funds

This chapter focuses on European money market funds defined by the guidelines on a common definition of European money market funds, which came into effect in May 2011, and are currently administered by the European Securities and Markets Authorities.[15] These funds, domiciled in the different EU countries, are governed by national laws of the respective country, whose interpretation of the common definition guidelines may vary. Furthermore, national regulators have discretion to introduce additional laws targeting money market fund, if warranted. Thus, European money market funds have historically had varying underlying legal regimes and varying risk characteristics, which in turn have resulted in a lack of cross-border comparability, as will be shown later in this section through the study of money market fund development in selected European countries.

To provide broader cross-border comparability and achieve greater distribution outside the country of domicile (referred to as a "home country"), European money market funds may choose to be authorized under the Undertakings for Collective Investments in Transferable Securities ("UCITS") Directive.[16] These UCITS authorized money market funds must follow risk-spreading rules laid out in the UCITS Directive, as transposed into the respective national laws. Finally, European money market funds are subject to other relevant notices and guidelines, which provide recommendations with respect to operational, accounting and risk management issues.[17] It is evident from the analysis below that the current structure of the European money market fund industry is geared towards meeting the needs of investors, with different types of fund products designed according to their operational and tax requirements as well as risk and return preferences. The following six sub-sections present the historical background of the money market fund industries in selected European countries and explain the fund development in the context of the prevailing market environment and regulation.

France

France led the development of European money market funds in the early 1980s (Lambrechts 1995). The reason for the emergence of money market funds in France was the restrictive banking regime where French bank regulation capped the interest rate that banks could pay their clients on savings accounts (Le Coz 2009). Thus, French money market funds were able to offer their investors a return consistent with the market rates, when banks could not. Coincidentally, in order to accelerate the post-recession economic recovery in the early 1980s, the French government increased issuance of short-term government obligations and encouraged retail investor participation by offering a tax credit (Poizot *et al.* 2006).[18] Due to both a relatively high yield and a tax credit, government securities have quickly become an attractive investment option for retail investors providing a strong impetus for development of *SICAV Monetaire*, French collective investment schemes that facilitated investor participation in this market.[19]

SICAV Monetaire invested in government and corporate obligations of relatively short duration, and tracking short-term interest rates were marketed as money market funds. Unlike the US money market funds, which developed to a considerable product standardization, the French money market funds have always featured varied risk profiles. Historically, three broad types of French money market funds were recognized: *regular* money market funds, *dynamic* money market funds and *dynamic plus* money market funds, although a classification of these funds has always presented a challenge owing to the diversity of investment strategies and the lack of a commonly accepted definition of European money market funds.[20] The most conservative *regular* French money market funds were managed to track short-term market indices, while *dynamic* and *dynamic plus* money market funds sought to obtain additional yield by investing a part of their portfolios in riskier assets.[21]

Because French money market funds were aimed at tracking short-term market indices, share prices of these funds could increase or decrease depending on the behaviour of the selected index. Therefore, French money market funds have been referred to as *variable net asset values* money market funds.[22] In practice, share prices of French money market funds generally exhibited a steady growth due to a continuing reinvestment of capital gains and dividends (Le Coz 2009).[23] A comforting perception of a steady increase in share price was facilitated by a lack of *market-based* pricing in French money market funds.[24] Until the early 2000s, French money market funds have fully relied on amortized cost accounting to smooth out share price fluctuations.[25] The distinctive attributes of French money market funds – an attractive yield relative to bank deposits, a tax advantage and an impression of a steady positive performance – explain why French money market funds quickly gained investors' acceptance and still command a substantial share of the European money market fund industry today.[26]

Ireland

In the early 1990s, Ireland, one of the two main fund administration centres in Europe, became a platform for the development of money market funds in

Europe. The demand for money market fund administration services came from the US asset managers, who observed growing interest from multinational corporations for professional cash management outside the US. This explains why the US-style money market funds in Europe to this day are mainly managed by the US asset managers for the benefit of their institutional clients operating multinationally. Money market funds transplanted to Europe from the US were managed just like their US peers and became known as the US-style money market funds, but denominated in various European currencies. The US-style funds were featuring constant net asset values per share and were managed in line with risk-limiting provisions that are supportive to low volatility of portfolio assets.

Arriving in Ireland, the US-style money market funds exported the US cash culture, its investment and operational practices. In the absence of de jure regulation, de facto US market practices were adopted by fund managers voluntarily. Ireland was able to harvest the benefits of development in international trade and cross-border cash flows that, in turn, prompted expansion of the US money market funds overseas by virtue of its flexible regulatory regime and responsive fund service industry.[27]

Luxembourg

Luxembourg, another major European fund administration centre, likewise benefitted from the acceleration of cross-border cash flows. However, due to its proximity to France, the early versions of Luxembourg money market funds originating in the 1980s strongly resembled their French peers. The main reason for the migration of French money market funds to Luxembourg was taxation. As mentioned previously, French money market funds provided investors with tax-advantageous income, but only if the funds invested at least 90 per cent of their assets domestically. Thus, while providing tax-advantaged income, these funds could only offer investors limited diversification options. Money market funds sought to enlarge their investment universe by allocating more assets to foreign securities, but they still wanted to do it in a tax-efficient way. These funds found Luxembourg in terms of its regulatory regime the right destination supporting this objective.

Advantageous tax treatment is the major factor behind the growth of Luxembourg money market funds featuring *floating net asset values* per share, which was widely accepted by investors in other European countries studied, e.g. in Germany, Spain and France. Following the development of US-style money market funds initially hosted mainly by Ireland, Luxembourg fund services quickly embraced the US-style funds offering *constant net asset values* per share. Both Ireland and Luxembourg transposed the UCITS Directive into their national laws by the late 1980s thus enabling their funds to pursue business freely across the EU on the basis of a single authorization issued by the host country authorities.[28]

The presence of the UCITS framework for marketing collective investment schemes throughout Europe has been the most important factor enabling distribution growth of the US-style money market funds. These funds were offered mainly to institutional investors who sought professional cash management services generated only nominal sales in the host country.[29] The US-style money market funds, whether domiciled in Ireland or Luxembourg, were almost exclusively sold cross-border as opposed to French money market funds which were mainly sold to French investors (Poizot *et al.* 2006).

Germany

In 1994, money market funds were introduced to Germany after considerable resistance by the Bundesbank.[30] Similar to the US banking industry, German banks were fully aware of the competitive threat of money market funds to the banking community. Another reason for the Bundesbank's resistance was a likely distortion to its control of the monetary base.[31] Similar to the money market funds operating in France, the core objective of German money market funds was a performance broadly in line with money market benchmarks (Le Coz 2009). German regulators limited final maturities of money market fund-eligible holdings to one year (Jank and Wedow 2009), which brought domestic money market funds in line with a "qualifying" money market fund definition adopted for statistical purposes by the European Central Bank in 1998.[32]

From the standpoint of asset valuation, German money market funds have always relied on *market-based* asset values and included interest income in the share price (Jank and Wedow 2009). German money market funds were managed with an implicit assumption that a share price of a conservatively managed fund would not decline significantly on any single day. The assumption boded well with retail clients, who were the main investors in German money market funds (Le Coz 2009: 1). The concept of a constant share price, so favoured by the US money market fund investors, never took hold in Germany. Its money market funds were not treated any differently for the purpose of asset pricing than any other collective investment scheme. Furthermore, it was too operationally burdensome and costly for asset managers to establish separate asset valuation practices and to fund accounting systems designed specifically for money market funds, given their limited size of assets under management.[33] Thus, a slow growth of assets under management in German money market funds could be explained by a low level of institutional investor participation. German business culture, with its traditional reliance on banks for all cash management needs by corporate entities, rendered money market funds predominantly retail-based.[34]

As mentioned earlier in this section, taxation played an important role in shaping the landscape of European money market funds. It was the issue of taxation that placed German money market funds in an unfair competitive position with other UCITS-authorized money market funds established elsewhere in Europe, and it ultimately inhibited the growth of *domestic* money market funds.[35] As much as money market fund investors loathed uncertainty, certainty of taxes is something they would prefer to avoid. While income derived from investments in German-based money market funds could be taxed at the same rate as income from cross-border money market funds, investors in *domestic* funds were disadvantaged in terms of the timing of tax payments. Tax on investment income from *domestic* funds was deducted at the time when an investor received such income. Therefore, an investor would receive a lower *after*-tax income. Money market funds sold cross-border paid out income *before* taxes and was taxed only in the following year after such income was received.

Thus, German money market funds have never become a significant factor in the German financial system, as the taxation issue and the strong banking culture have pre-empted widespread investor acceptance.

Spain

The Spanish money market developed in the mid-1980s, facilitated by the introduction of Letras de Tesoro (Treasury Bills) in 1987. In addition to government securities, Spanish banking and corporate sectors issued a variety of money market instruments, including commercial paper, certificates of deposit, medium-term notes and term deposits suitable for purchases of these funds. Spanish money market funds known as *fondos de inversion en activos del mercado monetario*, or investment funds in money market assets, were among the main investors in short-term government and corporate securities.

Notably, an investment objective of Spanish money market funds to track short-term interest rates was consistent with that of French and German money market funds; thus, Spanish money market funds' share prices were expected to fluctuate, reflecting the interest rate movements. In practice, investors in these funds expected the value of their shares to increase steadily due to accumulation of capital gain and interest income, consistent with investors' expectations of money market fund performance in France and Germany. Thus, due to similarities in investment objective, to track short-term interest rates, and an expectation of steady increases in fund share prices due to accumulation of capital gains and interest income, these types of funds are often considered as a homogenous group of *continental* European money market funds.[36]

The United Kingdom

The history of European money market funds would be incomplete without mentioning the UK, even though its own *domestic* money market fund industry is rather limited.[37] An example of the UK money market funds illustrates the importance of other factors for the industry development, including the position of banks and the presence of a deep and liquid public market. Fidelity Investments, one of the largest US asset managers, laid the foundation of the UK money market fund industry in the late 1980s, when it launched its first British pound sterling-denominated entity, Fidelity Cash Unit Trust.[38] It should be noted that money market funds were not permitted as authorized unit trusts until 1988 (Lambrechts 1995). Fidelity was one of the first fund management groups to offer an alternative means of managing cash to its institutional clients doing business in Europe.

Launched by a US asset manager, the fund mirrored investment and operational polices accepted by the US money market funds.[39]

It should be noted that local UK investors did not have any particular need to look beyond banks. The UK banking regulation did not limit deposit rates the way French regulators did. Therefore, the UK banks were able to offer market rates, thus causing emerging money market funds to lose a meaningful yield advantage. Another significant factor inhibiting the development of the UK money market funds was scarcity of government and corporate short-term issuance. The UK corporations relied mainly on bank financing for their borrowing needs and did not actively utilize the public market. These two factors, namely competition from banks and the limited public short-term market, curtailed the development of the UK money market fund industry.

Preliminary conclusion

Major themes can be drawn from this historical narrative relating to the early days of the European money market fund industry. First, domestic bank reg- ulation which limited interest rates on bank deposit accounts, was a strong positive factor for money market funds (e.g. France). A lack of such regulation left money market funds without a competitive advantage and hampered their development (e.g. the UK). Second, the development of *domestic* European money market funds has been strongly correlated with the depth of the local short-term markets. The limited size of the local corporate issuance restricted money market funds' investment options and prevented the funds from achiev- ing sufficient economy of scale to support their operations (e.g. in Germany and the UK). On the other hand, an active local short-term market promoted *domestic* money market funds (e.g. in France). Third, a favourable tax treat- ment helped *domestic* money market funds to gain investors' acceptance (e.g. in France). Alternatively, a disadvantaged tax regime inhibited growth of *domestic* money market funds and pushed fund origination and management to European fund administration centres (e.g. Germany).

European money market fund regulation

The perceived need to regulate money market funds in Europe has been made most explicit at the EU level, as evidenced in a number of normative documents. This chapter limits the discussion to what we consider to be the primary legislation relevant to money market funds administered throughout the EU. Specifically, the UCITS Directive,[40] and the guidelines on a common definition of European money market funds, referred to in this chapter as the "ESMA Guidelines",[41] all of which are currently administered by the European Securities and Markets Authority, and which represent the primary source of harmonized rules for European money market funds. We must also note a lengthy debate related to further codifying and reforming European money market fund regulation at the EU level.[42] That said, at the time of this chapter, no resolution of the debate has been reached.

It appears that the desire for developing a single market for financial services in the EU and the related quest for harmonizing regulation and oversight drives the policy debate towards providing regulation that controls investment activities and operations of money market funds throughout Europe. However, as opposed to the elevated profile of the money market fund-related debate at the EU level, it appears that this issue is rather insignificant for the great majority of national regulators. This could be explained by the relatively limited size of the local money market fund industries – with the notable exceptions of France, Ireland and Luxembourg – and a negligible impact of these funds on capital market activities in the majority of EU countries. The following sections examine how investment activities and marketing and distribution of money market funds in the EU are affected by the existing pan-European regulatory framework.

UCITS framework

While the UCITS Directive does not target money market funds specifically, it still serves as a primary source for harmonized rules at the Community level, applicable to European money market funds registered under the UCITS brand. There are, however, two general limitations of the UCITS regulatory framework regarding money market fund regulation. First, as explained later in this section, generic investment parameters established under the UCITS regime are too broad and, per se, do not satisfy the spirit of the low-risk investment product that money market funds are meant to be. Second, a UCITS authorization is not compulsory.

Since its adoption, the UCITS Directive has undergone a number of adjustments. The current version, known as the UCITS IV, was approved in July 2009.[43] Essential for establishing a harmonized investment product, the UCITS IV Directive outlines a general framework for investment schemes operating under the UCITS brand. First, a UCITS must operate on a *principle of risk spreading*.[44] Second, a UCITS must be open-ended, i.e. investors should be able to redeem shares or units on demand. Third, a UCITS must be liquid.[45] Fourth, assets must be entrusted to an independent custodian or depositary and held in a separate account on behalf of investors.[46] The UCITS-authorized money market funds adhere to these common product rules notwithstanding their long-standing differences in investment management culture, national tax laws and regulatory regimes discussed earlier.

In full accord with the general UCITS framework, money market funds operating under the UCITS brand seek to offer investors a convenient way to invest collectively in money market securities based on the principle of risk spreading. Besides its focus on facilitating cross-border distribution, the UCITS Directive laid out a set of standards related to eligible asset types and risk exposures in registered investment schemes. Specifically, the UCITS Directive sought to limit credit risk by restricting exposures to a single issuer, counterparty and a group of affiliated issuers, as well as investments in other UCITS.[47]

Given the UCITS's flexibility with respect to transposition to national laws, local versions of these prudential rules may vary reflecting the structure of national capital markets. In addition, as mentioned earlier, investment limitations of the UCITS IV Directive that were designed to address a wide range of investment products may not be sufficient to adequately restrict credit, market and liquidity risks in money market funds. Therefore, while achieving a great deal for a broad harmonization of European investment practices, the UCITS IV Directive was viewed as an insufficient tool to substitute for targeted pan-European money market fund regulation. The European Securities and Markets Authority, a successor of the Commission of European Securities Regulators, has become the regulatory body in charge of administering and enforcing guidelines related to a common definition of European money market funds.[48]

European Securities and Markets Authority

Regulatory oversight of the European Securities and Markets Authority to money market funds is multi-pronged and includes issuances of guidelines concerning investment and operational practices as well as information transparency. Importantly for money market funds, the guidelines legalized amortized cost valuation for money market instruments by all UCITS provided that amortized cost valuation "will not result in a material discrepancy between the value of [an instrument] and [its amortized cost value]".[49]

The guidelines further advise asset managers to monitor potential discrepancies between the market-based value of portfolio assets and their amortized cost to avoid *material* discrepancies between these two values. Furthermore, shares or units of those UCITS that invest solely in high quality, short maturity instruments may be valued at amortized cost.[50] This guideline mimics, albeit in a general and simplified way, the valuation approach employed by the US money market funds. Nonetheless, the Commission of European Securities Regulators' guideline does not define parameters of *material* discrepancies, thus UCITS including European money market funds may potentially have varying thresholds of materiality.[51] Thus, valuations may vary radically depending on individual fund practices. This variation, in practice, exemplifies the lack of specificity in EU regulation which should, but does not, address important micro-processes of market infrastructure. The lack of specificity, in turn, hinders the development of a uniform regulatory regime in financial services. In relation to our theory that successful de facto money market regulation should replicate de facto market practice, the current European de jure regulations provide too much discretion to managers in determining the essential meaning of money market funds. The effect of regulatory vagueness where specific market practice is not replicated has the effect of leading investors into believing that characteristics normally associated with money market funds exist when in fact they may be missing. To cure this fault in the regulatory regime, we would urge regulators to come up with definitions that are in accord with market practice expectations.

Conscious that the money market fund definition is crucial for market development, it is important to point out that the most significant regulation from the perspective of the money market fund industry is the European Securities and

Markets Authority's function of administering and enforcing a common definition of European money market funds that came into effect in July 2011.[52] European money market fund definitions used prior to 2011 were developed by the European Central Bank and MiFID and described these funds as collective investment schemes akin to bank demand deposits.[53] These definitions were tailored to the tasks of the respective organizations, but were not meant to cover the entire diverse landscape of European money market funds at that time. In May 2010, the Committee of European Securities Regulators issued the guidelines on a common definition, which codified specific portfolio management and operational rules deemed appropriate for European money market funds.[54] Given the diversity of these funds, the guidelines provided for a flexible two-tier structure of the European money market fund industry.

The two-tier structure sought to make de jure different kinds of money market funds already de facto in the European marketplace and assist investors in distinguishing between two major types of money market funds: those holding short-dated securities and those investing in relatively longer-dated assets. The majority of the US-style liquidity money market funds were expected to fall within the short-term money market fund category, and regular money market funds were expected to fall into the money market fund category.[55] This diversity in de jure structure illustrates the divergence of de facto market segments.

Notwithstanding the differences in risk profiles of the two fund types, both categories of money market funds must meet three requirements. First, the primary objective of the fund must be to maintain principal and provide returns in line with money market rates.[56] Second, the fund must invest in money market instruments that comply with criteria set out under the UCITS IV Directive or in deposits with credit institutions.[57] Third, the fund must provide daily price calculations and daily liquidity.[58] Definitional standards related to quality, diversification and maturity applicable to both fund categories are presented in Table 8.1. These standards apply to all European money market funds regardless of the country of domicile and cover both UCITS-authorized funds and ones regulated under national laws.[59]

As can be seen from Table 8.1 and the following discussion, these rules go some way in establishing certain investment benchmarks, but are not anywhere near sufficient in providing guidance for genuine pan-European de jure standardization, which would protect investors de facto. For example, the objective standard of high quality relies on credit ratings assigned by rating agencies.[60] The guidance does not seek to further spread credit risk in money market funds through any additional diversification requirements above and beyond those imposed by the UCITS IV Directive. Given this approach, those money market funds unauthorized by the UCITS IV Directive could be managed to varying diversification requirements based on national laws and thus exhibiting varying degrees of concentration risk.[61] Furthermore, (regular) money market funds are able to assume higher credit risk through investments in relatively low rated sovereign securities, driving the differences in credit profiles between short-term and (regular) money market funds farther apart.[62] Thus, extending to the relatively lower spectrum of credit risk, the rule may actually promote greater

Table 8.1 Risk-limiting provisions for European money market funds[63]

Elements	Provisions	
	Short-term money market fund	*(Regular) Money market fund*
Quality	Subjective standard: Each portfolio holding should be of high quality Objective standard: A security should not be considered of high quality unless it has been awarded one of the two highest available short-term credit ratings by each recognized credit rating agency	In addition, it may hold sovereign issuance of at least investment grade quality
Maturity	Objective standard: Each security must mature within 397 days	Each security must mature within two years
	Weighted average maturity may not exceed 60 days	Weighted average maturity may not exceed six months
	Weighted average life may not exceed 120 days	Weighted average life may not exceed 12 months

risk-taking by this type of fund, unfavourably for the fund investors seeking a low-risk investment option. Thus, in this sense, the purported de jure protection of diversification is not adequate de facto from a market practice perspective.

As another matter of de facto risk management, European money market funds manage their exposure to interest rate and market risk by limiting portfolio maturity. Table 8.1 points to three tests related to maturity. The first test limits final maturities of all eligible securities to 397 days for short-term money market funds and two years for (regular) money market funds, thus enabling (regular) money market funds to assume significantly greater market risk.[64] The other two portfolio maturity tests are designed to limit interest rate, spread and liquidity risks. Weighted-average portfolio maturity may not exceed 60 days in short-term money market funds, and six months in (regular) money market funds implies that (regular) money market funds are able to assume three times higher interest rate risk as compared to short-term money market funds.[65] To illustrate, an instant three per cent increase in interest rates would cause a short-term money market fund to lose 50 basis points, or a half of one per cent of its assets.[66] The same three per cent increase in interest rates would cause a (regular) money market fund to lose 150 basis points, or one and a half of one per cent of its assets.[67] For the sake of comparison with US money market funds, this price volatility would be deemed unacceptable by placing it well beyond the materiality threshold of 50 basis point, at which point the fund boards must consider corrective actions.[68]

European regulators also need to recognize the de facto implications of allowing a two-tiered market in money market funds. The potential for significant loss differential in two types of European money market funds – stemming mainly from the ability of (regular) money market funds to extend duration – raises concerns regarding the merits of a two-tier industry structure from the standpoint of investor protection.[69] A common definition of European money market funds attempted to address this concern by requiring the funds themselves to indicate to investors what type of money market funds they belong to.[70] No portfolio information is required to be disclosed to investors under the ESMA Guidelines, which is, in our view, one of their most significant weaknesses, since the efficient and sustainable operation of these markets depends on disclosure of such information. Without this de facto information, the de jure regulatory regime can only delude investors by lending credence to a process which does not support investor protection.

Notably, the ESMA Guidelines do not contain any specific asset liquidity standards. Instead, liquidity considerations are embedded in the asset credit quality assessment as one of the factors to consider in investment decisions.[71] This implies the regulatory view that high quality, short-term instruments are generally sufficiently liquid. However, this view ignores the abundance of credit risk and the lack of secondary market liquidity demonstrated during the financial crisis.

With respect to portfolio-level liquidity, the CESR's guidelines rely on Article 51 of the UCITS Directive requiring UCITS to employ a risk management process that enables them "to monitor and measure at any time the risk of the positions and their contribution to the overall risk profile of the portfolio".[72] Specifically related to money market funds, the risk management process should include "a prudent approach to the management of currency, credit, interest rate and liquidity risk" and stress testing.[73] Finally, with respect to liquidity of money market fund shares, the guidelines document refers to national authorities to establish an appropriate settlement process aligned to local practices.[74] Thus, as shown in this section, in establishing a de jure investment management framework for European money market funds, regulators were mainly focused on issues of credit and interest rate risk exposure in individual funds, but not very concerned with developing regulatory parameters that would promote the de facto market for European investors.

With respect to currency risk, the CESR's guidelines permit European money market funds' investments in securities denominated in other than the fund's base portfolio currencies provided exposure to the non-base currencies is fully hedged.[75] The EU regulator approached foreign currency risk by imposing disclosure requirements with respect to foreign currency trades in the funds' offering documents, but not through prohibiting or limiting transactions in foreign currencies.[76]

In the conclusion of our analysis of the common definition of European money market funds, we underscore that in introducing a uniform two-tier industry structure, the guidelines sought to provide a more detailed understanding of the de facto distinction between various types of funds operating in Europe and sold cross-border. The harmonized definition was expected "to play an active role in building a common supervisory culture by promoting common supervisory approaches and practices [within the EU]".[77] The common definition was not structured in isolation but built upon an existing framework for the regulation of harmonized investment schemes in the EU. A counterargument is that the UCITS regime implemented at the national level results in a certain degree of diversity and inconsistency. In addition, the ESMA Guidelines for a common definition cover non-harmonized collective investment undertakings established under the national laws of Member States.[78] Thus, the need to reconcile different objectives of various constituencies has weakened the regulatory response to the issue of standardization of the money market fund practices in the EU.

Notes

1 This chapter was originally prepared as a paper for the conference "Shadow Banking: A European Perspective" organized by the City Political Economy Centre at the City University London in February 2013. A later and more detailed version of the paper appears in the *Columbia Journal of European Law* (2013, 19(2), pp. 175–224). The authors are grateful to the conference participants and to Dr Anastasia Nesvetailova personally for their insightful comments. The paper also benefitted from conversations with David Vriesenga, the first head of the European money market fund business at Moody's Investors Service in the 1990s, David Hynes, one of the 'founding fathers' of the International Money Market Fund Association and Rudolf Siebel, ex-Moody's Investors Service's analyst, who is currently Managing Director/Head of Market and Service of BVI Bundesverband Investment and Asset Management e.V. All errors remain our own.

2 Dr Viktoria Baklanova, CFA, PRM is a former rating analyst at Moody's Investors Service and Fitch Ratings with over a decade of experience in the money market fund analysis. Dr Baklanova is Senior Financial Analyst at the Office of Financial Research. Views and opinions expressed are those of the authors and do not necessarily represent official Office of Financial Research or US Department of the Treasury positions or policy. Prof. Joseph Tanega is Reader International Financial Law, University of Westminster, School of Law School, Department of Advanced Legal Studies, Professor of Regulation & Supervision of Retail Banking, Alma Graduate School, University of Bologna, Adjunct Professor of Ethics & Governance, University of Grenoble, Grenoble Graduate Business School, and Professor of Law, King Abdulaziz University, Jeddah, Saudi Arabia.

3 Throughout this chapter, references to the financial crisis mean the time period starting in August 2007 through to the end of 2009 unless noted otherwise.

4 For the US regulations, see Money Market Fund Reform; Amendments to Form PF (Securities and Exchange Commission, July 2014) [MMF Reform]. Available at: www. sec.gov/rules/final/2014/33-9616.pdf (last visited 24.07.2016); for international regulation of money market funds, see Proposal for a Regulation of the European Parliament and of the Council on Money Market Funds (Council of the European Union, June 2016) [European MMF Proposal]. Available at: http://data.consilium.europa.eu/doc/document/ST-9874-2016-INIT/en/pdf (last visited 24.07.2016).

5 For the literature review related to money market funds on both sides of the Atlantic, see generally, Baklanova and Tanega (2014).

6 US money market funds are currently required by the applicable regulation to maintain at least 10 per cent of their assets in *daily liquid* securities, i.e. securities that mature on the next business day or eligible US Treasury debt securities. See 17 CFR § 270.2a-7.

7 In the money markets, high-quality securities are normally understood as securities having the strongest capacity for timely payment of financial commitments. Such securities are often rated by credit rating agencies in the highest short-term rating category, e.g. P-1 (by Moody's Investors Service, see www.moodys.com), A-1 (by Standard & Poor's, see www.standardandpoors.com) or F1 (by Fitch Ratings, see www.fitchratings.com) or judged to be of comparable quality by the money market fund's investment advisor.

8 For a discussion of what could be considered a "material loss" of value of an individual debt security, see Fisch and Roiter (2011). The materiality threshold could be as little as one tenth of one per cent. However, for a money market fund portfolio as a whole, a deviation of its per-share price of one half of one per cent from the fund's stable value is considered material enough for the fund's Board of Directors to consider actions with respect to such a deviation. See 17 CFR § 270.2a-7.

9 See also SEC, *Money Market Funds*, at www.sec.gov/spotlight/money-market.shtml (last visited 24.07.2016). The chapter highlights the use of money market funds as an alternative to the interest-bearing bank accounts.

10 As at the end of the first quarter 2016, the total assets under management of money market funds globally stood at $5 trillion, with the US money market funds accounting for $2.7 trillion, or approximately 54 per cent of the total assets. See Investment Company Institute, "Supplement: Worldwide Public Tables, First Quarter 2016, Data in US Dollars (xls) as of Jun 28, 2016". Available at: www.ici.org/research/stats/world wide. Last accessed 24.07.2016.

11 The principal characteristics of the US money market funds are codified in 17 CFR § 270.2a-7.

12 See generally, Baklanova (2010).

13 See, e.g. Birdthistle (2010), Stulz (2011).

14 For an alternative view of the massive failure of banking regulation during the financial crisis and numerous bank failures, see Volcker (2011). The response points to 2,800 cases of failures of insured depository institutions since the 1970s while only two money market funds failed during the same period of time. For literature advocating bank-like regulation for money market funds see, e.g. Ricks (2010, 2011). See also Gorton and Metrick (2010). The authors call for insurance of money market funds to guarantee their investors' payment and eliminate incentives to run.

15 CESR's Guidelines on a common definition of European money market funds (European Securities and Markets Authority 19 May 2010) [ESMA Guidelines]. Available at: www.esma.europa.eu/sites/default/files/library/2015/11/10-049_cesr_guidelines_mmfs_with_disclaimer.pdf (last accessed: 24.07.2016).

16 DIRECTIVE 2009/65/EC OF THE EUROPEAN PARLIAMENT AND OF THE COUNCIL of 13 July 2009 on the coordination of laws, regulations and administrative provisions relating to undertakings for collective investment in transferable securities (UCITS) (OJ L302/32 17 November 2009).

17 For an in-depth analysis of a regulatory framework applicable to European money market funds, see generally, Baklanova and Tanega (2014).

18 Initially, capital gains of up to FRF300,000 per year were not subject to personal tax. Starting in the mid-1990s, the limit on capital gain not subject to personal tax was lowered to FRF150,000.

19 SICAV is an open-ended collective investment scheme common in Western Europe, which is analogous to open-ended mutual funds in the US. The majority of European money market funds are SICAVs, but not all of them.

20 The use of a *money market fund* designation was standardized only in July 2011 under the guidelines on a common definition of European money market funds. See ESMA Guidelines supra note 15.

21 Short-term market indices include Euribor or Eonia. Euribor is a rate at which interbank term deposits denominated in euro currency are offered by one bank to another bank within the European Monetary Union. Eonia is an effective overnight reference rate for the euro. It is computed as a weighted average of all overnight unsecured lending transactions undertaken in the interbank market, initiated within the euro area by the contributing banks. See EMMI»EURIBOR® at www.emmi-benchmarks.eu/euribor-org/about-euribor.html (last accessed: 24.07.2016).

22 It is worth noting that many European money market funds are managed as *constant net asset value* money market funds, whose shares are sold and redeemed at a constant

price. These funds, often registered in Ireland and Luxembourg, the main Europe's fund administration centres, are sometimes referred to as *US-style* money market funds in reference to a prevailing practice in the US. After the US MMF Reform came into effect in October 2016, US institutional prime money market funds are not allowed to offer their shares at a constant price.

23 French money market funds operate with a *variable net asset value*, although they normally exhibit a *constantly increasing net asset value*.

24 See, e.g. Int'l Money Mkt. Fund Ass'n, Constant and Variable Net Asset Value Money Market Funds (Institutional Money Market Fund Association / Position paper 2011) (on file with the authors).

25 See, e.g. Poizot *et al.* (2006). In 2002 Autorité des Marchés Financiers, the French financial market regulator, imposed a mark-to-market accounting to replace an amortized-cost asset valuation for money market funds with the exception of assets maturing within three months that are still valued at amortized cost. The accounting changes came into effect on 31 December 2003.

26 See Investment Company Institute, "Supplement: Worldwide Public Tables, First Quarter 2016, Data in US Dollars (xls) as of Jun 28, 2016". Available at: www.ici. org/research/stats/worldwide (last accessed: 24.07.2016). As at the first quarter 2016, French money market funds managed over $375 billion in assets, or approximately 28 per cent of total European money market fund assets.

27 See, e.g. PriceWaterhouseCoopers, "Right Place Right Time. Ireland: The Domicile of Choice for Regulated Funds" 6 (Jan. 2012), available at: http://download.pwc.com/ie/pubs/2012_ right_place_right_time_ireland_the_domicile_of_choice_for_regulated_funds.pdf (last accessed: 24.07.2016). Ireland currently commands close to 38 per cent of assets under management of European money market funds, offers the highest quality fund administration services and an advantageous tax regime.

28 Adopted in 1985, the UCITS Directive refers to a series of European Union directives establishing a common regulatory framework for marketing collective investment schemes throughout Europe. Council Directive 85/611/EEC, On the Coordination of Laws, Regulations and Administrative Provisions Relating to Undertakings for Collective Investment in Transferable Securities (UCITS), 1985 O.J. (L 375) 3 (EC).

29 The cross-border nature of Irish money market funds is reflected in statistical methodologies for collecting data related to collective investments. To avoid double-counting of Irish funds' assets in the combined per-country statistics, these assets are normally excluded from available European investment fund statistics.

30 German money market funds were introduced as part of the II. Financial Promotion Act (Finanzmarktförderungsgesetz) enacted in July 1994. The first money market funds were launched in September 1994.

31 See Anderson (2006). Anderson provides a definition of the monetary base, which includes bank deposits. The definition does not include shares of money market funds although such shares have been viewed by some authors as a close substitute for bank deposits. This issue of monetary base has been resolved by the European Central Bank collecting statistics on assets under management of the "qualified" money market funds.

32 This regulation was last updated in September 2011 to better align the definition of money market funds qualifying for statistical purposes with ESMA Guidelines. See REGULATION OF THE EUROPEAN CENTRAL BANK (EU) No 883/2011 of 25 August 2011 amending Regulation (EC) No 25/2009 concerning the balance sheet of the monetary financial institutions sector (ECB/2008/32) (ECB/2011/12) (OJ L 228: 13–15, 03.09.2011).

33 We note that there is a special challenge in obtaining precise statistics regarding the size of the *domestic* money market fund industry in Germany. The great majority of money market funds sold to German investors are UCITS funds domiciled elsewhere, mainly in neighbouring Luxembourg. Available statistics only report home country assets

excluding assets of those funds sold cross-border. For example, assets under management of German money market funds are only reported for those fund organized in Germany, which stood at $10.5 billion, or 0.8 per cent of the total assets under management of European money market funds as of the first quarter of 2016. Supra note 10.

34 For example, German corporate treasurers prefer keeping operating funds in a bank deposit account. Cash in a bank can be accessed immediately, as opposed to money market fund investments, which entail a somewhat more operationally burdensome process of analysing a money market fund and authorizing share purchases and redemptions.

35 While precise data are difficult to obtain, anecdotal evidences suggest that a significant part of money market fund assets in Germany is managed by Luxembourg-based funds. German asset managers have long established subsidiaries in neighbouring Luxembourg to take advantage of responsive and flexible Luxembourg financial authorities that promptly authorized new products and had less restrictive investment regulation.

36 The group of *continental* European money market funds include money market funds domiciled in certain other countries of continental Europe pursuing a similar investment objective and offering a *variable net asset value* share price. Because assets under management of *domestic* money market funds in these countries are relatively small, they are omitted from this study.

37 Supra note 10. As at the first quarter of 2016, assets under management of the UK money market funds were $6.3 billion, or 0.5 per cent of total assets under management in European money market funds.

38 Fidelity International, Fidelity Cash Fund, "A Safe Haven for Your Cash". Available at: www.fidelity.co.uk/static/pdf/investor/forms-documents/cash-fund-brochure.pdf (last accessed: 24.07.2016).

39 As opposed to *continental* European money market funds, Fidelity Cash Unit Trust maintained *constant net asset values* per share and daily liquidity at par. The fund was marketed as an alternative to bank deposits and had no penalties for early withdrawals.

40 Parliament and Council Directive 2009/65, [2009] OJ L302/32.

41 See ESMA Guidelines supra note 15.

42 See the timeline of relevant regulatory proposals at "Better Regulation, Money Market Funds (MMFs)" at www.betterregulation.com/ie/hot-topic/money-market-funds-mmfs (last accessed: 24.07.2016).

43 Parliament and Council Directive 2009/65, [2009] OJ L302/32.

44 Ibid. at 63–64, in which the UCITS Directive spells out specific limits on the spread of investments and an allowable level of leverage.

45 See "The Rise of UCITS III" (BlackRock, ViewPoints, September 2010) (explaining that the underlying assumption of the UCITS Directive is that *transferable* securities, or those traded on organized exchanges are *liquid* securities. An asset manager must be able to sell fund assets in the secondary market to raise enough cash to meet redemptions in the fund and make payment for these redemptions at least on the next day. In practice, the vast majority of money market funds market themselves as being able to make payment for redemptions daily).

46 Listing the following safeguards, embedded in the UCITS Directive, also referred to as "the six pillars of investor protection in the asset management industry": authorization rules; risk management framework; management of conflicts of interest; information disclosure; regulatory and third-party oversight; and quality and integrity of investment professionals.

47 Parliament and Council Directive 2009/65, [2009] OJ L302/32 at 63.

48 ESMA Guidelines supra note 15.

49 CESR's guidelines concerning eligible assets for investment by UCITS (Committee of European Securities Regulators, March 2007) at article/paragraph 8 (stating that valuing a money market security with "a residual maturity of less than three months and

with no specific sensitivity to market parameters, including credit risk" at amortized cost would be appropriate).

50 Ibid. at 8 (defining eligible UCITS as those investing "solely in high-quality instruments with as a general rule a maturity or residual maturity of at most 397 days or regular yield adjustments [within 397 days] . . . and with a weighted average maturity of 60 days").

51 17 CFR § 270.2a-7 (c)(8)(ii) (defining a deviation between amortized cost-based net asset value per share and its market-based value of one half of one per cent as material).

52 ESMA Guidelines supra note 15.

53 For an analysis of these definitions, see ESMA Guidelines supra note 15, Chapter 3.

54 Ibid.

55 CESR, *Consultation Paper: A Common Definition of European Money Market Funds* at 5–6, CESR/09–850 (20 October 2009) (recognizing a distinction between those money market funds operating with objectives of capital preservation and daily liquidity, which are, in fact, US-style money market funds and other money market funds that operate with a longer duration and weighted-average life).

56 ESMA Guidelines supra note 15 at Box 2, paragraph 1 and Box 3, paragraph 1.

57 Ibid. at Box 2, paragraph 2 and Box 3, paragraph 1.

58 Ibid. at Box 2, paragraph 6 and Box 3, paragraph 1. Daily liquidity requirement means that the fund must allow daily subscriptions and redemptions of its shares or units. Exception is made for those non-UCITS money market funds marketed solely through employee savings schemes and/or to specific categories of investors. These funds may provide weekly subscriptions and redemptions.

59 Ibid. at paragraph 3.

60 ESMA Guidelines supra note 15 at 9, paragraph 11. This standard must be maintained at all times while the fund holds the security. If the rating no longer complies with the guidelines, a management company must take corrective actions.

61 Ibid. at 3.

62 Ibid. at 3. The allowance for investment grade sovereign securities was introduced to accommodate "possible difficulties" that would arise for funds based on lower rated European countries and the need for financing of short-term sovereign debt across the European Union.

63 Table 8.2 is our own elaboration. The linguistic ambiguity of the ESMA Guidelines with respect to the use of the term "a money market fund" should be noted. On the one hand, the ESMA Guidelines use the term "a money market fund" in a generic sense to encompass those collective investment schemes subject to the said Guidelines. On the other, the ESMA Guidelines refer to a special type of "money market funds" that is managed within a broader risk profile. Understandably, the readers could perceive this ambiguous definition as cumbersome and unduly confusing. To avoid confusion, in this chapter we refer to those funds managed within a broader risk profile under the ESMA Guidelines as (regular) *money market funds* inserting the word 'regular' in parenthesis to distinguish these funds from *short-term money market funds*.

64 Ibid. at 6. The two-tier approach has recognized the historical de facto structure of the European money market fund industry and codified "the distinction between short-term money market funds, which operate a very short weighted average maturity and weighted average life, and (regular) money market funds, which operate a longer weighted average maturity and weighted average life".

65 Weighted-average maturity serves as a measure of a portfolio's modified duration that indicates the charge in value of a fixed income security for a given change in the level of interest rates. See Stigum and Crescenzi (2007: 85). In this example, a fund portfolio as a whole is viewed as a single security.

66 Ibid. The calculation assumes that a short-term money market fund has a maximum allowable weighted-average maturity of 60 days.

67 Ibid. The calculation assumptions that a (regular) money market fund has a maximum allowable weighted-average maturity of six months.
68 17 CFR § 270.2a-7.
69 See CESR, *Feedback Statement: CESR's Guidelines on a Common Definition of European Money Market Funds*, CESR/10-545 (19 May 2010) at 4, paragraph 2 (noted that respondents expressed mixed views regarding the proposed names of the two categories of money market funds. Some respondents suggested replacing the longer-term money market funds denomination with short-term bond funds).
70 ESMA Guidelines supra note 15 at Box 1, paragraphs 3 and 4. In addition, all European money market funds must indicate in their prospectuses and, in the case of UCITS, in their Key Investor Information Document, whether it is a short-term money market fund or a (regular) money market fund.
71 Ibid. at Box 2, paragraph 3(d). In addition, money market instruments must comply with the criteria set forth in the Parliament and Council Directive 2009/65, [2009] OJ L302/32. Non-UCITS money market funds are mandated to ensure that the liquidity of the portfolio is assessed on an equivalent basis.
72 ESMA Guidelines supra note 15, 10, paragraph 20. See also Parliament and Council Directive 2009/65, [2009] OJ L302/32 at Article 51(1).
73 ESMA Guidelines supra note 15, at 10, paragraph 20. See also Parliament and Council Directive 2010/43/EU, [2010] OJ L176/42 at Article 12. An implementing Directive mandates every management company operating under the UCITS brand to establish a permanent risk management function.
74 ESMA Guidelines supra note 15 at 9, paragraph 14. Notwithstanding the derogation of the settlement to national authorities, it was expected that "as a matter of best practice for UCITS money market funds, settlement would not exceed T+3". This means that the payment for redeemed money market shares would be made by the management company within three days after the shares had been redeemed. Fund shares, however, could be redeemed on a daily basis in line with Article 84(1) of the Parliament and Council Directive 2009/65, [2009] OJ L302/32.
75 ESMA Guidelines supra note 15, at Box 2, paragraph 11 and Box 3, paragraph 1. European money market funds are invested in securities denominated in various currencies, with funds investing in securities denominated in US dollars, British pound sterling and euros being the most widely accepted by investors. Investments in securities denominated in other than the portfolio base currency present additional investment risks.
76 ESMA Guidelines supra note 15, at 10.
77 ESMA, Questions and Answers: A Common Definition of European Money Market Funds (European Securities and Markets Authority August 2011) ESMA/2012/113 at 3.
78 ESMA Guidelines supra note 15, at 3.

References

Anderson, R. G. (2006) *Monetary Base* 2. Fed. Reserve Bank of Saint Louis, Working Paper 2006–049A. Available at: http://research.stlouisfed.org/wp/2006/2006–049.pdf. Last accessed: 25.06.2016.

Baklanova, V. (2010) *Money Market Funds: An Introduction to the Literature*. Working Paper. Available at: http://papers.ssrn.com/sol3/papers.cfm?abstract_id=1542983. Last accessed: 24.07.2016.

Baklanova, V. and J. Tanega, eds. (2014) *Money Market Funds in the EU and the US: Regulation and Practice*. Oxford, UK: Oxford University Press.

Birdthistle, W. A. (2010) *Breaking Bucks in Money Market Funds*. 5 Wisconsin Law Review 1155. Available at: http://scholarship.kentlaw.iit.edu/cgi/viewcontent. cgi?article=1076&context=fac_schol. Last accessed: 06.04.2017.

Fisch, J. E. and E. D. Roiter (2011) *A Floating NAV for Money Market Funds: Fix or Fantasy?* University of Pennsylvania, Institute for Law and Economics Research Paper, no. 11–30. Available at: http://scholarship.law.upenn.edu/faculty_scholarship/379/. Last accessed 23.04.2017.

Gorton, G. B., and A. Metrick (2010) *Regulating the Shadow Banking System.* Brookings Papers on Economic Activity 261. Available at: www.brookings.edu/~/media/Files/Programs/ES/BPEA/2010_fall_bpea_papers/2010b_bpea_gorton.pdf. Last accessed: 06.04.2017.

Jank, S. and M. Wedow (2009) *Sturm und Drang in Money Market Funds: When Money Market Funds Cease to be Narrow.* Deutsche Bundesbank, Discussion Paper Series 2: Banking and Financial Studies. Available at: http://papers.ssrn.com/sol3/papers.cfm?abstract_id=1333024. Last accessed: 24.07.2016.

Lambrechts, H. A. (1995) "Money Market Funds: The Missing Link in the South African Unit Trust Industry". *Journal of the Investment Analysts Society of South Africa* 11(9). Available at: www.iassa.co.za/articles/041_win1995_01.pdf. Last accessed: 24.06.2016.

Le Coz, G. (2009) "The Importance of Definition". *Finance Director Europe.* Available at: http://www.the-financedirector.com/features/feature63565/. Last accessed: 06.04.2017.

Poizot, A. *et al.* (2006) *French Money Market Funds.* Fitch Ratings. Available at: www.fitchratings.com/creditdesk/reports/report_frame.cfm?rpt_id=275636. Last accessed: 25.01.2013. Pay to view report.

Ricks, M. (2010) *Shadow Banking and Financial Regulation.* Columbia Law and Economics Working Paper, no. 370. Available at: https://papers.ssrn.com/sol3/papers.cfm?abstract_id=1571290. Last accessed 06.04.2017.

Ricks, M. (2011) "Regulating Money Creation after the Crisis". *Harvard Business Law Review*, 75(1), pp. 75–143.

Sharpe, W. F. (1993) *Nuclear Financial Economics.* Stanford University, Graduate School of Business Research paper 1275. Available at: www.gsb.stanford.edu/faculty-research/working-papers/nuclear-financial-economics. Last accessed: 06.04.2017.

Stigum, M. and A. Crescenzi (2007) *Stigum's Money Market.* 4th ed. New York: McGraw-Hill.

Stulz, R. M. (2011) *The Squam Lake Group Comment Letter to the PWG's Report on Money Market Fund Reform.* Comment Letter to the PWG's Report on Money Market Fund Reform Options SEC Rel. No. IC-29497 (on file with The Securities and Exchange Committee).

Volcker, P. A. (2011) *Supplemental Comment of Federated Investors, Inc. in Response to Comment of Mr. Paul A. Volcker* in J. D. Hawke Jr. File No. 4–619; Release No. IC-29497 President's Working Group Report on Money Market Fund Reform; Supplemental Comment of Federated Investors, Inc. in Response to Comment of Mr. Paul A. Volcker (US Securities and Exchange Commission).

9 Shadow connections

On hierarchies of collateral in shadow banking

Daniela Gabor

> Can we hope to ever measure 'systemic risk'? Yes. It's all about inter-connectedness which mega-banks and regulators should be able to measure . . . Repos among financial institutions are treated as extremely low risk, even though excessive reliance on repo funding almost brought our system down. How dumb is that?
>
> (Sheila Bair, Chair of US Systemic Risk Council, 6 June 2013)

Introduction

In contemporary politics and heterodox political economy, it is well established that the 'management of money is political' (Kirshner 2003: 645; Dow 2012). Even mainstream economics recognizes that much since the crisis (see Caballero 2010), albeit by coaching this recognition in the language of models that have gone astray. Yet the political economy of one of the most important monetary phenomena of recent times, the rise of shadow banking, remains surprisingly under-examined. When scholars ask political economy questions, they typically focus on poorly designed regulatory regimes to explain the rapid growth in shadow banking (see Schwarcz 2012; also Rixen 2013). For this reason, the political economy of shadow banking has so far been the political economy of regulatory arbitrage. The chapter questions this narrow regulatory focus. It argues that the political economy of shadow banking is *also* the political economy of interconnectedness generated through shadow banking activities, securitization and collateral intermediation (FSB 2011; Claessens *et al.* 2012). The chapter focuses on collateral.

The New York Fed (Pozsar *et al.* 2010) first mapped the shadow banking universe, drawing on the term coined by McCulley (2007) and extended by Pozsar (2008). The Fed study presented an extraordinarily complex map of non-regulated institutions that fulfilled functions traditionally pertaining to banks. In line with this definition, the FSB (2011) set out a regulatory agenda for shadow banking defined as 'entities and activities structured outside the regular banking system that perform bank-like functions'. Among these non-bank entities, the study listed finance companies, money market funds, (some) hedge funds, special-purpose vehicles etc. In turn, it identified two activities specific to shadow banking: securitization and collateral intermediation (repos and securities lending).

For regulatory purposes, a focus on shadow entities turned out to be problematic (ECB 2012; Bank of Canada 2013). It first raised difficult questions of the institutions that should fall into the regulatory perimeter of shadow banking. Take for instance the European Commission's (2012) consultations. Many of the respondents objected to the 'shadow bank' term, either because of a perceived pejorative connotation, or because some non-bank institutions that were already subject to regulatory provisions worried about the additional regulatory burden. Indeed, the shadow banking scholarship, originally focused on the US, recognized that mutations and innovations would continuously outpace regulators' ability to identify the relevant shadow entities (see Claessens *et al.* 2012).

Second, the institutional texture of the shadow banking world appeared to be contingent on distinctive forms of capitalism – with the market-based financial system of liberal capitalisms more germane to the rise of non-bank financial entities than the bank-based characteristic of most European countries (Iversen and Soskice 2012). The analysis initially suggested that European shadow banking was much smaller, of less systemic relevance compared to the US case (sees ECB 2012).

Indeed, when early scholarship placed the European financial system on the shadow banking map, it did so by outlining the involvement of large European banks in the US market-based finance (Shin 2011). Consider for example the market for asset-backed commercial paper (ABCP), one of the largest supporting shadow banking (USD 1.2trn in 2007) and the first to undergo financial tensions in 2007. Of the ten largest bank sponsors of ABCP conduits, seven were European, while the ten largest bank conduits all had European bank sponsors, mostly owning assets issued in the US (see Acharya *et al.* 2010). In turn, when scholarship explored shadow activities, it privileged securitization (Nesvetailova and Palan 2013; Thiemann 2014). For Adrian (2011: 1) of the New York Fed 'securitization of credit and funding of securitized products were at the heart of shadow banking', and indeed, most studies defined shadow banking as 'securitization-based, non-bank credit intermediation' (Pozsar *et al.* 2010; Bouveret 2011: 1; also Stein 2010). Conversely, the famous map in Pozsar *et al.* (2010) placed shadow banks along securitization chains.

Securitization, rather than collateral intermediation, took centre stage for several reasons. First, securitization captured public attention as the crisis started with a run on complex securitized products relying on the subprime US housing market and then propagated throughout other secured funding markets, including the repo market (see Gorton and Metrick 2009). Second, the rapid pre-crisis growth of securitization had been at the core of policy discourses applauding the benefits of financial innovation as an efficiency improving, risk-spreading technique (Engelen *et al.* 2011). Once financial actors stopped trading, or found it impossible to value highly rated securities (ABCPs, CDOs, square CDOs), securitization came to embody the misleading promises and 'distorted incentives' underpinning financial innovation (Shin 2009). It vindicated Minskian analyses of financial instability and private leverage cycles (see Moe 2012; Nesvetailova and Palan 2013). Furthermore, the readily available data on securitization products – in contrast to the glaring data gaps in collateral intermediation – allowed regulators to make sense of the crisis and narrate it, given the urgency of regulatory reform, as a crisis of 'securitized banking' (Engelen *et al.* 2011). In sum, historical, political and policy-driven motives focused analytical attention on the securitization component of shadow banking activities. With notable exceptions (see Singh 2011; Claessens *et al.* 2012; Moe 2012; Gabor 2016; Gabor and Ban 2016), the early literature on shadow banking presented collateral intermediation as a subset of securitization activities.

Tradable collateral is critical for the functioning of modern global financial markets. With the increasing globalization of financial markets, the territory of collateral no longer coincides with the political frontiers bounding the issuer. Demand for and use of collateral can easily cross borders, as tools for managing counterparty and currency risk have proliferated. Before the crisis, demand for collateral was powered by the rapid growth in shadow banking and derivative markets. One shadow 'activity' or market, the repo market, connects cash rich with securities rich institutions, relationships mediated by collateral (Sissoko 2010). In derivative markets, both the over-the-counter (OTC) bilateral segment and centrally cleared segment, collateral usage increased markedly before Lehman, with two-thirds of all OTC derivative transactions subject to collateral agreements (ISDA 2010). Since Lehman, the central role of collateral in financial markets has been strengthened by regulatory reforms. Basel III liquidity rules require banks to hold high-quality liquid assets, as do reforms of derivative markets where collateral requirements now apply to both centralized and non-centralized derivatives. As BNY Mellon, the largest tri-party repo agent in the US noted in 2015, 'collateral is the new cash, as HQLA can now be viewed as the financial system's most important commodity' (BNY Mellon 2015: 3).

It is tempting to infer that a greater structural role for collateral would improve the resilience of the financial sector. This is indeed the argument guiding collateral-intensive regulatory regimes. Yet we know little of how collateral flows are structured and managed on a precise basis (for notable exceptions, see Singh 2011; Singh and Stella 2012), while grudgingly, regulators recognize that interconnectedness generated through collateral flows adds to 'complexity and opacity' and may exacerbate procyclicality (Houben and Slingenberg 2013). To make sense of this opacity and relate it to larger questions of macroeconomic governance, the chapter proposes a taxonomy of connections created through collateral flows: horizontal and vertical. Horizontal connections are forged between financial institutions through collateral risk practices. The concept of vertical connections stresses the analytical importance of collateral issuers, typically recognized in the securitization literature (see Lysandrou and Nesvetailova 2015; Thiemann 2014) but less so for other private and public issuers. It is useful to conceive of a hierarchy of collateral, mapped onto currency hierarchies (Kaltenbrunner 2011; Cohen 2015), with the debt issued by the US state at the top, followed by other private and public issuers. By examining the fragility of collateral connections, the chapter asks two questions: 'what are the benefits and potential costs for issuers, including states, of joining collateral hierarchies?' and 'if there is a hierarchy of collateral issuers, what are the costs associated with sliding down the hierarchy?'.

Horizontal connections

The shift to tradable collateral in financial transactions can be traced back to the 1980s (Gabor 2016a). It reflects structural changes in finance, most notably the increasing importance of institutional investors (pension funds and insurance companies), and global banks' embrace of capital market activities, funded in collateralized funding markets (Gabor 2016b; also Hardie *et al*. 2013).

The most important market that circulates collateral is the repo market. A repo transaction involves the exchange of an asset for cash or for another asset – termed securities lending – with the commitment to reverse that transaction at a later date (a day, a week, a month). That asset is usually described as collateral, and the transaction a repo transaction. In theory, any asset can be 'repo-ed' as long as the lender (the counterparty) accepts it. What distinguishes a repo from similar financial transactions such as secured lending (Garbade 2006), is that the practices of collateral risk management have evolved to enable the two counterparties to re-use collateral for a broad range of activities (see BIS 1999).

Consider this example. Santander owns Spanish BB-rated corporate bonds. Deutsche Bank accepts those corporate bonds as collateral in return for euro cash, but to protect itself it imposes an initial haircut: for every EUR 100 it will ask for EUR 130 corporate bonds at market value. In contrast to a secured lending transaction, in this repo Santander sells and commits to repurchase its bonds, parting temporarily with legal ownership of collateral. In a repo contractual relationship, Deutsche Bank is a buyer, and Santander a seller.

But the relationship does not end here because the *economic* interpretation of a repo is distinctive from the *legal* one. In economic terms, a repo is a collateralized *loan* from Deutsche Bank to Santander. The distinction matters for the collateral risk management regime, since the two parties remain involved on a daily basis with repos with maturities beyond a day. If Santander defaults, legal ownership allows Deutsche Bank to sell the collateral and recover its cash. To ensure that it does not lose in the process – when, for example, that collateral falls in market price – Deutsche Bank applies a complex set of risk practices to collateral: it calculates the market value of those corporate bonds on a daily basis (marking them to market) and makes margin calls – if the price of the corporate bonds falls, Santander has to post additional collateral to Deutsche Bank.

In turn, Santander retains the risks and returns associated with collateral, although Deutsche Bank is the legal owner. Deutsche Bank has the obligation to transfer any coupon payments to Santander (Comotto 2012). For this reason, repos and securities financing transactions are used interchangeably: Santander uses the corporate bonds as collateral to finance them in the repo market, while retaining the underlying exposure to the risks and returns of those BB-rated bonds.

The distinction between the economic and legal interpretations is crucial for creating horizontal links. It makes repo different from other forms of secured lending (see BIS 1999). A repo cash borrower is a seller of collateral because the transfer of ownership is crucial to protect the cash lender (the buyer of collateral) in case of default. In other words, the legal status of a repo transaction morphs the counterparty risk – that Santander defaults – into collateral risk – that the collateral provided by Santander falls in price below the value of the cash loan. This is repo 'magic': the move from counterparty risk to collateral risk means that both parties care most about 'the volatility . . . in the value of collateral' than about the other's credit worthiness (BIS 1999).

Yet this does not imply that counterparty risk disappears altogether: riskier counterparties may have more difficult access to repo funding, or pay higher haircuts (Comotto 2012). This is particularly the case during periods of market stress, when uncertainty about asset valuations rises and expectations of collateral quality worsen. However, interconnectedness plays out through collateral values since the parties remain connected throughout the duration of the repo through the collateral risk practices (mark-to-market and margin call).

Furthermore, horizontal connections increase in complexity through practices of re-use or re-hypothecation. This is crucial to understanding why repo transactions are intimately linked to cycles of private leverage (FSB 2012). Continuing with the previous example, Deutsche Bank can re-use the securities accepted in the repo with Santander to settle a short position, to hedge an interest rate exposure, or because as a market-maker it can re-lend those securities at more favourable rates in the same market. These various functions imply that collateral managers can lend and borrow the same piece of collateral repeatedly, if there are no legal restrictions that constrain re-use (re-hypothecation for broker-dealers). Singh (2011) describes these as collateral chains: the same asset can move between various counterparties in different repo transactions, so that all these counterparties have a common exposure to the movements in the market where collateral trades. Such dynamic chains generated leverage and systemic risk through the shadow banking sector:

> If this collateral is lodged in cash, it can be re-invested. These strategies generate dynamic collateral chains in which the same security is lent several times, often involving actors from the shadow banking system. This mechanism can contribute to a surreptitious increase in leverage and strengthens the pro-cyclical nature of the financial system, which then becomes vulnerable to bank runs and sudden deleveraging.
>
> (European Commission 2013)

Singh (2012) estimated that before the 2008 crisis, a high-quality asset typically sustained five different repo transactions. Put differently, five different financial institutions were connected through one financial instrument and were exposed, in a chain-like fashion, to its price volatility through the risk management practices.

Legal limits to re-use further contribute to expanding collateral chains. Some jurisdictions, such as the US, may enforce restrictions on re-use in repo transactions involving an intermediary (a tri-party repo, see FSB 2012). When demand for collateral outpaces supply and re-use possibilities, financial institutions 'mine' collateral, that is they identify pools of assets in the ownership of asset managers – hedge funds, sovereign wealth funds, pension funds, insurance companies or mutual funds – and borrow them through repo transactions (see Pozsar and Singh 2011). Collateral mining strengthens interconnectedness among financial actors that own assets and are willing to lend them out to be included in collateral chains. Many pension funds do so in order to gain some additional returns on buy-to-hold portfolios of low-risk, low-return assets.

While the shadow banking literature typically points to money market funds and investment banks as key nodes in collateral networks, it is important to note that European banks have become critical nodes in European wholesale funding markets (Liikanen 2012). In contrast to the relational model where banks fund lending activities from deposits and the shortfall from the uncollateralized interbank market, tradable or market-based banking is aptly described by Mehrling *et al.*'s (2013) definition of shadow banking as 'money market funding of capital market lending'. Banks with trading activities invariably engage in collateral networks, unless the regulatory regime makes it costly to do so or prohibits it altogether. Why should this be the case? First, financing portfolios of high-risk, high-return tradable assets (securities) is cheapest through repo markets (BIS 1999). Second, even low-return, low-risk assets held for regulatory purposes, such as AAA rated government bonds, can be 'yield-enhanced' if banks, in their capacity as market-makers, lend them out to, say, hedge funds that are engaged in short-selling.

The magnitude of repo activity for European banks can be gauged from two distinctive sources. First, statistics from ICMA, the private repo lobby, suggests that the volume of repo transactions in Europe has been roughly similar to the US, both before and since the crisis, around EUR 7 trillion, with a dip immediately after Lehman's collapse. According to BIS research, the 20 largest European banks transacted 3 out of every 4 euros passing through the European repo market (Hördhal and King 2008). In other words, the repo market in Europe is by and large an interbank market. Against this context, the European Commission's (2013) insistence that systemic risk lies at the intersection of bank and non-bank (shadow) repo connections is ill-informed. European banks are the key nodes in European collateral networks.

Horizontal collateral chains are not exclusively private. Central banks may also become key nodes through practices of collateral transformation and securities lending. Where central banks accept a broad range of collateral, banks manage collateral portfolios to use high-quality collateral for private repos and use less liquid collateral with the central bank. Banks may also issue debt instruments exclusively for use at the central bank window. For instance, around 80 per cent of securitized instruments issued by European banks since 2009 have been retained on their balance sheet to use as collateral at the ECB refinancing operations. Similarly, central banks with large portfolios of tradable securities acquired through quantitative easing programmes may choose to lend out these securities in order to mitigate the shortage of high-quality collateral in private repo markets.

Collateral flows thus connect private financial institutions, cash pools and central banks across securities markets, derivative markets and interbank money markets.

Vertical connections: bringing issuers in

One of the most puzzling aspects of shadow banking is its reliance on government debt collateral. Private repo markets mostly circulate sovereign collateral, with around 75 per cent of the collateral flowing through repo markets both in the US and Europe coming from highly rated governments (Hördahl and King 2008; ECB 2012; ICMA 2012). The market participants' preference for government collateral has been persuasively explained in the shadow banking literature as a story of costs and profitability: when using liquid government debt, repo lenders demand low or no haircuts, while collateral risk management generate less frequent margin calls. Government debt collateral allows repo market participants to economize on the costs of funding their securities portfolio (Giovannini 2013).

Until recently, the shadow banking literature had little to say about the factors prompting states, in their capacity as debt issuers, to become providers of collateral. Analytical interest focused instead on explaining the incentive governing the issuers of securitized instruments, incentives partly generated by the US state's refusal to connect the fiscal stance to the demand for high-quality collateral (Pozsar 2011; see also Thiemann 2014; Lysandrou and Nesvetailova 2015). A dwindling supply of US government debt in the early 2000s prompted shadow banking to manufacture new pools of collateral through securitization. Yet the story of securitization as a market response to collateral shortages sheds little light on two important questions about the consequences of states becoming issuers of collateral deployed in global shadow networks. The first question asks: 'what are the benefits and potential costs for states?' The question recognizes that however shadow the new financial order of collateral-based finance, it is unconceivable that states would fail to notice their debt being increasingly used as collateral in private repo markets. The second asks: 'if there is a hierarchy of collateral issuers, what are the costs associated with sliding down the hierarchy?' While the literature does not attempt to distinguish between highly rated and low-rated sovereign issuers, it is problematic to assume that regardless of its underlying fiscal position, a state's debt is as good collateral as any other. Rather that the quality of collateral issued by states is contingent on shifting structural and policy contexts.

Both these questions take us back to the 1980s' global push for financial liberalization, and to the attempts to separate monetary from fiscal policy due to the growing influence of the central bank independence discourse in academic literature and in policy practice (Gabor 2016a). The move to market financing of budget deficits raised a critical question for fiscal authorities no longer able to draw on central banks: how should government bond markets be organized to ensure continuous access at sustainable financing rates in the context of increased capital mobility that give investors a wider choice of instruments?

The question of how to design the architecture of bond markets lacks straightforward answers. Biais and Green (2007) ask why bonds – as opposed to stocks – are traded in OTC markets whose opacity and concentration create high entry barriers for retail investors. The historical experience of corporate and municipal bonds in the US, they argue, shows that trade migrated from the New York Stock Exchange to OTC markets because of the changing make-up of bond-holders. Rather than efficiency, market structure is a question of entrenched interest groups. The growing importance of institutional investors and dealers shifted trading to OTC markets where 'institutions and dealers could negotiate compensation that was strictly regulated on exchanges'.

States have designed their debt markets to try to harness market structure to their advantage. The typical arrangement before the era of central bank independence was for the central bank to act as the fiscal agent of the state, and work with a handful of private financial institutions – market-makers – to ensure that it would achieve the objective of monetary policy, then the interest rate on government debt. In the 1980s, two simultaneous developments brought changes to such an arrangement. First, the rise of monetarism in academia and policy practice presented a persuasive celebration of the stability benefits created by removing the printing press from the itchy fingers of populist governments. Full independence would truly be achieved where sovereign debt management moved to an autonomous agency that insulated debt management from other macroeconomic objectives. Second, increased capital mobility eroded states' captive base of domestic investors. Together, these two rendered market liquidity the single most important concern for states' new life as issuers of debt: investors' ability to buy and sell government debt without large price changes would be critical to a state's success in attracting foreign investors. Confronted with such pressures, states turned to the most liquid government bond market in the world, the US treasury market (Gabor 2016a).

The UK gilt market reform offers an interesting example of how states made sense of these new challenges. Almost ten years after the Big Bang liberalization of the financial sector, the UK Treasury undertook a review of debt management in close cooperation with the Bank of England. The 1995 report highlighted the growing competition for foreign investors, wherein success for the UK depended first on 'a clearer public statement of the allocation of roles between the Treasury and the Bank'. It then noted that bond markets across the world were converging on the UST model with the following preeminent features: 'regular and non-discretionary issuance, entirely through actions; a market-making structure based on primary dealers; an open repo market and a strips market'. In contrast, only UK gilt-edged market-makers were allowed to short gilts. The report noted that France was the European country that had made the fastest steps in this direction, implementing a 'rapid modernization on US lines'. In contrast, the UK was lagging behind in achieving 'an efficient and liquid gilt market' because it had hesitated in opening up the repo market. An open repo market would allow primary dealers – local and foreign – to finance purchases of new gilts before distributing them and to make secondary markets and financial institutions in general, take positions in secondary markets by borrowing them through (special) repos. The review proposed to liberalize immediately (January 1996).

The 1995 report concluded an ongoing struggle between the Bank of England and the UK Treasury. The Bank of England had opposed repo liberalization, concerned that expanding the list of institutions active in the repo gilt market to foreign investors – US securities houses for instance – would foment speculative position taking, enabling investors with short-term horizons to easily enter and exit, in what Ian Hardie (2011) described as the financialization of sovereign bond markets. On the continent, Bundesbank shared this concern and similarly held a tight grip on Bund repos by imposing a reserve requirement on repo funding (Gabor 2016a). Both central banks were forced to loosen that grip under pressure from a coalition of Ministries of Finance and private financial institutions narrating repo liberalization as the only answer to the growing French dominance of European finance. The promise of open repo markets was a promise that states could successfully compete with the US to secure government bond market liquidity.

European states went further than the US in radically altering their government bond markets. The US Federal Reserve remained the Treasury's fiscal agent, whereas debt management in Germany, France and UK moved to autonomous debt management offices by the early 2000s. Repo liberalization in Europe also went further. The legal treatment of collateral in the US distinguished between public and private securities until 2005. Before 2005, only repo buyers of UST and agency collateral enjoyed safe harbour privileges, after Paul Volcker persuaded the US Congress in 1984 that the stability of the US financial system fundamentally depended on ensuring that at least public collateral (UST and agency securities) was exempted from automatic stay in the Bankruptcy Code (Roe 2013). In contrast, the legal regime in Europe conferred legal ownership rights to all repo lenders.

Open repo markets and primary dealers' structures do not automatically create liquid government bond markets. Small government bond markets or conservative fiscal stances become an impediment in a world where size breeds liquidity (IMF 2001). This suggests that we can think of a hierarchy of repo collateral issuers that is closely mapped onto currency hierarchies (Mehrling *et al.* 2013). The US state sits at the top of the hierarchy by virtue of its 'monetary power' as issuer of the reserve currency (Kirshner 1995; Cohen 2015). Indeed, central banks around the world hold sizeable proportions of their dollar reserves in US sovereign debt, and lend these through US repo and securities lending markets, allowing them to circulate in collateral networks. When the US state appeared determined to pay off its public debt in the early 2000s (Fleming 2000), the IMF (2001) raised the question of the potential impact on the international role of the dollar, pointing to the safe-haven role that US treasury securities play during times of stress.

Further down the hierarchy, it becomes less obvious how to tap into the potential benefits of becoming a collateral issuer for private repo markets. The euro area's efforts to collectively create liquid sovereign debt markets that could support the early ambitions to position the euro as a credible competitor to the US dollar are instructive. At first, it was expected that the euro area government bond market would pose a significant challenge to the US treasury market (McCauley 2001). The aggregate stock of public debt of member states, all enjoying investment grade status and re-denominated in euros, reached a comparable size to the US, the type of size that would breed liquidity. Euro-denominated public debt could credibly challenge UST's position at the top of the hierarchy of collateral issuers.

Yet the move to issue debt in a single currency failed to eliminate the fragmentation of euro liquidity, even for the three largest markets (France, Germany and Italy at the time), as investors continued to view them as different 'habitats' suited for specific financial activities (Giovannini 2013). Fragmentation, the IMF (2001) noted, impaired the 'efficient use of government securities as collateral' and made Europe less competitive in supplying collateral to global market participants. At that time, European government securities accounted for around 5 per cent of collateral in use, while US treasury and agency securities accounted for around 40 per cent. Differences in legal framework made the cross-border use of collateral costly or outright impossible.

The solution that the ECB proposed, and market participants followed, was to create a 'synthetic' collateral pool for funding driven repos. In these general collateral (GC) repos, the buyer accepts any security specified in the GC collateral pool, so that a set of distinctive securities is treated as equivalent collateral. For instance, the ECB specified a GC pool that made no distinction between state debt issued in euros, regardless of the issuer. With this, its strategy was to use its position as repo market participant (lending to banks against collateral) to influence the collateral decisions of private financial institutions, and together push the less liquid collateral up the hierarchy.

Before 2008, the success of these efforts highlighted the importance of the market-developing strategies of the state through its central bank institution. Rapidly growing demand for collateral saw global banks bundle German, Portuguese or Greek sovereign bonds in the same collateral pool (Hördahl and King 2008; Liikanen 2012). To go up the hierarchy of collateral circulating through global repo markets, states could harness market forces moving the global financial system towards greater collateralization.

For private issuers, the liquidity benefits of repo markets are more difficult to translate into high-quality collateral status. While investment grade rating is an important condition, it does not automatically generate low-haircut, high-liquidity features. For instance, a Fitch study of money market funds in the US, active on the lending side in (tri-party) repo markets, suggests that funds 'calibrate haircuts based on the potential price volatility of collateral'. The Committee on the Global

Table 9.1 Haircuts on term repos

	Prime counterparty	Non-prime counterparty	Hedge funds and other unrated counterparties
G7 government bonds	0	0	0.5
US agencies	1	2	3
Prime MBS AAA	4	6	10
ABS	10	20	20
Structured products (AAA)	10	15	20
Investment grade bonds (AAA and AA)	1	2	5

Source: CGFS (2010).

Financial System (CGFS) (2010) study of repo markets, one of the few to provide some empirical evidence for haircut schedules applied to public and private collateral in term repos, shows that despite the efforts of the US Fed to support securitization markets as an alternative to the dwindling supply of US Treasuries (Gabor 2016), haircuts on AAA rated products remained significantly higher than on G7 government bonds up to 2007.

Sliding down the hierarchy: crisis of collateral in shadow banking

The system of private claims generated through leveraged shadow banking rests on collateral chains. This is crucial to the distinctiveness of crises in shadow banking, compared with relational banking. In relational banking, a run occurs when depositors loose confidence in a bank; the bank experiences funding problems that quickly become systemic (a run on banks) because the process through which banks create money – that is bank deposits – fundamentally relies on trust. The central bank steps in through the lender of last resort function, supplying banks with liquidity (reserves) and thus restoring confidence in the interbank money market.

In contrast, a crisis of shadow banking takes the form of liquidity spirals (Brunnermeier and Pedersen 2009; Gorton and Metrick 2009; Mehrling 2012; Gabor 2016a). Brunnermeier and Pedersen (2009) defined liquidity spirals as a combination of funding problems for individual financial institutions and falling asset prices. Liquidity spirals are essentially crises of collateral sharpened by the risk management regime specific to repos.

Financial institutions that are connected through collateral flows are exposed together to collateral price volatility. To use the previous example, when the asset that supports five distinctive repo transactions falls in price as a result of market turmoil, the five parties that have accepted the asset as collateral make margin calls on their respective counterparties because collateral is marked to market. Margin calls thus propagate through collateral chains and require each borrower to post additional collateral (or cash). Furthermore, on short-term repos that require rollover, the cash lenders may increase haircuts because they lose confidence both in their ability to evaluate the future price volatility of that collateral and in their counterparties. This implies that the five borrowers have a funding shortfall that must be matched by borrowing elsewhere. Yet if liquidity preference is high and nobody wants to lend cash or high-quality collateral, the five borrowers have no choice but to sell some assets in order to meet the margin calls. This leads to further falls in asset prices and further margin calls. As liquidity disappears from asset markets, marking-to-market sharpens funding problems, destabilizing asset prices (Plantin *et al.* 2007). Financial fragility is sharpened by the link between funding requirements and fluctuating asset values. Institutions engaged in shadow banking activities become involved in liquidity spirals, with systemic risk embedded in collateral networks.

The crucial question in a crisis of interconnectedness becomes: what is the likelihood that an asset experiences severe price volatility? Put differently, what determines the possible loss of good collateral status for issuers? Finance scholars distinguish between information-sensitive and information-insensitive assets (Gorton 2010); or safe and unsafe assets (Gourinchas and Jeanne 2012). The best type of collateral in a crisis is an information-insensitive asset. Even when private financial actors acquire additional information about the issuer, price does not change dramatically (Dang *et al.* 2010). This implies stable collateral values and stable funding conditions. In turn, private financial actors lose confidence in the pricing of information-sensitive assets. Uncertainty about pricing becomes uncertainty about quality, so that even the markets for private AAA rated debt lose liquidity rapidly. If information-sensitive assets are key nodes in collateral networks, financial stress results in a run on repo (Gorton and Metrick 2009).

A crisis of shadow banking will see a run up to the top of the collateral hierarchy. It is now well documented that financial actors reliant on repo funding responded to the crisis of US shadow banking by crowding into US government securities (Gorton and Metrick 2009; BIS 2011). In contrast, repo market participants stopped using structured debt instruments – even those rated AAA – as collateral. These supported a significant share of repo transactions: around 30 per cent were collateralized with structured debt. Instead, government debt remained the only collateral accepted in secured funding. In a crisis of shadow banking, the universe of high-quality collateral shrinks to the assets that actors perceive to be safest, that is most liquid and least likely to experience severe price volatility.

Does the US experience suggest that government debt is the perfect safe asset for shadow banking? Can public 'safe' assets remain safe without policy interventions from either the issuer of the safe asset – the government – or the institution in charge of financial stability – the central bank – just by virtue of being a 'safe-haven' asset that financial institutions require during crisis?

The Financial Stability Board (2012), in its work stream on shadow banking, proposed a mandatory minimum haircut that would apply to repos regardless of whether the underlying collateral (the security financed) is 'safe' or potentially information-sensitive:

> The policy goal is to restrict, or put a floor on the cost of, secured borrowing against assets subject to procyclical variation in valuations/volatility, to reduce the potential for the excessive leverage to build-up and for large swings in system leverage when the financial system is under stress.
>
> (Financial Stability Board 2012: 7)

In this quote, the FSB asserts that repo markets sharpen cyclical price behaviour across all asset markets, including government bonds. Whereas buoyant shadow banking increases demand for government bonds that can be used as collateral, crises of deleveraging may reduce liquidity and destabilize government bond markets. Mandatory minimum haircuts, used as a macroprudential tool, would reduce the link between leverage and liquidity conditions. The proposal met with resistance from the European private repo lobby, whose publications questioned the FSB's argument that haircuts were pro-cyclical: low during boom periods and rising rapidly during periods of market stress (Comotto 2012). This may be the case, Comotto agreed, but only for a narrow range of private securities used in repos. In turn, haircuts on the US government debt changed little throughout the run on repo with private collateral (Gorton and Metrick 2009). A similar view can be traced to the Basel III liquidity requirements that treat sovereign debt of high-income countries as a safe asset. Yet recent scholarly contributions raised doubts about the validity of this assumption (Flandreau 2013; Giovannini 2013).

The starting point is to recognize that the information (in)sensitive distinction is ultimately descriptive, albeit a useful one for modelling macro-financial instability. Yet so far, the finance scholarship has not produced a convincing theoretical account to explain why some assets remain 'safe' during crisis. That is not to imply that such questions have not been asked (see Fisher 2013). For example, Gourinchas and Jeanne (2012) envisage a world where 'nothing is really safe' but where central banks ultimately provide stability for public assets: its own liabilities (cash and bank reserves) and government bonds. This further highlights the importance of bringing institutions into the explanatory framework: beyond the individual characteristics of an asset, what matters is the institutional structure in which the asset (market) is embedded. This hints to mapping the safe/unsafe – or (in)sensitive – distinction along private vs. public lines.

In doing so, the politics of providing safe assets for shadow banking become apparent and rest on the following question: are there institutional settings in which the journey from safe into unsafe assets can also be made by government bonds? In 'traditional' financial systems, Flandreau (2013) argues, history shows that good sovereigns also default when the central bank and government do not coordinate. In the context of shadow banking, are there instances where the systemic risk generated through collateral networks cannot be handled by the existing institutional configurations, and where political issues hamper the emergence of new, innovative institutions?

To answer this question, it is useful to recall the history of traditional (relational banking). In this system, bank reserves – the money created by the central bank – are the safe assets. During periods of stability, banks trade reserves with each other, without collateral, to fulfil reserve requirements or dispose of excess reserves from deposits higher than lending. Financial distress manifests through higher liquidity preference, with banks reluctant to lend to each other and interbank interest rates increasing rapidly (Dow 2003). In order to restore financial stability, the central bank stands ready to create new money – bank reserves – and lend it to banks that have funding difficulties, what is known as the Bagehot principle (Mehrling 2012). The central bank thus facilitates the creation of private money (bank deposits) and in doing so, preserves the status of its reserves as a safe asset.

Crucially, the lender of last resort function has not come about without a political struggle. It appears normalized because struggles took place in the 19th century when economists like David Ricardo strongly opposed the idea that a central bank – the Bank of England – should be the lender of last resort to restore confidence in banks and their money (Gabor 2010). Indeed, the historical institutionalism literature reminds us that institutions are 'enduring legacies of political struggle' (Thelen 1999); and central banks are no exception. Now any central bank in the world has the instruments, the ideational legitimacy and the legal mandate to stabilize relational banking.

In contrast, to stabilize shadow banking Mehrling (2012) argues, the central bank has to focus on collateral markets. It must become a market-maker of last resort, standing ready to prevent liquidity spirals from contaminating collateral networks. The traditional lender of last resort is not enough since it gives extraordinary liquidity to banks but *without* stabilizing the prices of the assets that are used as collateral. That involves a direction intervention in systemic collateral markets, that is, across the shadow banking universe, in government bond markets. Indeed, the successive rounds of quantitative easing implemented by the US Federal Reserve achieved just that. Yet the European crisis shows that the transition to a new mode of central banking is not always smooth.

The successful strategy to push all euro area state debt up the collateral hierarchy meant that banks across Eurozone could follow idiosyncratic strategies for accumulating sovereign debt. Preference for their own sovereign, rather than an internationalized portfolio, mattered little from a financing perspective since both domestic and international portfolios could be funded through repos. According to data from the European Banking Authority, banks with exposure to the US shadow banking and centralized liquidity management – German, French or Dutch – preferred international portfolios of sovereign debt; with the share of foreign sovereigns rising above 50 per cent. In contrast, banks with less cross-border activity or with independent subsidiaries reliant on host funding markets chose to hold a large share of their government bond portfolios mostly in the home sovereign. Greece banks had almost 80 per cent of the portfolio of sovereign debt in Greek bonds, followed by Italian banks (80 per cent) and Portuguese banks (73 per cent). This would prove costly after Lehman collapsed.

Europe's crisis of shadow banking was triggered by the exposure of the European banks to the US financial crisis, and was sharpened by the European sovereign debt crisis. The first stage, the subprime crisis coupled with the collapse of Lehman Brothers, saw a substantial dollar funding shortage for large European bank sponsors of conduits in various asset-backed markets (Shin 2011). These banks – key nodes in European collateral networks – could not fund their portfolios of US assets in US dollar markets or access lender of last resort liquidity from the US Federal Reserve. The European lender of last resort, the ECB, in turn did not have sufficient dollar reserves to meet the dollar funding needs. In response, the ECB and the US Fed set up currency swap lines. The ECB could thus borrow dollar reserves from the Fed, and lend them to European banks through repo operations.

To access dollar liquidity, banks had to find eligible collateral to give the ECB. The scramble for eligible collateral sharpened shortages, particularly since the liquidity spiral in the US shortened collateral chains (Singh 2011) and increased hoarding of high-quality collateral. Whereas the ECB did expand its list of assets eligible as collateral, by imposing substantial haircuts on the lower quality collateral and daily mark-to-market practices, it further contributed to the scramble for high-quality collateral and to increased scrutiny from private banks towards the quality of collateral of the various European sovereigns. At that moment, banks began questioning the 'safe-asset' status of sovereigns with well-documented domestic vulnerabilities such as a housing boom fed by credit or high reliance on cross-border funding of their banking sector. European collateral markets began segmenting, with periphery states losing their privileged position near the top of the collateral hierarchy.

The sovereign collateral framework of LCH Clearnet illustrates neatly the practices that reproduce and reorder a hierarchical collateral structure. LCH Clearnet is one of the largest Central Clearing Counterparties (CCPs) in Europe. A CCP sits between two repo parties, requiring each to post initial margin (haircut) so that it builds buffers to mitigate potential risks. Whereas in a bilateral repo it is only the borrower (the collateral seller) that pays haircuts, in CCPs, both parties pay a margin to the CCP. In 2010, LCH introduced a sovereign risk framework that would take into account 'step changes in the liquidity of some sovereign securities' and wrong way risk 'where a clearing member is highly correlated with the underlying securities'. To judge whether the risks attached to collateral increased significantly, LCH used three indicators: a 450 basis points spread over a 10-year AAA rated benchmark (Germany), a 500 basis points 5-year CDS spread, or when an implied rating dropped to B1. After discussions with the ECB and the Irish Treasury, LCH invoked the framework for Irish sovereign bonds in October 2010, and then for Portugal in April 2011. In both cases, the trigger was the growing spread to AAA rated German Bunds. For both sovereign securities, haircuts peaked at 80 per cent, tightening funding conditions substantially for banks that held these as repo collateral. Thus, the impact of a crisis of shadow banking was to further strengthen the dominant position of German sovereign bonds – the de facto safe asset in the Eurozone – and to push collateral issued by some sovereigns down the hierarchy.

Conclusion

Political-economic conceptions of shadow banking should take into account interconnectedness. Rather than tracing institutions crossing porous regulatory perimeters, the chapter suggested that analytical efforts would be better placed to map collateral networks, the institutions that act as key nodes in those networks, the issuers and the common exposure they generate. Interconnectedness matters for European shadow banking in particular, because European banks are key nodes in collateral networks, moving and re-using sovereign collateral. This suggests that both scholars and policy makers should be careful in drawing borders between shadow banks and 'traditional' or regulated banks. The distinction collapses from the perspective of collateral intermediation, a key shadow banking activity.

Through repo transactions, collateral moves in networks connecting banks to other banks or non-bank financial institutions. These connections are both systemic and fragile. Repo connections are fragile because they are the cheapest source of funding for leveraged financial activity, but also because practices of risk management and re-use can amplify concerns about collateral quality and ignite liquidity spirals. They are systemic because repo markets are now the most significant source of market funding for banks and non-banks with large trading portfolios. A run on shadow banking occurs as a downsizing of collateral networks, with a smaller number of connections supported by the same collateral simultaneous with a narrower range of acceptable collateral. What counts as acceptable in a crisis of shadow banking fundamentally depends on the institutional structures in which the repo market is embedded. The European crisis shows that shadow connections built around sovereign collateral can quickly disintegrate in the absence of central bank support.

References

Acharya, V., P. Schnabl and G. Suarez (2010) *Securitization without Risk Transfer*. NBER Working Paper, no. 15730. Available at: http://pages.stern.nyu.edu/~pschnabl/public_html/AcharyaSchnablSuarez2013.pdf. Last accessed: 06.01.2017.

Adrian, T. (2011) *Dodd-Frank One Year On: Implications for Shadow Banking*. Federal Reserve Bank of New York Staff Report, no. 533. Available at: www.newyorkfed.org/medialibrary/media/research/staff_reports/sr533.pdf. Last accessed: 06.02.2017.

Bair, S. (2013) 'Everything The IMF Wanted to Know about Financial Regulation and Wasn't Afraid to Ask'. *Vox.eu*, 9 June. Available at: http://voxeu.org/article/everything-imf-wanted-know-about-financial-regulation-and-wasn-t-afraid-ask. Last accessed 25.04.2017.

Bank of Canada (2013) *Shedding Light on Shadow Banking*. Remarks by Timothy Lane, Deputy Governor of the Bank of Canada. Available at: www.bankofcanada.ca/wp-content/uploads/2013/06/remarks-260613.pdf. Last accessed: 06.02.2017.

Biais, B. and R. C. Green (2007) *The Microstructure of the Bond Market in the 20th Century*. Tepper School of Business, Mimeo. Research Paper. Available at: https://pdfs.semanticscholar.org/0e88/d996f2bfc85aa2e123c87f4dc51c37151b1b.pdf. Last accessed: 20.01.2017.

BIS (1999) *Implications of Repo Markets for Central Banks*. Bank for International Settlements. CGFS Working Paper, no. 10. Available at: www.bis.org/publ/cgfs10.htm. Last accessed: 14.08.2013.

BIS (2011) 'The Impact of Sovereign Credit Risk on Bank Funding Conditions'. CGFS Paper no. 43.

BNY Mellon (2015) *The Future of Wholesale Funding Markets*. Bank of New York Mellon, Working Paper. Available at: www.bnymellon.com/us/en/our-thinking/the-future-of-wholesale-funding-markets.jsp. Last accessed 23.09.2015.

Bouveret, A. (2011) *An Assessment of the Shadow Banking Sector in Europe*. SSRN Paper. Available at: https://papers.ssrn.com/sol3/papers.cfm?abstract_id=2027007. Last accessed: 06.01.2017.

Brunnermeier, M. K. and L. H. Pedersen (2009) 'Market Liquidity and Funding Liquidity'. *The Review of Financial Studies*, 22(6), pp. 2201–2238.

Caballero, R. (2010) 'Macroeconomics after the Crisis: Time to Deal with the Pretense-of-Knowledge Syndrome'. *Journal of Economic Perspectives. American Economic Association*, 24(4), pp. 85–102.

CGFS (2010) 'Funding Patterns and Liquidity Management of Internationally Active Banks'. CGFS paper no. 39, May.

Claessens, S., Z. Pozsar, L. Ratnovski and M. Singh (2012) *Shadow Banking: Economics and Policy*. IMF Staff Discussion Note. Available at: www.imf.org/external/pubs/ft/ sdn/2012/sdn1212.pdf. Last accessed: 16.12.2016.

Cohen, B. J. (2015) *Currency Power: Understanding Monetary Rivalry*. Princeton, NJ: Princeton University Press.

Comotto, R. (2012) *Shadow Banking and Repo*. European Repo Council. Working Paper. Available at: www.icmacentre.ac.uk/images/2011/08/shadow-banking-and-repo.pdf. Last accessed 14.08.2013.

Dang, T. V., G. Gorton and B. Holmström (2012) *Debt, Ignorance and Financial Crises*. Columbia University Working Paper, December (first draft). Available at: www.columbia. edu/~td2332/Paper_Ignorance.pdf. Last accessed: 20.01.2017.

Dow, S. C. (2003) 'Uncertainty and Monetary Policy'. SCEME Working Papers. *Advances in Economic Methodology 002/2003*. SCEME.

Dow, S. C. (2012) *Foundations for New Economic Thinking*. London: Palgrave Macmillan.

ECB (2012) *Commission's Green Paper on Shadow Banking: The Eurosystem's Reply*. European Central Bank. Available at: www.ecb.europa.eu/pub/pdf/other/commissions greenpaperonshadowbankingeurosystemreplyen.pdf?d1e9220eb98d5ac4a658dbf8234 24a45. Last accessed: 14.08.2013.

Engelen, E., I. Ertürk, J. Froud, S. Johal, A. Leaver, M. Moran, A. Nilsson and K. Williams (2011) *After the Great Complacence: Financial Crisis and the Politics of Reform*. Oxford, UK: Oxford University Press.

European Commission (2012) *Green Paper Shadow Banking*. Available at: http:// ec.europa.eu/internal_market/bank/docs/shadow/green-paper_en.pdf. Last accessed: 23.11.2012.

European Commission (2013) *Shadow Banking: Addressing New Sources of Risk in the Financial Sector*. Communication, September 4. Available at: http://ec.europa.eu/ internal_market/finances/docs/shadow-banking/130904_communication_en.pdf. Last accessed: 14.08.2014.

Fisher, P. (2013) *Global Safe Assets*. Bank for International Settlements. Working Paper, no. 399. Available at www.bis.org/publ/work399.pdf. Last accessed: 06.02.2017.

Flandreau, S. (2013) *Do Good Sovereigns Default? Lessons from History*. BIS Working Paper, no. 72. Available at: https://pdfs.semanticscholar.org/dd8f/ae2d4e3f054fc 280c3d00967b7ee5a9a05d7.pdf. Last accessed: 20.01.2017.

Fleming, M. (2000) 'Financial Market Implications of the Federal Debt Paydown'. Federal Reserve Bank of New York. Available at: www.newyorkfed.org/medialibrary/media/ research/staff_reports/sr120.pdf. *Last accessed 23.04.2017.*

FSB (2011) *Shadow Banking: Scoping the Issues*. 12 April. Available at: www.fsb. org/2011/04/shadow-banking-scoping-the-issues/. Last accessed: 06.01.2017.

FSB (2012) *Global Shadow Banking Monitoring Report*. Financial Stability Board. Report. Available at: www.financialstabilityboard.org/publications/r_121118c.pdf. Last accessed: 20.12.2016.

Gabor, D. (2010) *Central Banking and Financialisation: A Romanian Account of How Eastern Europe Became Subprime*. Basingstoke, UK: Palgrave Macmillan.

Gabor, D. (2016a) 'A Step Too Far? The European FTT on Shadow Banking'. *Journal of European Public Policy*, 23(6), pp. 925–945.

Gabor, D. (2016b) 'The (Impossible) Repo Trinity: The Political Economy of Repo Markets'. *Review of International Political Economy*, 23(6), pp. 1–34.

Gabor, D. and C. Ban (2016) 'Banking on Bonds: The New Links Between States and Markets'. *Journal of Common Market Studies*, 54(3), pp. 617–635.

Garbade, K. (2006) 'The Evolution of Repo Contracting Conventions in the 1980s'. *Federal Reserve Bank of New York Economic Policy Review*, 12(1), pp. 2–12.

Giovannini, A. (2013) *Risk-free Assets in Financial Markets*. BIS Working Paper, no. 72. Available at: http://citeseerx.ist.psu.edu/viewdoc/download?doi=10.1.1.649.8993&rep= rep1&type=pdf. Last accessed: 20.12.2016.

Gorton, G. (2010) *Slapped by the Invisible Hand: The Panic of 2007*. New York: Oxford University Press.

Gorton, G. and A. Metrick (2009) *Securitized Banking and the Run on Repo*. NBER Working Paper, no. 15233. Available at: www.nber.org/papers/w15223.pdf. Last accessed: 20.12.2016.

Gourinchas P. and O. Jeanne (2012) *Global Safe Assets*. BIS Working Papers, no. 399. Available at: www.bis.org/publ/work399.pdf. Last accessed: 20.01.2017.

Hardie, I. (2011) 'How Much Can Governments Borrow? Financialisation and Emerging Markets Government Borrowing Capacity'. *Review of International Political Economy*, 18(2), pp. 141–167.

Hardie, I., D. Howarth, S. Maxfield and A. Verdun (2013) 'Banks and the False Dichotomy in the Comparative Political Economy of Finance'. *World Politics*, 65(4), pp. 691–728.

Hördahl, P. and M. King (2008) *Developments in Repo Markets during the Financial Turmoil*. BIS Quarterly, Fourth Quarter. Available at: www.bis.org/publ/qtrpdf/r_ qt0812e.htm. Last accessed: 20.01.2017.

Houben, A. C. F. J. and J. W. Slingenberg (2013) *Collateral Scarcity and Asset Encumbrance: Implications for the European Financial System*. Financial Stability Review, Banque de France. Available at: https://publications.banque-france.fr/sites/default/files/medias/ documents/financial-stability-review-17_2013–04.pdf. Last accessed: 06.02.2017.

IMF (2001) *International Capital Markets, Developments, Prospects and Key Policy Issues*. Chapter 4 ('The Changing Structure of the Major Government Securities Markets'). Washington, DC: IMF, August.

International Swaps and Derivatives Association (2010) *Market Survey*. Available at: www.isda.org/statistics/pdf/ISDA-Market-Survey-annual-data.pdf. Last accessed: 06.02.2017.

Iversen, T. and D. Soskice (2012) 'Modern capitalism and the advanced nation state: understanding the causes of the crisis'. In N. Bermeo and J. Pontusson (eds) *Coping with Crisis: Government Reactions to the Great Recession*. New York: Russell Sage, pp. 35–64.

Kaltenbrunner, A. (2011) Currency Internationalization and Exchange Rate Dynamics in Emerging Markets: A Post-Keynesian Analysis of Brazil. PhD dissertation, School of Oriental and African Studies (SOAS), University of London.

Kirshner, J. (1995) *Currency and Coercion: The Political Economy of International Monetary Power*. Princeton, NJ: Princeton University Press.

Kirshner, J. (2003) 'Money Is Politics'. *Review of International Political Economy*. Vol. 10(4), pp. 645–660.

Liikanen, E. (2012) *Reforming the Structure of the EU Banking Sector*. High-level Expert Group Report. Available at: http://ec.europa.eu/finance/bank/docs/high-level_expert_ group/report_en.pdf. Last accessed 12.01.2017.

Lysandrou, P. and A. Nesvetailova (2015) 'The Role of Shadow Banking Entities in the Financial Crisis: A Disaggregated View'. *Review of International Political Economy*, 22(2), pp. 257–279.

McCauley, R. (2001) 'Benchmark tipping in the money and bond markets'. *BIS Quarterly Review*, March, pp 39–45.

McCulley, P. (2007) 'Teton Reflections'. Global Central Bank Focus, PIMCO, September 2007. Available at: www.pimco.com/en-us/insights/economic-and-market-commentary/global-central-bank-focus/teton-reflections. Last accessed 23.04.2017.

Mehrling, P. (2012) 'Three Principles for Market-Based Credit Regulation'. *The American Economic Review*, 102(3), pp. 107–112.

Mehrling, P., Z. Pozsar, J. Sweeney and D. H. Neilson (2013) *Bagehot Was a Shadow Banker: Shadow Banking, Central Banking, and the Future of Global Finance*. Working Paper. Available at: http://econ.as.nyu.edu/docs/IO/26329/Mehrling_10012012.pdf. Last accessed: 06.01.2017.

Moe, T. G. (2012) *Shadow Banking and the Limits of Central Bank Liquidity Support: How to Achieve a Better Balance between Global and Official Liquidity*. Working paper, no. 712. Available at: www.levyinstitute.org/pubs/wp_712.pdf. Last accessed: 12.01.2017.

Nesvetailova, A. and R. Palan (2013) 'Minsky in the Shadows: Securitization, Ponzi Finance, and the Crisis of Northern Rock'. *Review of Radical Political Economics*, 45(3), pp. 349–368.

Plantin, G., H. Sapra and H. S. Shin (2007) 'Marking-to-Market: Panacea or Pandora's Box?' *Journal of Accounting Research*, 46(2), pp. 435–460.

Pozsar, Z. (2008) 'The Rise and Fall of the Shadow Banking System', Moody's Economy.com, July. www.economy.com/sbs. *Last accessed 23.04.2017.*

Pozsar, Z. (2011) *Institutional Cash Pools and the Triffin Dilemma of the U.S. Banking System*. IMF Working Paper. Available at: www.imf.org/external/pubs/ft/wp/2011/wp11190.pdf. Last accessed: 16.12.2016.

Pozsar, Z. and M. Sing (2011) 'The Nonbank-Bank Nexus and the Shadow Banking System'. IMF Working Paper, WP 11/289.

Pozsar, Z., T. Adrian, A. Ashcraft and H. Boesky (2010) *Shadow Banking*. Federal Reserve Bank of NY Staff Reports, no. 458. Available at: www.newyorkfed.org/medialibrary/media/research/staff_reports/sr458_July_2010_version.pdf. Last accessed: 16.12.2016.

Rixen, T. (2013) 'Why Reregulation after the Crisis Is Feeble: Shadow Banking, Offshore Financial Centres, and Jurisdictional Competition'. *Regulation & Governance*, 7(4), pp. 435–459.

Roe, M. (2013) 'Derivate Markets in Bankruptcy'. *Comparative Economic Studies*, 55(3), pp. 519–534.

Schwarcz, S. (2012) *Regulating Shadow Banking*. Inaugural Address for the Inaugural Symposium of the Review of Banking and Financial Law. Available at: http://scholarship.law.duke.edu/cgi/viewcontent.cgi?article=3121&context=faculty_scholarship. Last accessed: 14.08.2013.

Shin, H. S. (2009) 'Securitisation and Financial Stability'. *The Economic Journal*, 119(536), pp. 309–332.

Shin, H. S. (2011) 'Global savings glut or global banking glut?' Paper presented at the 12th Jacques Polak Annual Research Conference Hosted by the International Monetary Fund, Washington, DC, November 10–11, 2011.

Singh, M. (2011) *Velocity of Pledged Collateral: Analysis and Implications*. IMF Working Paper, no. WP/11/256. Available at: http://nowandfutures.com/large/VelocityOfPledgedCollateral-wp11256(repo_hypothecation)(imf).pdf. Last accessed: 13.01.2017.

Singh, M. and P. Stella (2012) *Money and Collateral*. Available at: http://papers.ssrn.com/sol3/papers.cfm?abstract_id=2050268. Last accessed 14.08.2013.

Sissoko, C. (2010) 'The Legal Foundations of Financial Collapse'. *Journal of Financial Economic Policy,* 2(1), pp. 5–34.

Stein, J. C. (2010) 'Securitization, Shadow Banking and Financial Fragility'. *Daedalus,* 139(4), pp. 41–51.

Thelen, K. (1999) 'Historical Institutionalism in Comparative Politics'. *Annual Review of Political Science,* 2(1), pp. 369–404.

Thiemann, M. (2014) 'In the Shadow of Basel: How Competitive Politics Bred the Crisis'. *Review of International Political Economy,* 21(6), pp. 1203–1239.

10 Investment funds, shadow banking and systemic risk

Elias Bengtsson

1 Introduction

Credit intermediation – accepting deposits or other short-term funding from surplus agents and lending it on to corporations, households and public bodies with borrowing needs – is typically associated with banks. Traditionally credit intermediation has been provided through a business model where banks act as single intermediaries, managing all stages of the credit intermediation process. The role of other financial intermediaries, such as investment funds, has been limited. However, in recent decades, the provisioning of credit has become increasingly segmented, with the various stages of the intermediation process supplied by a variety of financial entities, specializing on one particular or several stages in the intermediation chain. The potential benefits from such segmentation are substantial. It allows for more efficient intermediation, provides opportunities to diversify risk, improves pricing and allocation of risk as well as avoids its concentration in (typically a few large) banks. It also increases supply of funding and liquidity, thereby lowering costs for banks, their clients and the overall economy (Duffie, 2008; Bengtsson, 2014a).

Involvement in the credit intermediation process by non-bank financial intermediaries, either by directly supplying credit or by taking part in one or more stages of the credit intermediation process, has become known as "shadow banking" (Pozsar *et al.*, 2010; FSB, 2011). It can hardly have escaped anyone with interest in financial markets that the segmentation of the credit intermediation process, coupled with various vulnerable business models of many shadow banks, contributed to the build-up and manifestation of the global financial crisis. No wonder then that regulating and improving oversight of these non-bank credit intermediaries have become a top policy priority. Since the request from G20 in November 2010, the Financial Stability Board (FSB) has undertaken considerable work in mapping and exploring possible regulatory reform to reduce systemic risk and opportunities for regulatory arbitrage in the shadow banking system (G20, 2010; FSB, 2011).

But despite this, it is fair to say that the understanding of shadow banking is still in its infancy. As sound understanding is a precondition for appropriate regulation, there is a need for exploratory studies that seek to unveil particular aspects of shadow banking. This can include studying single stages in the credit intermediation process or looking at the involvement of one particular type of non-bank entities. This chapter seeks to accomplish this by considering the role of investment funds in the credit intermediation process (Section 2) and discussing various forms of systemic risk it might give rise to (Section 3). Based on these findings, it draws some conclusions on various policy challenges facing authorities charged with overseeing and regulating shadow banking (Section 4).

The analysis includes both traditional investment funds and hedge funds. But it is important to note that, like any other broad group of financial intermediaries, investment funds display large variety in investment strategies and business models. Some are only involved in one link in the credit intermediation chain – many not at all. Throughout the chapter, findings from research and statistics are used to shed light on this. However, it should be stated from the outset however that statistical coverage on the role of investment funds is very limited. The fact that this chapter only manages to portray a picture that is sometimes old and sometimes incomplete is merely a reflection of the lack of sufficient and timely data to gauge the importance of shadow banking in the credit intermediation process.

2 The role of investment funds in credit intermediation

This section briefly describes the main roles investment funds have played in credit intermediation in recent years. These include providing short- and medium-term funding to other financial entities that provide credit; taking over credit risk from banks and reversing their liquidity and maturity transformations by investing in structured credit; and substituting the role of banks in bearing credit risk by investing in credit derivatives.

2.1 Funding credit intermediation: substituting maturity transformation

While funds with fixed income exposures display large variation in the combination of ratings and maturities in their asset allocation, money market and short-term credit funds in general provide significant funding to the banking sector. For short- and medium-term money and credit instruments issued by banks, these funds play a particularly important role. For example, the share of money market and short-term debt instruments issued by euro area credit institutions held by euro area money market funds (MMFs) varied from 25 to 52 per cent between 2006 and 2012 (Figure 10.1).

In addition, a significant amount of these investment funds' money travels across border. This means that the total proportion of money and short-term debt instruments issued by banks and held by investment funds is even higher. For example, in mid-2008, US MMFs placed around half their assets under management with non-US (primarily European) banks. This funding corresponded to around one-eighth of European banks' US\$ funding needs (Baba *et al.*, 2009).

In a shadow banking framework, the supply of funding by investment funds to banks corresponds to a partial substitution of banks' maturity and liquidity transformations. This relates to the funding profile of investment funds. For open-ended funds, fund shares are withdrawable at notice. This means that

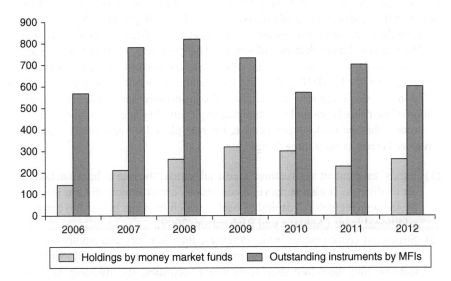

Figure 10.1 Money market and short-term credit instruments issued by credit institutions and held by MMFs in the Euro area 2006–2012 (EUR bn).

Source: ECB, Balance Sheet Items and Securities Issues Statistics (SEC).

Note: Data cover short-term (up to 1 year) debt securities issues by MFIs and held by MMFs in the euro area. Year-end statistics.

when such funds invest their immediately withdrawable funds in any financial instrument that has a longer tenure, the funds are engaged in maturity transformation. To the extent that banks replace deposit or other forms of short-term funding with funding with longer tenure from investment funds, their maturity transformation has decreased. However, the maturity transformation of banks has in fact been substituted by maturity transformation by investment funds.

2.2 Investing in structured credit: reversing maturity and liquidity transformation

In the context of credit intermediation, reversals of maturity and liquidity transformations are facilitated by investment funds investing in various forms of securitized loans. This includes a wide spectrum of structured credit instruments, ranging from simple asset-backed securities (ABSs) to various forms of more complex collateralized debt obligations (CDOs). Market data on structured credit is very limited, but investment funds and hedge funds play important roles as both buyers and sellers of these instruments (IMF, 2008; IOSCO, 2009). Estimates of holdings by the sector suggest that fund managers held around 28 per cent of US structured credit in the initial stages of the global financial crisis. (Figure 10.2).

Estimates of global CDO exposures by the end of 2006 corroborate this picture; hedge funds' share of total CDOs amounted to 47 per cent, whereas investment and pension funds together held around 19 per cent (Blundell-Wignall, 2007). In fact, hedge funds in particular played a decisive role in the development of the CDO market from the early 2000s and onwards (Lysandrou, 2011/2012). By 2008, structured credit represented more than half of total credit exposure to residential mortgages, and more than a quarter of total credit exposure to commercial mortgages and consumer credit in the US (IMF, 2008). The fact that the importance of structured credit in the intermediation process has diminished considerably since, is rather an illustration of the role of non-banks in strengthening cyclicality in credit supply.

From a shadow banking perspective, the role played by investment funds in structured credit implies three things:

(1) Funds' investment in structured credit substitutes the role of banks in taking on credit risk. It also supports a continuous credit intermediation process by freeing (regulatory) capital of banks, which then can be used to buttress additional loans (Acharya and Richardson, 2009).

(2) Structured credit enables banks to reverse their liquidity and maturity transformations, as securitizing credit implies taking long-term illiquid loans and transforming them into short-term liquid securities. By investing in these assets with short-term funding, investment funds reverse and take over banks' maturity and liquidity transformations.

(3) Just as for bank debt securities, the fact that investment funds frequently trade in structured credit means that they contribute to market liquidity for these instruments. This in turn is a precondition for the instruments to be effectively used as collateral in secured transactions.

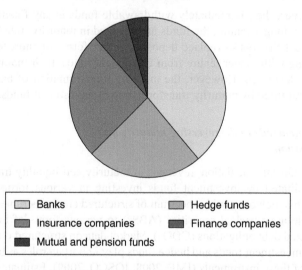

Figure 10.2 Holdings of US structured credit by sector (end 2007).

Source: Goldman Sachs in International Monetary Fund (2008) *Global Financial Stability*, Washington, DC, April.

Note: Figures cover par amounts for securities and notional amounts for derivatives. Data on banks includes investment banks.

2.3 Investing in credit derivatives: off-loading credit risk

Investing in credit derivatives represents another way in which investment funds substitute the traditional role of banks in the credit intermediation process. This involves credit default swaps (CDSs) – financial instruments that strip out the credit risk on an underlying asset. The market for such credit derivatives has grown tremendously during the past two decades – by mid-2000s, the gross market value of CDSs amounted to US\$ 294 billion, and by end 2012 to US\$ 848 billion (BIS, 2014).

The rapid growth in the market for unfunded credit derivatives is in fact attributable to the concurring growth in investment and hedge fund assets.[1] When the market for these credit derivatives developed in the mid-1990s, funds played a minor role. Even in 1999, hedge funds merely accounted for around 2 per cent of all credit risk protection sold. However, over the past decade, investment funds replaced insurance companies as the most visible and active non-bank market participant, with hedge funds' market share in selling credit risk protection reaching 28 per cent by end 2007 (Ong and Chan-Lau, 2006; Duffie, 2008). More recent figures suggest that, besides central clearing parties and primary dealers, hedge funds have become the most important category of financial institution in offering credit risk protection on a net basis (Figure 10.3).

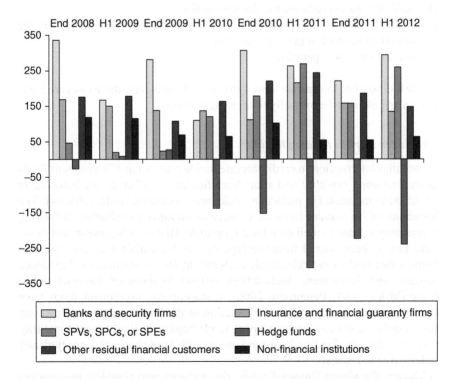

Figure 10.3 Net credit protection bought by sector 2008–2012 (notional amounts, USD bn).

Source: Bank for International Settlement.

From a shadow banking perspective, the holdings of credit derivatives by investment funds – just as their holdings of structured credit – can be considered as substituting banks in bearing credit risk. Indeed, the Committee on the Global Financial System has noted that credit derivatives have allowed funds to become competitors to the banks' credit intermediation business (CGFS, 2008). Also, just as for structured credit, it enables banks to reduce their required regulatory capital and thereby facilitates an ongoing supply of credit to the real economy.

3 Investment funds, shadow banking and systemic risk

The previous section illustrated important roles of investment funds in credit intermediation, by funding the banking sector, investing in structured credit and taking on credit risk through derivatives. These activities were considered from a shadow banking perspective in that funds substitute banks in taking on credit risk and engaging in maturity transformation, as well as providing opportunities for banks to reverse such transformations. In this section, risks that the credit intermediation process becomes interrupted due to the involvement of investment funds are considered. Three main systemic risks can be distinguished:

(1) sudden stops in credit intermediation funding;
(2) sudden reductions in market liquidity for financial instruments that are important to credit intermediation; and
(3) insufficient risk separation.

While it is possible to separate these systemic risks in theory, these risks are intertwined and likely to be mutually reinforcing in reality.

3.1 Sudden stops in funding liquidity

A potential interruption in credit intermediation may occur if investment funds cease providing liquidity and short-term funding to other actors involved in credit intermediation (in particular banks and structured credit vehicles). The instability of investment funds as a source of liquidity and short-term funding is primarily related to their own funding profile. Historically, investment funds have largely been spared from the type of massive withdrawals (or so-called "runs") that banks have recurrently suffered. In fact, some historical evidence suggests that investment funds attract inflows in times of financial turbulence (Miles, 2001; Pennacchi, 2006). Consequently, investment funds have been considered a stable source of funding to the banking system. However, this is quite surprising, as investment funds engage in liquidity and maturity transformation by funding long-term assets with fund shares that are typically redeemable at request.

During the global financial crisis, the maturity and liquidity mismatches of funds became a systemic problem. Runs occurred on both hedge funds and MMFs in several phases. Runs on investment funds in 2007 and 2008 meant that the supply of short-term funding to banks dropped sharply in both the USA and EU (Baba *et al.*, 2009; Mishkin, 2010). A similar pattern was observable in the summer of 2011 as US MMFs pulled out of European banks, putting pressure on the banks' dollar-denominated funding and trading. For instance, exposures of USA MMFs to French banks were reduced by 90 per cent between May 2011 and June 2012, resulting in a deficit of dollar funding of around US$ 100 billion (Chernenko and Sunderam, 2012). Part of this reduction in exposure was probably attributable to reallocation to reduce credit risk (see the following section), but investor redemptions was an important contributing factor. Assets of US prime MMFs fell by an estimated 10 per cent in summer 2011 (ICI, 2012).

There are at least three reasons why such runs occurred:

(1) *Many funds' long history of stable yields and protection of principal created an expectation of safety among fund investors*: These funds (MMFs in particular) have thereby attracted extremely risk-averse investors who are likely to withdraw from MMFs to avoid losses at the first sign of trouble. During the global financial crisis, relatively small losses trigged the runs in 2007 and 2008. In 2007, a widespread run on so-called enhanced MMFs occurred when news broke that losses were increasing on the subprime loans that backed the asset backed commercial papers (ABCPs) to which many funds were exposed.[2] Around 20 funds had to close for redemptions, and four funds had to be wound down. Again in 2008, following the bankruptcy of Lehman Brothers Inc., certain prime MMFs were facing losses on Lehman papers, which in turn led to withdrawals amounting to around US$ 300 billion (ICI, 2009).

(2) *Fund investors who redeem early can benefit from first mover advantages*: If the fund prices do not reflect the realizable market value of the fund's underlying assets (due to depreciation or lack of market liquidity), investors who redeem early will receive repayments based on the higher, unrealizable historical value. The remaining investors will be left with lower quality and less liquid assets, which forces them to bear a disproportionate share of the losses. To avoid ending up among the remaining investors, the collective behavior of fund investors may contribute to runs. First mover advantages are particularly strong for investors in debt instruments of leveraged funds. These investors have particularly strong incentives to run early, as those that do will receive their full investment at par. There are a number of examples of leveraged funds experiencing runs prior to the crisis, including LTCM and Amaranth Advisors (Kambhu *et al.*, 2007; King and Maier, 2009). During the crisis, this type of run occurred again on leveraged funds, and several funds closed due to inabilities to meet margin calls (Brunnermeier, 2009; Dwyer and Tkac, 2009). Leverage in an indirect sense may also partially explain the runs on constant net asset value (CNAV) MMFs during the crisis, in that investors expected repayment at par.

(3) *Information asymmetries*: Even if only one single fund is publicly known to be in trouble, a widespread run may occur. The reason is that investors may (correctly or not) suspect that – due to similar exposures among funds – other funds are also facing difficulties. As investors are not able to distinguish between those funds that do and those that do not, they face incentives to redeem. In 2008, such contagion between funds occurred following the Prime Reserve Fund's inability to repay investors at par ("breaking of the buck") (Fender *et al.*, 2008; Witmer, 2012). In Europe, the enhanced MMF segment suffered a similar fate in 2007 (Bengtsson, 2013).

Runs are also one explanation of why fund managers are prone to coordinated portfolio reallocations that in turn may hamper liquidity in the markets of financial instruments. The following section elaborates on how this may threaten credit intermediation.

3.2 Sudden reductions in market liquidity

Investment funds' aggregate portfolio reallocations – due to funding liquidity shortages or herding – may also impair market liquidity. While such "market runs" have occurred in niche markets, markets more important to credit intermediation have largely been spared. During the crisis, however, such runs manifested on several systemically important money and short-term credit markets (Aragon and Strahan, 2011). Market runs are associated with reductions in market liquidity which has two important consequences for financial stability. First, it puts pressure on those entities that have issued the instruments and rely on being able to roll them over to maintain funding liquidity. Second, in case the instruments are used in secured financing transactions, reduced market liquidity lowers the collateral value of the instruments (Gorton and Metrick, 2012).

The preconditions for a market run are typically built up in the expansive phase of the financial cycle. In this phase, investors (including fund investors and managers) tend to underestimate risk, which compresses the credit risk premium and increases asset prices. Once some trigger bursts the bubble and confidence evaporates in the markets, the consequences from such risk illusions may be detrimental (Minsky, 1992).[3] It often leads to situations where reduced market liquidity impairs price discovery, which leads to forced sales and depreciates asset prices. This may further reduce market liquidity. Such negative spirals are particularly driven by actors who themselves experience simultaneous strains on funding liquidity, including investment banks and investment funds that are leveraged or have leverage-like features (such as CNAV MMFs). The booms and busts of financial cycles are reinforced by intermediaries using collateralized funding (so-called "leverage cycles") to obtain leverage. Once the underestimation of risk becomes evident, collateral values decrease. This may force fire sales of assets to meet margin calls, which further depresses collateral values.

Structured credit and debt instruments issued by banks (and their various conduits or vehicles for structured credit) are two prominent examples of how

investment funds' reallocations may impair market liquidity with negative consequences for the credit intermediation process. In the build-up to the global
financial crisis, investment funds increased risk taking by leveraging their "balance sheets" and migrating to more risky assets. Leverage by credit hedge funds
fuelled the credit bubble for structured credit that burst in 2007, since hedge funds
could earn the spread between the credit instruments and the cheap funding they
could obtain by using those instruments as collateral (see previous section). It is
doubtable whether the volumes of structured credit would have reached the level
where the financial systems in the USA and EU were threatened, had it not been
for these funds (Lysandrou, 2011/2012). As an example of increasing risk exposure, several MMFs in the USA had up to 2008 gained market share by investing
in higher-yielding instruments, including Lehman Brothers' notes but also debt
instruments of longer tenure or lower ratings (Stecklow and Gullapalli, 2008).

For structured credit, the bubble burst when delinquencies on subprime mortgages increased in spring/summer 2007. These loans in turn backed commercial
papers issued by conduits sponsored by large banks. In August 2007, liquidity in
the instruments reached a level where obtaining a reliable market quote became
difficult. As it became apparent that certain investment funds held these papers,
investors started to redeem fund shares. Figures on net sales reveal that enhanced
MMFs in Europe lost around 20 per cent of total assets under management due
to investor redemptions in the third quarter of 2007.[4] For hedge funds, which
held the bulk of these instruments, the loss of liquidity in the instruments meant
that they no longer could use them as collateral for their funding (Lysandrou,
2011/2012). The sudden reduction of liquidity in structured credit had severe consequences for credit intermediation. Apart from rapidly falling asset prices with
direct losses for many financial intermediaries, the runs on conduits forced banks
to honor their contractual or implicit liquidity guarantees to those conduits. Also,
the sudden rupture to the process of off-loading credit to the shadow banking
system meant that banks had little choice but to retain those ABS they no longer
could sell on their balance sheets.

The run on the market for bank debt instruments was triggered in September
2008 when it became apparent that Lehman Brothers Inc. was facing serious trouble. Certain MMFs held securities issued by the troubled investment bank, but the
information asymmetries on individual MMF exposures led to significant withdrawal requests across the whole prime MMF segment. These withdrawals, in
turn, decreased the proportion of funds' liquid short-term assets, which forced up
the average maturities of portfolios. To avoid breaching regulatory requirements or
fund mandates, fund managers increased their allocation to very short-term cash-
like instruments. Also, as withdrawal requests increased, fund managers started
hoarding cash as a precaution against future withdrawals (Bengtsson, 2013).
Reduced liquidity also meant that fund managers had trouble obtaining reliable
quotes for longer-dated commercial paper, which in turn forced them to reallo-
cate toward very short-term securities. Eventually, market runs affected all but the
shortest debt instruments of the highest quality, and unprecedented public backstops were required to reinstate liquidity in the financial system.

The developments in structured credit and money markets are illustrative examples of how fund managers and their investors may contribute to procyclicality in credit and market liquidity as a consequence of their own funding liquidity shortages, asset reallocations and leverage. These market runs, in turn, put pressure on the funding liquidity of credit institutions, both directly and from the falling collateral values of instruments on their balance sheets. The inability to reverse maturity and liquidity transformation through markets in bank debt and structured finance is clearly a systemic risk related to the involvement of investment funds in the credit intermediation process.

3.3 Insufficient risk separation

Credit intermediation may also be threatened as a consequence of insufficient risk separation between fund managers and banks. The reason is that banks may suffer losses or liquidity shortages not provisioned for in their capital or liquidity planning due to insufficient risk separation, which in turn may reduce their supply of credit to the real economy.

One form of insufficient risk separation concerns implicit guarantees by sponsors of investment funds. Since the 1990s, banks have increasingly diversified into non-interest earning activities such as fund management (c.f. Bengtsson and Delbecque, 2011). Although such fund management services are typically offered through separately capitalized asset management subsidiaries, empirical evidence shows that risk of fund investors and managers can easily spill-over on their sponsors in the shape of non-contractual obligations to supply capital or liquidity. Banks honor these obligations for at least three reasons:

(1) Concerns with reputation and/or a wish to preserve the franchise value of the subsidiary or the financial group as a whole.
(2) Common or similar exposures between funds and banks, which may lead to losses for the sponsor if the assets of the fund are liquidated.
(3) Parent companies may rely on funding from their investment funds and may seek to prevent disruptions to their funding channels.

In the global financial crisis, the manifestation of such insufficient risk separation had serious consequences for the banking system. Much of this insufficiency related to runs on investment funds and markets discussed in Sections 3.1 and 3.2. Several hedge funds were supported by their parent companies when volatility in structured credit increased sharply in early 2007 (King and Maier, 2009). For example, Bear Stearns lent US$ 3.2 billion to a single hedge fund having trouble meeting margin calls (Brunnermeier, 2009). Similarly, several MMFs domiciled in Luxembourg took out short-term loans from their parent banks to meet redemptions in the turbulence of 2008 (CSSF, 2008). Capital support also occurred in the shape of fund assets purchased by banks above market value, to protect fund investors from losses. For instance, AXA, Société Générale and Credit Suisse all took part in such transactions with significant losses as a result. Another form of support during the crisis was to guarantee the value of fund assets (Kacperczyk and Schnabl, 2011; Brady *et al.*, 2012).

While it is difficult to gauge the potential impact on the sponsor from giving support, estimates show that assets of sponsored MMFs ranged between US$ 15 and 80 billion for European banks and between US$ 50 and 375 billion for US banks. This corresponded to 170 and 1,300 per cent, respectively, of the EU and US banks' core tier 1 capital (Bank of England, 2012). An estimate of the actual value of support, as opposed to the amounts guaranteed, suggests that the pretax value of parent support of MMFs in the EU was at least US$ 2 billion in 2008 alone (Ansidei *et al.*, 2012).

As these non-contractual contingent liabilities and commitments to provide capital or liquidity were typically not covered by existing capital adequacy frameworks, it is unlikely that sponsors had set aside sufficient capital or liquidity in relation to the risks. Also, the need for support tends to coincide with market stress, when sponsors may already face difficulties in maintaining sufficient "own" liquidity or capital. As most fund sponsors are banks, insufficient risk separation may constitute a systemic risk that can hamper the credit intermediation process.

Another form of insufficient risk separation relates to the significant role played by fund managers in credit derivatives (see Section 2.3). While credit derivatives enable banks to transfer credit risk to sellers of credit risk protection, in reality the transfer may be insufficient. This relates to situations where the originating bank's credit risk may merely have (fully or partially) transformed into counterpart risk to the seller of credit risk protection (Cole *et al.*, 2007). Insufficient risk separation in credit derivatives also concerns the settlement process following the triggering credit event. As demonstrated by the discussion on whether Greece in fact did default in 2012, the process of fulfilling credit derivatives contracts remains largely untested, and it still characterized by uncertainty (Buttonwood, 2012). If the settlement process is uncertain, a proportion of risk nevertheless remains with the entity with the original exposure to the borrower.[5] This implies that credit intermediaries may be exposed to risks that may elude managerial and supervisory oversight and lead to situations where banks lack ability to absorb losses from the manifestation of such risk and instead are forced to interrupt credit provisioning.

4 Concluding discussion

This chapter has sought to contribute to the understanding of system risk in shadow banking by investigating the role of investment funds in the credit intermediation process and associated systemic risks. On a general level, it showed that even though traditional investment funds and hedge funds may be very different in terms of their investment strategies and business models, some of them share several commonalities from a systemic risk perspective. More specifically, it was discussed how instability in the funding profile of investment funds may threaten their ability to substitute banks' maturity transformation; that funds' potential funding liquidity shortages, asset reallocations and leverage may contribute to procyclicality in credit and lead to market runs on systemic money and short-term credit markets; and that insufficient risk separation may elude managerial and supervisory oversight, and force banks to reduce or interrupt credit intermediation in periods of stress. These three forms of systemic risk are clearly related and may reinforce each other in times of financial turbulence.

On reflection, such interactions between risks speak in favor of the entity-based approach adopted in this chapter to analyze shadow banking and systemic risk. On the other hand, there are cross-sectoral interactions between different types of financial entities that also may give rise to systemic risk in credit interme-diation. The risk of omitting those types of interactions would be reduced by using an analytical approach based on a certain function or role in the credit intermedia-tion process. Regardless of the analytical approach, what clearly is a challenge is the lack of timely and comprehensive data for uncovering the entities involved in shadow banking and their respective roles. Without sufficient data, the task of policy bodies, regulators or macroprudential authorities to fully grasp shadow banking and its contribution to systemic risk is daunting.

While international work to improve data on shadow banking is underway by the FSB and others, designing appropriate regulation, which balances the economic benefits of activities or actors with their consequences for systemic risk, will be a challenge. One complicating factor is the potential (perceived) systemic importance of shadow banks, which may increase risk taking by them and their counterparts. In some jurisdictions during the crisis, shadow bank-ing entities and activities were offered public backstops on several occasions (Bengtsson, 2014a, 2014b). Such bail outs may foster a lack of vigilance among market actors, provide incentives for taking on additional risk and fuel future asset bubbles. This type of moral hazard is also likely to be influenced by the ongoing discussion on identifying and regulating systemically important non-bank financial institutions.

Another challenge for responsible authorities and policy bodies is the evolving character of shadow banking. It is innovative by nature, and there are many exam-ples throughout history of how shadow banking has been established primarily to exploit opportunities of regulatory arbitrage. As regulatory requirements are tightened on the regular banking sector (through Basel III and other reforms), the incentives for other entities to supply credit increase. Indeed, there are some indi-cations that asset managers are increasingly becoming involved in direct lending.[6] Similarly, if certain shadow banking entities or activities become subject to stricter regulation in the future, incentives arise for credit intermediation to migrate out-side the regulatory perimeter. Authorities are thus faced with a difficult boundary problem. The way responsible authorities deal with these challenges will indeed have consequences for the future of the financial system, and very likely for us all.

Acknowledgement

Reprinted with permission from Emerald Group Publishing Limited, originally pub-lished in *Journal of Financial Regulation and Compliance*, Volume 24, No. 1 © Emerald Group Publishing Limited 2016.

Further reading

Alternative Investment Management Association (AIMA) (2012), "The role of credit hedge funds in the financial system: Asset managers, not shadow banks", March.

Fitch Ratings (2006), "French money market funds", 23 May, available at: www.fitch ratings.com.

Gordon, J. and Gandia, C. (2012), "Money market funds run risk: Will floating net asset value fix the problem?", Columbia Law and Economics Working Paper No. 426.

Notes

1 There are numerous business models of hedge funds that take advantage of the opportunities provided by credit derivatives, including hedging and arbitrage trading. There are two main types of funds that offer credit risk protection: one is enhanced/dynamic money funds that seek to achieve above money market rates by investing in credit derivatives while simultaneously providing daily or near daily liquidity; another is specialized credit hedge funds that seek long credit exposure (BCBS, 2008).

2 Enhanced (or alternatively *dynamic, absolute performance* or *absolute return*) MMFs seek to bridge the gap between traditional MMFs and bond funds. This is achieved by taking on additional risk by investing in longer-dated and more volatile instruments such as short-term bonds, currencies and arbitrage on credit instruments (Standard and Poor's, 2007).

3 The trigger may be exogeneous (such as a macroeconomic shock) or endogeneous (a so-called "Minsky spiral").

4 According to data from Lipper FMI.

5 The case of AIG (an insurer) illustrates the counterparty credit risk associated with CDSs. A number of generic problems associated with adverse selection and moral hazard in CDS transactions are discussed in CGFS (2003).

6 For instance, estimates suggest loan origination for commercial real estate in the UK provided by non-banks was around 11 per cent of all new loans in 2013 (a doubling since 2012). A major part of this lending came from various hedge and debt funds and was driven by stricter regulation on traditional banks (Allen, 2014). Another example where fund managers' involvement in loan origination may increase is in Ireland, where a specific regulatory framework for loan origination investment funds was introduced in 2014 (Central Bank of Ireland, 2013).

References

Acharya, V. and Richardson, M. (2009), "Causes of the financial crisis", *Critical Review*, Vol. 21 Nos 2/3, pp. 195–210.

Allen, K. (2014), "Non-bank lenders rapidly expand into commercial property", *Financial Times*, 23 May.

Ansidei, J., Bengtsson, E., Frison, D. and Ward, G. (2012), "Money market funds in Europe and financial stability", Occasional Paper Series No. 1, European Systemic Risk Board, Frankfurt.

Aragon, G. and Strahan, P. (2011), "Hedge funds as liquidity providers: Evidence from the Lehman bankruptcy", *Journal of Financial Economics*, Vol. 103 No. 1, pp. 570–587.

Baba, N., McCauley, R. and Ramaswamy, S. (2009), "US dollar money market funds and non-US banks", *BIS Quarterly Review*, Vol. 65 No. 1, March.

Bank for International Settlement (BIS) (2014) "Statistical release: OTC derivatives statistics at end-December 2013", Monetary and Economic Department, May 2014, available at: www.bis.org/publ/otc_hy1405.pdf.

Bank of England (2012), Money Market Funds: Systemic risk indicators, Bank of England, Mimeo.

BCBS (2008) "Credit risk transfer developments from 2005 to 2007", The Joint Forum, July, available at: www.bis.org/publ/joint21.pdf.

Bengtsson, E. (2013), "Shadow banking and financial stability: European money market funds in the global financial crisis", *Journal of International Money and Finance*, Vol. 32 No. 1, pp. 579–594.

Bengtsson, E. (2014a), "Systemic risk regulation and money market funds", in Baklanova, V. and Tanega, J. (Eds), *Money Market Funds in the EU and the US – Regulation and Practice*, Oxford University Press, Oxford.

Bengtsson, E. (2014b), "Fund management and systemic risk: Lessons from the global financial crisis", *Financial Markets, Institutions & Instruments*, Vol. 23 No. 1, pp. 101–124.

Bengtsson, E. and Delbecque, B. (2011), "Revisiting the European asset management industry", *Financial Markets, Institutions & Instruments*, Vol. 20 No. 4, pp. 163–190.

Blundell-Wignall, A. (2007), "Structured products: Implications for financial market", *Financial Market Trends*, Vol. 93 No. 2, pp. 27–57.

Brady, A., Anadu, K. and Cooper, N. (2012), "The stability of prime money market mutual funds: Sponsor support from 2007 to 2011", Federal Reserve Bank of Boston Working Paper RPA 12–3, Boston, 13 August.

Brunnermeier, M. (2009), "Deciphering the liquidity and credit crunch 2007–08", *Journal of Economic Perspectives*, Vol. 23 No. 1, pp. 77–100.

Buttonwood (2012), "The euro zone crisis: When is a default not a default?", *The Economist*, 1 March.

Central Bank of Ireland (2013), "AIFMD questions and answers", May 2013.

CGFS (2003), *Annual Report*. Basle, Switzerland: Bank for International Settlement.

CGFS (2008), Credit Risk Transfer Statistics, Papers No. 35, Bank for International Settlement, Basel.

Chernenko, S. and Sunderam, A. (2012), "The quiet run of 2011: Money market funds and the European debt crisis", Fisher College of Business Working Paper No. 2012-4.

Cole, R., Feldberg, G. and Lynch, D. (2007), "Hedge funds, credit risk transfer and financial stability, Banque de France", *Financial Stability Review*, Vol. 10 No. 1, pp. 7–17.

CSSF (2008), "Annual report", available at: www.cssf.lu

Duffie, D. (2008), "Innovations in credit risk transfer: Implications for financial stability", BIS Working Papers No 255.

Dwyer, G. and Tkac, P. (2009), "The financial crisis of 2008 in fixed-income markets", *Journal of International Money and Finance*, Vol. 28 No. 8, pp. 1293–1316.

Fender, I., Frankel, A. and Gyntelberg, J. (2008), "Three market implications of the Lehman bankruptcy", *BIS Quarterly Review*, Vol. 1 No. 1, pp. 6–7.

FSB (2011), "Shadow banking: Strengthening oversight and regulation: Recommendations of the Financial Stability Board", 27 October.

G20 (2010), "The Seoul summit document", November 2010, Para. 41.

Gorton, G. and Metrick, A. (2012), "Who ran on repo?", NBER Working Paper No. 18455.

ICI (2009), "Report of the money market working group", 17 March.

ICI (2009) "Report of the Money Market Working Group", March 17 (2009).

ICI (2012), "Investment Company Fact Book: A review of trends and activity in the US", 52nd edition, available at: www.icifactbook.com

International Monetary Fund (2008), "Global Financial Stability", IMF, Washington, DC.

International Organization of Securities Commissions (IOSCO) (2009), "Transparency of structured finance products", Consultation Report, September.

Kacperczyk, M. and Schnabl, P. (2011), "Implicit guarantees and risk taking: Evidence from money market funds", NBER Working Paper No. 17321.

Kambhu, J., Schuermann, T. and Stiroh, K. (2007), "Hedge funds, financial intermediation and systemic risk", Staff Report No. 291, Federal Reserve Bank of New York, New York, NY.

King, M. and Maier, P. (2009), "Hedge funds and financial stability: Regulating prime brokers will mitigate systemic risks", *Journal of Financial Stability*, Vol. 5 No. 3, pp. 283–297.

Lysandrou, P. (2011/2012), "The primacy of hedge funds in the subprime crisis", *Journal of Post Keynesian Economics*, Vol. 34 No. 2, pp. 225–253.

Miles, W. (2001), "Can money market mutual funds provide sufficient liquidity to replace deposit insurance?", *Journal of Economics and Finance*, Vol. 25 No. 39, pp. 328–342.

Minsky, H. (1992), "The financial instability hypothesis", Jerome Levy Economics Institute Working Paper No. 74, Aldershot, UK. Available at: https://papers.ssrn.com/sol3/papers.cfm?abstract_id=161024.

Mishkin, F. (2010), "Over the cliff: From the subprime to the global financial crisis", NBER Working Paper series 16609.

Ong, l. and Chan-Lau, J. (2006), "The credit risk transfer market and stability implications for UK financial institutions", IMF Working Papers 06/139, International Monetary Fund, Washington, DC.

Pennacchi, G. (2006), "Deposit insurance, bank regulation, and financial system risks", *Journal of Monetary Economics*, Vol. 53 No. 1, pp. 1–30.

Pozsar, Z., Adrian, T., Ashcraft, A. and Boesky, H. (2010), "Shadow banking", Federal Reserve Bank of New York Staff Report No. 458, New York, NY, July.

Standard and Poor's (2007), "Money market funds intensify their focus on safety and liquidity", 24 September.

Stecklow, S. and Gullapalli, D. (2008), "A money-fund manger's fateful shift", *Wall Street Journal*, Vol. 8 No. 1, 8 December.

Witmer, J. (2012), "Does the Buck stop here? A comparison of withdrawals from money market mutual funds with floating and constant share prices", Working Paper 2012–25, Bank of Canada, Ottawa.

Part III

Banking on the future

The structural demand for financial innovation

11 Why overcapitalisation drives banks into the shadows

Jan Toporowski

Introduction

Shadow banking emerged into the light in the wake of the financial crisis that broke out in 2007, when banking regulators woke up to the realisation that their vassals had unreported or under-reported commitments to unregulated institutions whose claims could make regulated banks insolvent (Nesvetailova 2010). Subsequent reports and inquiries revealed networks of 'special investment vehicles' or 'special purpose vehicles' whose function seemed to be to absorb the off-balance sheet liabilities of banks that subsequently had to be rescued by governments. The outcome has been a series of investigations into shadow banking and what may be done to make their operations more transparent and prudent (Financial Stability Board 2011, 2012; Pozsar *et al.* 2012).

A particular difficulty that plagues the whole discussion of shadow banking is the absence of any agreed definition of what constitutes 'shadow banking'. There is general agreement that it refers to financial intermediation that takes place outside regulated banking. But there is little clarity over what constitutes the unregulated financial system, on the one hand, because this depends on regulations and financial structures that differ between countries at different stages of financial and economic development and, on the other, because what is not regulated is itself less visible. As a result, the discussion of shadow banking is beset by ambiguities and differences of meaning. Such differences of meaning make shadow banking a less efficient concept in communication between regulators, practitioners and academics. Discussions of theory and policy are thereby rendered less effective.

In many countries (e.g. mainland China) shadow banking has been taken to mean the system of informal or illegal banking (see Li and Hsu in this volume; e.g. 'Shadow Banking in China' *The Economist* 7 April 2012). However, in countries such as the United States or Great Britain, with developed capital markets, it has been taken to mean funds operating in those capital markets such as private equity funds or hedge funds, organised as limited partnerships and therefore with minimal disclosure requirements; or bank subsidiaries based in tax havens (Tucker 2010; Palan 2012). In the months before the financial crisis broke out, banks that were unable to sell bonds made up of securitised loans transferred ownership of those bonds to such funds established as special investment vehicles or special purpose vehicles, and financed from the inter-bank market. As the inter-bank market froze up in 2008, these funds were unable to roll over their borrowing, thereby precipitating the illiquidity and possible insolvency of their parent banks.

Accordingly, the shadow banking system has been viewed as a problem of regulation and so-called macro-prudential policy because it consists of claims and liabilities of an unknown scale to financial intermediaries with undisclosed balance sheets, by regulated banks, that are more or less guaranteed by the financial authorities (backed by the government). This is in contrast to regulated banks' claims and liabilities to other regulated banks, whose balance sheets are disclosed and more transparent and therefore easier to evaluate. In other words, the financial problems are seen as arising from the inter-locking balance sheets of banks and other intermediaries (banks holding as assets the liabilities of other financial intermediaries). This is supposed to be the source of 'contagion', or a tendency of illiquidity or insolvency in one bank or fund to spread to other banks or funds. A prodigious amount of effort has therefore gone into 'macro-mapping' the networks of such balance sheets' interdependencies (Financial Stability Board 2011, 2012; Pozsar *et al.* 2012). 'Incentive' problems are then supposed to be dealt with by the institutional separation of retail banking (under government or financial authorities' guarantee) from investment banking. The latter constitutes, allegedly, the 'speculative' part of banking whose role in the setting up of shadow banking funds is supposed to be responsible for the crisis. This is supposed to warrant separate capitalisation of retail and investment banking, if not an actual ban on retail bank involvement in investment banking (Independent Commission on Banking 2011. cf. Lysandrou 2012).

The fact that 'shadow banking' is unregulated has led to a widespread opinion that the very phenomenon of shadow banking is caused by regulation. Two kinds of regulation are supposed to be involved. On the one hand, central bank regulation of the money market rate of interest has encouraged large investment institutions to develop quasi money market instruments, such as repos and collateralised securities, often issued by special investment vehicles or special purpose vehicles that will offer higher yields than regulated money markets (see Gorton 2010, chapter 2).[1] The second kind of regulation is the regulation of balance sheets, in which financial regulators specify certain ratios and proportions in balance sheets that banks and other financial intermediaries must maintain. To prevent this kind of regulation from interfering with their business, financial intermediaries transfer unwanted parts of their balance sheets to shadow bank subsidiaries, or obtain desirable elements of their balance sheets from those subsidiaries or through the quasi money market. A key part in this process is played by securitisation, which transforms illiquid loans into liquid debt obligations that are sold through the bond market for ready money (bank deposits) and ended up accumulating on balance sheets in the shadow banking system (Pozsar *et al.* 2012). In this chapter, it is argued that a different kind of balance sheet regulation is responsible for creating the shadow banking system in the financially advanced economies. In such financially complex economies, the policy of setting high capital requirements for banks plays a particular part in creating and sustaining the shadow banking system.

Capital adequacy requirements

Capital adequacy requirements were first introduced at the end of the 1980s, following a number of crises in international banking, culminating in the international debt crisis that broke out in 1982 and continued to depress international banking until the 1990s. A committee of bank regulators, formed under the auspices of the Bank for International Settlements, made a number of recommendations for coordinating the regulation of international banks. A key recommendation of raising the amounts of capital held by banks was pushed through, principally by the UK and US representatives on that committee. These representatives from the two major global financial intermediary countries were crucial in framing the system of uniform regulation that is supposed to apply to banks in all countries participating in the international banking system. The banks regulated by those US and UK representatives had their capital base in the active capital markets of those countries – banks elsewhere in Europe and Asia have historically operated with much smaller equity bases. The result of their deliberations is well-known: banks henceforth were supposed to hold capital in proportion to their risk-weighted assets, those risk-weightings being higher for cross-border assets outside the OECD countries. The risk-weightings were modified at the end of the 1990s. Subsequently, in the wake of the financial crisis of 2008, capital requirements were raised and reinforced by limits on leverage (the ratio of a bank's borrowing to its equity) and higher minimum liquidity requirements (Basel Committee on Banking Supervision 2011).

The reasoning behind higher capital requirements is based on the function that a bank's equity or share capital has in its balance sheet of covering any shortfall in the value of assets relative to liabilities. In the first instance, that shortfall is supposed to be covered from reserves (accumulated retained profits, or shareholders' funds). If the reserves are insufficient, a bank is effectively insolvent. It follows from this that when a bank gets into financial difficulties, by definition it does not have enough equity to cover the shortfall in the value of its assets. However, this does not mean that increasing the share capital of all banks will strengthen them financially. The proposition that higher capital will strengthen the banking system contains a fallacy of composition. While higher capital may strengthen an individual bank, if all banks do this it can damage the asset value of the whole banking system (Toporowski 2009).

The reason for this is that the supply of capital in the main capital markets of the international banking system (in North America and Western Europe, including the UK) is dominated by institutional investors (insurance companies and pension funds) whose buying of new share issues is determined by the structure of their liabilities and regulatory requirements. In any one period, the scale and term structure of the liabilities of an institutional investor, together with the regulations that governments set for pension funds and insurance companies, determine the amount of shares that that investor may buy. This makes their demand for new stock in that period inelastic with respect to the price of that stock. In effect, the capital market is inflated if those investors wish to buy more stocks than are being issued, and capital is rationed if those investors do not have space in their regulated portfolios for all the new capital issues that are on offer, or that issuers would like to place on the market.[2] Where capital rationing prevails, banks that are obliged to sell new capital stocks do so by 'crowding out' non-bank issuers of new stocks. Those non-bank issuers are therefore obliged to finance their balance sheets through debt, rather than through their preferred equity. In turn, the greater indebtedness of non-bank borrowers reduces their expenditure on business investment, thereby reducing the liquidity and sales turnover of the non-bank private sector. Inevitably this leads to bad loans and deteriorating bank asset quality (Toporowski 2009, 2010).

In the section that follows, it is argued that raising capital requirements also fosters shadow banking.

Overcapitalisation and shadow banking

In the previous section, it was argued that the general imposition of high capital requirements (as opposed to increasing the capital of an individual bank, holding the capital of other banks constant) is a factor in the proliferation of bad assets on bank balance sheets. In this section, it is argued that shadow banking is the way in which banks 'cope' with the high capital requirements that this proliferation of bad assets entails.

Capital adequacy requirements are supposed to work by inducing banks to hold capital that matches the 'riskiness' of their assets. This riskiness is in practice unknown, in the sense that the banking future cannot be known, and banks, their customers and credit ratings agencies are notoriously prone to misjudge the quality of assets. The banking authorities set risk-weightings for banks either by rule of thumb or on the basis of past history. Given the length of credit cycles and the increasing integration of banking markets, such risk-weightings are biased towards avoiding the last banking crisis rather than the next one and inevitably give inadequate results. One has only to consider the incidence of default that might have been calculated in 2006, by comparison with the defaults that actually occurred.

Underlying the capital adequacy argument is a view of banking which assumes that banks will respond to the capital requirements by managing their capital issues, that the supply of equity capital is elastic in relation to the cost of capital and that the cost of capital serves as a disincentive to undertaking 'risks' in lending. However, if the supply of equity capital is inelastic, then the offer of a higher return on capital may not induce investors to buy new capital issues (possibly because that higher return might be viewed as an indicator of higher riskiness of a bank's assets). Banks are therefore obliged to meet capital adequacy requirements not by issuing new capital, but by managing their assets.

Well before the crisis, the liquidity and risk profile of assets could be managed by securitisation, that is the packaging of assets into bonds for sale into the capital market, because that capital market was being inflated. However, as the crisis approached, amid rumours of difficulties in selling new capital issues, banks started to remove their risky loans off their balance sheets into special investment vehicles and special purpose vehicles whose balance sheets were not disclosed as part of the reporting requirements of the parent bank. The clear motivation behind this was to show capital adequacy.

In other words, high capital requirements drive risky lending into the shadow banking system. On a reported bank balance sheet, risky lending may require the issue of costly new capital. The cost of the new capital then enters into the calculation of the credit rating for a bank. This therefore increases the cost of the bank's operations in the inter-bank market, as well as decreasing the scope of these operations, where there are counterparties that will not lend to a bank with a downgraded rating.

The higher capital cost of risky lending provides a second reason why high bank capital adequacy requirements encourage the expansion of shadow banking. Such requirements give shadow banks a competitive advantage in financial intermediation. A typical shadow bank (a hedge fund or a special purpose vehicle) has an opaque balance sheet, because it is based in a tax haven or organised as a partnership with minimal reporting requirements. It is often financed largely with inter-bank deposits, or deposits raised in the informal, quasi money market through repurchase agreements and foreign exchange swaps. The minimal, capital requirements mean that the profits of the shadow bank are distributed among its partners, rather than distributed around inactive institutional investors. The concentration of profits in a smaller group of partners is a greater incentive to form and operate shadow banks, relative to large banks that have to satisfy a bloated capital base.

Thus, more stringent capital adequacy requirements increase the incentive for banks to set up shadow bank subsidiaries to manage their risky lending. Because of the large amount of short-term borrowing from the inter-bank market that is used to finance shadow banks, such banks may have increased difficulties with maturity transformation (which caused the crisis in shadow banking in 2008). Such financing is likely to be facilitated in the foreseeable future as long as the inter-bank market is liquid, or central banks provide such liquidity through open market operations or quantitative easing.

Finally, there is the effect of bank capital adequacy requirements on non-financial businesses. As noted earlier, the crowding out of such businesses from the capital market drives those businesses to shadow banking for long-term borrowing.[3] Shadow banks that do not have expensive capital overheads can afford to treat these businesses more generously than regulated banks.

Conclusion

There is a complex relationship between the structure of financial intermediation, including the respective shares of shadow banking and formal banking, and the 'riskiness' of assets in the financial system, that is the 'riskiness' of the liabilities of the non-financial sector. The non-financial sector is vulnerable to business cycles, in which the equity of households and non-financial businesses is supposed to stabilise the finances of those businesses through down-turns in economic activity. If that equity is 'crowded out' by the capital issues of banks, households and non-financial businesses are obliged to finance themselves through down-turns with 'risky' debt (risky because it is incurred to defray losses or refinance existing assets rather than to buy remunerative assets). This risky debt would 'normally' appear on bank balance sheets as the counterpart of banks' greater equity. Risk-related bank capital requirements therefore determine what portion of the risky debt appears on the balance sheets of formal banks, and what portion appears on shadow banks' balance sheets.

It is no coincidence that the countries that most actively pursued the overcapital-isation of their banking systems were also the countries in which shadow banking has proliferated. This proliferation has occurred not just because of deregulation, but also because of the incentives that capital adequacy requirements create for the balance sheet management of banks, and the structural distortions that the requirements have imposed on capital markets. Those structural distortions arise because banks either have excess capital, in which case capital adequacy requirements do not constrain a bank's lending, or else banks have insufficient capital, or are on the margins of capital adequacy, so that (net) new lending requires additional capital. Capital adequacy regulation is only effective in the second case, because it is only in this case that banks' marginal cost of capital may act as a deterrent against risky lending, because banks must raise that additional capital.

Banks that do not have excess capital may respond to the requirement to hold more capital in different ways. One way is to raise the additional capital, paying whatever cost of capital may be required by the markets. In this case, the asset counterpart of this capital must generate a return large enough to cover that cost of capital. The consequences of adverse selection, from such a ramping up of lending rates, have been well-known since at least the time of Adam Smith (Stiglitz and Weiss 1981; Toporowski 2005: 20–25). Adverse selection would lead to poorer quality asset portfolios, requiring (if the regulators are engaged in dynamic provisioning, that is raising capital requirements as bank asset portfolios become more risky – see Brunnermeier *et al.* 2009) the raising of further capital. Where the supply of new capital is price-inelastic, which is the case when capital is supplied by institutional investors, the raising of additional regulatory capital by banks effectively 'crowds out' capital that should be available to non-financial businesses. Since non-financial businesses have comparatively minimal regulatory capital requirements, they can be more easily forced to satisfy their liquidity needs by resorting to debt markets. This rising indebtedness obliges them to hold more liquid assets (instead of using borrowing to finance business investment) as security against their higher borrowing. Those liquid assets are either claims on other companies or consumers or, in the case bank deposits, bank liabilities whose counterparts are the borrowings of other companies and consumers. But, since at least a part of this additional borrowing is due to the inability to obtain capital, forcing companies to use alternative debt instruments, much of that additional borrowing must necessarily be of worse quality. Worse quality borrowing which ends up on the books of regulated banks then requires them to raise additional capital, or hold onto their excess capital. In this way, bank capital requirements reinforce poor quality lending. The entry of non-financial businesses into financial intermediation feeds the shadow banking system both because non-financial businesses are not regulated as banks and because the declining quality of credit, due to this dysfunctional skewing of the capital market, and capital rationing create the incentive for transferring the resulting poor quality loans into shadow banking subsidiaries.

The second way, therefore, of coping with more demanding capital requirements is to eliminate poor quality loans by transferring them onto the balance sheets of non-bank subsidiaries, either through direct transfer, or through securitisation and market sale. The recent crisis showed how this can be achieved by cosmetic transformation of poor credit. That which ends up in shadow banks, financed with short-term borrowing from the money market or its fringe quasi money market, adds the problem of maturity transformation to the problem of bad credit. However, it should be pointed out that insofar as regulated banks engage in this kind of transfer of risky credit into the shadow banking system, this relieves the pressure on non-bank institutions of 'crowding out' by banks of those other institutions' demand for equity in the capital market.

Ultimately, shadow banking, like credit risk, is endogenous to the business cycle. The credit system (including financial institutions and banks) is the system that 'accommodates' the financing needs of governments, firms and consumers. The quality of its credit is determined by those processes, principally business investment, that can transform credit into income that can service debt (Toporowski 2012b). Balance sheet regulation in an accommodating credit system will evoke a shadow banking system to accommodate credit restricted by such regulation and capital rationing. The shadow banking system therefore expands at the end of a boom as the quality of credit deteriorates, with the shift of credit expansion from income generating processes to the (non-income-generating) refinancing of existing, already produced, assets. Similarly, the shadow banking system may contract as the quality of credit improves with a shift of credit expansion from the refinancing of existing, already produced, assets to income generating processes.

The above analysis suggests three ways to eliminate shadow banking. First of all, there is the elimination of all but minimal capital requirements for banks. This would remove the competitive advantage that shadow banks have in relation to regulated banks, and ease capital rationing constraints. Second, stricter regulation of investment banking, if necessary controlling new capital issues to direct new capital towards non-financial business, would provide capital most effectively to where it can stabilise the finances of the private sector, through refinancing debt into equity (Toporowski 2009). Finally, restrictions on the size of banks, and the range of business that regulated banks may do, need to be phased out. 'Too big to fail' also means 'big enough to regulate', and bank balance sheets accessible to regulation. While the apparent success of central bank policy in Canada has attracted much attention since the crisis broke out in 2008, not enough attention has been paid to the structure of the financial system that gave its central bank the favourable circumstances to ensure that success.

Notes

1 This unofficial money market is the foundation for the argument of Grahl and Lysandrou against a financial transactions tax. See Grahl and Lysandrou (2003).
2 Strictly speaking, sovereign wealth funds are in a position to respond to an increase in the amount of new capital issues by buying them in, and there are cases where, for example, Barclays Bank in the UK has raised capital from Middle Eastern funds. However, the continuing impairment of bank balance sheets seems to confirm that such funds can only really have a marginal impact on the situation outlined in this section. A second element of elasticity has been the rise of private equity, which offers institutional investors the opportunity to hold equity with the kind of assured liquidity that characterises medium-term debt. However, despite the rapid increase in private equity activity, it constitutes a relatively small part of institutional investors' portfolios (Toporowski 2012a). Nevertheless, many academics and policy-makers consider private equity to be a part of the shadow banking system (e.g. European Central Bank 2013). If banking is the business of taking deposits and making loans, then private equity cannot be considered as banking. However, insofar as it offers institutional investors opportunities for alternative ways of holding equity, and thereby evading regulations on their holding equity, then private equity has similarities to shadow banking.
3 It might be asked why non-financial firms do not simply go to the formal banking system for loans. Here it is worth pointing out that non-financial firms in search of equity capital usually require this to refinance existing debt and that equity capital is supposed not to be repaid except in the case of the winding up of a company. A failure to access the capital market to repay existing debt clearly indicates an inability, or at least an unwillingness, to repay, rather than refinance, that debt now *and in the foreseeable future*. It clearly signals the increased riskiness of any new borrowing that a firm may undertake. Such borrowing will be available, at a price, in the shadow banking system. A more general way of 'coping' with debt is to build up stocks of liquid assets. Such a build-up of liquidity has been very apparent in corporate balance sheets since the 2008 crisis, effectively shutting the capital market to non-financial corporations. According to the US Federal Reserve, US non-financial corporations held US$1,864.8 bn. in liquid assets at the end of 2009. By the end of 2013, this had risen to US$2,179.6bn (www.federal reserve.gov/releases/z1/Current/z1r-4.pdf). This growing engagement of non-financial corporations in financial intermediation constitutes a second shadow banking system whose incidents may be less dramatic than the financial crisis of 2008, but whose effects in under-investment and reduced economic activity, may be even more catastrophic than during that crisis.

References

Basel Committee on Banking Supervision (2011) *Basel III A Global Regulatory Framework for more Resilient Banks and Banking Systems*. Basel, Switzerland: Bank for International Settlements.

Brunnermeier, M., A. Crockett, C. A. E. Goodhart, A. D. Persaud and H. Shin (2009) *Fundamental Principles of Bank Regulation*. Geneva Reports on the World Economy. Geneva: Centre for Economic Policy Research.

European Central Bank (2013) *Enhancing the Monitoring of Shadow Banking*. Monthly Bulletin, February, pp. 89–99. Available at: www.ecb.europa.eu/pub/pdf/other/art2_mb201302en_pp89-99en.pdf. Last accessed 23.04.2017.

Financial Stability Board (2011) *Shadow Banking: Strengthening Oversight and Regulation Recommendations of the Financial Stability Board*. Report. London, 27 October. Available at: www.fsb.org/wp-content/uploads/r_111027a.pdf?page_moved=1. Last accessed 23.04.2017.

Financial Stability Board (2012) *Global Shadow Banking Monitoring Report*. Report. London, 18 November. Available at: www.fsb.org/wp-content/uploads/r_121118c.pdf. Last accessed 23.04.2017.

Gorton, G. (2010) *Slapped by the Invisible Hand: The Panic of 2007*. New York: Oxford University Press.

Grahl, J. and Lysandrou, P. (2003) 'Sand in the Wheels or Spanner in the Works? The Tobin Tax and Global Finance'. *Cambridge Journal of Economics*, 27(4), pp. 597–621.

Lysandrou, P. (2012) 'Hedge Funds'. In J. Toporowski and J. Michell (eds) *Handbook of Critical Issues in Finance*. Cheltenham, UK: Edward Elgar.

Nesvetailova, A. (2010). *Financial Alchemy in Crisis*. London: Pluto Press.

Palan, R. (2012) 'Tax Havens'. In J. Toporowski and J. Michell (eds) *Handbook of Critical Issues in Finance*. Cheltenham, UK: Edward Elgar.

Pozsar, Z., T. Adrian, A. Ashcraft and H. Boesky (2012) *Shadow Banking*. Staff Report, no. 458. New York: Federal Reserve Bank of New York (originally published in July 2010). Available at: www.newyorkfed.org/medialibrary/media/research/staff_reports/sr458.pdf. Last accessed 23.04.2017.

Stiglitz, J. E. and Weiss, A. (1981) 'Credit Rationing in Markets with Imperfect Information'. *American Economic Review*, 71, pp. 393–410.

The Economist (2012) 'Shadow Banking in China. The Wenzhou Experiment'. *The Economist*, 7 April 2012. Available at: www.economist.com/node/21552228. Last accessed 23.04.2017.

Toporowski, J. (2005) *Theories of Financial Disturbance: An Examination of Critical Theories of Finance from Adam Smith to the Present Day*. Cheltenham, UK: Edward Elgar.

Toporowski, J. (2009) *'Enforced Indebtedness' and Capital Adequacy Requirements*. Policy Note 2009/7. New York: The Levy Economics Institute of Bard College.

Toporowski, J. (2010) *A Theory of Capital Rationing*. Working Paper, no. 166. Economics Department, The School of Oriental and African Studies, University of London. Available at: www.soas.ac.uk/economics/research/workingpapers/file63670.pdf. Last accessed 23.04.2017.

Toporowski, J. (2012a) 'Private Equity Funds'. In J. Toporowski and J. Michell (eds) *A Handbook of Critical Issues in Finance*. Cheltenham, UK: Edward Elgar.

Toporowski, J. (2012b) *Corporate Liquidity and Financial Fragility: The Role of Investment, Debt and Interest*. Working Papers, no. 169. Department of Economics, The School of Oriental and African Studies, University of London, March. Available at: www.soas.ac.uk/economics/research/workingpapers/file74886.pdf. Last accessed 23.04.2017.

Tucker, P. (2010) *Shadow Banking, Financing Markets and Financial Stability*. Available at: www.bankofengland.co.uk/publications/Documents/speeches/2010/speech420.pdf. Last accessed: 19.12.2016.

12 The future for the top 0.1 per cent
The real role of hedge funds in the subprime crisis

Photis Lysandrou

Introduction

This chapter examines the role of the demand factors behind the process of the production of securities through the shadow banking system. It does so by focusing on the role of hedge funds in the global crisis and, specifically, their function as facilitators of the demand for shadow banking instruments (namely, collateralised debt obligations (CDOs)). While mainstream explanations for the 2007–09 meltdown have tended to focus on the banking system and supply-side factors of financial innovations, it is important not to ignore a central role of the hedge fund industry in driving the demand for new and alternative financial securities.

This chapter concurs that the hedge funds might have played no part in the actual construction of shadow banking instruments. However, it is their intermediary position between the investors seeking yield on the one hand and the banks that create the high yielding securities on the other that accounts for the expanding supply of these securities. Without hedge funds being active participants in this process, the volume of investable securities would never have reached the proportions that became critical in precipitating the near collapse of the whole financial system in 2007–09. To articulate this argument, this chapter is structured as follows. After first outlining the brief history of the evolution of hedge funds and some of their strategies, I examine hedge fund CDO holdings between 2002 and 2007 and show these holdings to have been an important demand-pull force behind the expansion of the shadow banking system. The final section reflects on some of the post-2009 shifts in the regulatory approach to finance. In particular, I argue that the search of yield from the growing wealth management industry is likely to continue to facilitate the growth of the hedge fund sector, a development that will both parallel and reinforce the trend growth of the global shadow banking system post-2009.

Hedge funds

Hedge funds are a unique type of financial institution. Unlike banks that traditionally perform a 'transformation' function (liquidity, risk or maturity transformation) hedge funds merely perform a 'transfer' function: assets placed under their management by clients are redeployed with the aim of generating better returns than is otherwise possible for those clients. Freed from the type of regulatory and fiduciary constraints that are binding on other institutional investors such as pension and mutual funds, hedge funds are not obliged to factor risk on anything like the same scale into their return generating strategies, a feature which explains why the latter are usually classified as 'absolute return' strategies. Finally, the multiplicity of their investment strategies is what distinguishes hedge funds from private equity firms that represent the other major type of 'alternative investment' vehicle.

The story of hedge funds is usually said to begin with Alfred Jones' partnership, A. W. Jones and Co., established in the US in 1949. Their basic strategy, based on what Jones called his 'hedge principle', was to combine long positions in stocks that were deemed undervalued with the short selling of stocks that were deemed overvalued. Jones' success in generating unusually high returns over the next two decades (one estimation puts the cumulative returns between 1949 and 1968 at around 5,000 per cent) helped to spawn imitators, particularly following the publication of a profile of Jones in Fortune magazine in 1966 in which the term 'hedge fund' was first used. A 1968 survey by the Securities Exchange Commission found that about 140 hedge funds had been established in the US by that time. Since then, the hedge fund industry has grown to a size sufficient to make it a powerful force in the global financial landscape: an estimated 10,000 funds were operating in 2007 on the eve of the financial crisis (approximately 70 per cent of which were based in New York, with a further 26 per cent based in London), with assets under their management totalling approximately $1.5 trillion. Although the hedge fund sector, in common with many other financial sectors, suffered a decline in 2009–2010 in the wake of the subprime crisis, this decline has since been more than reversed as evidenced by the fact that by mid-2015 assets under hedge fund management were in the region of $2.7 trillion (Barclay Hedge 2015).

The expansion of the hedge fund industry over the past seven decades can be divided into three distinct phases: (i) 1950–1980; (ii) 1980–2000; (iii) 2000–present. The factors demarcating the first and second of these growth phases broadly relate to differences in the general investment philosophy of the hedge funds, on the one hand, and to differences in the general economic environment in which they operate, on the other. Where the hedge funds of both periods were quintessentially speculative vehicles, borrowing heavily to leverage up their bets, the early hedge funds would typically avoid market risk by combining their bets in a particular asset class with offsetting positions in the same asset class, while their later counterparts would on the contrary typically embrace market risk. This is why some commentators argue that 'wager' or 'speculative' funds are now a more accurate description of hedge funds than is this latter term. Similarly, while the conservative, market risk avoiding approach of the early hedge funds was broadly reflective of an era where a battery of government controls and regulations ensured that the financial sector remained relatively small in scale and largely passive in character, the aggressive, market risk embracing approach of the later hedge funds was entirely in keeping with the opportunities offered by the new realities of the post Bretton Woods era, chief among these realities being the huge growth in the scale and volatility of the now largely deregulated financial markets.

The third period of hedge fund growth beginning in the early 2000s sees further changes in hedge fund investment strategy, but the more significant change that occurred at this time was the 'institutionalisation' of the hedge fund client base. From 1950 right through to 2000, rich individuals (the so-called 'high net worth individuals') were the only major source of money pouring into the hedge funds. From this time on, however, institutional investors, including pension funds, endowments and funds of funds, also became an important source of investments in hedge funds as can be gauged by the fact that while individuals accounted for 95 per cent of hedge fund assets in 2000, their percentage share had fallen to approximately 50 per cent in 2007 (IFSL 2008). The principal development triggering this very sudden change in the hedge fund client base was the fall in yields in all of the major US bond markets in the early to mid-2000s (initially caused by the low federal fund rate and then sustained by the huge influx of foreign public and private investments funds into the US).[1] In their search for yield, institutional investors turned to the hedge funds as part of the solution to the problem.

The role of the hedge funds in the subprime crisis

During the 1990s, hedge funds were associated with a number of financial crises around the world. Perhaps the most spectacular collapse of a hedge fund came in 1999, when Long Term Capital Managements faced bankruptcy amidst the collapse of emerging market economies in 1997–98, and Russia's default in particular. The evidence and realisation that hedge funds have the potential to seriously disrupt the financial markets has prompted calls for these private investment vehicles to be made subject to the same disclosure standards and regulatory constraints as are currently binding on the public investment vehicles.

While these calls began to be made before the outbreak of the subprime crisis in 2007, they became louder and more insistent after the crisis. Given that what began as a crisis in the market for subprime-backed securities rapidly mutated into the worst global economic crisis since the Great Depression, it stands to reason that the hedge funds would have been clamped down very quickly had it been generally recognised that these institutions bore the major responsibility for the growth of the toxic securities. However, this was not the case. Rather, the general consensus was that it was the banks and their associates who created the structured finance CDOs that were chiefly responsible for the subprime crisis. Even in continental Europe, where the drive towards closer regulation of the hedge funds is at its most powerful, it is still widely accepted that the hedge funds played a secondary, amplifying role in the crisis rather than a primary, causal one. To quote from a report published in February 2009 by the High-Level Group on Financial Supervision in the EU: "Concerning hedge funds, the Group considers they did not play a major role in the emergence of the crisis. Their role has largely been limited to a transmission function, notably through massive selling of shares and short-selling transactions".[2]

This argument is wrong. The hedge funds may indeed have played no part in the actual construction of the CDOs that were at the epicentre of the crisis, but this is not the point. The point is that had it not been for the hedge funds' *unique intermediary position* between the investors seeking yield on the one side and the banks who created the high yielding securities on the other, the supply of these securities could never have reached the proportions that were critical to causing the collapse of the whole financial system. There should never have existed a mass market for CDOs given that their complex and opaque structure broke all the rules of commodity exchange, and without the hedge funds such a market would not in fact have existed. Wealthy individuals did not have the requisite expertise to participate in this market, while liquidity, fiduciary and other considerations prevented institutional asset managers from having more than a limited participation. In both cases, the preferred solution to the yield problem, which was becoming increasingly acute after 2001, was to pour money into the hedge funds who in turn believed that one of the surest ways of satisfying the demand for yield was to redirect substantial proportions of this money into CDOs.[3]

CDOs and the shadow banking system

In conceptualising the shadow banking system, I follow Lysandrou and Nesvetailova (2015) and focus on the reasons behind the expansion of the system to the point where it could cause serious systemic damage. To this end, shadow banking can be best understood as:

> [a] system of unregulated off-bank balance sheet credit intermediation and maturity and liquidity transformation activities conducted by bank owned or sponsored entities in the capital and money market domains for the primary purpose of expanding the rate of production of yield bearing debt securities required by the global investor community.
>
> (Lysandrou and Nesvetailova 2015: 5)

The securities supplied by the shadow banking system right up to the outbreak of the crisis essentially fell into two categories: short-term and long-term. The predominant type of short-term security was asset-backed commercial paper (ABCP). From a flow perspective, ABCP merely represents a form of short-term funding of the long-term assets held by the conduits and special investment vehicles (SIVs). Yet from a stock perspective it represents an important type of value container demanded by short-term investors and most notably by the money market mutual funds. The predominant types of long-term securities were asset-backed securities and CDOs. While these credit instruments in one sense merely represent forms of capital market lending funded by money market borrowing (Mehrling *et al.* 2013), they also represent important supplements to the world's stocks of investable securities demanded by long-term investors such as insurance companies and pension and mutual funds.

In the mainstream explanations of the crisis, it is the financial institutions that created and distributed the CDOs that tend to be singled out for blame, with overconfidence and greed identified as the two principal motivating factors.[4] Insofar as more general environmental factors enter into the picture, they do so in ways that bolster this supply-side story behind the growth of CDOs, one argument being that the years of the "great moderation" and the concomitant relaxation of monetary policies and of bank supervision contributed to the undervaluation and mispricing of risk, and another being that the build-up of a "savings glut" in Asia and other parts of the world contributed to the unusually low borrowing costs and the resulting excessive leverage and risk taking in the Western banking system.

CDOs were first introduced in the 1980s, but their rate of growth remained slow until the early 2000s when that rate suddenly rocketed, as shown in Figure 12.1. In 2002, there was an estimated $250 billion worth of CDOs outstanding, but by the end of 2006 that sum had multiplied twelvefold to about $3 trillion, with about one-third of this sum comprised of 'cash' CDOs and the two-thirds comprised of 'synthetic' CDOs, that is CDOs artificially created by taking cash CDOs as reference entities for credit default swap agreements.

The period between 2002 and 2006 witnessed a phenomenal growth in the hedge fund industry: hedge fund assets tripled, rising from $500 billion to about $1.5 trillion, and the number of firms operating within the industry doubled, rising

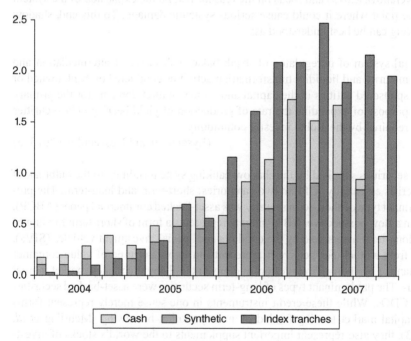

Figure 12.1 Growth of CDOs (US$ trillions).

Source: Borio (2008).

from about 5,000 to about 10,000. As already noted, one of the key drivers behind the growth of the hedge fund industry was its "institutionalisation", a trend that, as also noted, was largely the result of the unusually low yields that persisted in all of the major bond markets during this period.[5] Although CDOs offered what seemed to be a good solution to the yield problem that was becoming increasingly acute, the opaque, high-risk and difficult-to-trade nature of these financial products meant that the pension and mutual funds and various other institutional investors had to strictly limit their involvement with them and look for additional solutions to the yield problem. This included the placement of large sums with the hedge funds, which, not being subject to the same regulatory and prudential constraints that were binding on the public investment vehicles, used a substantial proportion of these sums to buy large amounts of CDOs. There were other buyers of these products as has often been pointed out, not only by the hedge funds themselves but also by many other commentators, but as we will now see, the hedge funds were by far the most important buyers.

By the end of 2006, there were approximately \$3 trillion worth of CDOs outstanding, with about one-third of this sum comprised of 'cash' CDOs and the other two-thirds comprised of 'synthetic' CDOs (Borio 2008). It has been estimated that the hedge funds held about 60 per cent of the cash CDOs and about 30 per cent of the synthetic CDOs, while the banks, insurance companies and pension and mutual funds held the rest.[6] After the subprime crisis, the hedge funds are often seen to have played the role of the innocent and gullible investor.[7] Yet far from being lured by the banks into buying the CDOs, they on the contrary pressured the banks into accelerating the rate of supply of these products, particularly of the super senior and senior varieties. They did so because these triple-A rated products served a double purpose for the hedge funds in that, on the one hand, they generated a higher return than did US treasuries even while having the same rating, and, on the other, they could be used as collateral in credit arrangements on account of their high rating. Given that hedge funds borrowed heavily from their prime brokers to leverage up their various exposures, it was only logical that they should use CDOs as collateral to reduce borrowing costs, while the prime brokers for their part were obliged to accept the CDOs as collateral in reverse repos given that it was they themselves who helped to create these structured credit products in the first place.

As I have shown in a number of studies (Lysandrou 2011, 2012; Lysandrou and Shabani 2016), the expansion of CDO growth from 2002 onwards bears a close correlation with the growth of hedge fund assets. A strong indication that this correlation is no coincidence but a manifestation of a deeper, causal link is given by the hedge funds' share of CDO holdings at the end of 2006 as documented above. From the start of the CDO explosion, it was observed that the hedge funds and CDOs were mutually suited: the high yields on CDOs were extremely attractive for the hedge funds, whereas the latter's structure and expertise meant that they could handle the complex and high-risk nature of these products with comparative ease. Indeed, the hedge funds became so important a part of the CDO universe that some commentators have attributed the growth of synthetic CDOs, which barely existed in 2002, to the shortage of cash CDOs created by the heavy demand from the hedge funds. As to the actual composition of CDOs, hedge funds held significant amounts of triple-A-rated senior tranches. In fact, the common perception that the hedge funds were only interested in holding the higher yield bearing equity and mezzanine tranches of CDOs is not correct. It is certainly true that the hedge funds did hold relatively more of these tranches than did other investors because they were better placed to do so. To quote from a report in April 2007:

> Hedge fund managers' expertise, experience and appetite for high returns provides them with an incentive to invest in the riskiest component of an issue such as CDO equity tranches. Other investors, like most institutional investors, naturally avoid these areas due to regulation or a lack of knowledge.
>
> (Mustier and Dubois 2007: 89)

For hedge funds, these tranches served a double purpose for them: on the one hand, they gave better returns than did other high quality government and corporate securities even while having the same superior credit rating, and, on the other, they could be used as collateral in borrowing arrangements because of their superior rating. If it is asked why the investment banks, which are the primary lenders of money to the hedge funds, were bound to accept these securities as collateral, the simple answer, to repeat, is that it was these very same banks that helped to create the CDOs in the first place.

The growth of CDOs: the pull of demand

The supply of CDOs was based on two key elements: securities backed by conventional loans, including conforming residential mortgage loans, and securities backed by nonconforming residential mortgage loans. I argue that in their search for yield, investors pressured the investment banks to supply structured credit products in ever greater quantities, and to do this, these banks needed the mortgage originators to take whatever steps were necessary to induce as many subprime borrowers as possible to take out mortgage loans. To quote from one testimony given by Gerald Corrigan of Goldman Sachs at a House of Commons hearing on the financial crisis: "To a significant degree it has been the reach for yield on the part of institutional investors in particular that goes a considerable distance in explaining this very rapid growth of structured credit products" (House of Commons 2008: 16). As already noted, these clues that attest to the strength of demand for CDOs have been ignored in most of the academic and official accounts of the subprime crisis because of the assumption that for the demand for any product to be one of the driving forces behind its supply, the product in question has to be sufficiently transparent as to allow it to be priced and traded against general market standards, and CDOs quite clearly do not meet this criterion.

In fact, a demand-led market for CDOs did exist between 2002 and 2007, albeit that it was based not so much on a system of arm's-length and impersonal exchanges as on a dense network of personal relations between pairs of agents at the very centre of which was the relation between the hedge funds and the investment banks (see Guttmann, this volume). This relationship has always been a particularly close one. In some instances, this closeness was cemented by the fact that investment banks owned the hedge funds that they were dealing with; in many other instances, it was cemented by the fact that the personnel employed by the hedge funds had been previously employed by investment banks. However, what was universally true and did more than anything else to bind the investment banks and hedge funds together, was the fact that they needed each other: hedge funds simply could not carry out their function to the extent that they did without the range of prime brokerage and other support services provided by the investment banks, while the latter could not maintain profit margins at the level that they did without the interest, fees and commissions that they charge the hedge funds (it is estimated that about a quarter of all investment banks' income comes from hedge funds).

When the problem of yield started to become serious from about 2002, the close-knit and mutually advantageous nature of the relationship between the hedge funds and the investment banks made it the perfect funnel through which the pressure of demand for higher yields emanating from investors at one end of the financial spectrum was passed onto the institutions supplying the high-yield securities at the other end. Just as the hedge funds were more than willing to plough substantial amounts of their clients' money into CDOs, because these helped to enhance returns while also helping to reduce leverage costs, the investment banks were equally willing to press the commercial banks and others into helping them to supply the hedge funds with CDOs, because in addition to the fees and commissions earned directly from the sale of these products, they could also expect the extra income from the extra business with hedge funds, much of which would have been generated with the help of CDOs.

In sum, my analysis of shadow banking indicates that one of the key factors driving the expansion of the system – the demand for CDOs – was by no means the passive accommodator of their supply as is often implied in conventional explanations of the crisis and in emerging theories of shadow banking. The rate of growth of CDOs between 2002 and 2007 could only have been so extraordinarily high because of the dynamic interaction between the push of supply factors on the one hand and the pull of demand factors on the other. This argument takes us back, of course, to the question as to why the hedge funds have not taken any major blame for the subprime crisis.

With the onset of the subprime crisis, the hedge funds seemed to have vanished from view by leaving the foreground to the banks that supplied the subprime products and mingling in the background with the other investors that bought these products. An important additional factor that helps to explain why this vanishing act has worked so well, concerns the relatively small amounts of losses incurred by the hedge funds as compared to those incurred by the banks. Yet as I show elsewhere (Lysandrou 2011, 2012), the roles played respectively by the hedge funds and the bank-sponsored conduits in the subprime crisis were the exact reverse of those that they are generally assumed to have played: it was the hedge funds together with the mortgage companies and the banks' SPEs and SIVs that caused the subprime crisis, while the banks' conduits helped to turn that crisis into a full-scale banking crisis. It is, of course, possible that even without a CDO crisis, a panic may still have broken out in the money markets in the summer of 2007 for some other particular reason, but this is conjecture. What is not conjecture is that it was the abrupt collapse of the $3 trillion CDO market that triggered the collapse of confidence in the money markets in general and in the interbank market in particular. Furthermore, it is also possible that had the CDO market remained as small in 2007 as it had been in 2002, the emergence of problems in that market may not have had any significant spill over effect in the other financial markets. Again, this is conjecture. The truth of the matter is that by 2007 the CDO market had grown to such a size as to be able to wreak general havoc when it eventually collapsed.

It is this single but absolutely crucial fact that explains why the hedge funds must carry the same primary responsibility for causing the subprime crisis as that carried by the SPEs and SIVs sponsored or operated by the commercial and investment banks. The logic is inescapable: if the hedge funds had not played as prominent a role on the buy side of the CDO market as that played by the commercial and investment banks on the supply side, that market would not have grown twelvefold between 2002 and mid-2007, and its collapse at this latter point in time would not have set in motion a liquidity-solvency crisis that rapidly spiralled out of control.

Hedge funds today

Following a temporary stall in the immediate post-subprime crisis period, assets under hedge fund management have again started to grow at a rapid pace. In parallel to the post-2009 expansion of the shadow banking system, the hedge fund resurgence is likely to continue for the foreseeable future for two sets of reasons, one to do with enablement and the other to do with motivation.

The key enabling factor is that hedge funds will continue to face far lighter regulation than do other types of institutional investor. Hedge funds may find the new transparency and reporting constraints to be an unwelcome nuisance, but these constraints will do little to hamper their use of unconventional, and often unethical, techniques and strategies to generate above average yields, which is what after all gives hedge funds their raison d'être. It should be further noted that hedge funds have escaped heavier and more effective regulation not only because they were largely absolved from complicity in causing the subprime crisis but also because of the political weight that they carry in the two major countries where they are based, the US and the UK. If the Republican Party in the US is opposed to any further tightening of hedge fund regulation, this is not a little to do with the fact that hedge funds are an important donor of funds to the Party, as holds true in the case of the UK's Conservative Party where hedge funds, together with private equity firms, now account for about 27 per cent of all donations (Mathiason and Bessaoud 2011).

Foremost among the motivating factors driving hedge fund resurgence is the parallel resurgence of global wealth concentration. While the combined wealth of the world's high net worth individuals fell from about $40 trillion in 2007 to an average of $36 trillion in 2008–9, that wealth has again grown, reaching $56.4 trillion in 2014 (Capgemini-RBC Wealth Management 2015). Much of this wealth is stored in an assortment of relatively safe assets (ranging from blue chip corporate securities and government bonds to real estate and cash), but a significant proportion continues to be allocated to the higher yield–higher risk alternative investment classes, including hedge funds. Another, equally important, driver behind the new phase of hedge fund growth is the extremely low yields on major government securities, a fact that recalls similar developments in the run up to the financial crisis. The problem is that although the global demand for safe-haven US treasuries and other advanced economy government bonds continues to rise in the current era of low economic growth and heighted uncertainty, the rate of supply of good quality investable government bonds has been constrained by fears that overstepping a specified government debt to GDP threshold (the Reinhart-Rogoff 90 per cent threshold figure being the most widely invoked) would spell disaster. As if these fears did not have a powerful enough dampening effect on government bond supplies, and thus on bond yields, what has served to make matters even worse is the reliance on monetary policy, in the form of quantitative easing, as a major way of lifting domestic economies out of recession. With bond yields at or close to zero by virtue of central bank bond purchases, it is little wonder that institutional investors such as pension and mutual funds, who have to meet obligations to their clients, are increasing their investments in hedge funds in a desperate attempt to find extra yield. There can be no better illustration of this desperation than the fact that despite facing heavy criticism in bartering its moral principles for material gain, the Church of England has recently increased its exposure to hedge funds from about 4 per cent of its £600 million pension fund to over 10 per cent (Jones 2012).

Conclusion

Despite the range of unresolved problems of accountability in the financial sector post-2007, governments are still hesitant as to how far they should go in tightening the controls on hedge funds. An important factor behind this hesitation is the continuing uncertainty over the extent to which the hedge funds were responsible for the subprime crisis that subsequently mutated by stages into the worst economic crisis since the Great Depression. As things stand, the supply-side story of the growth of toxic securities that absolves the hedge funds from major blame continues to be far more compelling than the demand-side story that fully implicates them, and the reason for this is that the latter story still contains too many gaps. This chapter has attempted to close some of these gaps.

Notes

1 For more detail on this point, see Goda *et al.* (2013).
2 The High Level Group on Financial Supervision in the EU (2009).
3 For a more detailed exposition of this argument, see Lysandrou (2011, 2012).
4 See, for example, Bank of England (2008) and Chailloux *et al.* (2008).
5 See Goda *et al.* (2013).
6 See Blundell-Wignall (2007); House of Commons (2008).
7 When the heads of some of the biggest US hedge funds were called before a US Senate hearing on the sub-prime crisis in November 2008, they declared that they were in no way to blame for the financial carnage. The "focal point of carnage", to quote Kenneth Griffin, one of the hedge fund chiefs, was not us "but the regulated institutions, the commercial banks who originated and securitised the sub-prime mortgages and the investment banks who then used these securities as backing for Collateralised Debt Obligations and other structured financial products". By their "fanciful" ratings of these products, to quote James Simmons, another of the hedge fund chiefs, the credit ratings agencies must take particular blame for the carnage in that they facilitated the sale of "sow's ears as silk purses" Kirchgaessner and Sender (2008).

References

Bank of England (2008) *Financial Stability Report*. Available at: www.bankofengland. co.uk/publications/Pages/fsr/2008/fsr24.aspx. Last accessed: 12.01.2017.

Barclay Hedge (2015) *Alternative Income Database*. Available at: www.barclayhedge. com/cgi-bin/public_baid/search.cgi. Last accessed: 12.01.2017.

Blundell-Wignall, A. (2007) *An Overview of Hedge Funds and Structured Products: Issues of Leverage and Risk*. OECD Working Paper. Available at: www.oecd.org/finance/ financial-markets/40972327.pdf. Last accessed: 12.01.2017.

Borio, C. (2008) *The Financial Turmoil of 2007: A Preliminary Assessment and Some Policy Considerations*. BIS Working Papers, No. 251. Available at: www.bis.org/publ/ work251.htm. Last accessed: 12.01.2017.

Capgemini-RBC Wealth Management (2015) *World Wealth Report*. Available at: www. uk.capgemini.com/thought-leadership/world-wealth-report-2015-from-capgemini- and-rbc-wealth-management. Last accessed: 12.01.2017.

Chailloux, A., S. Gray and R. McCaughrin (2008) *Central Bank Collateral Frameworks: Principles and Policies*. IMF Working Paper, No. 08/222. Available at: www.imf.org/ external/pubs/ft/wp/2008/wp08222.pdf. Last accessed: 12.01.2017.

Goda, T., P. Lysandrou and C. Stewart (2013), "The Contribution of US Bond Demand to the US Bond Yield Conundrum of 2004 to 2007: An Empirical Investigation". *Journal of International Financial Markets, Institutions and Money*, 27, pp. 113–136.

House of Commons (2008) *Report on Financial Stability and Transparency*. Treasury Committee Report. Available at: www.publications.parliament.uk/pa/cm200708/cm select/cmtreasy/371/371.pdf. Last accessed: 12.01.2017.

IFSL (2008) *Hedge Funds 2008*. International Financial Service London Report. Available at: www.finyear.com/attachment/98053. Last accessed: 12.01.2017.

Jones, S. (2012) "Church of England Doubles Hedge Fund Investments". *Financial Times*, 30 November. Available at: www.ft.com/content/9659eefa-4e86-11e1-8670-00144 feabdc0. Last accessed 24.04.2017.

Kirchgaessner, S. and H. Sender (2008) "Hedge Fund Chiefs Blame the System for Financial Crisis". *Financial Times*, 13 November. Available at: www.ft.com/content/0f8c0216- b193-11dd-b97a-0000779fd18c. Last accessed 24.04.2017.

Lysandrou, P. (2011) "The Primacy of Hedge Funds in the Subprime Crisis". *Journal of Post-Keynesian Economics*, 34(2), pp. 225–254.

Lysandrou, P. (2012) "Hedge Funds". In J. Toporowski and J. Michell (eds) *Handbook of Critical Issues in Finance*. Cheltenham, UK: Edward Elgar.

Lysandrou, P. and A. Nesvetailova (2015) "The Role of Shadow Banking Entities in the Financial Crisis: A Disaggregated View". *Review of International Political Economy*, 22(2), pp. 257–279.

Lysandrou, P. and M. Shabani (2016) *The Explosive Growth of the US ABCP Market Between 2004 and 2007: A Search for Yield Story*. CITYPERC Working Paper. Available at: www.city.ac.uk/__data/assets/pdf_file/0009/353736/CITYPERC-WPS-201603.pdf. Last accessed 25.04.2017.

Mathiason, N. and Y. Bessaoud (2011) "Tory Party Funding from City Doubles under Cameron". *The Bureau of Investigative Journalism*, 8 February. Available at: www. thebureauinvestigates.com/stories/2011-02-08/tory-party-funding-from-city-doubles-under-cameron. Last accessed 25.04.2017.

Mehrling, P., Z. Pozsar, J. Sweeney and D. H. Neilson (2013) *Bagehot was a Shadow Banker: Shadow Banking, Central Banking, and the Future of Global Finance*. Working Paper. Available at: https://ssrn.com/abstract=2232016. Last accessed: 16.12.2016.

Mustier, J.-P. and A. Dubois (2007) *Risks and Return on Banking Activities Related to Hedge Funds*. Banque de France, Financial Stability Review, No. 10. Available at: https://publications.banque-france.fr/sites/default/files/medias/documents/financial-stability-review-10_2007–04.pdf. Last accessed: 12.01.2017.

13 The economy of deferral and displacement

Finance, shadow banking and fiscal arbitrage

Ronen Palan and Duncan Wigan

Introduction

This chapter analyses one of the most important 'proximate' causes of the development of the shadow banking system. Our key proposition here is that shadow banking entities and transaction structures that have developed in and around them are deeply linked to the tax and regulatory flexibility they offer to companies, financial institutions and individuals. Indeed, we suggest that exploring tax arbitrage in particular may help researchers and policy makers to integrate the so-called 'endogenous' and 'exogenous' explanations of shadow banking (Lysandrou and Nesvetailova 2015). Tax arbitrage helps to mobilize the ability to leverage financial innovations within banking, and reduce taxation costs from forms of financialized assets and income streams, which help to offer both fee income for shadow banking institutions and after-tax yield to bond and securitized asset holders. We also suggest that taxation issues help to bridge another open question about shadow banking – whether these are mainly a monetary or financial phenomenon. One of the key achievements of shadow banking is not so much just that their activities are outside of prudential regulatory spaces, but that they have developed hybrid institutions and instruments that bridge the older descriptive boundaries of money and finance.

A veteran observer of the Irish financial centre, Jim Stewart, concluded a study of Irish-based subprime special purpose vehicles (SPVs) with the observation that 'the shadow banking sector developed in tax havens and low tax centres to facilitate regulatory and tax arbitrage' (2012: 3). The rapidly emerging body of literature on the shadow banking industry, reported on in this book, has generally tended to overlook the not insignificant fact that many security-based swap entities (SBSs), possibly even the majority of such entities, including hedge funds, SPVs, structured investment vehicles, and money market funds are registered in jurisdictions known colloquially as tax havens. Perhaps due to an understandable focus on speculative dynamics and the complexity, opacity and fragility of global financial markets in general, the growing literature on the financial crisis has tended to ignore that a good portion of the failed subprime loans were held by SPVs, at least nominally, in jurisdictions such as Ireland and the Caymans (Adrian and Ashcraft 2012; Perotti 2013; Tarullo 2013). The problem here, however, is that the issue too readily becomes a policy-oriented challenge of how to get this activity back inside the prudential scope of central banks, rather than an effort to understand what was driving (and continues to drive) the growth of these activities in the first place.

Equally, despite the fact that it is common knowledge over-the-counter (OTC) derivatives markets 'turbo charge tax shelters' (Sheppard 1999), little attention has been afforded to the fiscal implications of financial derivatives.

That seems to be changing, and the current chapter attempts to contribute to that change. The U.S. Inland Revenue Service recently estimated that $100bn of tax is lost annually due to the corporate use of derivatives in tax planning (Donohue 2012). Although disputed, this is undoubtedly a significant figure that questions the exclusive focus in orthodox finance literature on derivatives as simply hedging and trading instruments. By way of comparison, the total tax paid by the top 30 European banks at the height of the financial bubble in 2007 was 33.9 billion euros (ECB 2007). Does this mean that as a previous Chancellor to the British Exchequer, Nigel Lawson, once observed, 'complex structured finance is a euphemism for tax avoidance'? We do not think that the SBS is merely a euphemism for tax avoidance, there are clearly demand and supply issues that are fulfilled by the SBS as described in this book, but there is little doubt that one of the primary (and what we term 'proximate') drivers of the emergence of the entities, products and markets that make up the shadow banking industry is tax avoidance. We suggest that while tax and regulatory avoidance is not the only reason for the growth of shadow banking, it has been critical to its structure and evolution in ways that are often underappreciated.

This chapter aims to present some of the evidence that suggests that the key instruments of the shadow banking world, derivatives, SPVs and hedge funds, are motivated at least to a degree by tax avoidance, or what the industry would term tax and regulatory arbitrage.

An economy of deferral and displacement

For most of the twentieth century, economic paradigms and regulatory frameworks have been built on the clear separation of national and international jurisdictional space, and within nations, between fiscal and financial phenomena. One the one hand, tax evasion and avoidance were dealt with largely by domestic regulations, bilateral treaties and, more recently, OECD-led international initiatives. Financial supervision, on the other hand, was oriented towards market stability and did not take the issue of complex inter-connectedness between financial and fiscal matters into account.

The separation between the two realms is replicated in academia as well. Financial economists rarely devote much attention to fiscal considerations, whereas accountants and tax lawyers usually profess to knowing very little about financial matters. This is not unreasonable considering the diverging types of expertise needed to operate in the two realms. Yet, financial entities are, as economists are fond of emphasizing, profit oriented businesses. Economists do not pay sufficient attention to the blurring of the boundaries between the national and international,[1] nor to the differences between the concepts of pre-tax and post-tax profit-orientation of the firm. Rather, the assumption seems to be that transactions that directly or indirectly have cross-border implications are both marginal and do not affect the basic structure of the national–international divide. Similarly, there is a presumption that pre- and post-tax positions arise from similar positions and are closely correlated, only that the post-tax position of an entity is simply its pre-tax minus the necessary tax that is paid to government. Post-tax profit can, in this perspective and given known statutory tax rates, be read off the pre-tax position.

This view, if it were ever true, is increasingly obsolete. As businesses operate in a world of notionally separate states, each with different treatments of different assets and income streams, the 'bottom line' for companies, to all intents and purposes, is their post-tax position in the jurisdictions in which they operate. As businesses increasingly operate across multiple jurisdictional spaces (either directly or indirectly), they can and do structure their corporate organization, costs, expenses and financial transfers in such way as to minimize taxation – just like any other costs. And this means that however odd these resulting structures may appear from a conventional productivist and methodologically nationalist economic perspective, financial and organizational innovation has changed our understanding of national and corporate juridical space. In conventional accounts the world of states consists of political entities that are in control of landed territories, including adjacent waters, each of which are sovereign independent states and have a right to regulate businesses located, domiciled or licensed in their territories as well as levy tax on them. From an international businesses' perspective, the world consists of easily traversed diverging sovereign platforms, each of which offers a distinct bundle of regulatory, taxation and market attributes. There are no particular reasons why business would tend to ensure that activities are recorded, and hence tax is paid where income accrues, costs incurred or profits are made. On the contrary, business would aim to structure activities in such a way that profits accumulate where tax is minimal, while expenses are recorded where subsidies and deductions are maximized. Tax is therefore integral to evaluating a spread, or how much above a risk-free rate a product must return. Modern systems of taxation have developed on the basis of a relatively simple world where corporeal property is exchanged in the provision of goods and services, where costs and income accrue and corporate entities have a recognizable national home. Taxation is typically levied on an entity at the point of assumed completion of the series of transactions (where the good or services are delivered). But two changes in economic activity have changed these assumptions. First, the growth of the services sector activity has meant that more and more of economic exchange occurs in or is based around incorporeal property, and these activities make locational, ownership and valuation issues far more fungible and mobile. Second, in the inherently incorporeal world of finance and commerce, these simple attributes of ownership, location, forms of capital can be unbundled, rearranged and relocated to achieve one of the following:

- That the issuing business in charge of final transactions, or that the business that appears to gain from the final transactions and hence where 'profit' is logged, happen to be located in territories that levy minimal or no taxation on such entities. Hence, for instance, most hedge funds will be registered in territories known colloquially as tax havens.

- Or that final transactions are structured in such a way that they are 'logged' or registered in political platforms that levy minimal taxation on a particular form of final transaction that is used for such cases – hence tax is minimized. Businesses set up 'holding companies' and various types of 'SPVs' in offshore locations for that purpose. They also use financial engineering to alter the character of income subject to taxation and minimize a tax contribution.
- Or that final transaction is structured in such a way that the maturity point of the transaction that triggers taxation is deferred to some point in the future, but the future never truly materializes, and/or the transaction is structured in such a way that it takes place in a simulated realm that is not easily recognizable by the tax authorities, and hence the transaction may disappear completely from their radar. That is where derivatives come into play.

Indeed, it is not too much to argue that much of the financial innovation and corporate restructuring (which tax economist Desai (2009) has referred to as 'de-centring' of the firm), has involved fiscal arbitrage in which potential tax liabilities can be deferred or displaced. An economy of deferral and displacement has emerged, supported and sustained by a large and sprawling army of accountants, lawyers and financiers, which according to a recent estimate by a UK parliamentary committee (House of Commons 2013), is worth about $US55bn a year, to consult businesses on how to take advantage of either strategy a, b or c, or ideally, all three, to ensure their post-tax position is minimized. Importantly for this chapter, we argue, tax arbitrage has been one of the key drivers for the emergence of the shadow banking industry.

Derivatives

In the early phase of the development of derivatives, researchers seemed to be very aware of the tax advantages offered by such transactions and their role in international capital flows. The development of parallel loans, the precursor to swaps, was stimulated by US capital controls and the tax wedge imposed as part of those controls (Mehrling 2011). Peter Garber (1998) similarly, provides examples of how derivatives were being used to relocate assets, activities and claims to income to offshore jurisdictions to take advantage of low or no tax opportunities.

In 2013, the Group Chief Executive of the UK bank Barclays, Anthony Jenkins, stated:

> There are some areas that relied on sophisticated and complex structures, where transactions were carried out primarily to access the tax benefits. Although this was legal, going forward such activity is incompatible with our purpose. We will not engage in it again.
>
> (Barclays 2013)

The Structured Capital Markets division reportedly contributed as much as £1bn a year to Barclays' profits by selling complex structured products which had the effect of reducing tax charges or providing artificial deductions – accounting items that can be set against taxes due (Lawrence 2013). A comprehensive review of the use of derivatives in tax planning concludes that "derivatives are appealing because they can replicate financial positions, blur economic substance, and introduce considerable ambiguity in tax reports" and refers to an annual $100bn lost to the U.S. Inland Revenue Service due to corporate use of derivatives in tax planning (Donohue 2012).

Financial derivatives, which emerged in the immediate wake of the collapse of the Bretton Woods System as a mechanism to harness and navigate the volatility of market driven finance, are contracts the value of which derives from the performance of underlying securities prices, interest rates, foreign exchange rates, commodities and market indexes.[2]

The industry is the largest in the world. The notional value of all OTC contracts at the end of December 2012 was $633 trillion, down from an all-time high of $706 trillion at the end of June 2011(BIS 2013). Derivatives challenge fiscal efficacy via the capacity to transform when a fiscal claim is applicable (timing) where that fiscal claim should be applied (source) and to what the fiscal claim is applied (income character or asset identity). Derivatives can be used to defer or displace taxation in one of the following ways:

- Deferring gains to future periods or accelerating losses to the present can be advantageous.
- Derivatives can reduce taxes by altering the character of gains in order to release suspended capital losses.
- By transforming capital losses into ordinary losses, derivatives can reduce taxable income.
- Derivatives can displace the site at which income or expenses accrue.
- Derivatives can also modify the source of gains and losses.
- Derivatives are often used to increase debt-to-equity ratios in order to reduce tax.

These capacities are exercised through the ability of derivatives to permit contracting parties to synthetically replicate the economics of a position, without taking on the legal form of that position. As a result, the transaction may go under the radar of tax authorities or simply be misidentified. As mentioned earlier, tax rates vary across jurisdictions and asset types. This legal-geographical differentiation is the grounds upon which the transforming, synthesizing and switching functions of derivatives perform.[3] Further, source, timing and character rules apply differently for equity, debt, options, forwards and swaps, but these contracts can be recombined in various ways to produce the returns of any underlying asset. As a result, derivatives are, to borrow a phrase, potentially 'fiscal weapons of mass destruction' because they afford the ability to replicate the commercial outcome of a transaction without entering into the transaction and incurring the tax exposure associated with such a transaction.

Simply, a position on a bond can be synthesized through a position in equity options by entering into put and call contracts. In this example, the value of the bond which will be replicated is 100. The put and the call are written so that the investor has a right to sell at a given fixed price and buy at a given fixed price at the same time. If the underlying equity moves below 100 the investor can exercise the put at 100. If the equity moves above 100, the call written with a strike price of 100 will be exercised and the investor will receive 100. In effect a position on a fixed income asset (one that returns a predefined sum, such as the bond) has been replicated by a put and a call. The put and call as opposed to providing fixed returns, provide the investor with contingent returns. A position with fixed returns and one with contingent returns may be taxed differently. Consequently, an investor can choose a preferred tax exposure. Further, a swap allows an investor to switch between asset forms and where an asset is located providing the investor with a choice of where tax is due and on what basis.

A core fiscal principle is the determination of when and where an item of income or expense becomes subject to tax. This matters because of the time value of money. A taxpayer is likely to prefer to pay €100 in two years time than pay €100 tomorrow. In a situation where a tax charge arises on the basis of a triggering event, such as an asset sale, it is possible via a derivative structure to replicate the payoff from the asset sale without making the sale. In effect, income can be realized but tax will not be. This is a function of constructing a sale of some attributes of an asset and postponing a transfer of direct ownership, perhaps almost indefinitely. An investor who holds shares the price of which has increased may wish to realize that profit. If the investor sells the shares, a capital gains tax will be imposed. On the other hand, an investor could, where legally admissible, buy a put option on the equity from a bank with a strike price of 100 that matures in two years. The current share price is 100. The investor then sells a call option with the same strike price and maturity. Simultaneously, the investor borrows from the counterparty the full value of all the shares owned using the shares as collateral for the loan. The end effect is stark. The investor realizes gains in the present, but owes no tax now. Furthermore, due to the options the investor is no longer exposed to changes in share value. If the share price is higher than 100 when the option matures, the loss on the call offsets this gain. If the share price is lower than 100, the gain on the put option offsets this loss (Martin and Zailer 2001). Eventually the loan will have to repaid, but the contract could be renewed nearing maturity.

The transformation of source rules follows similar principles. A foreign investor in equities subject to withholding tax on the sale of the equities may turn to an equity swap to alter where the income is sourced for tax purposes. For instance, returns from an investment in US equity by a foreigner will usually be subject to a withholding tax of 30 per cent. However, the investor can receive the same returns through an equity swap in which she receives payments from a counterparty if the value of the equity increases or dividends are paid, and makes payments to that counterparty on the basis of interest on the value of equity referenced in the swap and in the event that the value of the equity declines. The source of the income in a swap is based on the residence of the investor, while a direct purchase of equity is sourced where that purchase is made. If that investor is resident or registered in an offshore jurisdiction, income from the swap may be subject to no tax at all (Levin 2012: 5–6). By artificially replicating a desired equity position, a foreign investor can receive the economic benefits of direct ownership without the fiscal obligations attached to it.

Central to fiscal systems and the character of assets for tax purposes is the distinction between income and capital, with income usually taxed at a higher rate than capital gains. Derivatives can transform ownership of an asset from one to the other. Warren (1993) outlines how this can be achieved. As noted, the basis of modern finance theory is that any asset can be replicated with a combination of put and call options on another asset or assets (Scholes 2004). When assets with fixed returns, like a bond, are taxed as income but those with a contingent return, such as a share, are taxed as capital, an investor may prefer to replicate the position on a bond via a position in equity combined with put and call options. The investor produces a synthetic zero coupon bond (a bond that pays yield only on maturity), which pays £110 in two years. To replicate this position in assets with contingent returns, returns that will be taxed at the lower income tax rate, the investor buys a share of the same value and two options, enacting what is termed 'put-call parity'. The first option is a put, a right to sell a share at a specified time, two years hence, for a specific price, £110. The second option is a call, obliging the investor to sell a share at a specified time, two years, for a specific price, £110. If the share price is below £110 in two years, the investor will exercise the put and 'put' the shares to the market at £110. If the share price is above £110 in two years, the holder of the call option will exercise that option and pay the investor £110. The investor has thus replicated a risk-free position in a bond. As such, the investor will be taxed on these assets as capital rather than income. A tax inspector would need to combine the three separate contracts to recognize this equivalence.

Hybrid instruments blend features of debt and equity, as well as blend asset and derivative elements. Different jurisdictions will treat an instrument as debt or equity depending on local rules for doing so. Firms that make cross-border investments can take advantage of this identity-based differential tax treatment. For example, a US firm may make an investment in a subsidiary that issues a hybrid instrument from Luxembourg. That subsidiary will make payments to the US based parent. In Luxembourg, since the hybrid instrument is characterized as debt, the subsidiary will be afforded tax deductions on the interest it pays for the debt and no withholding tax will be levied on those payments as they exit the jurisdiction. However, in the US, that payment is not recorded as interest income, but as dividend income, which is subject to less tax (JCT 2011; Johannesen 2012). In the example of a convertible bond, an issuer may sell a bond with an in-built trigger dictating that when the issuer's share price reaches a certain level, the bond is converted into a certain number of shares. This raises the question of whether the instrument should be characterized as debt or equity for tax purposes. The instrument provides the issuer with deductions on interest paid, while reducing the level of that interest on the basis of the value imputed to the contingent position on the stock. That the same instrument in another jurisdiction may be treated as equity implies that interest that is deductible in the offshore jurisdiction will not lead to taxable interest income in the second jurisdiction where the instrument is treated as equity. This is a case of 'double non-taxation'.

The UK Public Accounts Committee held a hearing in 2012 investigating the marketing of tax avoidance schemes (UK PAC 2013). Evidence was provided by the directors of three firms specializing in the sale of 'tax mitigation schemes': Tax Trade, Future Capital Partners and Ingenious Media. These witnesses stated that they relied upon legal opinions of highly ranked barristers, Queen's Counsel (QC), to ratify the legality of schemes they sold. Rex Bretten, then recently retired from the London firm Tax Chambers, was named as one of a handful of QCs who 'prostitute themselves' to schemes devised to create 'tax relief'. Somewhat ironically, Rex Bretten four months subsequently had an appeal against Her Majesty's Revenue and Customs' (HMRC) decision not to allow him to claim tax relief on a £475,000 loss on an avoidance scheme of his own devising, quashed. In February 2003, Bretten with family members had become trustees of two trusts set up by Oakwood Consultants, owned by a firm of accountants. Oakwood exchanged loan notes with a face value of £500,000 with Bretten in return for £500,000. The loan notes were constructed to be redeemable for £25,000 15 days after issue, thereby creating the tax-deductible loss. However, the scheme included a call option on the notes held by one of the trustees, which could be redeemed 9 days after issue and before the 15th day of issue for 99.5 per cent of face value. This option was exercised resulting in one of the trusts holding £499,500 and the liability on the loan notes being held by the other trust (UK FTT 2013: 189). HMRC deemed the scheme wholly artificial and therefore disallowed the tax-deductible loss on the notes. This case reveals both actors that are central to derivative-driven tax avoidance and the relative simplicity of some of these schemes. Not all are so simple.

Special purpose vehicles

Financial instruments such as subprime funds, derivatives and other financial instruments are often issued and controlled through SPVs, known also as special purpose entities (SPEs), or as the EU now prefers to call them, financial vehicle corporations. The terminology, however, can be confusing because such entities conduct a wide variety of transactions, including synthetic and cash flow collateralized debt obligations (CDOs), mortgages securitizations, asset-backed commercial paper programmes, credit card receivables and a host of other receivables financing transactions.

The BIS provide the following definition:

> [an] SPE is a legal entity created at the direction of a sponsoring firm (which may also be referred to as the sponsor, originator, seller, or administrator) . . . An SPE can take the form of a corporation, trust, partnership, corporation or a limited liability company.

The BIS differentiates between two broad types of SPEs, asset securitization and liability securitization. Asset securitizations are usually undertaken by banks and finance companies, and typically involve issuing bonds that are backed by the cash flows of income-generating assets (ranging from credit card receivables to residential mortgage loans). Liability securitizations are usually undertaken by insurance companies and typically involve issuing bonds that assume the risk of a potential insurance liability (ranging from a catastrophic natural event to an unexpected claims level on a certain product type).

These funds are controversial. Already in 2004, the IMF statistical department raised questions on the apparent location or residency of SPEs for statistical purposes. The IMF's concern was initially of a technical nature. These funds, it noted, were 'intentionally created as separate legal entities with various degrees of operational autonomy, and various arrangements establishing their relationships to the originators, partners and investors' (IMF 2004: 3). The statistical department simply wanted to have some clarity about the true location of SPEs for its 'balance of payment issue'.[4] The statisticians were not clear whether SPEs can be treated as separate entities in balance of payments statistics, or whether they were 'brain dead' units with no autonomy at all.

That proved a problem. Many of the subprime loans were established through offshore SPEs. But the crisis also revealed large gaps in information and regulation of such SPEs. Following the crisis, the BIS commissioned a report in 2008 on SPEs. In line with the division between monetary and fiscal expertise discussed above, the BIS has taken a rather benign view of SPEs, viewing them through the lens of orthodox finance theory as "a way of disaggregating the risks of an underlying pool of exposures held by the SPE and reallocating these risks to those parties most willing to take on those risks". The BIS notes that the choice of jurisdiction for incorporation of the SPE was typically decided in order to "maintain tax neutrality of the structure and keep potential additional tax liability to a minimum [thus it] plays a role in ensuring that the SPE can be perceived as being bankruptcy remote" (BIS 2009: 10). Indeed, the BIS report argues that 'tax neutrality' is advantageous because it ensures that the SPE has more funds to deal with potential bankruptcies!

The attraction of a Cayman registration, for instance, is obvious. A Cayman legal structure allows companies to raise capital off balance sheets. Costs are modest. To set up an SPV, government fees range between US$574 and US$2,400, depending on the amount of capital involved, and total costs generally range between US$2,000 and US$3,000. The regulatory framework is extremely flexible and red tape is minimal. "No governmental authorizations or licenses are necessary in order to establish an SPV in the Cayman Islands. Incorporation generally takes less than 24 hours. Most SPVs are established as 'exempted companies'" (Willington Trust Corporation 2013). As such, they are not permitted to conduct business within the Cayman Islands, but in return, they are entitled to a complete tax holiday for 20 years, with a possibility of a 10-year extension. As there are no direct taxes in the islands, an exempted company will not have to pay any form of income tax, capital gains tax or corporation tax. Similarly, no taxes will be withheld on any cash flows. Perhaps the greatest attraction of Cayman registration is that, as a provider website specializing in such companies boasts, "A properly structured SPV may reduce or even eliminate taxes owed to the sponsor's home country".[5]

SPEs have also been used to hide debt, hide ownership and obscure relationships between different legal entities which are in fact related to each other. This proved a key problem in the collapse of a number of large companies like Enron, Paramalat, as well as in some high profile failures during the crisis. Jim Stewart notes that many of the subprime mortgages that failed during the crisis were controlled SPEs registered in Ireland. Currently, there are more than 4,000 investment funds in Ireland, and many more sub-funds, and many of those consisted of subprime loans prior to the crisis (Stewart 2012: 4). These companies – if they are to be treated as independent companies – were registered in Ireland but were controlled from the financial centres of London, New York and the like. The reason for the popularity of Ireland and other tax havens Arthur Cox's website explains, voted the Irish Law Firm of the Year 2010 and 2014, is ease of incorporation and because "favourable tax laws allow the structures to be, in most cases, tax neutral and a 'Eurobond exemption', together with an extensive range of domestic provisions and double taxation treaties, permits interest on debts to be paid gross in most cases" (Arthur Cox 2012, 1).

SPEs were created largely for bankruptcy provisions. The trend in US courts was not to accept the 'sham' of offshore incorporation, so the concept of bankruptcy remoteness that is at the heart of SPVs, was challenged. For example, in the bankruptcy case of Bear Stearns, two high-grade funds were both subject to scrutiny. They were both open ended investment companies that invested in asset-backed securities (ABSs), mortgage-backed securities, derivatives, options, swaps, futures, equities and currencies. They were Cayman Islands exempted limited liability companies with registered offices in the Cayman Islands. Yet, PFPC Inc., a Massachusetts corporation, administered the funds and performed all back office functions, including accounting and clerical functions. The books and records of these funds were maintained and stored in Delaware, while Deloitte & Touche, Cayman Islands, performed the most recent audit. The New York Courts took the view that since the investment manager, Bear Stearns Asset Management Inc., was a New York corporation, liabilities were subject to that company and not the Cayman SPEs.

It also became clear during the crisis that neither Ireland nor Cayman nor Bermuda nor any other offshore jurisdictions that hosted such entities considered taking any responsibility for their failure. Their responsibility towards these entities and their clients was the equivalent of the parking attendant's responsibility for its transient clientele; with the minor difference that most carparks would tend to display a large poster reminding their clients that the carpark takes no responsibility for its clients' vehicles. Scrutiny of such funds in Ireland is minimal. Indeed, in 2008, Luxembourg introduced a new law, so that as long as the fund manager 'notifies' the regulator within a month of launch, the fund can enjoy pre-authorization approval. Unlike the Irish regulator that applies some light touch regulations, the regulator in Luxembourg does not 'scrutinize promoters' at all (Stewart 2012).

In addition to economic and financial accounting considerations, financial institutions subject to capital adequacy requirements may issue or hold financial instruments designed to produce favourable results under those rules. In other words, SPEs may be used for transforming the impact of taxation rules, but also capital adequacy requirements such as Basel III. Indeed, it is not clear right now whether all SPEs are treated equally under Basel III rules as part of a bank's balance sheet provisions. While securitizations enabled banks to circumvent capital adequacy requirements, dissolve the substance of their fiduciary obligations to clients and accelerate issuance and hence fees, tax benefits played an important role in their proliferation.

In the US, mortgage securitization benefitted from a tax advantage early on. The 1986 Tax Act exempts real estate mortgage investment conduits from taxation so that the tax liability flows through to the investors in the securitization. This means that the sponsor or issuer avoids the tax liability of the conduit and of holding mortgages on the balance sheet. In turn, the taxable event after securitization shifts from the repayment of principal and interest to the securities issued by the SPV. This not only creates an opportunity for re-characterizing cash flows but also represents a simple deferral mechanism. The taxable event shifts from the mortgage repayment on one credit to the life of the securitization – repeated offsetting between income and losses can postpone the taxable event until the SPV distributes proceeds (Ceriani *et al.* 2011: 81). A tax pound tomorrow is worth more than a tax pound today. Correlation across the portfolio of assets within the securitization is the basis of this tax arbitrage. As far as the performance of the underlying assets is uncorrelated and therefore losses on some assets can be offset against gains on other assets, the overall tax liability of the securitization is reduced. Capital losses across the asset pool are worth more in the securitization because they can be offset against the higher rate income tax. Indeed, that losses within the asset pool can create a tax advantage may have played into what have been termed 'poor underwriting standards', when originators seem to have passed poorly performing credits, or 'toxic assets', onto unsuspecting investors. The attraction of originating weak credit is obviously increased due to the tax arbitrage available on capital losses. Securitizations also afford opportunities to re-characterize cash flows. An inflow comprising of $95 principal and $10 interest can be re-characterized as $100 principal and $5 interest (Eddins 2009: 14–15). As far as investors pay less tax on capital and more on income, this provides a clear tax benefit. Of course, in a situation where an investor may be either long or short a securitization, the arbitrage can be played inversely.

The admixture of credit default swaps (CDS) and securitization in CDOs turbo charged this arbitrage process. First, the income character of the assets flowing into the SPV is ignored under US rules and only the income character flowing out of the SPV is tax liable. Second, a CDS premium from a US investor to a non-resident SPV is tax exempt (Ceriani *et al.* 2011: 84). These, and the fact that the SPV is not subject corporate tax as is the case in offshore jurisdictions, is a necessary pre-condition for the arbitrage to work. The arbitrage relies on the different tax treatments of buy and hold investors and business traders subject to mark-to-market rules (Eddins 2009: 16–18).[6] Buy and hold investors pay income tax on interest and capital tax on losses. Mark-to-market business traders pay income tax on both interest and capital. The buy and hold investor is exposed to the credit performance of an underlying pool of assets. This investor will offset losses at the lower capital tax rate and be willing to pay a premium based on the higher tax liability to the mark-to-market trader for protection against deterioration in a credit exposure. As the mark-to-market credit protection seller is not subject to the tax arising from the different tax treatment of interest and capital, the seller receives a fee for protection that is higher than its ultimate exposure. The credit protection seller then buys protection on a synthetic pool of assets mirroring the cash flows of the original credits, to be left in receipt of a tax enhanced premium without further contingent exposures.

Ostensibly, securitization represents an efficient means of reducing the risk of individual credits (by permitting them to be orphaned from the issuing institution and sold to those with the risk appetite for holding them) and therefore reducing the costs of borrowing and the efficiency of capital markets. The GFC revealed this to be only part of the story. This corner of the SBS allowed banks to disavow themselves of responsibility for the quality of the credit they issued or traded and fuelled the meteoric build-up of easy credit prior to the crisis. The degree of diversification within securitizations was systematically underestimated and counterparty risk insufficiently appreciated. However, little attention has been afforded the fiscal aspects of the market's extraordinary growth.

Concluding remarks

Debates in legal scholarship, especially in what has become known as critical legal scholarship, may point the way forward for political economy's engagement with shadow banking. For instance, Gunther Teubner (1997) and others have developed a thesis that we are seeing the emergence of almost a 'global law without a state' (or a new 'lex mercatoria'). In particular, what they suggest we are seeing is the growth of commercial and financial activity operating entirely independently of national and regulatory orders. This is a conception of financial and commercial activity that has 'lifted off' national regulatory spaces. In the context of our analysis of shadow banking, we might term this a conception of 'shadow' commerce.

By contrast with this national thesis, Robert Wai (2002, 2005, 2008) and John Biggins (2012) challenge that conception and contend that 'lift off' can never be entirely achieved in international transactions. Institutions and transactions have to 'touch down' in some jurisdictions to achieve certain benefits (such as property rights protection, etc.). Rather, in a plural and fragmented jurisdictional world (where each jurisdiction is "rife with contradictions, gaps and ambiguities"), 'partial lift off' can be achieved. But institutions are still faced with (now) strategic choices about which transaction types 'touch down' where and when. Biggins calls this forum selection decision-making "targeted touchdown". We would submit that the tax arbitrage role of shadow banking gives us access to that process of targeted touchdown in jurisdictional placement of monetary and financial transactions. Indeed, this is a point that the finance theorist and Nobel laureate Merton Miller made more than two decades ago:

The income tax system of virtually every country that is advanced enough to have one seeks to maintain . . . different rates of tax for different sources of income – between income from capital and income from labour; between interest and dividends; between dividends and capital gains; between personal and corporate income; between business income paid out and business income retained between income earned at home and abroad; and so on. At the same time . . . securities can be used to transmute one form of income into another – in particular, higher taxed forms to lower taxed ones . . . Although I have chosen to emphasise tax changes as an initiating force in financial innovation, the same process can be seen to work in any financial area subject to state regulation, which is to say, virtually everyone.

(Miller 1991: 5–6)

Miller's comments could also now be supplemented by the additional point that financial innovation has also permitted different sources of income and wealth to be relocated across juridical boundaries. Considered this way, Miller offers us a prescient statement of both deferral and displacement, and partial lift off and targeted touchdown. While political economists and finance scholars have often seen tax arbitrage as an impetus for financial innovation, including developments being studied under the rubric of shadow banking, closer inspection reveals a tax arbitrage story of innovation and rapid growth.

Notes

1 Fujita *et al.* (1999: 209) pose the dilemma of that blurring rhetorically: "Given that national boundaries no longer provide the most natural unit of economic analysis, what should replace them?".
2 For a thorough review of the mechanics of derivatives markets and products, see Kolb (1995).
3 In a similar vein, Bryan and Rafferty (2006) refer to the binding and blending potentials of derivatives – binding referring to the ability of derivatives to link capital across time and space; blending referring to the potential to mix up different claims and liabilities without having to change possession or even ownership.
4 According to available data, the world runs a balance of payments deficit with itself. Undoubtedly, the interactions between financial innovation, the shadow banking system and the system of national accounts contribute to this. This deficit is also a proxy for fiscal incapacity.
5 Willington Trust Corporation (2013).
6 The illustration draws directly from Eddins (2009) Tax Arbitrage Feedback Theory which specifies the role of tax arbitrage in altering the spreads available on a given range of products and thereby incentivizing investment in those markets and securities where those opportunities are most extenuated. This was in the credit default and securitization markets and is a necessary component of any explanation of the GFC.

References

Adrian, T. and A. Ashcraft (2012) *Shadow Banking: A Review of the Literature*. Federal Reserve Bank of New York Staff Report, no. 580. Available at: www.newyorkfed.org/medialibrary/media/research/staff_reports/sr580.pdf. Last accessed: 20.12.2016.

Barclays (2013) *Barclays PLC Strategic Review*. Anthony Jenkins, Group Chief Executive, February 12. Available at: www.home.barclays/content/dam/barclayspublic/docs/ InvestorRelations/IRNewsPresentations/2012News/12-feb-barclays-strategic-review-announcement.pdf. Last accessed: 20.12.2016.

Biggins, J. (2012) "'Targeted Touchdown' and 'Partial Liftoff': Post Crisis Dispute Resolution in the OTC Derivatives Markets and the Challenge for ISDA". *German Law Journal*, 13(12), pp. 1299–1328.

BIS (2009) *Report on Special Purpose Entities*. Basel Committee on Banking Supervision. September. Basle, Switzerland: Bank for International Settlements.

BIS (2013) *Quarterly Review*. The International Banking Market, Statistical Annex, Bank for International Settlements: Basel, September. Available at: www.bis.org/publ/ qtrpdf/r_qs1306.p hdf. Last accessed 24.04.17.

Bryan, D. and M. Rafferty (2006) "Financial Derivatives: The New Gold?". *Competition & Change*, 10(3), pp. 265–282.

Ceriani, V., S. Manestra, G. Ricotti, A. Sanelli and E. Zangari (2011) "The Tax System and the Financial Crisis". *PSL Quarterly Review*, 64(256), pp. 39–94.

Cox, A. (2012) *Establishing Special Purpose Vehicles in Ireland for Structured Finance Transactions*. Available at: www.yumpu.com/en/document/view/22706577/establishing-special-purpose-vehicles-in-ireland-securitizationnet. Last accessed: 20.12.2016.

Desai, M. A. (2009) "The Decentering of the Global Firm". *The World Economy*, 32(9), pp. 1271–1290.

Donohue, M. (2012) *Financial Derivatives in Corporate Tax Avoidance: Why, How and Who?* AAA Annual Meeting – Tax Concurrent Sessions. Available at: http://ssrn.com/ abstract=2097994. Last accessed: 20.12.2016.

ECB (2007) *EU Banking Sector Stability*. European Central Bank.

Eddins, S. T. (2009) *Tax Arbitrage Feedback Theory*. Ironbridge Capital Management LLP. Available at SSRN: http://ssrn.com/abstract=1356159. Last accessed: 20.12.2016.

Fujita, M., P. Krugman and T. Mori (1999) "On the Evolution of Hierarchical Urban Systems". *European Economic Review*, 43(2), pp. 209–251.

Garber, P. (1998) *Derivatives in International Capital Flows*. NBER Working Paper, no. 6623. Available at: www.nber.org/papers/w6623. Last accessed: 20.12.2016.

House of Commons (2013) *Tax Avoidance: tackling Marketed Avoidance Schemes*. 29th Report of Session 2012–13, London: House of Commons. Available at: www.publications. parliament.uk/pa/cm201213/cmselect/cmpubacc/788/788.pdf. Last accessed 25.04.2017.

International Monetary Fund (2004) *Special Purpose Entities*. IMF Committee on Balance of Payments Statistics, Balance of Payment Technical Expert Group (BOPTEG), Issues Paper (BOPTEG), no. 94. Available at: www.imf.org/external/pubs/ft/bop/2004/04-24. pdf. Last accessed: 20.12.2016.

Johannesen, N. (2012) *Cross-Border Hybrid Instruments*. Department of Economics, University of Copenhagen. Unpublished Manuscript. Available at: www.nielsjohannesen. net/wp-content/uploads/2012/04/NielsJohannesen_2012_Crossborder-hybrid-instruments. pdf. Last accessed: 20.12.2016.

Joint Committee on Taxation (2011) *Present Law and Issues Related to the Taxation of Financial Instruments and Products*. Joint Committee on Taxation: Washington. Last accessed: 20.12.2016. Available at: www.jct.gov/publications. html?func=startdown&id=4372. Last accessed 24.04.2017.

Kolb, R. W. (1995) *The Financial Derivatives Reader*. London: Blackwell Lawrence.

Lawrence, F. (2013) "Barclays secret tax avoidance factory that made £1bn a year profit disbanded". *The Guardian*, February 11. Available at: http://www.theguardian.com/ business/2013/feb/11/barclays-investment-banking-tax-avoidance). Last accessed 25.04.2017.

Levin, C. (2012) *Closing Ten Offshore Tax Loopholes*. Permanent Subcommittee on Investigations, United States Senate: Committee on Homeland Security and Governmental Affairs. Available at: www.hsgac.senate.gov/download/levin-letter-re-10-offshore-tax-loopholes-october-5-2012. Last accessed: 20.12.2016.

Lysandrou, P and A. Nesvetailova (2015) "The Role of Shadow Banking Entities in the Financial Crisis: A Disaggregated View". *Review of International Political Economy*, 22(2), pp. 257–279.

Martin, D. and I. Zailer (2001) "Derivatives Products and Tax Planning". *Derivatives Use, Trading & Regulation*, 7(1), pp. 8–16.

Mehrling, P. (2011) *The New Lombard Street: How the Fed Became the Dealer of Last Resort*. Princeton, NJ: Princeton University Press.

Miller, M. (1991) "Financial Innovations: The Past Twenty Years and the Next". In M. Miller (ed.) *Financial Innovations and Market Volatility*. Cambridge, UK: Blackwell.

Perotti, E. (2013) *The Roots of Shadow Banking*. Centre for Economic Policy Research, Policy Insight, no. 69. Available at: http://cepr.org/content/roots-shadow-banking. Last accessed: 20.12.2016.

Scholes, M. S. (2004) "The Future of Hedge Funds". *Journal of Financial Transformation*, 10, pp. 8–11.

Sheppard, L. (1999) *Slow and Steady Progress on Corporate Tax Shelters*. Tax Notes, no. 19.

Stewart, J. (2012) *Low Tax Financial Centres and the Financial Crisis: The Case of the Irish Financial Services Centre, Dublin*. IIIS Discussion Paper, no. 420. Available at: www.tcd.ie/iiis/documents/discussion/pdfs/iiisdp420.pdf. Last accessed: 20.12.2016.

Tarullo, D. K. (2013) *Shadow Banking and Systemic Risk Regulation*. Speech at the Americans for Financial Reform and Economic Policy Institute Conference, Washington, DC, 22 November. Available at: www.federalreserve.gov/newsevents/speech/tarullo20131122a.htm. Last accessed 25.04.2017.

Teubner, G. (1997) "Global Bukowina: Legal Pluralism in the World Society". In G. Teubner (ed.) *Global Law Without a State*. Dartmouth, NH: Ashgate Press.

UK FTT (2013) *Bretten v Revenue & Customs*. Available at: www.bailii.org/uk/cases/UKFTT/TC/2013/TC02604.html. Last accessed: 20.12.2016.

UK PAC (2013) *Tax Avoidance: Tackling Marketed Avoidance Schemes*. Twenty-Ninth Report of Session 2012–13, House of Commons Committee of Public Accounts, House of Commons London: The Stationery Office Limited. Available at: www.publications.parliament.uk/pa/cm201213/cmselect/cmpubacc/788/788.pdf. Last accessed: 20.12.2016.

Wai, R. (2002) "Transnational Liftoff and Juridical Touchdown: The Regulatory Function of Private International Law in an Era of Globalization". *Columbia Journal of Transnational Law*, 40, pp. 209–265.

Wai, R. (2005) "Transnational Private Law and Private Ordering in a Contested Global Society". *Harvard International Law Journal*, 46, pp. 471–488.

Wai, R. (2008) "The Interlegality of International Private Law". *Law and Contemporary Problems*, 107, pp. 107–128.

Warren, A. C., Jr (1993) "Financial Contract Innovation and Income Tax Policy". *Harvard Law Review*, 107, pp. 460–492.

Willington Trust Corporation (2013) *Cayman Islands SPVs*. Available at: www.wilmington trust.com/wtcom/index.jsp?fileid=3000129. Last accessed: 20.12.2016.

14 Shadow banking and the challenges for central banks

Thorvald Grung Moe

Introduction

The depth and length of the current financial crisis have been exceptional. The global financial system was close to a meltdown after Lehman Brothers filed for bankruptcy in September 2008. Central banks responded with unprecedented force and were able to restore stability to financial markets. As the recession dragged on, they broadened their tool kit and extended their liquidity support from single institutions to key markets. Many central banks also provided additional liquidity support through asset purchases, large-scale market interventions and other creative ways of easing credit conditions. As a result, central banks' balance sheets have grown dramatically compared to GDP.

Scholars broadly agree that these untraditional polices saved the global financial system from a systemic meltdown in 2008. There is less agreement about the way forward and how central banks should conduct their liquidity policies in the future. Some want central banks to expand their discount window lending and become "market makers of last resort" (MMLR) (Carney 2008, 2011, 2013). Others are wary of such extensions of the government safety net and would prefer to rein in the expansion of the shadow financial system with stricter regulation (Tarullo 2013; Turner 2013; Wolf 2013).

The shadow banking system represents a special policy challenge for central banks, since its growth is closely linked to the introduction of stricter rules for the regulated banking system. The two parts of the financial system are also closely linked through a network of securities lending, rehypothecation, and repo- and derivatives markets. Recent proposals by international regulatory bodies to increase transparency and restrict the uncontrolled leverage of this highly pro-cyclical system should help, but will probably not be enough. Unless the expansion of the shadow banking system is curbed, central banks could risk becoming implicit guarantors of shadow banking liabilities.

My intuition is that there must be some limit to how far central banks should go in supporting the broader financial market in a crisis, especially when much of the on-going expansion is based on a "liquidity illusion" (Nesvetailova 2010) that markets are deep and safe and will be supported by central banks – almost for free. This has led to under-pricing of the true risk embedded in shadow banking instruments, and made them an artificially cheap source of funding. Even if central banks can create abundant amounts of *official* liquidity, there should be limits to their support of the *private* financial sector. But recent relaxations in the proposed liquidity regulations and suggestions that central bank facilities should be included in banks' liquidity reserves reflect the pressure on central banks to support core financial markets in a new crisis. Such an accommodative policy stance could, however, contribute to further financial fragility and ultimately lead to another government bailout – if asset prices collapse, central banks intervene and fiscal transfers are subsequently required to recapitalize central banks. This would be ironic, after the recent focus on ending taxpayer bailout of too-big-to-fail institutions.

Shadow banking redefined

There is a growing awareness that the shadow banking system is not a financial system distinctly different from regulated banking. Banks are big players in the shadow banking system, both as collateral providers and as repo participants. Money market funds are major funding sources for the big banks, and the over-the-counter (OTC) derivatives market is an integral part of the shadow banking system through its extensive reliance on pledged collateral. Gabor (2013) shows that big banks are dominant in the shadow banking system in Europe, and a Bank for International Settlements report notes that a few global banks dominate the global OTC market (BIS 2013). By recasting the shadow banking debate in this light, we can appreciate that many of the on-going regulatory debates on collateral policies, minimum haircuts, liquidity rules, high-quality liquid assets, risk weights for sovereign debt, and the central banks' role as liquidity back-stoppers (be it LLR (Lender of Last Resort) or MMLR) are indeed tightly connected.

Key to this "new" understanding of the shadow banking complex is the collateral intermediation function that underpins the financial plumbing of our market-based financial system (Singh 2013b). The pro-cyclical nature of this collateral-based financial system through funding and asset price fluctuations, is now seen by many as the essential feature of the shadow banking system. Our understanding of the interaction between the regulated banking system, other regulated financial entities, and privately organized markets is still incomplete, partly due to lack of data, but recent papers study the role of shadow banking liabilities in the money supply (Sunderam 2012) and explore the impact of shadow money creation on macroeconomic fluctuations (Moreira and Savov 2013).

This "new view" of shadow banking is reflected in the recommendations by the Financial Stability Board (FSB) (2013a) and the European Commission (2013), where the focus is now squarely on financial *activities*, like money markets, securitization, securities lending, and repo markets, rather than on *institutions*. The EU *Communication on Shadow Banking* therefore recommends measures that will increase the transparency of shadow banking activities, as well as specific measures addressing the risk in money market funds and investment funds. The EU Commission also wants to reduce the risk associated with securities financing transactions; including measures to limit the extent of rehypothecation.[1]

"This mechanism can contribute to increased leverage and strengthen the pro-cyclical nature of the financial system, which then becomes vulnerable to bank runs and sudden deleveraging" (EU 2013: 11).

The growth in shadow banking activities has coincided with a sharp decline in the role of direct bank credit intermediation. While almost three-quarters of all credit was funded by short-term bank liabilities back in the mid-1940s in the US (bank and non-bank credit), that number fell to 15 per cent just before the financial crisis (Adrian *et al.* 2013). But Adrian *et al.* also show how banks have retained important functions related to shadow finance, such as issuers of securities, underwriters in charge of placement, and servicers that take care of the revenue streams from securitization. As a result, very little securitization activity is conducted without participation of regulated banking entities (Cetorelli and Peristiani 2012). So, while the term "shadow banking" implies activity outside the purview of regulatory oversight, "regulated institutions are in fact heavily involved in these activities, both in funding their own operations and in extending credit and liquidity support to shadow banks beyond the regulatory perimeter" (Tarullo 2013).

This capacity of the shadow banking system to operate on a large scale in a way that creates bank-like liabilities through a complex chain on collateral transactions, has created multiple forms of feedbacks into the regulated banking system. The use and re-use of collateral exacerbates pro-cyclical dynamics and makes the whole financial system more fragile. When times are good, market participants tend to be more willing to let counterparties re-use collateral, increase market liquidity, and thereby lower the cost of capital. But in more stressed market conditions, market participants become more sensitive to counterparty risk and more reluctant to re-use their collateral. This puts additional strains on already tight liquidity conditions and tends to amplify the pro-cyclicality of the shadow banking system.

The challenge of endogenous money

That private money is not cash and that all IOUs are not equal should not come as a surprise. The collapse of the shadow banking system during the recent global financial crisis is not unprecedented if we look closer at earlier crises. Hyman Minsky (1982) noted that this desire for more cash than is available from its usual source sows the seeds for the next financial crisis. During a boom, the margin of safety decreases and economic units take on more and more leverage. Money markets have a tendency to expand during boom periods, providing an elastic source of private credit. As money markets expand, a general decline in the liquidity of households and firms follows. This makes them vulnerable to a fall in asset values. There will be a general expectation about liquidity in key asset markets that cannot be sustained unless the central bank moves in and supports the price, i.e. monetization by the central bank. But this is surely "fair-weather" liquidity, since "no one would seriously defend the proposition that all things should be made liquid" (Simmons 1947).

Andrew Haldane (2012) adds that "cycles in money and banking credit were indeed familiar from centuries past" and yet, for some odd reason, these insights were ignored for perhaps a generation, with near-fatal consequences for us all. The perception that claims on trust companies (or shadow banks) were as good as cash was based on explicit or implicit promises by their sponsors to provide liquidity and credit support. Or the perception was based on the high ratings of the securitized assets on their balance sheets (Tarullo 2013). But as a BIS report noted:

> The presumed superior liquidity of securitized assets over conventional bank loans may turn out to be a mirage if a substantial number of the creditors attempt to liquidate their holdings simultaneously.
>
> (BIS 1986)

The resulting fire sales in 2008 resembled the panic liquidation by trust companies in 1907. The sudden withdrawal of funding led to rapid deleveraging and "repo runs". Fire sales of securities into falling markets created adverse feedback loops of mark-to-market losses, margin calls, and further liquidations. This "unwinding of the risk illusion, that is, the assumption that lending to shadow banks was essentially risk-free, helped transform a dramatic correction in real estate valuations into a crisis that engulfed the entire economy" (Tarullo 2013).

This endogenous nature of private credit (and liquidity) was not sufficiently appreciated before the crisis. Inside money expands like ripples in the pond during the upswing on the back of private promises to pay (back).[2] As Hayek observed in 1931:

> [t]he characteristic peculiarity of these circulating forms of credit is that they spring up without being subject to any central control, but once they have come into existence their convertibility into other forms of money must be possible if a collapse of credit is to be avoided.
>
> (Hayek 1931)

This convertibility of inside money (bank money) into outside money (cash) is achieved when central banks intervene in a crisis to support vanishing market liquidity. But how far should central banks stretch their balance sheets to support liquidity in these private, spontaneous markets? This becomes a pressing question when markets have grown at an exponential pace, like the repo and OTC derivatives markets. Should taxpayers' money be put at risk to support a financial system with "excess credit elasticity?"[3]

The rapid growth of shadow banking has challenged the traditional view of banking where banks would receive savings and then intermediate it towards the most productive uses. Banks were supposed to receive a tangible "good" – savings – and pass it on to the investor; nothing would be lost in the process. The alternative, and more realistic, view of banking now recognizes that "banks can create money out of nothing" (Borio 2012; Turner 2013). It then follows logically that privately created money can disappear as well. As Adrian and Shin (2009a) note, "when liquidity dries up, it disappears altogether rather than being re-allocated elsewhere".

The global financial crisis showed how funding and market liquidity interacted to support rapid growth in credit and asset markets, but also how fast this liquidity can disappear. The shadow banking system became a key provider of funding liquidity to both financial institutions and market makers (FSB 2013b). Shadow banking activities were indeed central to the provision of liquidity in core funding markets. These core markets underpin the liquidity creation process within the financial system itself, and a failure could easily lead to a "liquidity spiral" and a generalized liquidity crisis (Johnson and Santor 2013). The pro-cyclical nature of bank credit and the interaction with the shadow banking system have been studied intensively since the global financial crisis. Since the seminal paper on the shadow banking system by Pozsar *et al.* (2010), a range of other in-depth studies on shadow banking, the repurchase market, and securities lending has followed. Through this more recent work, we have gained a better understanding of the "repo machine" that was at the centre of the financial crisis in the US.

Adrian and Shin (2009b) explore the hypothesis that "the financial intermediary sector, far from being passive, is instead the engine that drives the boom-bust cycle". They note that securitization was intended to disperse risks associated with bank lending so that investors who were better able to absorb losses would share the risks (2009a):

> But in reality, securitization worked to concentrate risks in the banking sector. There was a simple reason for this. Banks and other intermediaries wanted to increase their leverage – to become more indebted – so as to spice up their short-term profit. So, rather than dispersing risks evenly throughout the economy, banks and other intermediaries bought each other's securities with borrowed money. As a result, far from dispersing risks, securitization had the perverse effect of concentrating all the risks in the banking system itself.

Hyman Minsky described this pro-cyclical nature of financial markets long before the recent financial crisis. He noted: "Securitization implies that there is no limit to bank initiative in creating credits, for there is no recourse to bank capital" (Minsky 1987). This makes the supply of credit almost infinitely elastic as every new "euphoric era means that an investment boom is combined with pervasive liquidity-decreasing portfolio transformations" (Minsky 1982; and also Borio (2013) on the "excess elasticity" of the financial system).

More recently, the experience with quantitative easing has shown that bank credit is quite autonomous and difficult to influence, as the link between bank credit and central bank money is very weak. Private liquidity tends to move quite independently of the prevailing stance of monetary policy, reflecting private sector risk perceptions ("the risk channel") and the ease of arranging non-bank financing (via the "shadow banking infrastructure"). These liquidity cycles are then amplified by the rise and fall in collateral prices, which again propagate through the collateral chains of the shadow banking system. Banks and shadow banks are not just allocating pre-existing savings; collectively they create both credit and deposits (Turner 2012). Their cyclical behaviour is now at the heart of the more violent swings in the financial cycles that we have experienced since the late 1990s.

This new financial landscape requires a reorientation in both theory and policy. Before the crisis, money and credit were seen as either redundant or at least inessential in the mainstream New Keynesian paradigm (Borio and Disyatat 2010). Standard models were based on one representative, risk-less agent, so anyone's IOU could and would be immediately and fully acceptable in payment for goods or services (Goodhart and Tsomocos 2011). There was no need for money! Building new models that capture the interaction between the financial and the real sectors and the role of credit should now be a key preoccupation of academics and policymakers. This may require some novel approaches, as mainstream theory needs to interact with and build on insights from non-traditional schools of thought. As Borio and Disyatat (2011: 31) note, a deeper understanding of financial crises and the workings of our modern finance-based global economy will require "a rediscovery of the essence of monetary analysis".

The increased pro-cyclicality of the financial system has led to a reorientation in policy. In addition to policy measures aimed at strengthening the robustness of financial institutions, there is now a greater willingness to address the endogenous credit cycles more directly. Macroprudential instruments will be targeted at excessive credit growth, and central banks and supervisory authorities will work together to improve underwriting standards (IMF 2013). In addition, there is also a greater willingness among policymakers to intervene in the free workings of financial markets, as "markets are no longer viewed as self-stabilizing" (Tett 2013). Even structural solutions are no longer taboo and governments (belatedly) now want to create some controls on shadow banks (ibid.).

It remains to be seen if the proposed reforms will be enough to dampen the endogenous cycles of finance. The extraordinary expansion of shadow banking credit is still supported by the preferential treatment of repo and derivative transactions under bankruptcy law (Perotti 2012, 2013).[4] And lax rehypothecation rules still encourage the build-up of collateral chains that propagate failures between key actors in core funding markets. As noted earlier, such breakdowns in market liquidity could again lead to pressure for central bank interventions. Central banks' liquidity policies are thus closely related to the developments in the shadow banking sector and the "changing collateral space" (Singh 2013a).

Shadow banking and collateral pressures

The shadow banking sector is both a user of collateral and a collateral provider. As Manmohan Singh of the IMF has argued in several papers, shadow banking is really a network of collateral transactions that today constitutes our modern financial system (Singh 2012, 2013a). This "collateral landscape" is now changing due to regulatory initiatives and the general move towards more secured financial transactions. The result is a scramble for safe assets and increasing concerns about collateral shortages in the future (IMF 2012).

The increased preference for collateralized transactions has led to asset encumbrance of banks' balance sheets (BIS 2013; EBA 2013). Banks try to secure cheaper funding by offering collateral for new loans. Examples of such secured funding include covered bonds, repurchase agreements and derivatives trades. But the sum total is too many claims against the banking sector's aggregate balance sheet, concern about too much asset encumbrance and a markedly weakened position for unsecured creditors, including non-guaranteed depositors. The scale of this extra demand for collateral is not yet known, but estimates vary from $2 trillion to $6 trillion (Hauser 2013; IMF 2012; US Treasury 2013)! The new liquidity rules for banks under the Basel III agreement (LCR and NSFR) add somewhere between $1 to $2.5 trillion in demand for high-quality liquid assets (HQLA). Then there is the additional demand coming from the new derivatives regulation, where counterparties will have to post HQLA for the default fund (initial margin) and variation margins. This might add another $1 to $2 trillion in HQLA demand.[5] In addition, banks will have to provide far more collateral for their remaining bilateral derivatives trades, with estimates varying between another $1 and $2 trillion dollars.[6] Several reports have recently analysed the potential shortages of highly liquid collateral (BIS 2013; IMF 2012). Many argue that there will not be a *shortage* of HQLA, since primary issuance is expected to remain fairly high going forward (US Treasury 2013). However, there could be *scarcity* of HQLA, especially if markets become stressed again (BIS 2013).

The scale of the required collateral in the OTC markets (for bilateral and central clearing counterparty (CCP) margins) is also highly uncertain. These markets are huge, estimated by the BIS to be almost $700 trillion (in notional amounts outstanding) as at June 2013 (BIS 2013).[7] The concentration is also very high in these markets, with a few international dealers holding up to 60–70 per cent of all outstanding contracts (OCC 2013; Smyth and Wetherilt 2011). This concentration creates risk of rapid propagation of distress across the financial system should any one of these major dealers become distressed. In addition, the widespread use of rehypothecation and margining is amplifying the pro-cyclicality of the financial system (Deryugina 2009; Sidanius and Zikes 2012).

There is indeed concern that tighter market conditions for safe assets could impact financial stability (IMF 2012). As investors search for HQLA, there could be more short-term market volatility, herding behaviour and sharp price movements. Tying up high-quality collateral in CCP guarantee funds and initial margins could also reduce liquidity in the derivatives and repo markets, and lead to increased risk of price spikes and shortages of high-grade collateral (ibid). One predictable effect of the upcoming scramble for HQLA is "collateral transformation services" that can expand the HQLA universe. These could take the form of collateral mobilization (from insurance companies and pension funds), increased collateral velocity (i.e. re-use), collateral pooling (among firms in the same company) or the re-emergence of asset creation (creating "HQLA" as was customary before the recent crisis) (Hauser 2013). There will be a huge market for collateral upgrading, by connecting those with good collateral with, for example, a hedge fund that does not have good collateral but needs it to post initial margin with a CCP.

Such a development is even supported by regulators; board member Benoît Cœuré from the European Central Bank (ECB) has encouraged market participants to analyse solutions that optimize the use of collateral (Cœuré 2013). And the IMF proposes "some flexibility in the definition of acceptable safe assets" to avoid undue pressure in the market (IMF 2012), while the European Systemic Risk Board (ESRB) notes that there is a clear incentive for a more prominent role for collateral transformation services to emerge in one form or another (ESRB 2013). The downside of such transformation is, however, more interconnections between key players in the financial market and increased risk of contagion. As M. Singh (2013b) notes: "Collateral transformation is likely to fill the void, but will increase the nexus between banks and non-banks". Furthermore, these new interconnections between financial institutions will weaken the resilience of the financial system in adverse conditions (Heath *et al.* 2013). Policymakers therefore need to strike a balance between the desire to ensure the soundness of financial institutions and the costs associated with a potentially too-rapid acquisition of safe assets to meet this goal (IMF 2012).

This concern with shortages or scarcity of HQLA has recently led to increased pressure on central banks to relax their liquidity policies; banks want cheaper funding and wider collateral pools. The new collateral-intensive financial system confronts central banks and governments with a deeply political question: How should the potential systemic risk generated by the shadow banking system be managed, especially in times of stress (Gabor 2013)? As regulators try to instil more safety in the system, transaction costs will increase, prices go up and volumes fall. But scaling back the profitable OTC market may be like putting the genie back in the bottle. The pushback from the financial industry over the proposed OTC reforms shows that this will be a tough battle.[8] Also, the new market equilibrium for highly liquid assets is indeed "hard to fully fathom in advance" (Stein 2013a).

There is also the risk that pressure to securitize the huge unsecured repo and OTC positions may expose CCPs to new and unexplored concentration risk. This could put pressure on central banks to provide even more liquidity in a crisis to avoid a new systemic meltdown (Murphy 2013; Tucker 2014).[9] And increased collateral requirements would also expose the financial system to pro-cyclical and self-reinforcing spirals as market participants will repo, swap or sell assets to meet collateral calls in times of stress (ESRB 2013).

"The huge scale of the collateral based shadow banking system represents a dilemma for central banks" (Moe 2012). Unless the endogenous growth in shadow banking liabilities is somehow constrained, there will continue to be pressure on central banks to stop fire sales and create outside liquidity in periods of stress (Mehrling *et al.* 2013; Perotti 2012). To prevent the new Basel liquidity regulations (LCR and NSFR) from "dissolving from within" (Schmitz 2012), it is important that central banks review their liquidity policies carefully and avoid relaxing their lending standards further (Goodfriend 2013). With many sovereigns under pressure due to weak fiscal positions and low economic growth, central banks cannot afford to be lax in their provision of central bank money. Faced with a shadow banking system with "excess elasticity" (Borio 2013), central banks should limit their liquidity support to further market-based finance, and instead support structural reforms that can reduce the need for massive liquidity assistance in the future.[10]

Collateral dilemmas

Central banks' liquidity policies were transformed during and after the financial crisis. In the wake of Lehman's collapse, the risk of a worldwide systemic crisis was considered by many to be very real. Against this background, many central banks initiated new and innovative liquidity facilities to provide liquidity to a wider set of counterparties, at much longer maturities and against a gradually much wider set of collateral.[11] Without this timely liquidity support, the breakdown in market liquidity would most likely have led to the disorderly failure of a number of major financial institutions.

Ben Bernanke (2013) has argued that this expanded role for the Federal Reserve in liquidity provision was a natural extension of the classical lender-of-last policy prescribed by Walter Bagehot.[12]

> The Fed lent not only to banks, but, seeking to stem the panic in wholesale funding markets, it also extended its lender-of-last-resort facilities to support nonbank institutions, such as investment banks and money market funds, and key financial markets, such as those for commercial paper and asset-backed securities.
>
> (ibid.)

The scale of liquidity support was massive, as "the Fed's balance sheet was being used to directly replace the decline in balance sheet capacity of the financial intermediary sector" (Adrian and Shin 2009a).

The huge increase in central banks' balance sheets obviously led to changes in their collateral policies. In principle, central bank credit should only be granted to solvent firms against good collateral.[13] This would act as a safeguard against reckless money growth, limit the central bank's exposure to financial loss and lessen the need for counterparty credit assessment (Cheun 2009). A shortage of eligible collateral would then act as a brake on central bank credit, acting as an anchor much like gold under the gold system of international finance. A strict collateral policy would in this way help preserve the integrity of the fiat money system. Central banks should, according to this view, only extend credit backed by "real value assets".[14]

Most central banks are by law prevented from issuing (central bank or outside) money without some sort of collateral backing. The issuance of claims against oneself is in principle indefinitely augmentable and therefore not well qualified as collateral. The same goes for government credit, as the government could then pledge self-issued debt as collateral for loans from the central bank. The central bank can, however, issue new money against government securities purchased in the secondary market for monetary policy purposes (Jácome *et al.* 2012). Thus, government securities provided by third parties are normally considered HQLA.[15]

But the breakdown in unsecured interbank credit after the crisis put commercial banks in a squeeze. Their own liquidity needs increased dramatically, while their counterparties at the same time withdrew their posted collateral. In response, central banks relaxed their traditional strict collateral requirements in order to accommodate the bank's desperate need for liquidity. And banks became more creative in finding ways to post low quality, but acceptable collateral at the central bank, because better quality collateral had alternative uses with better returns. This type of behaviour was well known even before the crisis, as observed by an ECB executive board member (quoted in Chailloux *et al.* 2008: 5).[16]

> Quite understandably, central bank counterparties have economized on the use of central government bonds, which has often been the only collateral counterparties could still use in interbank repo markets. Instead they have brought forward less liquid collateral . . . including ABSs, for which primary and secondary markets have basically dried up.

By facilitating this type of "collateral manufacturing", central banks' collateral policies facilitated the build-up of leverage before the crisis in the banking and the shadow banking systems. Banks could use their high-quality collateral to obtain repo financing, thereby providing pledgeable collateral for the daisy chains of rehypothecation in the shadow banking system. By running an accommodative collateral policy before the crisis, many central banks supported the excessive market growth that they eventually had to support during the crisis with even more relaxed collateral standards. The recent changes in collateral policies of the Bank of England can be seen as a natural extension of this accommodative liquidity policy (BoE 2013).

If central banks insist on only highly liquid assets as collateral for liquidity support in a crisis, some otherwise solvent banks with liquidity problems may fail. *This is obviously a policy dilemma for central banks.* They risk amplifying the financial crisis by tightening their lending standards during a crisis. This is counterintuitive, as they are supposed to rescue the financial markets in a crisis. But it illustrates well the tensions between "finance-based" collateral guidelines and "macro-based" crisis management policies. A countercyclical collateral policy could indeed be useful in dampening the financial cycle and provide some funding alternatives when conditions in the market become tight and build an illiquidity discount into some asset prices (Chailloux *et al.* 2008). However, such countercyclical behaviour can only be viable if "collateral neutrality" is restored in normal times. "Otherwise, central banks would increasingly ease their collateral requirements and end up undermining public confidence in the soundness of their balance sheet, potentially weakening the trust in money" (ibid.).

Going forward, central bank collateral policy will have to grapple with these conflicting goals. Central bank collateral policy also needs to be integrated with the broader policy shift towards macroprudential policy (Allen 2013). Central bank collateral policy will be important not only for short-term liquidity policy, but also for the longer-term development of core funding markets. Somehow, they will have to decide which funding markets are systemic and how far they should go in accommodating the endogenous growth of shadow bank liabilities.

Looking into the future: policy challenges

This on-going collateral policy debate relates to fundamental principles of central banking. According to Andrew Sheng, "at the heart of the current debate is whether central banks, as agents for monetary discipline, should re-impose the hard budget constraint on global fiat money and by what rule" (Sheng 2011). But is it reasonable for central banks to impose strict limits on their official liquidity support when private credit remains largely unconstrained? As Borio and Disyatat (2011) have noted:

> The fundamental weaknesses in the international monetary and financial system stem from the problem of "excess elasticity": the system lacks sufficiently strong anchors to prevent the build-up of unsustainable booms in credit and asset prices (financial imbalances) which can eventually lead to serious financial strains and derail the world economy.

We should therefore start by exploring ways to limit the unconstrained growth of shadow banking liquidity creation before we impose severe limitations on central bank official liquidity. After all, the provision of an elastic (official) currency is one of the key functions of central banks in a crisis. We therefore need to find the right balance between the legitimate need for market liquidity support in a crisis and unwarranted central bank support for purely speculative credit creation.[17]

The sharp growth in shadow banking activities combined with a shift from unsecured to secured credit has created pressure on HQLA and central bank liquidity facilities. The new focus on asset encumbrance is just a reflection of this sharp growth, as unsecured creditors collectively try to protect their positions. But this rush to safety cannot remove the aggregate risk in the financial system, so we have a classic case of "fallacy of composition": what may be individually rational can produce bad collective outcomes. We need to find a better balance between the growth of finance, secured and unsecured funding, and central banks' liquidity facilities.

Limiting the growth of the shadow banking system is one key element in this new balance. As Borio (2013) notes:

> The Achilles heel of the international monetary and financial system is not so much the risk of a structural excess demand for safe assets, but rather the "excess elasticity" of the same system, i.e. the inability of policy regimes in place – monetary, prudential and fiscal – to prevent successive financial boom and bust cycles.

Reforming the non-bank financial sector has been high on the policy agenda for quite some time. After the crisis, the G20 leaders agreed to deal with the fault lines exposed by the crisis in the "shadow banking system". Their focus has been on the excessive reliance on short-term wholesale funding (money market funds), the growth of repo and securities lending transactions, and the general lack of transparency that hid growing amounts of leverage and mismatch between long-term credit extension and short-term funding (FSB 2013a).

The European Commission has followed up with a proposal to improve the transparency of securities financing transactions (EU 2014b). This proposal will increase the reporting requirements of such transactions and allow supervisors to better identify the links between banks and shadow banking entities. The Commission also wants to improve the transparency of the rehypothecation activity and impose minimum conditions to be met by the parties involved.[18] It remains to be seen if these proposals will be sufficient to stem the growth of non-bank finance and remove the current opaqueness in the shadow banking sector. As long as the underlying incentives are strongly supportive of continued growth in non-bank credit, in large part due to low risk weights and the preferential status of collateral-based credit transactions, the reporting requirement may well be in vain (Perotti 2012). Sheila Bair (2013) is blunter when she notes: "Repos among financial institutions are treated as extremely low risk, even though excessive reliance on repo funding almost brought our system down. How dumb is that?" Central banks will therefore continue to be under pressure "to stop fire sales and create outside liquidity" in a crisis (Perotti 2012), and banks will argue that "diminishing the repo market could reduce liquidity in the assets that are loaned out, such as government bonds and even stocks".[19] As the pressure builds, central bankers have already conceded that the definition of HQLA could be relaxed or that committed liquidity facilities (CLF) at central banks could be adopted. Governor Stein of the Federal Reserve notes:

> It is worth keeping an open mind about more widespread use of CLF-like mechanisms . . . If a scarcity of HQLA-eligible assets turns out to be more of a problem than we expect, something along those lines has the potential to be a useful safety valve, as it puts a cap on the cost of liquidity regulation. Such a safety valve would have a direct economic benefit, in the sense of preventing the burden of regulation from getting unduly heavy in any one country.
>
> (Stein 2013a)

Some would also like to see central banks talking on a wider role as "MMLR". Mehrling *et al.* (2013) argue that "central banks have the power and responsibility to support the shadow banking markets in times of crisis as well as in normal times". They argue that the private collateral-based credit system is a natural extension of the existing national credit systems, and that the international dollar money market has in fact become the funding market for all credit needs today, both private and public. Supporting this new dealer system of finance should, in their view, be the new role for central banks operating in the spirit of Bagehot.

As Allen (2013) also notes: "The hard truth, as Bagehot pointed out, is that in a liquidity emergency, a central bank has to be ready to lend, possibly in large amounts, and against a wide range of collateral".

The question is again how far central banks should go in embracing this potentially costly function? Johnson and Santor (2013) from the Bank of Canada support this new MMLR function, since some core funding markets now are so critical for our financial system that "a shock could have catastrophic consequences". If funding liquidity vanished, there would simply not be any substitutes. These funding markets therefore need to be "continuously open even under stress" (Carney 2008). As a consequence, central bank support should be permanently available and the traditional LLR function should be expanded to include support of core funding markets, "with the central bank being a 'market maker' of last resort if necessary" (Johnson and Santor 2013).

However, before venturing into this uncharted territory of MMLR, some more analysis should be conducted on which markets are especially important to the real economy, or to the financial system itself, and what qualities those markets need to avoid egregious risks to stability (Tucker 2014). "We simply need a solid debate about central banks' role in supporting financial markets" (ibid.). According to Paul Tucker, we need a better framework for discussing the robustness of market and funding liquidity, whether there are ready substitutes if a market should close, and about the resilience of liquidity in systemically relevant markets. Such a framework "would have focused policymakers' attention on the workings of the ABS markets and, in particular, on the associated repo markets well before the crisis" (ibid.).

On the other hand, one could argue that it is not the job of central banks to decide how big the financial sector should be or which markets should be supported or not. Their job is just to ensure that the financial system is safe, as stated by the Governor of Bank of England (Carney 2013): "the Bank stands ready to provide solvent counterparties with highly liquid assets in exchange for a wide range of collateral assets of good credit quality but lower market liquidity". But this is exactly the sticking point: When is a counterparty solvent and how far should the bank be stretching its collateral criteria, assuming the counterparty is solvent?[20]

It is well known that the determination of solvency in a crisis is always tricky and subject to subjective judgments. As Governor Stein notes (Stein 2013a):

> A key point in this regard – and one that has been reinforced by the experience of the past several years – is that the line between illiquidity and insolvency is far blurrier in real life than it is sometimes assumed to be in theory. Indeed, one might argue that a bank or broker-dealer that experiences a liquidity crunch must have some probability of having solvency problems as well; otherwise, it is hard to see why it could not attract short-term funding from the private market.

When a central bank acts as an LLR in a crisis, it necessarily takes on some credit risk. And if it experiences losses, these losses will ultimately fall on the shoulders of taxpayers. So relaxing collateral standards with reference to the presumed solvency of counterparties in a crisis is absolutely not risk free. There is a distinct possibility that central banks will then be subject to the "time inconsistency" of their collateral policies, as they relax collateral requirements for presumed solvent counterparties, in order to support vanishing funding liquidity in systemic, core financial markets.

A better policy would be to add conditions to such liquidity support. Hyman Minsky (1985) supported an elastic currency in the midst of a crisis (when all other options had been exhausted), but suggested that such a flexible liquidity policy should be combined with tough regulatory measures both before and after the crisis: "Clearly, central bank lender-of-last-resort interventions must lead to legislated or administered changes that favour hedge financing and . . . the central bank should continuously 'lean against' the use of speculative and Ponzi financing" (ibid.).[21]

Central bank liquidity support should not be made available for core funding markets without a solid test of their integrity and robustness. And structural reforms should also be considered to bring a better balance between the size of the shadow banking activities and central banks' capacity and willingness to provide backup liquidity. "The idea that a huge expansion even of a reformed financial system would bring great global benefit is doubtful" (Wolf 2013), and "even right-wing voices now think it makes sense to restrict the size and behaviour of banks" (Turner 2013). Such policy measures would be in line with recent research that finds that "financial development is good only up to a point, after which it becomes a drag on growth" (Cecchetti and Kharroubi 2012).

Unless the endogenous creation of shadow banking credit is somehow constrained (especially the exponential growth of OTC derivative and repo markets), growing debt will eventually outpace by far the available pool of HQLA. It is vital to strengthen the robustness of core funding markets now, when markets are calm, in order to improve their resiliency before the next crisis occurs. "This is especially important in light of the heightened threshold established by the Dodd-Frank Act for future central bank interventions in the event of a market disruption" (Dudley 2013).

Today, there is an increasing consensus that we need to take financial booms and busts – financial cycles – more systematically into account and that central banks should lean more deliberately against booms and ease less aggressively during busts (Borio 2014). But so far there have been few concrete suggestions for limiting the strong credit growth in the shadow banking system.[22] And the dynamics of endogenous finance are still inadequately explained in mainstream theory compared to the classic accounts of Keynes (1936), Simons (1936) and Minsky (1982). They directed us to the critical importance of controlling "near-moneys", especially in the upswing. Since the capitalist economy is inherently unstable, and the shadow banking sector is an important source of this instability, we will need stronger medicine than just "leaning against the wind". As Henry Simons (1936) suggested, only radical changes in the financial sector's structure can prevent future crises (Moe 2013).

Central banks should be especially concerned with providing support to core financial markets without any form of structural reform. A judicious review of the robustness of such markets is at least needed before central banks commit fully to such a new and expanded role as MMLR. Until it can be shown that these markets are reasonably able to stand on their own without central bank support in a crisis, authorities should insist on further reforms.[23] It would indeed be ironic if central banks declared victory in the fight against too-big-to-fail institutions, just to end up bankrolling core funding markets.[24]

Notes

1 See Deryugina (2009) for an instructive discussion of rehypothecation issues.
2 See Gurley and Shaw (1960) for the distinction between inside and outside money.
3 Borio and Disyatat (2011) introduced the term "excess elasticity" of the financial system.
4 Without this "safe harbour" protection, a party to a repo contract would be a regular debtor in bankruptcy proceedings.
5 Proposed limitations on rehypothecation will "freeze" collateral, thereby eliminating its velocity entirely (see US Treasury TBAC presentation Q2 2013 for details).
6 Note that these estimates are for "normal" market conditions. In stressed markets the demand for HQLA would increase substantially.
7 The gross market value is far less, around $20 trillion, whereas gross credit exposure – after netting – is around $4 trillion (BIS 2013).
8 The last adjustments in the liquidity rules reduced the largest US banks' need for liquid assets from $840bn to $192bn; see also *Financial Times*: "Banks win Basel Concessions on Debt Rules", 13 January 2014 on the recent tweaking of the leverage ratio regulation. Available at: www.ft.com/content/d920db5e-7bb6-11e3-84af-00144feabdc0. Last accessed 25.04.2017.
9 Murphy (2013) notes that "without access to a central bank, a CCP could find itself unable to fund itself in the event of a crisis".
10 See (EU 2014a) for the new structural reform proposal from the European Commission in response to the Liikanen report (Liikanen 2012).
11 Madigan (2009) provides the rationale for the new liquidity policies of the Federal Reserve during the crisis.
12 The Bagehot Rule (Bagehot 1873) states that central banks should lend early and freely to solvent firms against good collateral and at high rates.
13 How to determine if a counterparty is indeed solvent is an equally challenging task, ref. Stein (2013a): "The line between illiquidity and insolvency is far blurrier in real life than it is sometimes assumed to be in theory".
14 See Lehmbecker (2008) for a statement of the German Property School of Economics' view on collateralized money.
15 With the recent financial crisis in the EU, there is now a discussion about the credit quality of sovereign debt of countries without their own central bank.
16 José Manuel González-Páramo, ECB Executive Board Member, June 2008.
17 There is a growing consensus that financial deepening is not always a good thing (see Cecchetti and Kharroubi 2012).
18 On 29 January 2014, the European Commission also adopted a proposal for a regulation to stop the biggest banks from engaging in proprietary trading and to give supervisors the power to require those banks to separate other risky trading activities from their deposit-taking business (EU 2014a).
19 *Financial Times*: "Repo Market Clampdown Could Hurt", August 29, 2013. Available at: www.ft.com/content/27c4d406-10b7-11e3-b291-00144feabdc0. Last accessed 25.04.2017.
20 The BoE argument seems to be that as long as the counterparty is considered solvent, it is fair to accept "even raw loans" as collateral for liquidity support.

21 Note that Minsky here anticipated the recent macroprudential policy trend of "leaning against the wind" by some thirty years!
22 The emphasis so far is on data collection and better monitoring; this will improve our knowledge of the interconnections, but can surely only be a first step?
23 The Federal Reserve Bank of New York has long been fighting for structural changes in the tri-party repo market (Stein 2013b), and the Federal Reserve System has been equally vocal in its call for reform of the money market industry (Federal Reserve 2013).
24 Thomas Baxter, General Counsel of the New York Fed, recently noted that broad based liquidity support, like the Primary Dealer Credit Facility during the crisis, would still be permitted as a form of "macroprudential" policy, while institution-specific liquidity support, like the support for AIG, would be prohibited according to the new Dodd-Frank law (Baxter 2013).

References

Adrian, T. and H. S. Shin (2009a) *The Shadow Banking System: Implications for Financial Regulation.* Federal Reserve Bank of New York Staff Report, no. 382. Available at: www.newyorkfed.org/medialibrary/media/research/staff_reports/sr382.pdf. Last accessed: 06.01.2017.

Adrian, T. and H. S. Shin (2009b) *Financial Intermediaries and Monetary Economics* Federal Reserve Bank of New York Staff Report, no. 398. Available at: www.newyorkfed.org/medialibrary/media/research/staff_reports/sr398.pdf. Last accessed: 06.01.2017.

Adrian, T., A. B. Ashcraft and N. Cetorelli (2013) *Shadow Bank Monitoring.* Federal Reserve Bank of New York Staff Report, No. 638. Available at: www.newyorkfed.org/medialibrary/media/research/staff_reports/sr638.pdf. Last accessed: 06.01.2017.

Allen, W. A. (2013) *A New and Explicit Policy on Liquidity Provision.* Available at: www.centralbanking.com. Last accessed: 06.01.2017.

Bagehot, W. (1873) *Lombard Street: A Description of the Money Market.* London: Henry S. King and Co.

Bair, S. (2013) "Everything the IMF Wanted to Know about Financial Regulation and Wasn't Afraid to Ask". *Voxeu.org*, 9 June. Available at: http://voxeu.org/article/everything-imf-wanted-know-about-financial-regulation-and-wasn-t-afraid-ask. Last accessed 25.04.2017.

Bank of England (2013) *Liquidity Insurance at the Bank of England: Developments in the Sterling Monetary Framework.* Report. Available at: www.bankofengland.co.uk/markets/Documents/money/publications/liquidityinsurance.pdf. Last accessed: 12.01.2017.

Baxter, T. C. (2013) *From Bagehot to Bernanke and Draghi: Emergency Liquidity, Macroprudential Supervision and the Rediscovery of the Lender of Last Resort Function.* Remarks at the Committee on International Monetary Law, Madrid, September 19, 2013. Available at: www.newyorkfed.org/newsevents/speeches/2013/bax130919. Last accessed: 06.01.2017.

Bernanke, B. S. (2013) *Remarks at Fourteenth Jacques Polak Annual Research Conference.* IMF. Available at: www.imf.org/external/np/res/seminars/2013/arc/. Last accessed: 12.01.2017.

BIS (1986) "The Management of Banks' Off-Balance Sheet Exposures. Basle, Switzerland: Bank for International Settlements. Available at: www.bis.org/publ/bcbsc134.pdf. Last accessed 25.04.2017.

BIS (2013) *Quarterly Review.* The International Banking Market, Statistical Annex, Bank for International Settlements: Basel, September. Available at: www.bis.org/publ/qtrpdf/r_qt1312.pdf. Last accessed: 12.01.2017.

Borio, C. (2012) *The Financial Cycle and Macroeconomics: What Have We Learnt?* BIS Working Papers, no. 395. Available at: www.bis.org/publ/work395.htm. Last accessed: 12.01.2017.

Borio, C. (2013) *Comments on Jean-Pierre Landau's Paper.* Jackson Hole Symposium, Federal Reserve Bank of Kansas City. Available at: http://citeseerx.ist.psu.edu/view doc/download;jsessionid=E3FFC1A186C0EDDE5CF347C4B9B56848?doi=10.1.1.59 3.5609&rep=rep1&type=pdf. Last accessed: 12.01.2017.

Borio, C. (2014) "The Financial Cycle and Macroeconomics: What Have We Learnt?" *Journal of Banking and Finance*, 45, August, pp. 182–198.

Borio, C and P Disyatat (2010) "Unconventional Monetary Policies: An Appraisal". *The Manchester School*, 78(s1), pp. 53–89, September. Also available as *BIS Working Papers*, no 292, November 2009.

Borio, C. and P. Disyatat (2011) *Global Imbalances and the Financial Crisis: Link or No Link?* Working Paper, no. 346. Available at: www.bis.org/publ/work346.pdf. Last accessed: 12.01.2017.

Carney, M. (2008) *Principles for Liquid Markets.* Remarks to the New York Association for Business Economics, New York, 22 May. Available at: www.bankofcanada. ca/2008/05/principles-for-liquid-markets/. Last accessed: 12.01.2017.

Carney, M. (2011) *Global Liquidity.* Remarks to the Canada–United Kingdom Chamber of Commerce, London, 8 November. Available at: http://business.financialpost.com/ news/economy/text-of-bank-of-canada-governor-mark-carneys-speech-to-the-canada-united-kingdom-chamber-of-commerce. Last accessed: 12.01.2017.

Carney, M. (2013) *The UK at the Heart of a Renewed Globalization.* Speech, 24 October. Available at: www.bankofengland.co.uk/publications/Documents/speeches/2013/speech 690.pdf. Last accessed: 12.01.2017.

Cecchetti, S. G. and E. Kharroubi (2012) *Reassessing the Impact of Finance on Growth.* BIS Working Papers, no. 381. Available at: www.bis.org/publ/work381.pdf. Last accessed: 12.01.2017.

Cetorelli, N. and S. Peristiani (2012) "The Role of Banks in Asset Securitization". *Federal Reserve Bank of New York Economic Policy Review.* Vol. 18(2), pp. 47–64.

Chailloux, A., S. Gray and R. McCaughrin (2008) Central Bank Collateral Frameworks: Principles and Policies. IMF Working Paper, No. 08/222. Available at: www.imf.org/ external/pubs/ft/wp/2008/wp08222.pdf. Last accessed: 12.01.2017.

Cheun, S., I. Von Köppen-Mertes and B. Weller (2009) *The Collateral Frameworks of the Eurosystem, the Federal Reserve system and the Bank of England and the Financial Market Turmoil.* ECB Occasional Paper, no. 207. Available at: www.ecb.europa.eu/pub/pdf/ scpops/ecbocp107.pdf?b300d2d3429520e80560256735eed7fb. Last accessed: 12.01.2017.

Cœuré, B. (2013) *COGESI Workshop on Collateral Eligibility Requirements.* Speech, 15 July. Available at: www.ecb.europa.eu/press/key/date/2013/html/sp130715_1.en.html. Last accessed: 12.01.2017.

Deryugina, M. (2009) "Standardization of Securities Regulation: Rehypothecation and Securities Commingling in the United States and the United Kingdom". *Review of Banking and Financial Law*, 29, pp. 254–288.

Dudley, W. C. (2013) *Remarks at Workshop on "Fire Sales" as a Driver of Systemic Risk in Tri-Party Repo and Other Secured Funding Markets.* 4 October. Available at: www. newyorkfed.org/research/conference/2013/fire_sales_driver.html. Last accessed 25.04.2017.

ESRB (2013) *Macroprudential Stance on Eligible Collateral for Central Counterparties.* Report. Available at: www.esrb.europa.eu/pub/pdf/commentaries/ESRB_commentary_ 1311.pdf?c7bdc8da2a559dc321fd51018bfc9502. Last accessed: 12.01.2017.

European Banking Authority (EBA) (2013) *On Asset Encumbrance Reporting under Article 100 of Capital Requirements Regulation (CRR)*. Report. Available at: www. eba.europa.eu/-/eba-publishes-final-draft-technical-standards-on-asset-encumbrance. Last accessed: 12.01.2017.

European Union/European Commission (2013) *Communication on Shadow Banking and Proposal on Money Market Funds*. Available at: http://europa.eu/rapid/press-release_ IP-13–812_en.htm?locale=en. Last accessed: 12.01.2017.

European Union/European Commission (2014a) *Structural Reform of the EU Banking Sector*. Available at: http://ec.europa.eu/finance/bank/structural-reform/index_en.htm. Last accessed: 12.01.2017.

European Union/European Commission (2014b) *Proposal on Transparency of Securities Financing Transactions*. Available at: http://ec.europa.eu/finance/financial-markets/ securities-financing-transactions/index_en.htm. Last accessed: 12.01.2017.

Federal Reserve Bank of Boston (2013) *The 12 Federal Reserve Bank Presidents Encourage Money Market Mutual Fund Reform*. Submit Joint Letter Commenting on the SEC's Proposal. Available at: www.bostonfed.org/news/press/2013/pr091213.htm. Last accessed: 12.01.2017.

FSB (2013a) *Strengthening Oversight and Regulation of Shadow Banking: An Overview of Policy Recommendations*. FSB Report. Available at: www.ny.frb.org/research/ epr/12v18n2/1207peri.pdf. Last accessed: 12.01.2017.

FSB (2013b) *Global Shadow Banking Monitoring Report*. FSB Report. Available at: www. financialstabilityboard.org/publications/r_131114.htm. Last accessed: 12.01.2017.

Gabor, D. (2013) *Shadow Interconnectedness: The Political Economy of (European) Shadow Banking*. SSRN Working Paper. Available at: https://papers.ssrn.com/sol3/ papers.cfm?abstract_id=2326645. Last accessed: 20.12.2016.

Goodfriend, M. (2013) *Lessons Learned from a Century of Federal Reserve Last Resort Lending*. Testimony before the Subcommittee on Monetary Policy and Trade Committee on Financial Services. U.S. House of Representatives, Washington, DC. Available at: http://financialservices.house.gov/uploadedfiles/hhrg-113-ba19-wstate-mgoodfriend-20130911.pdf. Last accessed: 20.12.2016.

Goodhart, C. A. E. and D. P. Tsomocos (2011) *The Role of Default in Macroeconomics*. IMES Discussion Paper, no. 2011-E-23. Available at: www.imes.boj.or.jp/research/ papers/english/11-E-23.pdf. Last accessed: 12.01.2017.

Gurley, J. G. and E. S. Shaw (1960) *Money in a Theory of Finance*. Washington, DC: Brookings Institution.

Haldane, A. (2012) "What Have the Economists Ever Done for Us?" *www.voxeu.com*, 1 October. Available at: http://voxeu.org/article/what-have-economists-ever-done-us. Last accessed 25.04.2017.

Hauser, A. (2013) *The Future of Repo: "Too Much" or "Too Little"?* Speech given at the ICMA Conference on the Future of the Repo Market, London, 11 June. Available at: www.bankofengland.co.uk/publications/Documents/speeches/2013/speech665.pdf. Last accessed: 12.01.2017.

Hayek, F. A. (1931) *Prices and Production*. New York: Augustus M. Kelly. Available at: http://mises.org/books/pricesproduction.pdf. Last accessed 12.01.2017.

Heath, A., G. Kelly and M. Manning (2013) "OTC Derivatives Reform: Netting and Networks". In A. Heath, M. Lilley and M. Manning (eds) *Liquidity and Funding Markets*. Reserve Bank of Australia. Available at: www.rba.gov.au/publications/ confs/2013/pdf/conf-vol-2013.pdf. Last accessed 12.01.2017.

International Monetary Fund (2012) *Safe Assets: Financial System Cornerstone?* In *Global Financial Stability Report* (Chapter 3). Available at: www.imf.org/External/Pubs/FT/GFSR/2012/01/pdf/text.pdf. Last accessed 12.01.2017.

International Monetary Fund (2013) *Key Aspects of Macroprudential Policy.* IMF Staff Paper. Available at: www.imf.org/external/np/pp/eng/2013/061013b.pdf. Last accessed 12.01.2017.

Jácome, L. I., M. Matamoros-Indorf, M. Sharma and S. Townsend (2012) *Central Bank Credit to the Government: What Can We Learn from International Practices?* IMF Working Paper, no. 12/16. Available at: https://pdfs.semanticscholar.org/6f78/4926a64552fe2fc308c6dbeade9228d9c6ee.pdf. Last accessed 12.01.2017.

Johnson, G. and E. Santor (2013) "Central Bank Liquidity Provision and Core Funding Markets". In A. Heath, M. Lilley and M. Manning (eds) *Liquidity and Funding Markets.* Reserve Bank of Australia. Available at: www.rba.gov.au/publications/confs/2013/pdf/conf-vol-2013.pdf. Last accessed 12.01.2017.

Keynes, J. M. (1936) *The General Theory of Employment, Interest and Money.* New York: Harcourt, Brace & Co.

Lehmbecker, P. (2008) *The Quality of Eligible Collateral and Monetary Stability.* Discussion Paper, no. 3. Faculty of Business Studies and Economics, University of Bremen. Available at: https://core.ac.uk/download/pdf/39406179.pdf. Last accessed 12.01.2017.

Liikanen, E. (2012) *Reforming the Structure of the EU Banking Sector.* High-level Expert Group Report. Available at: http://ec.europa.eu/finance/bank/docs/high-level_expert_group/report_en.pdf. Last accessed 12.01.2017.

Madigan, B. F. (2009) *Bagehot's Dictum in Practice: Formulating and Implementing Policies to Combat the Financial Crisis.* Jackson Hole Symposium, Federal Reserve Bank of Kansas City. Available at: www.federalreserve.gov/newsevents/speech/madigan20090821a.htm. Last accessed 12.01.2017.

Mehrling, P., Z. Pozsar, J. Sweeney and D. H. Neilson (2013) *Bagehot was a Shadow Banker: Shadow Banking, Central Banking, and the Future of Global Finance.* Working Paper. Available at: https://ssrn.com/abstract=2232016. Last accessed: 16.12.2016.

Minsky, H. P. (1982) *Can "It" Happen Again? Essays on Instability and Finance.* Armonk, NY: M. E. Sharpe.

Minsky, H. P. (1985) "Money and the Lender of Last Resort". *Challenge*, 28(1), pp. 12–18.

Minsky, H. P. (1987) *Securitization.* Policy Note. Available at: www.levyinstitute.org/pubs/pn_08_2.pdf. Last accessed: 16.12.2016.

Moe, T. G. (2012) *Shadow Banking and the Limits of Central Bank Liquidity Support: How to Achieve a Better Balance between Global and Official Liquidity.* Working Paper, no. 712. Available at: www.levyinstitute.org/pubs/wp_712.pdf. Last accessed: 12.01.2017.

Moe, T. G. (2013) "Control of Finance as a Prerequisite for Successful Monetary Policy: A Reinterpretation of Henry Simons' 'Rules versus Authorities in Monetary Policy'". *Accounting, Economics, and Law*, 3(3), pp. 261–276.

Moreira, A. and A. Savov (2013) *The Macroeconomics of Shadow Banking.* Working Paper. Available at: www.frbsf.org/economic-research/files/P3-Moreira-Shavov.pdf. Last accessed: 12.01.2017.

Murphy, D. (2013) *OTC Derivatives, Bilateral Trading and Central Clearing: An Introduction to Regulatory Policy, Market Impact and Systemic Risk.* New York: Palgrave Macmillan.

Nesvetailova, A. (2010) *Financial Alchemy in Crisis: The Great Liquidity Illusion.* London: Pluto Press.

Office of the Comptroller of the Currency (OCC) (2013) *OCC's Quarterly Report on Bank Trading and Derivatives Activities*. Second Quarter 2013. Available at: www.occ.treas.gov/topics/capital-markets/financial-markets/derivatives/derivatives-quarterly-report.html. Last accessed: 12.01.2017.

Perotti, E. (2012) "The Roots of Shadow Banking". *Voxeu.org*, 21 June.

Perotti, E. (2013) *The Roots of Shadow Banking*. Centre for Economic Policy Research, Policy Insight, no. 69. Available at: http://cepr.org/sites/default/files/policy_insights/PolicyInsight69.pdf. Last accessed: 12.01.2017.

Pozsar, Z., T. Adrian, A. Ashcraft and H. Boesky (2010) *Shadow Banking*. Federal Reserve Bank of New York Staff Report, no. 458. Available at: www.newyorkfed.org/media library/media/research/staff_reports/sr458.pdf. Last accessed: 06.01.2017.

Schmitz, S. W. (2012) "The Liquidity Coverage Ratio under Siege". *Voxeu.org*, 28 July. Available at: www.economonitor.com/blog/2012/07/the-liquidity-coverage-ratio-under-siege/. Last accessed 25.04.2017.

Sheng, A. (2011) *Central Banking in an Era of Quantitative Easing*. The Levy Economics Institute of Bard College. Working Paper, no. 684. Available at: www.levyinstitute.org/publications/central-banking-in-an-era-of-quantitative-easing. Last accessed: 06.01.2017.

Sidanius, C. and F. Zikes (2012) *OTC Derivatives Reform and Collateral Demand Impact*. Financial Stability Working Paper, no. 18. Available at: www.bankofengland.co.uk/financialstability/Documents/fpc/fspapers/fs_paper18.pdf. Last accessed: 06.01.2017.

Simmons, E. C. (1947) "The Relative Liquidity of Money and Other Things". *American Economic Review*, 37(2), pp. 308–311.

Simons, H. (1936) "Rules versus Authorities in Monetary Policy". *Journal of Political Economy*, 44(1), pp. 1–30.

Singh, M. (2012) *Puts in the Shadow*. IMF Working Paper, no. 122/229. Available at: www.imf.org/external/pubs/ft/wp/2012/wp12229.pdf. Last accessed: 12.01.2017.

Singh, M. (2013a) *The Changing Collateral Space*. IMF Working Paper, no. 13/25. Available at: www.imf.org/external/pubs/ft/wp/2013/wp1325.pdf. Last accessed: 12.01.2017.

Singh, M. (2013b) "The Economics of Shadow Banking". In A. Heath, M. Lilley and M. Manning (eds) *Liquidity and Funding Markets*. Reserve Bank of Australia. Available at: www.rba.gov.au/publications/confs/2013/pdf/conf-vol-2013.pdf. Last accessed: 12.01.2017.

Smyth, N. and A. Wetherilt (2011) *Trading Models and Liquidity Provision in OTC Derivatives Markets*. Bank of England Quarterly Bulletin. 4th Quarter. Available at: www.bankofengland.co.uk/publications/Documents/quarterlybulletin/qb110404.pdf. Last accessed: 12.01.2017.

Stein, J. C. (2013a) *Liquidity Regulation and Central Banking*. Federal Reserve Bank of Richmond. Credit Markets Symposium. Available at: www.federalreserve.gov/news events/speech/stein20130419a.htm. Last accessed: 12.01.2017.

Stein, J. C. (2013b) *The Fire-Sales Problem and Securities Financing Transactions*. Federal Reserve Bank of New York. Workshop on Fire Sales as a Driver of Systemic Risk in Tri-Party Repo and other Secured Funding Markets. Available at: www.federal reserve.gov/newsevents/speech/stein20131107a.htm. Last accessed: 12.01.2017.

Sunderam, A. (2012) *Money Creation and the Shadow Banking System*. Harvard Business School. Working Paper. Available at: www.hbs.edu/faculty/Publication%20 Files/money_20120624_4c0f90d8-e8db-42e8-91fe-9e1c3688c35b.pdf. Last accessed: 12.01.2017.

Tarullo, D. K. (2013) *Shadow Banking and Systemic Risk Regulation.* Speech at the Americans for Financial Reform and Economic Policy Institute Conference, Washington, DC, 22 November. Available at: www.federalreserve.gov/newsevents/speech/tarullo20131122a.htm. Last accessed: 12.01.2017.

Tett, G. (2013) "Ideas Adjust to New 'Facts' of Finance". *Financial Times*, 26 December. Available at: www.ft.com/content/a5d434b6-6e24-11e3-8dff-00144feabdc0. Last accessed 25.04.2017.

Tucker, P. (2014) *Regulatory Reform, Stability and Central Banking.* Brookings, Hutchins Center on Fiscal and Monetary Policy. Report. Available at: www.brookings.edu/wp-content/uploads/2016/06/16-regulatory-reform-stability-central-banking-tucker.pdf. Last accessed: 12.01.2017.

Turner, A. (2012) "Shadow Banking and Financial Instability". Lecture at Cass Business School. 14th March *2012*. Available at: www.cass.city.ac.uk/__data/assets/pdf.../004-CASS-LECTURE-20120308.pdf. *Last accessed 25.04.2017.*

Turner, A. (2013) *Debt, Money, and Mephistopheles: How Do We Get Out of this Mess?.* Speech at the Cass Business School, 6 February. Available at: www.fca.org.uk/publication/archive/debt-money-mephistopheles-speech.pdf. Last accessed: 12.01.2017.

US Treasury (2013) *The Scarcity Value of Treasury Collateral: Repo Market Effects of Security-Specific Supply and Demand Factors.* Working Paper, no. 22. Available at: www.chicagofed.org/publications/working-papers/2013/wp-22. Last accessed: 12.01.2017.

US Treasury TBAC presentation Q2 (2013) *Availability of High-Quality Collateral.* Treasury Borrowing Advisory Committee Discussion Charts by Calendar Year. Available at: www.treasury.gov/press-center/press-releases/Pages/jl1923.aspx. Last accessed: 12.01.2017.

Wolf, M. (2013) "Bank of England's Mark Carney Places a Bet on Big Finance". *Financial Times*, 29 October. Available at: www.ft.com/content/08dea9d4-4002-11e3-8882-00144feabdc0. Last accessed 25.04.2017.

Conclusion
Shadow banking
Into the limelight

Anastasia Nesvetailova

Much of the research that has underpinned this volume is closely associated with the lessons drawn from the financial crisis of 2007–09. At the same time, as the contributors also show, shadow banking extends far beyond the frames of the 2007–09 crisis, not only in longevity but also in scope.

Against this background, any definitive diagnoses of the scope and role of the shadow banking system are likely to be short-lived, because it proves to be a constantly evolving system. It is embedded in diverse institutional contexts and, driven by innovation, has been marked not only by diversity and shifts within its elements but by changes in the system as a whole (Pozsar, this volume). For instance, while most existing data may indicate that shadow banking is a problem of advanced financialised Anglo-Saxon capitalism, non-bank credit intermediaries and capital markets play an increasingly important role in continental economies (chapters by Engelen, Bouveret, Kessler and Wilhelm, Gabor, this volume). In the emerging markets, as Li and Hsu, and Kaurova show in their chapters, shadow banking systems accommodate growing demand for alternative sources of funding and specialised financial services in otherwise tightly regulated banking systems.

The debates about the scope and constitution of shadow banking are set to continue for some time. They illustrate, among other things, that any definition of shadow banking is an outcome of a particular set of ideational values and often carries an observer's bias (Engelen, and Kessler and Whilhelm, this volume). This in turn, may help explain why relatively little progress in terms of regulation of the shadow banking system has been made since 2007. Notwithstanding the slow pace, however, as Moe argues in his chapter, in light of the 2007–09 experience, any policy on financial stability should focus not only on the traditional banking sector but on the shadow banking system as well.

Against this background, the main conclusions of this volume can be best summarised as key areas of continuing discussion on shadow banking and its future challenges, a discussion where disagreement and contention are more prominent than consensus, at least for now.

Scope

Broadly, shadow banking can be understood as a system of credit creation and intermediation outside the traditional banking sector. Within this broad definition, however, shadow banking is geographically and politically diverse, as is its relationship to the traditional sectors of the economy, including banking.

This book discussed three sets of approaches to shadow banking: an *entities-based* approach; an *activities-based* approach; and a *systemic- or network-based* approach. The entities-based approach remains the chosen method of many regulatory bodies which aim to address the problems of the regulation of shadow banking post-2009. Championed most centrally by the FSB, this perspective prioritises the focus on non-banking entities and their functions as a necessary tool in helping to monitor the financial stability risks stemming from shadow banking. Here, specific principles upon which the regulation of shadow banking is based include:

> [d]efining and updating the regulatory perimeter; collecting information and assessing shadow banking risks;[1] enhancing public disclosure to help market participants understand these risks; adopting appropriate policy tools to mitigate identified risks; and participating in an information-sharing exercise within the FSB on assessments and tools.
>
> (FSB 2016)

Any engagement with the products and institutions of financial innovation is a welcome departure from some of the pre-2007 regulatory dogmas. However, as Daniela Gabor notes in her chapter, analytically, it is the activities, rather than institutions of shadow banking, that are more important. An activities-based view allows for a fuller and more reflective understanding of the shadow banking system not simply as a multitude of individual entities engaged in credit transformation, but as the political economy of interconnectedness generated through shadow banking activities, securitisation and collateral intermediation (also Claessens *et al.* 2012; FSB 2011a, 2011b). For example, according to Gabor and others, collateral-intensive finance connects government bond markets to financial stability, and in doing so, entangles macroeconomic relationships between central banks, governments and private financial institutions.

An activities-based view of shadow banking also gives different insights into the regulatory framework. First, although a better recognition of risks stemming from the shadow banking system is seen as paramount to financial stability, it is not clear how insights into such risks are best gained. Many shadow banking entities are seen as 'bank-like' structures, which prompted some observers to suggest extending banking regulations onto the shadow banking system. As Adair Turner once put it, 'if it looks like a bank and quacks like a bank, it has got to be subject to bank-like safeguards' (Masters 2012). Others, however, have warned against a simple extension of bank regulations to the shadow banking sector. Jon Cunliffe, the deputy governor of the Bank of England, has warned that one 'can't wheel up the machine that we've built for banks . . . and say that the same laws apply to shadow banks'. A US Federal Reserve Governor Daniel Tarullo also suggested that the amount of capital an institution holds should 'focus firstly on the liabilities they bear rather than whether they are a bank, an insurer or asset manager' (Reuters 2015).

Furthermore, it is not clear as to *where* the regulations should really be applied. Detecting systemic risks associated with shadow banking is challenging, not only because of the multitude of entities and activities comprising the shadow banking system but because of the often hidden connections within the shadow banking system, and between shadow banking systems and the rest of the economy (cf. contributions by Gabor and Guttmann, this volume). A network-based or a systemic view of shadow banking challenges both the entities-based and activities-focused perspectives which implicitly assume a neatly demarked realm of shadow and non-shadow banking systems. In reality, as Guttmann explains in his chapter, they are tightly intertwined, rendering the whole not only more than the sum of its parts but also more opaque and complex.

Indeed, many functions performed by the shadow banking system are an important part of the everyday operation of modern finance: repo markets, non-bank financial institutions and asset management firms perform critical functions of liquidity provision, credit and collateral intermediation. Yet the opacity of collateral chains and products, as well as undetected risks thriving in unregulated 'in-between' legal spaces of the financial system, make shadow banking particularly prone to the build-up of risks, including systemic risks. As Guttmann explains, both in the design and circulation of the financial claims, shadow banking encourages opacity and facilitates complexity. It fosters customisation by avoiding the standardisation of claims in favour of broker-dealer networks which can accommodate in personalised fashion a much greater variety of funding arrangements for their clients. As a result, while the gestation of risks often goes unnoticed during periods of economic and financial booms, in times of financial stress and crisis they often require radical political solutions, as illustrated by the 2007–09 crisis.

Origins

Most commonly, the emergence and growth of shadow banking is attributed to the regulatory and policy context. This context includes monetary policy regimes as well as the regulations imposed on the traditional banks and financial institutions. Throughout history, financial innovation has always had a regulation-evading intent built into its techniques (Guttmann, this volume). This can be seen both in the evolution of the Eurodollar markets in London (Burn 2006; Palan 2003), and more recently, in the growth of money market networks (Baklanova and Tanega, Bengtsson, this volume).

Regulatory avoidance by relying on financial and legal techniques, as well as political leverage is 'part and parcel of how the world's leading banks operate today' (Guttmann, this volume). On both sides of the Atlantic, loose and fragmented regulations have enabled the expansion of shadow banking which continues to thrive in regulatory niches. In Europe, as Antoine Bouveret argues in his chapter, the flexible monetary policy framework of the ECB allowed it to support the shadow banking system, even without it having a global understanding of the system. Mainly this was due to the high interconnectedness between banks and shadow banks. Elsewhere in the money markets too, the lack of oversight contributed to the gestation of systemic risks due to the effect of regulatory vagueness: in areas where specific market practice is not replicated, this led investors into believing that characteristics normally associated with money market funds exist when in fact they may be missing (Baklanova and Tanega, this volume). More generally, the entry of non-financial businesses into financial intermediation continues to feed the shadow banking system both because non-financial businesses are not regulated as banks and because of the declining quality of credit (Toporowski, this volume).

Yet regulatory fragmentation and arbitrage provide only part of the story of the expansion of shadow banking. Both historical and current records of financial innovations illustrate that structural factors shaping the demand for products and services offered through the shadow banking system, along with the changes within the financial institutions, drive the expansion and mutation of the shadow banking system. As Jan Toporowski explains in his chapter, ultimately, shadow banking, like credit risk, is endogenous to the business cycle. The credit system in turn, (including financial institutions and banks) is the system that 'accommodates' the financing needs of governments, firms and consumers. The quality of its credit is determined by those processes, principally business investment, that can transform credit into income that can service debt (Toporowski 2012). Understood in this light, shadow banking has to be seen not as a mere institutional outcome of regulatory fragmentation and arbitrage, but as a vital infrastructure of the financial system that sustains debt-based funding mechanisms and converts debt-based funding into income, capital and wealth.

Theories

If one tries to tease out the broader theoretical implications of the multi-disciplinary work presented in this volume, two strands stand out. On the one hand, the prevalent vision of shadow banking as an institutional reaction to regulatory constraints on traditional banking builds into a set of supply-side theories of shadow banking. These tend to emphasise the incentive structure of financial institutions, the techniques of legal and financial innovation, and the functions of the markets in creating new financial practices, products and institutions. As noted earlier, it is on this particular aspect of the shadow banking system that the work of monetary and financial authorities on financial stability has focused.

On the other hand, several contributions to the volume find the regulatory arbitrage theory delimited, and discuss alternative conceptualisations of shadow banking. In these visions, shadow banking, while accommodating the quest for regulatory arbitrage between existing rules and norms of finance, is a functional response to the structural problem of yield and scarcity of investables in the economy. Partly, this process is driven by the evolutionary development of fiscal elements of the financial system.

As Photis Lysandrou argues in his chapter, the supply-side theories of shadow banking have tended to focus on banks and regulatory contexts, often ignoring other participants of the financial system and the wider drive for yield, a fact that has become increasingly important in the context of low returns on traditional financial securities. According to Lysandrou, although the hedge funds might have played no part in the actual construction of shadow banking instruments, it is their intermediary position between the investors seeking yield on the one hand and the banks that create the high yielding securities on the other that accounts for the expanding supply of these securities. Without hedge funds being active participants in this process, the volume of investable securities would never have reached the proportions that became critical in precipitating the near collapse of the whole financial system in 2007–09.

The focus on structural changes in the economy, as well as on non-monetary mechanisms of finance, helps us understand that shadow banking is a vital set of institutional mechanisms that enable the operation of the financial system today. Shadow banking serves as an infrastructure of the credit-based economy, where current wealth and incomes are critically dependent on our valuations of the future. Palan and Wigan add an evolutionary element to the demand-side theory of shadow banking by examining the role of taxation and fiscal jurisdictions in the shadow banking system. Specifically, they suggest that 'one of the key achievements of shadow banking is not so much that their activities are outside of prudential regu-latory spaces, but that they have developed hybrid institutions and instruments that bridge the older descriptive boundaries of money and finance' (Palan and Wigan this volume). The authors' survey of the universe of elements that populate the shadow banking system, e.g. derivatives, special purpose vehicles and hedge funds, points out that while the use of these elements is at least partially motivated by tax avoidance, over time they build into a network that enables the expansion of shadow banking services, products and facilities, and thus should be understood as an important part in the supply-side theorisations of shadow banking.

With the wealth management industry expected to expand even further by the late 2020s, these trends are likely to play an even bigger role in the political econ-omy of shadow banking. In particular, as Lysandrou predicts, the search for yield from the growing wealth management industry is likely to continue to facilitate the growth of the hedge fund sector, a development that will both parallel and reinforce the trend growth of the global shadow banking system post-2009.

These insights in turn, suggest a paradoxical conclusion about shadow banking and its functions. On the one hand, academic literature and public debate have come to associate shadow banking with the global financial crisis of 2007–09. Yet as the thrust of post-2009 regulatory efforts has been directed at traditional banks, critics stress that shadow banking practices, entities and networks have enabled the gestation of hidden risks and have aggravated the complexity and opacity of lending. Post-2009, the shadow banking system continues to evolve, and there has been a widening of potential sources of financial fragility and, therefore, systemic risk in various segments of the shadow banking system.

On the other hand, it is now clear that even if the crisis of 2007–09 had not happened, the phenomenon of shadow banking was bound to come to the fore of policy and academic research. A decade after the first outbreak of the crisis, driven by innovation, regulatory arbitrage, technological change and structural economic factors, shadow banking continues to evolve. This evolution further embeds the processes and institutions of financial innovation and shadow banking in our everyday lives, making any definitive diagnoses of its nature and dynamics premature at best. Spurred to attention by the crisis of 2007–09 therefore, the shadow banking system is likely to remain at the centre of economic activity and policy-making, not only because of its role in financial stability but due to its importance to the everyday operations of capital markets, banks and the wider economy anchored in debt.

A deeper insight into the dynamics of this economy suggests that shadow banking is not simply an institutional outcome of a particular regulatory and policy context. Instead, as this volume aimed to show, it is best understood as an evolving infrastructure of a debt-anchored economy and a system of wealth dependent on valorisation of the future.

Note

1 In other words, maturity/liquidity transformation, imperfect credit risk transfer and/or leverage.

References

Burn, G. (2006) *The Re-emergence of Global Finance*. Basingstoke, UK: Palgrave Macmillan.

Claessens, S., Z. Pozsar, L. Ratnovski and M. Singh (2012) *Shadow Banking: Economics and Policy*. IMF Staff Discussion Note. Available at: www.imf.org/external/pubs/ft/sdn/2012/sdn1212.pdf. Last accessed: 16.12.2016.

FSB (2011a) *Shadow Banking: Strengthening Oversight and Regulation*. Recommendations of the Financial Stability Board, 27 October. Available at: www.fsb.org/wp-content/uploads/r_110412a.pdf. Last accessed: 13.01.2017.

FSB (2011b) *Shadow Banking: Scoping the Issues. A Background Note of the Financial Stability Board*. Financial Stability Board. Available at: www.fsb.org/2011/04/shadow-banking-scoping-the-issues/. Last accessed: 20.12.2016.

FSB (2016) *Thematic Review on the Implementation of the FSB Policy Framework for Shadow Banking Entities*. Financial Stability Board Report. Available at www.fsb.org/wp-content/uploads/Shadow-banking-peer-review-press-release.pdf. Last accessed: 19.12.2016.

Masters, B. (2012) 'FSB Seeks to Tame Shadow Banking'. *Financial Times*, 18 November. Available at: www.ft.com/content/23eefd10-3175-11e2-b68b-00144feabdc0. Last accessed 25.04.2017.

Palan, R. (2003) *The Offshore World*. Ithaca, NY and London: Cornell University Press.

Reuters (2015) 'Central Bankers Warn Against Extending Bank Regulations to Shadow Banks'. *Reuters*, 28 September. Available at: http://uk.reuters.com/article/regulations-financing-idUKL5N11Y1Z020150928. Last accessed 25.04.2017.

Toporowski, J. (2012) *Corporate Liquidity and Financial Fragility: The Role of Investment, Debt and Interest*. SOAS Department of Economics Working Paper Series, no. 169. Available at: www.soas.ac.uk/economics/research/workingpapers/file74886.pdf. Last accessed: 13.01.2017.

Index